Arthur Miller is regarded as one of the most important playwrights of the twentieth century. His work is performed and studied around the world and this Companion provides an introduction to this influential dramatist.

In addition to analyses of Miller's plays, including *All My Sons*, *Death of a Salesman*, and *The Crucible*, his work is also placed within the context of the social and political climate of the time. The impact of the Depression, the Holocaust, and McCarthyism on his plays is examined, and the contributors also discuss Miller's fiction and work in film. In the last twenty years Miller has written a host of new plays and the Companion examines these works, including *The Ride Down Mount Morgan*, *The Last Yankee*, and *Broken Glass*. The volume closes with a bibliographic essay which reviews the key studies of Miller.

The Companion also contains a detailed chronology of Miller's work and illustrations from important productions.

THE CAMBRIDGE
COMPANION TO
ARTHUR MILLER

CAMBRIDGE COMPANIONS TO LITERATURE

THE CAMBRIDGE
COMPANION TO
ARTHUR MILLER

EDITED BY

CHRISTOPHER BIGSBY

CAMBRIDGE
UNIVERSITY PRESS

PUBLISHED BY THE PRESS SYNDICATE OF THE UNIVERSITY OF CAMBRIDGE
The Pitt Building, Trumpington Street, Cambridge CB2 1RP, United Kingdom

CAMBRIDGE UNIVERSITY PRESS
The Edinburgh Building, Cambridge CB2 2RU, United Kingdom
40 West 20th Street, New York, NY 10011–4211, USA
10 Stamford Road, Oakleigh, Melbourne 3166, Australia

© Cambridge University Press 1997

First published 1997

Printed in the United Kingdom at the University Press, Cambridge

Typeset in Sabon 10/13 pt.

A catalogue record for this book is available from the British Library

Library of Congress cataloging in publication data

The Cambridge companion to Arthur Miller / edited by Christopher Bigsby.
p.   cm. – (Cambridge companions to literature)
Includes bibliographical references and index.
ISBN 0 521 55019 X (hardback). – ISBN 0 521 55992 8 (paperback)
1. Miller, Arthur, 1915– Criticism and interpretation.
I. Bigsby, C. W. E. II. Series.
PS3525.I5156Z548   1997
812'.52–dc21   97–37707
CIP

ISBN 0 521 55019 X hardback
ISBN 0 521 55992 8 paperback

CE

CONTENTS

ILLUSTRATIONS

NOTES ON CONTRIBUTORS

THOMAS P. ADLER (AB, AM, Boston College; PhD, University of Illinois) is Professor of English and Interim Dean of Liberal Arts at Purdue University, where he has taught dramatic literature for over twenty-five years. He has written widely on modern British and American playwrights, including Harold Pinter, Eugene O'Neill, Edward Albee, and, most extensively, Tennessee Williams. His most recent books are *"A Streetcar Named Desire": The Moth and the Lantern* (1990); and *American Drama, 1940–1960: A Critical History* (1994). He has also contributed essays on Lillian Hellman and on Williams to two other volumes in the *Cambridge Companion* series.

JANET N. BALAKIAN is Assistant Professor of English at Kean College, New Jersey. She has published interviews with Miller, Ionesco, Wasserstein, and her essays on Williams's *Camino Real* and on Wendy Wasserstein are forthcoming in *The Cambridge Companion to Tennessee Williams* and *The Cambridge Companion to American Women Playwrights*. She is also working on a study of Wendy Wasserstein's plays.

STEPHEN BARKER is Associate Dean and Chair of the Department of Studio Art in the School of the Arts at the University of California–Irvine. Formerly Chair of the Department of Drama at UC–Irvine, he has written on drama theory and practice, and on literary and aesthetic theory. He is the author of *Autoaesthetics: Strategies of the Self After Nietzsche* (1992); and the editor of *Excavations and Their Objects: Freud's Collection of Antiquity* (1995); and *Signs of Change: Premodern, Modern, Postmodern* (1996), as well as articles and chapters on Nietzsche, Derrida, Beckett, Blanchot, Faulkner, Cocteau, Miller, Muller, and others. He has recently completed a book on Samuel Beckett and the idea of action.

CHRISTOPHER BIGSBY is Professor of American Studies at the University of East Anglia and has published more than twenty books on British and American culture, including *Confrontation and Commitment: A Study of Contemporary American Drama 1959–1966* (1967); *Albee* (1969); *The Black American Writer*, two volumes (1969); *The Second Black Renaissance* (1980); *Joe*

Orton (1982); *A Critical Introduction to Twentieth Century American Drama*, three volumes (1982–85); *David Mamet* (1985); *Modern American Drama 1940–1990* (1992). He is the editor of *Contemporary English Drama* (1991); *Arthur Miller and Company* (1990); and *The Portable Arthur Miller* (1995). He is also the author of three novels: *Hester* (1994); *Pearl* (1995); and *Still Lives* (1996).

MALCOLM BRADBURY is a novelist, critic, and writer of film and television screenplays. He was formerly Professor of American Studies at the University of East Anglia, where he founded the American Studies programme and also Britain's first MA in Creative Writing, which has had many distinguished graduates. His novels include *Eating People is Wrong* (1959); *Stepping Westward* (1965); *The History Man* (1975), which won the Royal Society of Literature Heinemann Prize; *Rates of Exchange* (1983), which was shortlisted for the Booker Prize; and *Doctor Criminale* (1993). His critical works include *Modernism: A Guide to European Literature* (with J.W. McFarlane, 1976; revised 1991); *Saul Bellow* (1982); *The Modern American Novel* (1984, revised 1992); *The Modern World: Ten Great Writers* (1989); *From Puritanism to Postmodernism: A History of American Literature* (with Richard Ruland, 1991); *The Modern British Novel* (1994), and *Dangerous Pilgrimages: Trans-Atlantic Mythologies and the Novel* (1995). His screenplays include adaptations of Tom Sharpe's *Porterhouse Blue* and Kingsley Amis's *The Green Man*; John Schlesinger directed his film adaptation of Stella Gibbons's *Cold Comfort Farm*. He was nominated one of the twenty "Best of British Writers" in 1983, has honorary degrees from Leicester, Hull, Birmingham, and Nottingham Universities, and in 1991 was awarded the CBE.

STEVEN R. CENTOLA, Professor of English at Millersville University in Pennsylvania, teaches courses in drama and American literature. He is the founder and President of the Arthur Miller Society. He has interviewed Arthur Miller three times and has published these interviews as well as numerous articles on Miller's drama in various scholarly journals. Dr. Centola is also the author of the books *Arthur Miller in Conversation* (1993); *The Achievement of Arthur Miller: New Essays* (1995); and the revised and expanded version of *The Theater Essays of Arthur Miller* (1996). He has recently completed a study guide to the film version of *The Crucible* for the Twentieth Century Fox movie studio and is currently under contract with Greenwood Press for the forthcoming book, *The Critical Response to Arthur Miller.*

WILLIAM W. DEMASTES is Professor of English at Louisiana State University, Baton Rouge. In addition to numerous articles, he is the author of *Beyond Naturalism: A New Realism in American Theatre* (1988); *Clifford Odets: A Research and Production Sourcebook* (1991); and *Theatre of Chaos* (forthcoming). He is the editor of *American Playwrights, 1880–1945*; *British Playwrights, 1956–1995* (1996); and *Realism and the American Dramatic*

Tradition (1996); as well as coeditor of two forthcoming volumes, *British Playwrights, 1880–1956* and *Irish Playwrights, 1880–1995*.

SUSAN HAEDICKE teaches drama in the English Department at the George Washington University and has taught dramaturgy at the University of Massachusetts and Mount Holyoke College. She is currently writing a book on Robert Alexander and the Living Stage Theatre Company, the community-based theatre associated with Arena Stage in Washington DC, and is editing a book on urban community-based theatres around the world. Her articles have appeared in several journals, including *Theatre Topics, Journal of Dramatic Theory and Criticism,* and *Essays in Theatre,* and she has contributed essays to volumes on Arthur Miller and Israel Horovitz. She is also a dramaturg who has worked professionally for Le Neon French–American Theatre Company and Horizons Theatre in Washington DC and for New World Theatre in Massachusetts.

BRENDA MURPHY is Professor of English at the University of Connecticut and the author of *Miller: Death of a Salesman* (1995); *Tennessee Williams and Elia Kazan: A Collaboration in the Theatre* (1992); *A Realist in the American Theatre: Selected Drama Criticism of William Dean Howells* (1992); *American Realism and American Drama, 1880–1940,* Cambridge Studies in American Literature and Culture (1987); and, with George Monteiro, *John Hay-Howells Letters* (1980), as well as numerous articles on modern drama and American literature.

R. BARTON PALMER is Calhoun Lemon Professor of Literature at Clemson University in South Carolina and also serves as Executive Director of the South Atlantic Modern Language Association. As a medievalist, he has edited and translated six volumes of the narrative poetry of Guillaume de Machaut, Chaucer's most famous French contemporary. Two of these have been selected by *Choice* magazine as "outstanding academic books." As a film scholar, he has published *Hollywood's Dark Cinema: The American Film Noir* (1994) and *Perspectives on Film Noir* (1995), and edited a collection on film theory, *The Cinematic Text: Methods and Approaches* (1998). Forthcoming books include *Screening Modern Literature: W. Somerset Maugham and the Cinema* (with Robert Calder) and *Joseph L. Mankiewicz: A Critical Guide* (with Cheryl Lower).

MATTHEW C. ROUDANÉ is Professor of English at Georgia State University in Atlanta. He has published a number of books on modern American drama, including *Conversations with Arthur Miller* (1987) and *Approaches to Teaching Miller's "Death of a Salesman"* (1995). His most recent book is *American Drama since 1960: A Critical History* (1996) and he is the editor of *The Cambridge Companion to Tennessee Williams* (1997). He also serves as editor for the *South Atlantic Review.*

JUNE SCHLUETER, Charles A. Dana Professor of English at Lafayette College, Easton, Pennsylvania, holds a PhD from Columbia University. She is the author of *Metafictional Characters in Modern Drama* (1979); *The Plays and Novels of Peter Handke* (1981); *Arthur Miller* (with James K. Flanagan, 1987); *Reading Shakespeare in Performance: King Lear* (with James P. Lusardi, 1991); and *Dramatic Closure: Reading the End* (1995). She has edited *The English Novel: Twentieth Century Criticism, Volume II: Twentieth Century Novelists* (1982); *Modern American Literature, Supplement II* (1985); and *An Encyclopedia of British Women Writers* (1988) (all with Paul Schlueter); *Approaches to Teaching Beckett's Waiting for Godot* (with Enoch Brater, 1991); *Feminist Rereadings of Modern American Drama* (1989); and *Modern American Drama: The Female Canon* (1990). She has also published essays and reviews on modern drama and Shakespeare and is the coeditor of *Shakespeare Bulletin*. She held a Fulbright lectureship in West Germany in 1978–79.

ALBERT WERTHEIM, is Professor of English and of Theatre and Drama at Indiana University. He is the author of numerous articles on modern American and South African drama, and on classic and modern British drama. He is the editor of *Essays on Contemporary American Drama* (1984) and *Essays on Contemporary British Drama* (1984), a past President of the Eugene O'Neill Society, Treasurer of the American Society for Theatre Research, and a member of the editorial boards of *American Drama* and *Theatre Survey*. He is currently at work on a critical study of the plays of Athol Fugard.

CHRONOLOGY

1915   Arthur Asher Miller born on 17 October in New York City to Isidore and Augusta Miller. Second of three children.

1929   Father's clothing business declines because of the Depression, forcing the family to move to Brooklyn.

1933   Miller graduates from high school, but is rejected from Cornell University and University of Michigan. Works at a variety of jobs and writes his first short story "In Memoriam" depicting an aging salesman. Reapplies to University of Michigan and is granted a conditional acceptance after writing to Dean that he is now "a much more serious fellow."

1934   Studies journalism at University of Michigan where he becomes night editor of *Michigan Daily*. Studies playwriting under Professor Kenneth T. Rowe.

1936   First play, *No Villain*, is produced and wins University of Michigan's Avery Hopwood Award.

1937   Receives second Avery Hopwood Award for *Honors at Dawn*, but the play is never produced. Receives the Theatre Guild's Bureau of New Plays Award for *They Too Arise* (revision of *No Villain*).

1938   Comes in second for Avery Hopwood Award for *The Great Disobedience*, which is produced at University of Michigan. Graduates and moves to New York.

1939   Completes another revision of *They Too Arise* (now entitled *The Grass Still Grows*). Writes scripts for Federal Theatre Project until it is closed by Congress. He then writes radio plays for CBS and NBC.

1940   Completes *The Golden Years*. Marries Mary Grace Slattery. They will have two children, Jane (1944) and Robert (1947).

1941   Completes two radio plays, *The Pussycat and the Expert Plumber Who Was a Man* and *William Ireland's Confession*. Also works at various odd jobs.

1942   Completes radio play, *The Four Freedoms*.

1943   Completes *The Half-Bridge*.

1944   Tours army camps gathering material for screenplay, *The Story of G.I. Joe*, and book, *Situation Normal*. First Broadway production, *The Man Who Had All the Luck*, closes after four performances, but wins Theatre Guild National Award and is published in *Cross-Section: A Collection of New American Writing*.

1945   Publishes first novel, *Focus*, on anti-semitism. Completes radio play, *Grandpa and the Statue*, and a one-act play, *That They May Win*. Attacks Ezra Pound for his pro-Fascist activities.

1947   *All My Sons* opens on Broadway and wins New York Drama Critics' Circle Award. Auctions off manuscript on behalf of Progressive Citizens of America. Becomes involved in variety of anti-Fascist and pro-Communist activities.

1949   *Death of a Salesman* (originally entitled *The Inside of His Head*) opens in New York with Lee J. Cobb in the title role. Jo Mielziner designs the innovative set. Wins the Pulitzer Prize and the New York Drama Critics' Circle Award. Miller publishes the first of his many theatrical and political essays.

1950   Adaptation of Ibsen's *An Enemy of the People* opens; but closes after thirty-six performances.

1953   *The Crucible* opens in New York to mixed reviews that differ on play's relevance to McCarthyism. Play wins Antoinette Perry and Donaldson Awards.

1954   Denied passport by State Department to attend opening of *The Crucible* in Brussels because of his alleged support of the Communist movement. Miller supporters claim this move is a retaliation for the parallels between McCarthy era tactics and the Salem witch trials evident in *The Crucible*.

1955   Contracts to write a film script for New York City Youth Board, but is dropped from film after a condemnation of his leftist activities appears in a New York City newspaper. *A Memory of Two Mondays* and the one-act version of *A View from the Bridge* produced as double-bill in New York.

1956   Two-act version of *A View from the Bridge* opens in London. Testifies before the House Un-American Activities Committee and refuses to name names of others attending meetings organized by Communist sympathizers. Divorces Mary Slattery and marries Marilyn Monroe.

1957   Indicted on charges of contempt of Congress for refusing to name suspected Communists. Publishes *Collected Plays*.

1958   US Court of Appeals reverses contempt of Congress conviction. Filming begins of Miller's *The Misfits*, starring Marilyn Monroe.

1959   Awarded Gold Medal for Drama by National Institute of Arts and Letters.

1961   *The Misfits* released. Divorces Marilyn Monroe. Opera versions of *A View from the Bridge* and *The Crucible* produced.

1962   Marries Ingeborg Morath, an Austrian-born photographer. Daughter, Rebecca (1963).

1964   *After the Fall* and *Incident at Vichy* open in New York.

1965   Elected president of PEN (Poets, Essayists and Novelists), an international literary association.

1967   Publishes *I Don't Need You Any More*, a collection of short stories.

1968   *The Price* opens on Broadway. Serves as a delegate to the
        Democratic Party National Convention.

1969   Publishes *In Russia* (travel journal) with photographs by his wife,
        Inge Morath. Films *The Reason Why*, an anti-war allegory. Refuses
        to be published in Greece to show his opposition to the
        government's oppression of writers.

1970   Two one-act plays, *Fame* and *The Reason Why*, performed at New
        York's New Theatre Workshop. The Soviet Union, in response to
        In Russia, bans all of Miller's works.

1971   *The Portable Arthur Miller* published. *The Price* and *Memory of
        Two Mondays* appear on television. Helps win release of Brazilian
        director/playwright Augusto Boal.

1972   *The Creation of the World and Other Business* produced in New
        York, but closes after twenty performances. Protests oppression of
        artists worldwide – very active politically through the 1970s.
        Permission granted for all-black production of *Death of a
        Salesman* in Baltimore. Revival of *The Crucible* in New
        York.

1973   Revival of *Death of a Salesman* in Philadelphia – first time the play
        is performed within one hundred miles of Broadway since 1949.

1974   *Up from Paradise* (musical version of *The Creation of the World
        and Other Business*) produced in Ann Arbor, Michigan. *After the
        Fall* appears on television.

1975   Revival of *Death of a Salesman* in New York at Circle in the
        Square.

1977   *The Archbishop's Ceiling* has limited run in Washington DC.
        Publishes *In the Country* (travel journal) with photographs by Inge
        Morath.

1978   Visits China. *The Theater Essays of Arthur Miller* published. *Fame*
        appears on television. Protests the arrests of dissidents in Soviet
        Union.

1979   Publishes *Chinese Encounters* (travel journal) with photographs by Inge Morath.

1980   *The American Clock* opens in New York. In spite of its success in South Carolina, the play closes in New York after a few performances. *Playing for Time*, adaptation of Fania Fenelon's book, appears on television.

1981   Arthur Miller's *Collected Plays*, vol. II is published.

1982   Two one-act plays, *Some Kind of Love Story* and *Elegy for a Lady*, open in New Haven.

1983   Directs *Death of a Salesman* in Beijing with Chinese cast. Revival of *A View from the Bridge* in New York. Revision and revival of *Up from Paradise* in New York.

1984   Publishes *Salesman in Beijing* with photographs by Inge Morath. *Death of a Salesman* is revived on Broadway with Dustin Hoffman in lead role. Involved in dispute with the Wooster Group over their unauthorized use of scenes from *The Crucible* for their production of *LSD*.

1985   Revival of *The Price* opens successfully on Broadway. Hoffman version of *Death of a Salesman* produced on television. *Playing for Time* produced in Washington DC.

1986   *The American Clock* and *The Archbishop's Ceiling* produced in London. Revival of *The Crucible* in New York and Washington DC.

1987   *Timebends: A Life* (Miller's autobiography) published. *Danger: Memory!* (two one-act plays, *I Can't Remember Anything* and *Clara*) produced in New York. *All My Sons* appears on television.

1989   Revival of *The Crucible* in New Haven. Opening of The Arthur Miller Centre, University of East Anglia, Norwich, UK.

1990   Revival of *The Crucible* in New York and London. Screenplay for motion picture *Everybody Wins*.

1991   *The Ride Down Mount Morgan* opens in London.

1992   *Homely Girl, A Life* published.

1993   *The Last Yankee* opens in New York. Continuing a life-long commitment to the freedom of writers, Miller contributes to volume on censorship entitled *Censored Books: Critical Viewpoints*.

1994   *Broken Glass* opens in New York and London.

1995   *Plain Girl* published in England. Eightieth birthday marked by Gala Performance at the Royal National Theatre in London and Gala Dinner at the Arthur Miller Centre.

1996   Film version of *The Crucible* released.

I

CHRISTOPHER BIGSBY

Introduction

The plays are my autobiography. I can't write plays that don't sum up where I am. I'm in all of them. I don't know how else to go about writing.[1]

Arthur Miller was born in Harlem, on 17 October 1915, a long way from the Connecticut hills where he has lived for nearly half a century, though not quite as far as it may seem. Harlem, then, was an elegant and mixed neighborhood, partly German, partly Italian, Jewish, and black. There was open space. His mother could watch him walk to a school which she herself had attended, down unthreatening streets.

The family was wealthy. His father, an all but illiterate immigrant from Poland, had built up a clothing business which employed a thousand workers. That all ended with the 1929 Wall Street Crash. The houses grew smaller, family life more tense. They moved to Brooklyn. At thirteen he wanted to be a soldier and go to West Point. Three years later, with the Depression biting hard, he "wanted to be anything that was going." The "anything" extended to being a crooner. For a brief while he had a radio programme of his own: "I sang the latest hits and had a blind pianist with lots of dandruff."

The impact of the Depression was traumatizing: "there were three suicides on the little block where we lived. They couldn't cope. The impact was incalculable. These people were profound believers in the American dream. The day the money stopped their identity was gone . . . America is hope, even when it doesn't work . . . America is promises . . . I don't think America ever got over the Depression." Certainly the Depression haunts his plays. The lesson which he drew from it, though, had little to do with economics. He learned that "there is a feeling at the back of the brain that the whole thing can sink at a moment's notice . . . everything else is ephemeral. It is going to blow away, except what a person is and what a relationship is." The Depression nearly ended plans for his education. The family business was gone, along with the stocks and shares. There was no money left to support him. He earned his way to university through a succession of small jobs, including delivering bread at four in the morning for four dollars a week.

The University of Michigan had a reputation as a radical campus. With a group of others he ran the student newspaper. Five of his friends went to the Spanish Civil War: one died, another was severely wounded. He was tempted to go himself but there were causes closer to home. Down the road in Detroit Henry Ford hired "Nazi storm troopers" to run the factory. "Spain," he insisted, "was in Detroit." His radicalism now poured into a series of student plays, two of which won, and another was runner-up for, the annual Hopwood Award.

Miller knew little of theatre. He had seen few plays and was unsure even how long an act should be. "I chose theatre," though, he has explained, because "it was the cockpit of literary activity and you could talk directly to an audience and radicalize the people." There was something real about theatre which appealed to a man who, beyond anything, liked to make things. From the age of six he had worked with wood. He has continued to do so, building the shed in which he wrote *Death of a Salesman* and subsequently a bed, a dinner table, and an array of chairs and cabinets. A play, he has suggested, is like that: "it has an architectural structure. You could walk around in it. I like to make things, mostly furniture, and create as I go along. I improvise designs. I never make a drawing. I just get a couple of pieces of wood and start to fiddle around until something happens. A play is a real object."

On leaving university Miller briefly joined the Federal Theatre, a nation-wide organization designed to give work to unemployed writers, actors, directors, and designers. Among other works he submitted was a play about Montezuma and Cortes called *The Golden Years*, which was finally produced, for the first time, in a radio and television version, nearly fifty years later. Thereafter he wrote radio plays, mostly for Du Pont's drama series Cavalcade of America, while also working at the Brooklyn Navy Yard, a school injury ruling him out of the military.

His first Broadway play, *The Man Who Had All the Luck* (1944), closed after four days; though, nearly fifty years later, the Bristol Old Vic in Britain successfully produced the same play. His response was to turn to the novel. *Focus*, a work about anti-semitism in America, proved remarkably successful. He nonetheless returned to the theatre with *All My Sons*, a play written during wartime but produced in 1947. It was an immediate success.

Despite this success, or perhaps because of it, he took a job in a factory, for wages, because, as he has explained, "I wanted to be with the salt of the earth." His radical days in Michigan had left him feeling guilt for his sudden wealth. The job lasted a week: "I couldn't think of myself any longer as being allied to the working class because the working class were busy being middle class." Miller followed *All My Sons* with *Death of a*

Salesman which, while responding to the new American affluence, still seemed to him to bear the mark of the Depression. It was, he has explained, about "what happens when everybody has a refrigerator and a car. I wrote *Salesman* at the beginning of the greatest boom in world history but I felt that the reality was Depression, the whole thing coming down in a heap of ashes. There was still the feel of the Depression, the fear that everything would disappear." One thing that did begin to disappear was his audience.

His own response to the growing anti-Communist hysteria of the early fifties was to write an adaptation of Henrik Ibsen's *An Enemy of the People* and then *The Crucible*, set during the 1692 Salem witch trials but with obvious relevance to Senator Joseph McCarthy and to the House Un-American Activities Committee (HUAC), a committee of the House of Representatives which set itself to identify present and former Communists and so-called fellow travelers in all branches of American life. His audience began to edge away. *Death of a Salesman* ran for 742 performances; *An Enemy of the People* managed 36, and *The Crucible* 197. The play was sustained on Broadway only with the help of a cast willing to accept pay cuts while those who attended were likely to be partisan. On the night Ethel and Julius Rosenberg were executed as Communist spies, audience and cast stood for a moment's silence. It was not a good time to be a liberal: "the isolation was terrible. No part of society would support you."

In the early fifties a cabin appeared half a mile from Miller's home, where men sat for twenty-four hours a day watching out for Russian bombers passing over Connecticut: "If you told them you didn't think there would be any they looked at you suspiciously." Decades later he read the FBI reports and discovered that he and his friends had been under observation throughout this period. He joined a group of writers, publishers, and journalists whose objective was to write articles attacking McCarthy. No newspaper would publish them and the group broke up when it was infiltrated by the FBI. Called before HUAC in 1956 and asked to identify those who had attended meetings which might be construed as being subversive he refused, was fined, and sentenced to prison for contempt of Congress, a sentence later quashed on appeal.

His last play of the 1950s, *A View from the Bridge*, which focused on the figure of the informer, ran for 149 performances. Eddie Carbone, its protagonist, precipitates his own death as a means of denying a truth he cannot face, his feelings of sexual attraction to his own niece, Catherine. Forty years later, in *Broken Glass*, Phillip Gellburg cannot claim his life as his own because he, too, cannot accept his own nature. Denial, indeed, lies at the heart of Miller's work. Time after time he explores the lives of those who fail to acknowledge their freedom to act. They are observers of their own fate, unwilling, often through guilt, sometimes through fear, to intervene on their own behalf or to acknowledge their responsibility toward others. Some, like Joe Keller in *All My Sons*, John Proctor in *The Crucible*, or Phillip Gellburg in *Broken Glass*, win their way through to understanding, albeit on the edge of death; others, like Willy Loman and Eddie Carbone, die rather than accept a truth which they fear will render their lives retrospectively meaningless. Willy Loman believes himself no more than his function, which is why the play bears the title it does. He has another life but fails to value it because his society seems to afford it no value. Miller's characters seek some confirmation of their identity, some recognition that they have left their mark on the world, in a context in which that significance seems denied them. The persistence of that need, however, is evidence for the survival of an instinct otherwise threatened by the power of coercive myths.

There followed a nine-year period in which no new Miller play appeared on the American stage. A gap had opened up between him and his audience. He turned instead to the cinema, though largely because of his marriage to Marilyn Monroe. When she lost a child in pregnancy Miller wrote the screenplay of *The Misfits* for her as a gift. "It was also," he explained, "an expression of some kind of belief in her as an actress. But by the time we got to make the film three years had gone by and we were no longer man and wife. The film was there but the marriage wasn't."

He returned to the theatre in 1964. He and Monroe had divorced not long before her death and critics saw *After the Fall* as in part his attempt to deal with this period of his life. It was, however, a work of much greater scope than this suggests, braiding together, as it does, the Holocaust and the anti-Communist hysteria of the fifties in an attempt to locate the connective tissue linking private and public betrayals. *After the Fall* was perhaps the first of his plays to establish a greater reputation outside the United States than within. Playing in repertory at the new Lincoln Center, it ran for fifty-nine performances. Its companion piece, *Incident at Vichy*, which also addressed the question of the Holocaust and the nature of human betrayal, ran for ninety-nine performances. It was not, however, a work without contemporary relevance. The play, he explained, "was written at a time when all values were up in the air. You're a Nazi. That's OK. You could be a vegetarian. I am there to say that vegetarians don't kill people . . . In other words the message of the time was that there was no such thing as society . . . just people doing what they wanted." This was a theme to which he would return in subsequent decades.

The fact is that two events, above all, proved definitional for Miller – the Depression and the Holocaust. One changed a particular model of social organization, a national myth, an interpretation of history; the other seemed to destroy the very meaning of the individual and the concept of society as a network of sustaining obligations. To write after such events was to face a challenge, for how could art itself be said to have survived. Viewed in one way the ironies of the theatre of the absurd (as presented by Samuel Beckett and Eugene Ionesco) were a logical response. But for Miller this was to make art complicit with the forces it existed to resist. In the presence of such defining events, art, Miller implies, has a special responsibility. It either accommodates itself to, acquiesces in, social and metaphysical irony or it resists it. And in that context theatre becomes central as a direct expression of a fundamental community of mutually dependent individuals.

Despite the ambiguous American response to *After the Fall* and *Incident at Vichy*, Miller concluded the sixties with his most successful play since *Death of a Salesman*. *The Price*, in which two brothers meet one another after years of hostility and separation, appeared in 1968, a year characterised by trauma in Vietnam and assassinations at home.

Indeed, the real theatre in late sixties America seemed to be taking place on the street, as America staged its social and political conficts in rallies and marches. Miller played his role in these. In particular he stood up against the Vietnam war, which he characterized as a "criminal engagement which showed a side of American civilization I would rather not think about." He was a delegate to the chaotic and violent National Democratic Party Convention in Chicago in 1968 and worked for the anti-war movement. Abroad, he became President of PEN, the international writers' organization, and spoke in defense of imprisoned writers, an activity which gave him the subject for a new play.

In the late 1970s Arthur Miller sat at a dinner table in Czechoslovakia with a group of writers. Outside the window, in the street below, was a car filled with secret police. But the real threat did not lie outside the window. It lay in the microphones which, they could be reasonably sure, were concealed in the apartment. The writers' awareness of other, unseen, listeners put a pressure on language, turning those present into actors who performed for two audiences. Words had to carry a double meaning, one for those in the room, whose eyes they could meet, and another for those who would listen later to a tape recording which recorded everything but the truth. It was a game which writers were especially well equipped to play but it was a dangerous game nonetheless in that language became suspect and deeply problematic.

In 1977 Miller wrote a play based on this experience. It was called *The Archbishop's Ceiling* and was set in an old archbishop's palace in an unnamed city in eastern Europe (clearly Prague). In the ceiling there may or may not be concealed microphones. Beyond the obvious reference to a totalitarian world in which reality is defined by those who control political power and, indeed, language, it would have been hard for audiences not to see the relevance of the play to an American society in which the President of the United States, Richard Nixon, had not only bugged his own office but, from time to time, had plainly forgotten that he had done so. In such circumstances the real becomes increasingly difficult to define, a fact which intrigued Miller. In answer to a question from a member of the audience at the National Theatre in London in 1984, he remarked that "what I've become more and more fascinated by is the question of reality and what it is, and whether there is any, and how one invites it into oneself. That's a moral issue, finally ."[2]

In 1980, however, he appeared to turn the clock back in a work which borrowed from the very first play he ever wrote, *No Villain*. *The American Clock* is set during the Depression years. It was, he explained, "a conscious attempt to invoke the past and its necessities at a time when self-interest seemed the order of the day . . . I wanted to remind people of a totally different period. We always wanted to wipe out the past. We don't give a damn about it any more. It has no utilitarian value." His 1992 play, *The Ride Down Mount Morgan*, a play about a man who believes "you can have it all," made a similar point.

In 1994 he once again returned to the past in a play set in 1938. *Broken Glass* is set at the time of the Nazi persecution of the Jews, but relates to a sense of moral and political paralysis which he saw being recreated in contemporary Europe. "We are living," he suggested in 1995, "at a time when nothing has a relationship to anything else. Just for my own sanity I wanted to write about something that showed a relationship, that A led to B. It is in relation to a culture that has severed connectiveness. We are now one individual and another individual and another in the face of the fact that it is perfectly obvious that there is a society, that we are all in the grip of various forces that are raging around us. The reigning philosophy is that you are on your own."

In his autobiography, *Timebends*, Arthur Miller remarks on his talent for "being contemporary," his conviction of the need always to stay "involved in transition." It is, he suggests, a natural inheritance of the child and grandchild of immigrants. Change was a birthright, while survival depended on an ability to read the shifting text of society. And yet along with the need to decode the moment went a desire to reach back beyond some temporal divide and acknowledge continuity. Growing up alongside his father and grandfather, both from Poland, the past existed for him as present fact. That simple truth lies behind virtually all of his work as he resists the American desire to deny history in the name of a future which contains the essence of its promise of new beginnings. Indeed, he has remarked on the tendency of American authors themselves to write "as though the tongue had been cut out of the past, leaving him alone to begin from the beginning, from the Creation and the first naming of things seen for the first time . . . American writers spring as though from the ground itself or drop out of the air all new and self-conceived and self-made, quite like the businessmen they despise."[3]

Miller has spoken of his concern to penetrate his own feelings about himself and the times in which he lived. It is in that sense that he sees Willy Loman as a representative figure because he, as Miller once remarked, carried in his pocket the "coinage of our day" (*Timebends*, p. 176). But Willy Loman has a past and for Miller the present moment always has a history. Nor is it simply that he hears echoes of the past, so that the anti-Communist hysteria of the 1950s, for example, can be seen to be a reenactment of the witch-hunts of colonial New England. It is that, believing in a moral world in which actions have consequences for which individual and state must be held accountable, it becomes necessary to dramatize causality in the lives of his characters. It is in that sense that he says that "the job of the artist . . . is to remind people of what they have chosen to forget" (*Arthur Miller and Company*, p. 200),[4] and asserts, as he does in *After the Fall*, that the past is holy. As he has explained, "I've come out of the playwriting tradition which is Greek and Ibsen where the past is the burden of man and it's got to be placed on the stage so that he can grapple with it. That's the way these plays are built. It's *now* grappling with *then*, it's the story of how the birds come home to roost. Every play" (*Arthur Miller and Company*, p. 201). The very structure of *Death of a Salesman*, of *After the Fall*, and, indeed, *Timebends* itself, brings past and present together precisely because the past which we carry in our heads is the substance of our present.

The reference to Ibsen is both accurate and misleading, accurate in that it draws attention to the logic of plays which do, indeed, insist on the moral relevance of the past, and misleading in that his acknowledgment of the significance of Ibsen is often taken to imply a commitment to realism on Miller's part. In fact, as he has frequently lamented, only *All My Sons* genuinely fitted that model. It is true that he is not a formalist, insisting that stylistic invention, without an explicit commitment of some kind to a more humane vision of life, is "a boat without a rudder." On the other hand his commitment to stylistic innovation is apparent in *Death of a Salesman* and *A View from the Bridge*, as it is in *After the Fall* and *Two Way Mirror*. The structure of a play, he has insisted, is its essential poem. It is as much a metaphor as are the characters, as is the action, while his concern with the suspect nature of the real, the fictive component of memory, and the plasticity of language, is evident in *The Crucible, The Archbishop's Ceiling,* and *The Ride Down Mount Morgan.* For Miller there are if not realities then urgencies, and beneath the contingencies of the body politic a skeletal structure of individual human relationships. Public behavior does not corrupt private relations: it is a projection of them. In other words, his central subject is human fallibility. The problem was never capitalism or a coercive conformity, anti-semitism or totalitarianism, but the very human nature which in other respects is the only possible defense against those reductive forces. Private and public history alike begin and end with the individual, with the self. Miller's characters are deeply flawed. That is what led him to speak of modern tragedy, but that flaw is the essence of their humanity.

At the center of his work, then, is a concern to see in private lives the origins of public issues. As he has said, "the way I see life there are no public issues; they are all private issues." The dilemma of Willy Loman, of John Proctor, and of Phillip Gellburg, has to do with the substance and integrity of their identities, yet the battles which they wage with themselves are related to larger issues. Denial and betrayal are marks not only of the individual but of a society whose leaders deny that very mutuality which is their justification for existence.

Arthur Miller is Jewish. This means nothing to him in terms of formal observances. Beyond that, however, it is a significant fact. It is not for nothing that the Holocaust lurks behind *The Crucible* and is a subject of *After the Fall, Incident at Vichy,* and *Broken Glass.* Not merely does he believe that his liberal instincts may be rooted in the Jewish experience but the knowledge that the sky can fall has given a greater urgency and a sharper edge to his commitment to reinventing the moral world whose historical irrelevance was declared so peremptorily nearly sixty years ago. The lessons which he learned from the Depression, as the familiar world dissolved leaving only the necessities of survival, were projected to some ultimate point in Nazi Germany. His public statements in defense of writers are thus of a piece with his work for he believes the writer to be a truth teller whose function is in part to warn against the coercive power of myth and the constant temptation to deny responsibility for the world we make. As at the beginning of his career, he remains committed to theatre because he believes it can change people – no longer in that direct sense that he once thought possible, but change them nonetheless: "I've given up the idea objectively that anything I write was going to get anyone elected. But I do think that in a very small way, probably historically of no importance, what one writes can change people in the sense that it gives them a new idea of themselves . . . You will shift the consciousness of a certain number of people."

NOTES

1 Unless otherwise indicated all quotations are from an interview with Arthur Miller, recorded at his home in Roxbury, Connecticut in Summer 1995, for a series of four BBC radio programmes transmitted to mark his 80th birthday.
2 *Platform Papers: 7. Arthur Miller* (London: Royal National Theatre, 1995), p. 11.
3 Arthur Miller, *Timebends* (New York: Grove Press, 1987, and London: Methuen, 1991), pp. 114–15
4 Christopher Bigsby (ed.), *Arthur Miller and Company* (London: Methuen, 1990).

2

BRENDA MURPHY

The tradition of social drama: Miller and his forebears

By his own account, Arthur Miller's admiration for the classical Greek dramatists began with his earliest efforts at playwriting, when he was a student at the University of Michigan. "When I began to write," he has said in an interview, "one assumed inevitably that one was in the mainstream that began with Aeschylus and went through about twenty-five hundred years of playwriting."[1] Asked in 1966 which playwrights he admired most when he was young, he replied, "first the Greeks, for their magnificent form, the symmetry. Half the time I couldn't really repeat the story because the characters in the mythology were completely blank to me. I had no background at that time to know really what was involved in these plays, but the architecture was clear . . . That form has never left me; I suppose it just got burned in" (Martin, *Theater Essays*, pp. 265–66). He has written in his autobiography *Timebends*[2] that, once he began to write plays and "confront dramatic problems" himself, he "read differently than [he] had before, in every period of Western drama" (p. 232). Regarding these plays no longer as "marble masterworks but improvisations that their authors had simply given up trying to perfect" gave Miller a new perspective on the classics:

> Regarding them as provisional, I could not find as common an identity among various Greek plays as Aristotle described, *Ajax*, for example, being of an entirely different nature than *Oedipus at Colonus*, and so it all devolved into the practical and familiar business of storytelling and the sustaining of tension by hewing to inner theme or paradox. My mind was taken over by the basic Greek structural concept of a past stretching so far back that its origins were lost in myth, surfacing in the present and donating a dilemma to the persons on the stage, who were astounded and awestruck by the wonderful train of seeming accidents that unveiled their connections to that past.
>
> (*Timebends*, pp. 232–33)

Over the years, Miller has come to see that it was not only form that he learned from the classical Greeks, but a sense of the nature and function of drama itself. A major focus of his thought has been the social and ritual function that Greek drama exerted within the culture of the Greek *polis*. After his own work on *The Crucible* (1953), Miller has said that he had "a changed view of the Greek tragedies; they must have had their therapeutic effect by raising to conscious awareness the clan's capacity for brutal and unredeemed violence so that it could be sublimated and contained by new institutions, like the law Athena brings to tame the primordial, chainlike vendetta" (*Timebends*, p. 342). In a 1985 interview he noted that "the great Greek plays taught the western mind the law. They taught the western mind how to settle tribal conflicts without murdering each other."[3]

In 1955, Miller published a rather lengthy essay as an introduction to the volume *A View from the Bridge*, which contains the original one-act version of that play as well as the one-act play *A Memory of Two Mondays*.[4] This essay, entitled "On Social Plays," is his most extended treatment of the classical Greek playwrights and their contribution to the tradition of Western drama and its conception of drama's nature and function. In 1955, Miller was writing in the context of a theatre that was preoccupied, in the United States particularly, with the individual, and with psychological analysis divorced from the social context beyond the domestic confines of the family. In a theatre where the works of Tennessee Williams and William Inge held sway, Miller was trying to define a tradition that would encompass both the psychological and the social. He found this in classical Greek drama. As he explained: "the Greek dramatist had more than a passing interest in psychology and character on the stage. But for him these were means to a larger end, and the end was what we isolate today as social. That is, the relations of man as a social animal, rather than his definition as a separated entity, was the dramatic goal" (*A View from the Bridge*, p. 1). The great achievement of the classical Greeks, as Miller saw it, was the integration of the psychological and the social. Drama, he thought, "gains its weight as it deals with more and more of the whole man, not either his subjective or his social life alone, and the Greek was unable to conceive of man or anything else except as a whole" (*A View from the Bridge*, p. 4). This wholeness or integration could be achieved by the individual only when the individual considered himself as a citizen of an entity larger than the nuclear family:

In Greece the tragic victory consisted in demonstrating that the polis – the whole people – had discovered some aspect of the Grand Design which also was the right way to live *together*. If the American playwrights of serious intent are in any way the sub-conscience of the country, our claims to have found that way are less than proved. For when the Greek thought of the right way to live it was a whole concept; it meant a way to live that would create citizens who were brave in a war, had a sense of responsibility to the polis in peace, and were also developed as individual personalities.

(A View from the Bridge, p. 5).

The concept of the drama of the "whole" man – psyche and citizen, individual subject and social actor – has driven Miller's own playwriting from very early on. The dialectic of personal self-actualization in conflict with social responsibility informs his work from beginning to end.

As the play written with the classical Greek drama most consciously in mind, *A View from the Bridge* provides the clearest sense of the dramatic agenda Miller derived from this tradition. Most fundamental is the story itself, a story that came to Miller as a particular experience, but that quickly proved to have mythic resonance within the Italian community of Brooklyn. "It's a vendetta story," he said in 1976, "which is the basis of so much Greek drama. They are people who have a blood debt that they have to pay. That story came from a true story – I was partially a witness to it – and it struck me then that somehow something was being re-enacted: that I was telling a very old story as well as a contemporary one" (Roudané, *Conversations*, p. 262). The elements of the tale – the man who harbors an illicit passion for a young woman who has been placed in his protection; the breaking of a community taboo because of this passion; the rejection of the man by the community; the forming of a vendetta against him; his destruction by those he has wronged – proved to be well known: "To anybody who knows plain Sicilians or Calabrian people – that story is age-old . . . It had a myth-like resonance for me. I didn't feel I was making anything up, but rather recording something old and marvelous" (Roudané, *Conversations*, p. 192).

While the mythic resonance of the story came as something of a surprise to Miller, the play's form was an intentional allusion to Greek dramatic architectonics. The form, he has said, was influenced by his curiosity "as to whether we could in a contemporary theater deal with life in some way like the Greeks did . . . everything that is said in the Greek classic play is going to advance the order, the theme, in manifest ways . . . They thought art is form; a conscious but at the same time an inspired act" (Roudané, *Conversations*, p. 366). Miller wrote the original one-act version of the play "with the feeling that [he] would make one single constantly rising trajectory, until its fall, rather like an arrow shot from a bow; and this form would declare rather than conceal itself" (Roudané, *Conversations*, p. 367). Like the Greek playwrights he was taking as his models, Miller "wanted to reveal the method nakedly to everybody so that from the beginning of the play we are to know that this man can't make it, and yet might reveal himself somehow in his struggle" (Roudané, *Conversations*, p. 367). For Miller, writing for an American theatre dominated by psychological realism, the play represented an experiment: "I wanted to see whether I could write a play with one single arch instead of three acts in which it rises to some kind of a crescendo before the curtain comes down, then another crescendo before the curtain comes down again, then finally an explosion before the curtain comes down for good. I wanted to have one long line with one explosion, which is rather the Greek way. We have all forgotten that the Greek plays were all one-act plays, a continuous action."[5]

In conceiving the play, Miller made use of the classical Greek convention of the chorus to provide a contemporary point of view on the mythic tale as it unfolds. Alfieri, the narrator, is "a minor character," Miller has said, "except that he is very crucial to that play. He's a kind of chorus in that he represents common sense in the way that Greek choruses did. That is, common sense in relation to excess. Disaster comes from excess, and he is trying to keep Eddie Carbone in the middle of the road and not let his truth – that is to say, his real nature – come out" (Roudané, *Conversations*, p. 263). Miller uses his choral character as an intermediary between the mythic world he creates in the play and the world of the audience. A Cassandra-like prophet, Alfieri has the ability to see the course of destruction down which Eddie is heading, and to articulate it for the audience, but he is unable to stop it. Having left the culture of Red Hook, the Brooklyn waterfront, to make his career as a lawyer, Alfieri is a liminal figure in both cultures, explaining Red Hook to mainstream America and mainstream America to Red Hook, but unable to act in any consequential way or to influence the actions of others.

More important to Miller, however, were the psychological and social forces that lead inevitably to Eddie Carbone's destruction, the primal sexual passion that he feels for his niece Catherine – "a passion which, despite its contradicting the self-interest of the individual it inhabits, despite every kind of warning, despite even its destruction of the moral beliefs of the individual, proceeds to magnify its power over him until it destroys him" (Martin, *Theater Essays*, p. 163) – and his destruction by what Miller has called the "conscience of the community": "A solidarity that may be primitive but which finally administers a self-preserving blow against its violators . . . there is a search for some fundamental fiat, not moral in itself but ultimately so, which keeps a certain order among us, enough to keep us from barbarism" (Martin, *Theater Essays*, pp. 260–61).

To establish Eddie as the victim of a passion over which he has no control, Miller has Alfieri describe him in the familiar terms that describe the traditional Aristotelian tragic hero. Eddie is "as good a man as he had to be / In a life that was hard and even" (*A View from the Bridge*, p. 96). His visitation by sexual passion is represented as a catastrophe over which he has no control, the kind of tragic accident that causes Oedipus to kill his father and marry his mother, "a passion / That had moved into his body, like a stranger" (p. 115). Like that of a classical Greek protagonist, Eddie's fate is inexorable, easily predictable both by characters in the play and by the audience, but impossible to alter. Playing his combined role of prophet–chorus–intermediary, Alfieri explains: "I could see every step coming, step after step, / And I sat here many afternoons, / Asking myself why, being an intelligent man, / I was so powerless to stop it" (p. 121).

The overwhelming force in *A View from the Bridge* is nature, a force that Miller implies, works equally on the individual and the community. Wanting to believe that Catherine's fiancé Rodolpho is homosexual, and that he only wants to marry her in order to become a citizen, Eddie insists to Alfieri that there must be some law that will stop the marriage, some legal expression of the community taboo against what he sees as a perversion of nature. Alfieri tells him that he has no legal rights over Catherine: "The law is nature. / The law is only a word for what has a right to happen" (p. 140). Alfieri's position that the law of the community follows from the laws of nature is brought into question by the events of the play, however. Desperate, and acting blindly on his passion when he gets no support from the law, Eddie violates a deeper taboo of his community when he informs on Rodolpho and his brother Marco, cousins of Eddie's wife Beatrice, who are in the United States illegally, and thus subject to deportation. Not only is Marco Beatrice's blood kin, but the play amply establishes that sending him back to Italy will mean dire poverty for his wife and children. In turning Marco and Rodolpho in to the immigration authorities, Eddie obeys the laws of the United States, but, Miller implies, violates the more fundamental law of kinship, the preservation of the family. Obeying another fundamental law, Marco now feels he must avenge Eddie's wrong to him and his family. When Alfieri tries to dissuade him from killing Eddie in revenge, Marco asks, "then what is done with such a man?" (p. 153). Alfieri replies, "nothing. If he obeys the law, he lives. That's all" (p. 153). When Marco stabs Eddie, the implication is that the law of nature has spoken, that Eddie, who is guilty of an illicit passion and a violation of the laws of kinship, must be purged from the community. The events of the play clearly demonstrate that, as Marco says, "all the law is not in a book." Alfieri is wrong when he says that "the law is nature."

What then of Miller's contention that "the great Greek plays taught the western mind the law. They taught the western mind how to settle tribal conflicts without murdering each other" (Roudané, *Conversations*, p. 374)? The law in this play, the force that sends Marco back to Italy, is itself unnatural, and is responsible for part of the chain of events that leads to Marco's stabbing of Eddie. The law, civilization, is in fact the antithesis of nature in the play. In the person of Alfieri, civilization wages a constant battle throughout the play to defeat nature. By allying the audience with Alfieri through the play's structure, Miller places us on the side of civilization and against the forces of nature which, the events of the play suggest, are ultimately destructive. Imperfect though it may be, Miller implies, civilization is what keeps us from the fate of an Eddie Carbone. In the contest between law and nature, the civilized citizen must choose law.

Miller discovered Henrik Ibsen at about the same time that he discovered the classical Greek playwrights, while he was a student at the University of Michigan. He has explained several times in interviews the connections he sees between the two. He told Christopher Bigsby: "I assumed then that everyone was aware that [Ibsen] was carrying the Greeks into nineteenth-century Europe, principally because they were both obsessed with the birds coming home to roost . . . there's something in me that understood that very well" (Bigsby, *Arthur Miller*, p. 49).[6] Miller's affinity with Ibsen is much deeper than technique, however. The first play he remembers seeing was *Ghosts*. Miller has written several times about Ibsen, most significantly in the Introduction to his *Collected Plays* (1957) and in a *New York Times* article entitled "Ibsen's Message for Today's World," which was later published as the Preface to his adaptation of *An Enemy of the People*. In the *Collected Plays* essay, Miller carefully laid out the elements of Ibsen's dramatic technique which he thought had influenced him in the writing of *All My Sons* (1947), his most consciously Ibsenesque play. They include what is commonly referred to as the "late point of attack," or what Miller calls "bringing the past into the present" (Martin, *Theater Essays*, p. 132), which allows the present to be "comprehended with wholeness, as a moment in a flow of time, and not – as with so many modern plays – as a situation without roots" (Martin, *Theater Essays*, p. 133), and, perhaps equally important to Miller at this time, Ibsen's "insistence upon valid causation" in his plots (Martin, *Theater Essays*, p. 133).

In mid-career, Miller became impatient with what he saw as an over-emphasis of Ibsen's influence on his work by critics.[7] He complained in a 1966 interview that he had become "known really by virtue of the single play [he] had ever tried to do in completely realistic Ibsen-like form, which was *All My Sons*" (Martin, *Theater Essays*, p. 282). In 1970 he said Ibsen "was a strong influence on my early youth but I have no debt to him in the sense that one is insisting upon re-creating him all the time."[8] A number of critical studies over the years have demonstrated that Ibsen's influence was pervasive in Miller's early career. Critics have recognized from the beginning the traces of Ibsen's *Pillars of Society* in *All My Sons*, and others have pointed out that the story of Joe Keller and Steve Deever in that play is derived from that of Håkon Werle and Old Ekdal in *The Wild Duck*.[9] Useful as they are in pointing out Miller's direct debt to Ibsen, however, these studies only begin to indicate the extent to which Ibsen's ideas and images permeated Miller's creative imagination at the beginning of his career. *The Man Who Had All the Luck* (1944), Miller's first play to reach Broadway, has such a close affinity to Ibsen's *Master Builder* that it might be seen as an adaptation if it were not for the fundamental thematic divergence in Miller's play. Miller has told in *Timebends* the stories related to his first wife's Aunt Helen and his own cousin Jean that planted the idea for the play and the germ for its plot in his imagination. Missing from this account is the equally important presence of Ibsen's *Master Builder* in Miller's creative imagination as he composed *The Man Who Had All the Luck*. Juxtaposing the two reveals a nexus of ideas that was perhaps obscured by Miller's direct engagement with the stories with which he was working.

Halvard Solness, the master builder of Ibsen's play, believes that he has a special power of will that can turn people into his willing and abject servants and force events to happen. This power, he believes, is what makes him appear lucky to others. When congratulated for having "had luck on [his] side," however, Solness replies, "yes, but that's exactly why I've got this horrible fear . . . it racks me, morning and night. Because someday things have to change, you'll see."[10] Solness believes that he has no right to his luck, and that his own destruction is inevitable. And beyond the natural justice of the universe, Solness believes in a divine retribution as well. Ibsen suggests that Solness is right about his guilt, the inevitability of his destruction, and even its source, although he understands it only imperfectly. His representation of Solness is deeply tragic. As the recipient of "luck," or good fortune, he is doomed to destruction, caused in part by the frailties of his own nature and his defiance of divine order. In Ibsen's play, the assertion of individual will is an evil and destructive thing, associated with hidden and uncontrollable forces referred to as trolls or devils. As a tragic hero, Solness is both guilty and victimized, the cause of a self-destruction that he cannot avoid.

In *The Man Who Had All the Luck*, Miller complicates Ibsen's tragic statement by opening it up to contemporary interpretation. David Frieber is confronted with the same fundamental dilemma as Solness. Like Solness, he is blessed with "the smell of luck; it hangs on him like a coat."[11] Also like Solness, however, David thinks that his good fortune is undeserved: "Does a thing really belong to you because your name is on it? Don't you have to feel you're smart enough, or strong enough, or good enough, or something enough to have won it before it's really yours?" (p. 521). Like Solness, David fears the disaster that will compensate for his luck: "I mean you begin to wonder when something's going to come along for you . . . a big unhappiness of some kind; a loss" (p. 525). Since David has come by his prosperity unjustly, by taking credit for another man's work, he believes that his downfall is inevitable. Like Solness, he lives in fear of the force that will destroy him. Like Solness trying to neutralize his young potential rival Ragnar Brovik, he hopes he can head off the coming disaster: "It may be that a man – say, a man like me – can live a whole life from the beginning to the end, all nice and sweet and even, if he just looks sharp, sharp as hell, and grabs onto what's going to smash him down before it gets started" (p. 530).

Miller sets up an existential alternative to the tragic universe that Ibsen represents. While Solness does indeed bring about a form of divine retribution through his own self-destruction, David's friends Gus and J. B. suggest that there is no need either to fear or to hope, for his world is not ordered by divine justice; it proceeds by random chance. When David's test comes, however, Miller presents a third alternative in the view of his wife Hester. In the climactic third-act discussion scene, Hester explains that she has come to understand David's fears. Expecting what he called "a great smash down" (p. 545), to pay for his luck, he had believed that their baby would be born dead: "The baby would die, it had to because he wanted it so much – and once it was dead everything else would be safe. This was his curse; he would finally pay for his happiness. And then we'd be safe" (p. 545). When the baby was born healthy, Hester explains, David no longer felt safe, "again he'd got what he wanted. Now he had everything, now he really had it all. And the God or the devil he lives by hadn't been paid" (p. 545). David has now mortgaged all of his property and invested the money in mink. If the mink die, his prosperity, his luck, will be destroyed, but he will feel that he and his family are safe. On this night, when the mink are about to whelp, and make a real fortune for David, Hester gets a call telling her that the fish he is feeding them are diseased. Hester decides that the best thing to do is to let the mink die, to bring on the disaster that David is waiting for. When he tries to save them, she says that she will leave him and take the baby away if he doesn't let the mink die: "I'm not going to have him learn his words from a man who shakes at every rumbling in the sky, and looks in all the corners of the dark for a devil that isn't there . . . He's not going to look to devils for what he'll have in the world . . . No matter what he comes to own he'll never believe he has to pay for it with the life of his son!" (p. 549). Hester's position is a rejection of both *The Master Builder*'s tragic romanticism and the existential futility of the other characters in the play. Denying the existence of the forces that David fears, Hester asserts the efficacy of human will. If there is a "great smash down," Hester tells him, "I want you to do it, and I want you to know once and for all that it was you who did it!" (p. 550). Like Hilda Wangel in *The Master Builder*, Hester urges her man to defy his deity, but the effect is very different. In destroying the mink, she destroys a bad dream, and at the same time she restores her husband to his family.

In his appropriation of *The Master Builder*, Miller was attempting to counter both the dark romanticism of Ibsen's later plays and the existential *angst* of the 1940s. Miller rejected Ibsen's belief in supernatural forces represented by trolls and devils as well as his belief in a just universe. But he also rejected the view of some of his contemporaries that the lack of a demonstrable divine justice implied a futility of human action and an absence of human responsibility for one's actions. In the face of a universe where luck is a matter of random chance, Miller placed his faith in the efficacy of praxis – willed action. He rejected what he saw as an increasing retreat into a romantic preoccupation with the self in Ibsen's later work.

For Miller, Ibsen's significant statements were in his social plays – *The Pillars of Society*, *Ghosts*, *An Enemy of the People* – where he articulated the conflict between individual desire and social responsibility that has been at the center of Miller's own work throughout his career. In 1950, Miller decided to adapt *An Enemy of the People* at the request of the actors Fredric March and Florence Eldridge, who, victims of McCarthyist attacks themselves, "were alarmed that some kind of pre-Fascist period was developing in the United States because of McCarthyism" (Bigsby, *Arthur Miller*, p. 80). In the *New York Times* article that he used as a preface to the published play, Miller stated clearly: "I believe this play could be alive for us because its central theme is, in my opinion, the central theme of our social life today. Simply, it is the question of whether the democratic guarantees protecting political minorities ought to be set aside in time of crisis" (Martin, *Theater Essays*, p. 17). Miller was troubled by the elitism implied in Ibsen's play, and even changed Dr. Stockmann's often-quoted line which ends the play, "the strongest man in the world is the man who stands alone,"[12] to the more Milleresque "You are fighting for the truth, and that's why you're alone. And that makes you strong. We're the strongest people in the world."[13] He saw the play's fundamental statement as an assertion of the right of the individual to tell the truth as he sees it in the face of opposition by the majority. Miller has been criticized for eliding the elitism of Ibsen's original version and taking the ambiguity and complexity out of Stockmann's character by his "over-insistence on a moral stance",[14] but he insists that the play's fundamental idea is "that before many people can know something one man has to know it. The majority in that sense is always wrong, always trailing behind that one man" (Roudané, *Conversations*, p. 371).

All My Sons has long been recognized as Miller's most Ibsenesque play, both by himself and by others. Although he has acknowledged his technical debt to Ibsen in showing him how to bring the past into the present and how to represent the principle of causality in the play of events, the most Ibsenesque aspect of the play is its theme, that of the individual's responsibility to society even when that means the sacrifice of the claims of family. In his Introduction to the *Collected Plays*, Miller explained that "the fortress which *All My Sons* lays siege to is the fortress of unrelatedness" (Martin, *Theater Essays*, p. 131). In the play it is Chris Keller who articulates the "responsibility to something bigger," trying to make his father see that the well-being of his family is no counterbalance to his crime against humankind. To his father's defense that he sent out the faulty parts that resulted in the deaths of twenty-one pilots in order to save his business for his sons, Chris replies: "What are you made of, dollar bills? What the hell do you mean you did it for me? Don't you have a country? Don't you live in the world?"[15] When Joe Keller comes to see that the pilots were all "his sons," Chris's mission, and Miller's, is complete, although, because this is a tragedy, Keller must die for his crime.

Viewed over all, the influence of the powerful playwrights Miller discovered as a university student, the classical Greeks and Henrik Ibsen, the "contemporary Greek" (Roudané, *Conversations*, p. 322), was palpable in the early years of his career, not only in providing him with a technical arsenal from which to work out his own techniques, but in providing an example of the kind of theatre Miller wanted to create, a moral theatre which argued a case as well as enacting a story. Their central concerns were his concerns as well, and although he left their dramatic techniques behind as he discovered his own, he has continued to pursue the implications of their common concern, the question of what the individual must do in the world, of how to reconcile the rights and desires of individual citizens, whether they be of the *polis* or of the world, to the good of the whole.

NOTES

1 Robert A. Martin (ed.), *The Theater Essays of Arthur Miller* (New York: Viking Press, 1978), p. 265.
2 *Timebends* (New York: Grove Press, 1987).
3 Matthew C. Roudané (ed.), *Conversations with Arthur Miller* (Jackson: University Press of Mississippi, 1987), p. 374.
4 *A View from the Bridge* (New York: Viking Press, 1955).
5 Christopher Bigsby (ed.), *Arthur Miller and Company* (London: Methuen, 1990), p. 113.
6 See also Roudané, *Conversations*, pp. 291–92 and 322.
7 See for example, Mary McCarthy, "American Realists, Playwrights," *Encounter* 17 (1961): 24–31; Seymour L. Flaxman, "The Debt of Williams and Miller to Ibsen and Strindberg," *Comparative Literature Studies* Special Advance Issue (1963): 51–60; Raymond Williams, "The Realism of Arthur Miller," *Critical Quarterly* 1 (1959): 140–49; David Bronson, "*An Enemy of the People*: A Key to Arthur Miller's Art and Ethics," *Comparative Drama* 2 (1968–69): 229–47; and, later, Einar Haugen, "Ibsen as a Fellow Traveler: Arthur Miller's Adaptation of *An Enemy of the People*," *Scandinavian Studies* 51 (1979): 343–53; Peter J. Burgard, "Two Parts Ibsen, One Part American Dream: On Derivation and Originality in Arthur Miller's *Death of a Salesman*," *Orbis Litterarum* 43.4 (1988): 336–53.
8 Ronald Hayman, *Arthur Miller* (New York: Frederick Ungar, 1972), p. 6.
9 For general reference to Ibsen's influences, see John Gassner, *The Theatre in Our Times* (New York: Crown, 1954), p. 345, and Benjamin Nelson, *Arthur Miller: Portrait of a Playwright* (New York: David McKay, 1970), pp. 80–81; for a discussion of the play's debt to *The Pillars of Society*, see McCarthy, "American Realists, Playwrights," p. 30, and Gassner, *The Theatre in Our Times*, pp. 344–45; for a discussion of the parallels with *The Wild Duck*, see Christopher Bigsby, *Confrontation and Commitment: A Study of Contemporary American Drama 1959–66* (Columbia: University of Missouri Press, 1968), pp. 28–29, and Leonard Moss, *Arthur Miller*, revised edn. (New York: Twayne, 1980). In his notebook for *All My Sons*, located at the Harry Ransom Humanities Research Center, University of Texas at Austin, Miller's original name for Joe Keller's accuser was "Ekhart," echoing Ibsen's "Ekdal."
10 *The Master Builder*, trans. Rolf Fjelde, 1965; reprinted in *Henrik Ibsen: Four Major Plays* (New York: Penguin, 1990), p. 323.
11 *The Man Who Had All the Luck*, in Edwin Seaver (ed.), *Cross-Section* (New York: L. B. Fischer, 1944), pp. 490–91.
12 *An Enemy of the People*, trans. Eva Le Gallienne, in *Six Plays by Henrik Ibsen* (New York: Modern Library, 1951). Ibsen's original Norwegian reads as follows: "Sagen er den, ser I, at den stærkste mand i verden, det er han, som står mest alene" (*En Folkefiende* [Copenhagen: Gyldenalske Boghandels Forlag, 1882], p. 219).
13 *An Enemy of the People*, adaptation, 1951 (reprinted Harmondsworth and New York: Penguin, 1979), pp. 124–25.
14 David Bronson, "*An Enemy of the People*," p. 243. See also Haugen, "Ibsen as a Fellow Traveler." Miller discussed the play's elitism in his introduction.
15 *All My Sons* (New York: Reynal and Hitchcock, 1947), pp. 68–69.

3

CHRISTOPHER BIGSBY

The early plays

If we think of Arthur Miller's career as essentially beginning in 1944, with the disastrous Broadway production of *The Man Who Had All the Luck*, we ignore nearly a decade of playwriting, a decade in which he was shaping his ideas and experimenting with form. Writing as a student at the University of Michigan, he won two prestigious Hopwood Awards and was a runner-up with his third play. He wrote his first, *No Villain*, in 1936, and followed it with a series of plays in which he tested his skills and explored his response to private and public issues. Not all of them were by any means five-finger exercises. *They Too Arise*, a version of *No Villain*, was produced by both a local group and the Chicago division of the Federal Theatre. Even *Honors at Dawn* and *The Great Disobedience*, more obviously apprentice work, compare not unfavorably with the products of 1930s radical theatre whose own melodrama frequently matched that of the period. A further play, written in 1939–40, though lost for many years, did finally receive both a radio and television production nearly fifty years later and was warmly received. *The Golden Years*, a play which takes place during the conquest of Mexico by Cortes, is a work of considerable subtlety and power which was written in response to the growing power of Hitler.

The Michigan plays express the vaguely held beliefs of a writer trying to make sense of the economic crisis which had come close to ruining his own family and which had challenged the most fundamental myths and basic political and social conventions of a nation. The rhetoric lacks the control of his later work, a control he was often to achieve through writing first in verse and then in prose. In these plays meaning undeniably bubbles too freely to the surface. He frequently discharges in words what he would later be content to express through character and action. There is also plainly a good deal more than a whiff of melodrama. But a starkly Manichaean decade generated its own necessities and urgencies and he simply responded to those pressures in common with others who were joining in a national debate about the meaning and direction of American society.

The initial typescript of the play entitled *No Villain* is shorter and simpler than the various versions that followed. Abe Simon, a coat manufacturer, is faced with ruin when a strike of shipping clerks prevents him delivering his goods. The bank is about to call in his credit note. One son, Ben, who has grudgingly gone into business, supports him, despite his own left-wing convictions. Another son, Arnold, back from college and imbued with Communist theory, will not. There are hints of a possible solution if Ben will marry the daughter of a rich manufacturer but this is a sub-plot which is dealt with in a perfunctory way. The conflict, in essence, is that between private interest and the general well-being, but there are, as the title suggests, no villains; the characters are all victims of a system which alone is evil. This sets man against man and places material rather than human values at the centre of affairs. Thus, Abe insists, much as Isidore Miller had done, that "If you don't get them they'll get you. You gotta be on one side or the other in this business. In any business . . . It's dog eat dog."[1] His son, Arnold, sees things differently: "You've got to get out and on top and look down and see, see what one thing is worth against another. The world is different now than when you were young. It's not there to be made now. Now we've got to change the world!"

Nothing is resolved in the play. Arnold is not pressed to the point at which he has to balance the demands of personal loyalty against those of social conscience; Ben is allowed to brush off the temptation of a marital alliance in little more than a casual aside. Marxist theory is alluded to but permitted no articulate spokesman, while the manufacturers' resort to strong-arm tactics is only hinted at but never explored or allowed to become dramatically relevant. Nevertheless, the main structure of the argument is in place, as are those tensions within the family and between the family and the public world which would be expanded in later versions. What tends to disappear in those later versions, however, or at least to be muted, is the specifically Jewish context. So, here, the maternal grandfather (who, incidentally, was to crop up again in the *The American Clock*) is seen observing Jewish ritual, and, when he dies of a heart attack, is laid out in a coffin which becomes the focus for the required Jewish ceremonial. The suggestion seems to be that something more than personal and national values are being abrogated; but like so much else in this first effort this is alluded to but not really engaged. *No Villain* ends with a ringing declaration of the need for new beginnings, as Ben draws the conclusions from what we have seen:

For us it begins, Arny and I . . . For us there begins not work toward a business, but just a . . . sort of a battle . . . sort of a fight . . . so that you'll know that this (covers the scene with an arc motion of his hand), this will never be in our lives. We'll never have to sit like you sit there now for the reasons you are sitting there . . . Dad, now we not only are working people . . . we *know* we are. Maybe I'm afraid . . . I don't know. But I couldn't start this thing over again. I've got to build something bigger . . . Something that won't allow this to happen . . . Something that'll change this deeply . . . to the bottom . . . It's the only way Dad . . . it's the only way.

It is, of course, a piece of rhetoric whose very vagueness is both its strength and its weakness. For all the fact that both brothers have read Marx, and the play has an epigraph from Engels ("Now for the first time a class arose which, without in any way participating in production, won for itself the directing role over production as a whole and threw the producers into economic subjection; a class which made itself the indispensable mediator between every two producers and exploited them both"), no clear model for this new world emerges, any more than it does in most 1930s literature in America. In large part this is because Marxism seems to be accommodated to an older and more specifically American ideology. There is a whiff of Jefferson as there is, for that matter, in the work of John Steinbeck. If change is necessary then life, liberty, and the pursuit of happiness are liable to determine the parameters of the new every bit as much as an awakened working class who make as little appearance in this play (sixteen workers are listed in the cast but none, except a shipping clerk, are allowed to speak) as they do in that work which so startled America the previous year, Clifford Odets's *Awake and Sing* (a play, incidentally, which also features a grandfather who, like the one in Miller's play, feels like a boarder and dies in the course of the play). The concluding speech of Odets's play, indeed, is very close in spirit to Ben's call for a new life:

My days won't be for nothing . . . I's twenty-two and kickin'. I'll get along. Did Jake [the grandfather] die for us to fight about nickels? No! "Awake and sing," he said. Right here he stood and said it. The night he died, I saw it like a thunderbolt! I saw he was dead and I was born! I swear to God, I'm one week old! I want the whole city to hear it – fresh blood, arms. We got 'em. We're glad we're living.'[2]

Again, no definite model of the new world in process of being born but a call for a new generation to escape from the sterile and destructive materialism which had corrupted the 1920s, a spirit embodied in the titles which Miller chose to give to two subsequent revisions of the play: *They Too Arise* and *The Grass Still Grows*.

The play which was performed by the Hillel Players on 12 and 13 March

1937 was a considerably revised and improved version of *No Villain*. The dilemma in which the Simon family finds itself is now sharpened by the inclusion of a meeting of the Manufacturers' Association which debates the hiring of strike-breakers. The figure of Grandfather Stein is elaborated, becoming not merely a comic focus but also a crucial test of Abe's faltering humanity. More significantly, *They Too Arise*, as it was now called, is no longer a play about a simple conflict between capital and labor. It is also centrally concerned with betrayal: the betrayal by the Jewish manufacturers of their religious precepts and moral principles, of workers by their employers, and vice versa, of Abe by his son Arnold, and, in some degree, too, of his sons by Abe, as he seems willing to sacrifice Arnold's principles and Ben's freedom in order to sustain his dreams and substantiate his myths. It has become, in other words, not merely a protest play but, more importantly (given the number of such plays generated by the New Playwrights' Theatre, the Theatre Collective, Theatre of Action, the New Theatre League and Theatre Union, among others), a drama which concerns itself with contrasting views of the meaning and nature of experience. It debates the relationship between the individual and the society which he inhabits and shapes, and it proposes a connection between private values and public principles. In other words, it addresses issues which were to become central to Miller throughout his career.

Moreover, at the very beginning of that career he chooses to focus on the family, finding there a microcosm of those tensions which equally characterize a society in transition. The father is presented as an embodiment of the past and of an authority which must be challenged: the sons are an expression of a necessary revolt which nonetheless is tainted with guilt. If these complexities are not as yet addressed with any great subtlety Miller is already discovering the dramatic energy to be generated by familial relationships in which loyalty clashes with belief, moral value with social theory, and personal commitment with public form. So, here, Abe builds a business in order to pass it on to his sons. Their acceptance will be the mark of his achievement, an endorsement of his values, an expression of their love and a perpetuation of his name and hence of his existence ("I wanna leave ya with a . . . with a name . . . with a clean name and a . . . and a healthy business"). But their independent existence depends on a resistance which love and a sense of duty inhibit them from offering. So, Ben has given up college after two years in order to help his father, while Arnold, who has not, collaborates in the process which destroys his father's business. Years, later, in *The Price*, Miller was to play elaborate games with a similar situation but the tension is equally there in *All My Sons* and *Death of a Salesman*. Will the sons be captured by their father's myth, and hence justify his life at the expense of their personal identities and even moral beings, or will they, like Arnold, turn their backs on that life in the name of abstract values (justice, ideology, faith) or personal fulfillment, thereby vindicating themselves and declaring their innocence, at the price of an implicit indictment of their father?

All the elements which were to go to make Miller's first Broadway successes so effective were already visible in *They Too Arise*. He had simply not yet developed his sense of character to the point at which Ben and Arnold, for example, carry total conviction. Arnold remains altogether too vague. It is clear *that* he believes, but precisely *what* he believes is less certain. Is it a workers' state he wants or simply some control over monopoly capitalism? What precisely does he feel about his father? Ben comes into clearer focus but it is difficult entirely to believe in the gesture whereby he agrees to marry the daughter of a rival manufacturer in order to bail out his father and their faltering company, though this scene was to be effectively reworked, in an ironic and amusing way, in *The American Clock*, a play which contains more than one echo of *They Too Arise* (including the conversation between Arnold and his grandfather about the Soviet Union's attitude toward private enterprise, which is reproduced virtually verbatim).

This, then, is not a play without its faults, especially when compared to Miller's later work; but already, in the course of a single year, he had succeeded in turning his first prize-winning version into something more complex, more theatrically convincing and more morally demanding. The Abe Simon who finds his civic precepts in collision with his moral convictions is a worthy predecessor to Willy Loman. Convinced that "most of the people oughta know what's right and what's wrong" he finds himself, apparently for the first time in his life, forced to question a basic tenet of his belief. He resolves it at the level of language by invoking other principles ("the way an honest man does business," "it ain't no way for Jewish men to act") only to discover that this leaves him a social victim without becoming an ally of those who he is, incidentally, trying to protect – his own sons. His bafflement is close to that felt by Joe Keller in *All My Sons* and Willy Loman in *Death of a Salesman*. In those plays, however, the sense of guilt could not be acknowledged or expiated, unless by death. Here history, in the shape of economic forces, relieves Abe of the dilemma since financial ruin removes him from the arena of corruption. The family survives because, under pressure, Abe is allowed the grace of self-knowledge; the absolution of bankruptcy leaves him innocent of the crimes in which the other manufacturers had invited him to be complicit. In short, he can walk away or rather is forced to walk away. Later Miller chose to turn the screw that much further, no longer permitting his characters to side-step their fate or the consequences of their actions. The Simon family is ruined financially but redeemed spiritually. And in this version of the play it is Abe, not Ben, who is able to sense a new possibility, to have a new vision, and because it has been wrung out of him, because it comes directly out of a moment in which he has been forced to acknowledge the failure of his own dreams, it has a force missing from the earlier draft.

There is still, to be sure, an echo of Odets, but now the rhetoric comes from a character whose own myths have collapsed. There is a desperation which in some way leavens and perhaps even slightly ironizes the ringing declaration of faith in the future in a way that was never quite true of the earlier version and certainly not true of *Awake and Sing*. So, the man who had struck out at his own father-in-law, rather as Billy Budd had at Claggart, simply because he could not find a language commensurate with his own sense of affront and injustice, now insists of his own sons that

> they ain't gonna get rich by killing! They ain't gonna go through what I went through in my life for nothing . . . I wasted my life for what? They're young yet Esther, they got a life to live! . . . I'm gonna see that they don't waste it like I did trying to get rich! . . . When I lifted that hand against the old man it was like some kind of a . . . of a thing ya can't see was pushing me . . . it was like a . . . Esther that was something . . . dirty . . . something rotten was pushing me . . . I know it Esther and it's gotta be wiped out! I dasn't say no more! I don't know how, I don't know where but I gotta do it! I will not see my sons laughing at it the way I did till it drags them so far they gotta hit an old man to stand up! . . . We oughta be able to learn a lot . . . we can change a lot . . . A lotta changing we can do . . .

It is a speech, of course, that could have come out of any one of dozens of plays or novels of the period, a speech, moreover, which resolves none of the social issues which precipitate it; but it occurs in a play, written originally by a second-year student and revised only a year later, which stands up well against much of the drama that was so exciting America at the time; and it is worth reminding ourselves that committed drama was by now reaching far greater numbers than at any time in the history of the United States, thanks not so much to the small New York based radical companies as to the enormous success, across the country, of the newly formed Federal Theatre created as part of Roosevelt's Works Progress Administration. And, as the scattered references to the situation of the Jews in Europe make plain, this is a play, too, whose concern with the necessity to resist the gangster tactics of the powerful had a relevance which went beyond the confines of the garment district in New York City.

A third version of the play seems to be that prepared for the Theatre Guild's Bureau of New Plays, whose $1,250 award it received. Certainly the copy in the Theatre Collection of the New York Public Library at Lincoln Center is so marked. The principal difference between this and the earlier versions lies in the fact that Arnold is now permitted several speeches in which he makes clear the nature of his ideological stance and, incidentally, the basic proposition of the play. This meets the problem of the vagueness of his motives but does so at the price of a certain credibility as his father obligingly listens, largely without demur, to an analysis fundamentally at odds with his own beliefs. However, there is a polemical force to his remarks which is reminiscent of the famous passage in F. Scott Fitzgerald's *Tender is the Night* in which the world economy is shown to be operating in the interests of the rich, as these are embodied in the person of Nicole Diver. As Arnold observes:

> A man in Chicago gets up in the morning and goes to the Pit – the grain exchange. A man in Chicago a thousand miles away, a place you've never been in and never will be, lifts his finger and suddenly one morning in New York Esther Simon finds that she can't buy her daughter a dress. Why? Because a man in Chicago bought wheat and bought something else on the exchange and raised the price of food in Esther Simon's grocery store. See? A finger lifts in Chicago, and in New York Esther Simon can't buy her daughter a dress. Esther never saw the finger, the finger never saw Esther.

In this version Arnold is very explicit as to why he is unwilling to help his father by delivering coats and thus undermining the strike of shipping clerks. The enemy, he insists, is not the impoverished workers but those who command economic and commercial power and who choose to exercise it with a total disregard for economic results. His new faith resides in the need to weaken the grasp of the wealthy and work for the triumph of the working class:

> if we take the right of ownership away from that little finger in Chicago, then Esther Simon will be able to buy her daughter a new dress. Because the grain is there! The farmers grew that. But by being able to command credit and money, a finger can lift and hold back that grain from the people. And the people will have to pay and pay and pay until that finger stops. But when it drops it isn't the same finger. It's fatter. But Esther Simon still couldn't buy that dress.
>
> But how are we going to make it impossible for one man to control the lives of so many people? The best way – the most common sense way is for the people to take that power away . . . I'm a Communist because I want the people to take the power that comes from ownership away from the little class of capitalists who have it now. I didn't work because the shipping clerks

are organizing to help take that power away some day. They are the people
. . . some day the working class will own what they've built all these years.

In *The Grapes of Wrath* Steinbeck speaks of ownership destroying communal values in the name of self-interest. What is needed, he suggests, is a revolt by the people, working together against the alienation of the laborer from his work and a system of monopoly capitalism which placed profit before human need. However, the passage of time has turned such social analysis into piety and such a social program into sentimental rhetoric. That this seemed less true at the time is evidenced not only by the prizes which Miller's play attracted, and by the evident success, in all genres, of works which embodied much the same sentiments, but also by the extent to which New Deal policies seemed to be moving the whole culture to the left. The language of radical change was adopted even by those charged with shaping national economic and social policy and, thereby, national destiny. And the theatre seemed at the heart of this change as the Federal Theatre sought out new audiences – consisting to a remarkable degree of the unemployed and near destitute – and confronted them with a radical view of their own society in such plays as *One Third of a Nation* and *Triple A Ploughed Under*. Certainly anyone recognizing a Manichaean tendency in Miller's early plays would do well to consult these most famous products of the only truly national theatre America has ever known.

The Group Theatre, meanwhile, though not politically radical in intent, discovered and promoted the career of a man – Clifford Odets – whose challenge to the prevailing system could be regarded as radical, at least in the context of a society whose own political system has rarely found a place for a truly ideological left. Thus, when Arnold addresses his parents and accuses them of closing their eyes to the larger political issues of the day he is making a case not only for his own involvement but also for a theatre which must be similarly engaged:

> You think that because you close your door in front of the house then everything that happens outside doesn't have anything to do with you. That's the way you've always been and that's why when something happens you get all excited and you bang your head against the wall; because you don't want to understand causes. You only want things to "get better." Well the time has come when things don't get better unless you make them better.

Yet even here, and despite his own convictions, Miller is aware of the personal cost of presenting what Ibsen had called the "demand of the ideal." Arnold's confident analysis is tainted by the detachment which is its precondition and he is shown arguing with his brother as his grandfather suffers a fatal heart attack, for his is indeed a social philosophy which has a hard time making space for the individual, and not the least interesting aspect of this version is that Miller feels obliged to acknowledge this even while permitting Arnold an articulate defense of his position.

In this third version of the play Abe Simon is no longer given the concluding speeches. Rather like Willy Loman he remains committed to the idea of personal success ("I wanna see you on top. You can do it Ben, without me. Ya gotta do it Ben. It ain't fair that I should give my life like this and go out with – with nothing."). It is in fact Ben who changes most conclusively (as, later, in *Death of a Salesman*, it was to be Biff), exclaiming, in a slightly unlikely manner:

> we are being sorted out every day like letters in the Post Office. Some on this side, some on the other . . . Yesterday *we* were sorted. We were thrown with most. That's where we belong. That's where we're going to stay because the other side is holding up the world. The day is coming Dad when the people are going to take back what's been stolen from them. When it comes I'm holding a gun, not an injunction.

In that context Abe and Esther's final commitment – "A lotta things we gotta learn" – is deliberately ambiguous if not destabilizing since violence is certainly a long way from their minds. But Ben's remark, "We were thrown with most. That's where we belong," casts an interesting light on Biff's confession in *Salesman* that he is a dime a dozen, a dollar a day man. Rather than being an acknowledgment of a limited capacity or, more cogently, evidence that he is willing to settle for a life drained of pointless striving, it is perhaps a remnant of that sense of solidarity which came with opting out of the brutal and self-destructive competition for success.

They Too Arise underwent one further revision – quite the most radical, as it turned out. Miller completed this one in New York a year after graduation. The manuscript is dated "8.6.39" and is considerably more than twice the length of any of the other typescripts. Never performed, it is entitled *The Grass Still Grows* and is described as "a comedy." The basic situation remains the same except that Arnold is now a newly qualified doctor and Ben a would-be writer who has abandoned his novel because "the world doesn't need writing to fix it," and, besides, "I look for a loveable trait in everybody and when I find it, I hang on to it for dear life . . . I have no perspective . . . I cannot appreciate real evil. I don't know what to do when it confronts me." This was to be a real issue in another play which Miller wrote that year (*The Golden Years*) as it was to be in one which he wrote a couple of years later (*The Half-Bridge*), but, as it happens, he never really has to confront it here. In a comedy it would have been out of place. To be sure, Roth, the rival manufacturer, whose daughter

Ben is being urged to marry, is now shown as an employer of scab labor (including Abe's brother, Dave, who now makes a first appearance) but the political radicalism of the earlier versions has all but disappeared, as it had equally begun to fade in American society itself. Arnold is no longer a radical (Marxism sitting somewhat uneasily with the medical profession).

The dilemma of the Simon Coat Company is adroitly settled when Abe accepts a proposal to turn it into a cooperative. Instead we are presented with a comedy about the victory of love over parental opposition. Ben is allowed to marry Louise, a new character introduced here for the first time, while Arnold is paired off with Helen, who now plainly knows her own mind where affairs of the heart are concerned. Abe remains a man who needs to find justification in his sons ("You never built. How could you want it? But whatever you are . . . you're still my son, Ben . . . and as my son I'd like you to take this from me that I made . . . I'm in it like I'm in you, and I don't want to see it die . . . that's the only reason why it's here"), but he is no longer a principal focus. What the play does not resolve is Ben's future. Having married the company's book-keeper, will he remain in the family business or become a writer? Where did Arnold's sudden affection for Helen come from? Is it likely that Abe can so easily become adjusted to losing control of his own business? In a comedy, though, such issues are perhaps hardly central.

In the course of three years, then, the play moved from being a committed social work to a light comedy, with all reference to the shipping clerks' strike eliminated. The final version is witty and articulate but lacking in dramatic conviction. Character is sacrificed to plot as the social drama becomes the pretext rather than the essence of the play. Abe is simply too detached from his own fate for his dilemma to carry any force while, drained of any real social convictions, Arnold and Ben become insubstantial figures lacking in self-knowledge and hence self-doubt. For her part, Esther emerges as something of a clichéd Jewish mother, and, indeed, the play's humor relies in part on the stereotype.

The version which today seems the most convincing is the one first performed fifty years ago. Whatever its imperfections – and compared to much that was then being produced both on Broadway and further afield, it was by no means an insubstantial piece of work – it expressed a genuine social anger which was no less plausible for being on occasion naively expressed by characters reaching for a language which they themselves barely understood. And indeed not the least interesting aspect of the play is the concern with language. In the final version Abe Simon was to object that his own need to build something, to create something which would be an expression of his life, was finally incommunicable because "It's a language that they don't speak any more in this country. It's a language that went out thirty years ago" (partly Willy Loman's problem a decade later). But he, in turn, finds his own father-in-law difficult to understand as the old man, in turn, dependent as he is on a faulty hearing aid, quite literally has difficulty in decoding the world in which he finds himself. Arnold's Marxist rhetoric may contain the essence of Miller's critique of monopoly capitalism but it is itself suspect in so far as a space opens up between his theoretical analysis and the individual human lives to which he tries to apply it. So, too, the coded language which the employers use, to describe their plans to hire scab labor and gangsters to break the strike, underlines the extent to which words no longer seem adequate to human need and rhetoric itself becomes a symptom of that collapse of values and communality which it is designed to address.

Something of the naivety of the characters, in other words, is an expression of the fact that they are people who suddenly find themselves in circumstances for which nothing has prepared them. And that was precisely the situation in which America found itself in the thirties. The old values, the animating myths of the culture, the language of individual endeavor and the Puritan ethic no longer seemed to apply. People encountered one another in a new context in which all available vocabularies seemed rendered void or merely ironic. In a way the attraction of the Communist Party lay in the fact that it offered a new lexicon, a route back to communality and forward to a new justice through a grammar, compounded out of history and economics, which offered some kind of structure to experience and relationship. The promise was that to accept the holy wafer offered by the Party, to acknowledge its scriptures, confess to sins of omission and commission, was in some way to reinvent an older vocabulary. Ernest Hemingway, who, in *A Farewell to Arms*, had announced the corruption of the language of abstract idealism, now, in 1937, with *To Have and Have Not*, reinvoked precisely that language. He was never a member of the Party but in common with many, indeed most, intellectuals he was announcing the bankruptcy of more than the financial system. Miller, too, was never a Party member; radicalism simply constituted the available vocabulary, an analysis of social process which seemed more plausible than any offered by those rendered dumb by the collapse of their fundamental beliefs. It was a vocabulary and an analysis of which he quickly became skeptical (and the various versions of this play plot that change with some precision). On the other hand its appeal as an explanatory model was considerable and its stress on human interconnectiveness compelling.

In common with so many others Miller responded to its powerful images of human community, to its inclusive myths and persuasive polemic; also in common with many others, however, he came to feel the inadequacy of its deterministic philosophy, its steadfast materialism and its disregard for the individual. Never being a true convert he never felt the trauma of apostasy. The fact that social drama could dissolve so quickly into comedy suggests the extent to which he had the detachment whose absence Ben – the putative writer – had regretted. And while it is true that the social commitments which led Miller toward Marxism have never left him, it is equally true that skepticism toward the language with which people choose to defend their commitments and explain their actions – a skepticism fleetingly apparent in these early plays – has also remained fundamental to his work.

As a first play *They Too Arise* was a work of considerable promise. As a drama to be seen alongside *Waiting for Lefty* or, indeed, any of the committed plays of a committed decade, it can more than hold its own.

Sorting out the chronology of Miller's early plays is not easy, not least because the dates on some of the typescripts prove to be unreliable. As a result, a number of critics (including myself in *A Critical Introduction to Twentieth Century American Drama*) list *Honors at Dawn* as his first play, written in the course of a few days in 1936. In fact this was a product of 1937 and with it he received his second Avery Hopwood Award, the judges being Susan Glaspell, herself an outstanding playwright and regional director for the Federal Theatre; Allardyce Nicoll, the drama critic; and Percival Wilde, a prolific playwright whose work was especially popular with amateurs. Not as accomplished as *They Too Arise*, it nonetheless comes out of the same concern with the battle for human rights in a world apparently dedicated to serving the interests of big business and the careers of captains of industry. Miller, the committed playwright, was doing battle for the working class, who this time do make more than a fleeting appearance.

Honors at Dawn is another strike play, rooted to some degree in personal experience, drawing, as it does, on the time he had spent in an automobile parts warehouse and his experience of university life. Once again there are two brothers, representing different responses to life and adopting radically different stances with respect to an economically and socially divided country. Harry celebrates the American dream. The son of a Polish immigrant, he embraces the myths and prejudices of a society whose chief virtue seems to lie in the economic rewards which it offers to those with the energy and ruthlessness to claim them. His brother, Max, seems uninterested in the siren call of success. He is a practical man who takes pleasure in his ability to maintain and improve machinery, a talent which he is invited to extend to the perfection of society by his workmates at the Castle Parts factory. They are involved in a fight for higher pay and union recognition and persuade Max to assist them by distributing leaflets. When he is seen doing this he is offered a bribe to inform on his fellow workers but refuses, joining his brother at university as a means of avoiding the dilemma. When precisely the same offer is made to Harry by the university authorities, themselves under pressure from the factory owner whose donations to the university give him a hold over the institution, he readily agrees in return for a loan to finance his extravagant lifestyle. His job is to report back on radical students and on a professor whose views have brought him into conflict with the same factory owner.

The professor is fired and the degrees of his student supporters withheld. At first Max is unwilling to believe in a connection between the university authorities and the industrialist at whose hands he had already suffered; he certainly resists the notion that his own brother might be involved. But confronted with the evidence of corruption he returns to those he regards as his natural allies. He has no illusions about the lives which they live: "A worker's house is gray. Rain is the only paint they get. They're gray inside and out. Outside there's the rain, inside the tears . . . when you live in barracks like that, you don't live . . . you're like coal . . . just there to be shuttled in. Gray houses and gray people with bumpy faces like the bulging paper on their walls." But if their lives are two-dimensional they have the integrity of confronting necessity. They are free of deceit. They see one another not as rivals for the few rewards society has to offer but as comrades. Accordingly, Max goes back to the factory and joins them in their fight, where, in the process of making an impromptu speech, he is shot.

The play lacks the subtlety of Miller's later work. Thus Harry is gauche and strident as well as socially reactionary. He despises those who work with their hands, including his own family, and obligingly enunciates his single-minded pursuit of success. He manipulates the system and in turn allows himself to be manipulated in an ironic version of the social contract. By contrast, Max is a plodding idealist, a natural engineer who combines honest work with enlightened values which he derives from experience rather than from the social theories which seem to motivate his fellow students. To be sure, in *Death of a Salesman* Happy and Biff are similarly juxtaposed, each representing one aspect of Willy Loman's sensibility; but neither is self-parodying, as at times Harry and Max are, nor are his later characters forced to become the mere embodiments of social values.

Honors at Dawn is a melodrama in which character, language, and plot are pressed to extremes. It ends, fittingly, with a pistol shot. But then *All My Sons*, *Death of a Salesman*, and *A View from the Bridge* all end in violent death and *The Man Who Had All the Luck* was to have done, Miller finally changing the ending some forty-two years later. The difference is that where in those plays the death of the protagonists is a logical extension of their internal development, the only route they can take when face to face with a self-generated fate, Max's death is another noble sacrifice in the cause of humanity. He joins that panoply of secular saints which was a product of 1930s literature.

While it is not possible to make a case for this play in the way that it is for *They Too Arise* and, even more so, *The Golden Years*, it is possible to recognize Miller's search for a way in which he can bring together his social concerns and his interest in the individual's commitment to self-invention. Max Zabriski spends much of the time struggling toward an articulateness which will finally enable him to express himself no less than his convictions. At the beginning of the play he is described as a man who "don't say nothin'." At the end he is able to stand up and rally his fellow workers. But even then he is hardly fluent and not the least interesting aspect of *Honors at Dawn* is the extent to which it expresses doubts about the articulateness on which it relies.

A family friend, Smygli, can only speak in broken English but there is little doubting his wisdom. He is, in fact, a graduate in philosophy from Warsaw University who finds himself in a society which has no use for the non-utilitarian and whose language is partly closed to him. Here he survives as a farmer. A venture into the fast-food business (he sets up a hot-dog stall) fails. His importance is that he values America for reasons which do not primarily have anything to do with money or commercial success. It is the freedom of America which he celebrates. The irony is that no one seems interested. He is incapable of communicating his enthusiasm, partly because of his difficulty with the language but partly because no one wishes to hear. Articulateness seems to have taken the American people away from the meaning of their country no less than their lives. Harry is fluent, but he uses language for deceit. So, too, does the university, finding a formula which will allow it to dismiss radical students without specifying the precise nature of their offense. This is a society whose goals are expressed in the acceptable language of individual endeavor and civic duty but which appears to sanction crude injustice and hypocrisy. Nor, finally, can Max distill the meaning of his life into words, any more than Willy Loman was to be able to do. His impulse is to make things and through that to make himself. But forces in society, which he can himself barely understand, conspire to prevent him from doing this as they were similarly conspiring to prevent others from so doing at a time when the soup kitchen was still a central reality and image.

Max's genuine needs are no more apparent to him than are John Proctor's or Eddie Carbone's. Like Proctor, he discovers himself at the very moment of losing himself, of losing his life. That this never becomes entirely convincing in *Honors at Dawn* is because the opposing forces are as yet too crudely dramatized and because neither Max nor Harry really escape the polemical roles they are assigned. A social debate is staged but those who participate in it lack, as yet, that individualized human reality that would make them anything more than mechanistic embodiments of the views they express.

There are, however, hints of something more. As in *They Too Arise* Miller is plainly fascinated not only by the suspect nature of language – deeply implicated in the processes of betrayal – but also by betrayal itself. At the heart of the play is the informer, a decade and a half before the McCarthyite witch-hunts were popularly supposed to have motivated him to write about the subject in *The Crucible* and *A View from the Bridge* and a quarter of a century before he was to make this a central concern of *After the Fall*. To an extent, of course, all this does is to remind us of the obvious fact that the social tensions of the Depression bred that kind of corruption as readily as did the hysteria of the 1950s. But, more than that, the informer stands here, as in a more sophisticated way he does in Miller's later work, as a perfect symbol of that betrayal of selfhood and identity which may be socially inspired but which is generated out of the self. This was, in other words, the beginnings of an investigation which was eventually to lead him, in *After the Fall*, to see betrayal as the mark of humanity, as, ironically, that impulse which links us together even as it is a denial of the fact of communality. If Max and Harry are seen as two aspects of the same self then this conviction can be traced to the very beginnings of Miller's career, selflessness doing battle with selfishness within the same sensibility.

Harry's problem is not that he believes nothing but that he believes altogether too much. Like Willy Loman he believes in the valuation which others are prepared to place on him. The intangible attracts him so long as it offers a promise and a description of the tangible world he hopes to inherit. He has no feelings. Even the girl he dates is just one more merit badge to qualify him for a world of inevitable success. Max, by contrast, is instinctive. He is baffled by abstraction, at home only with the practical realities of machinery. Marxist theory bounces off him. His final speech, as he calls out to his fellow workers, is not an expression of convictions rationally learned but of a spontaneous impulse. He is, in other words, Miller's attempt to create a working-class character who is denied access to the language which would make it possible for him to express the real nature of his feelings. He is a deliberate contrast to the middle-class

Marxists at the university and as such something of an improvement on the working-class heroes created by writers anxious to celebrate a class about whom they knew little. Miller did know such people. This was the pay-off for the years he had spent earning enough money to go to the university. That he was not yet able to find a convincing dramatic shape for such a character is hardly surprising in a man who was still an undergraduate student.

In awarding Miller his second Avery Hopwood Award, Susan Glaspell must have found something reassuringly familiar about *Honors at Dawn*. For in the form of *Inheritors*, which she wrote in 1921, she had also written about the corruption of a university and the threatened firing of a radical professor as the result of external pressure, seeing in that a symbol of the collapse of national values. Both plays have epic pretensions, relating family conflict to public issues. But where Susan Glaspell's admittedly much more assured work was produced by the Provincetown Players and secured national attention, Miller's failed to secure even a laboratory production at his own university, something that was accorded to his next play.

The Great Disobedience was the third play Miller submitted for an Avery Hopwood Award and the only one not to win; it came second. Based on his visit to Jackson prison, it set out, as did Tennessee Williams in his early unpublished play *Not About Nightingales*, to identify the need for prison reform. Just as *Honors at Dawn* had detected the hand of big business in university affairs so *The Great Disobedience* sees the prison system as intimately involved in capitalism's efforts to protect its profits and maintain its control. Victor Matthews, who has become an inconvenience to the rubber company for which he works as a compensation doctor, is sent to prison, ostensibly for performing an illegal abortion but in fact because of his failure to protect the interests of his employer. This is presented as doubly evil in so far as the abortion itself is seen as a life-saving gesture (the young girl in question was contemplating suicide) offered to someone already suffering as a consequence of an inequitable society. The penal system not only corruptly cooperates with big business, it becomes a symbol of the power of capital and industry to rob individuals of their freedom and even their lives. Once inside, the prisoners are further destroyed as wardens conspire to sell them drugs, an image of an economic system in which demand is created by those who control supply.

Between Victor and his fate (he is classified as a high-security prisoner, on the instructions of his employer, and as such is sentenced in effect to solitary confinement) stand two people; Caroline, the woman who loves him, and Dr. Karl Mannheim, an old college friend who is now the prison psychiatrist. Only two years earlier they had all been at university together,

Caroline then being Karl's girl. Now Victor's career is in ruins and Karl's depends on the goodwill of a sadistic Deputy Warden. The question is whether Karl will side with a corrupt system or with his friend. He is certainly liberal in his approach to the men in his care and tries to mitigate the worst effects of the world in which they find themselves. He attempts to change the system in subtle ways. He is, in effect, a liberal reformer who rather than destroy the system tries to modify it and treat the symptoms of those it damages. Understanding the nature of the mechanism which would humiliate and corrupt those it touches he is frozen into inaction by the blunt irrationalism of its representatives. When he might act, he does not.

Karl Mannheim is methodical. Everything has to be in its place. System substitutes for value, and method for action. Placed under stress he quickly loses control of the world he thought he could dominate. He fills his office with works of art which hint at a sensibility he lacks the courage to translate into decisive acts. Though he accumulates evidence of corruption he forbears to use it until shocked out of the rational and systematic mode of thought which he had mistaken for a genuine intervention.

The Great Disobedience is, if anything, more melodramatic than *Honors at Dawn*. Victor Matthews becomes psychotic, convinced that Caroline carries the child who will one day grow up to denounce the system which has destroyed its father and to claim the freedom which is denied to him. Karl also slips to the very edge of madness, overcome by guilt at his failure to intervene in the lives of others, and by shame at his inability to shape his own life into something he can claim with any pride. Though his revelations of drug trafficking do eventually precipitate an inquiry, this merely serves to deflect attention from the real villain, Stephen Riker, owner of the Riker Rubber Company, for whom the prison system exists as a means of removing troublemakers. Though the Deputy Warden is dismissed, he is replaced by another Riker man, transferred from the South where Riker has also been using the prison system for his own advantage. The play ends ambiguously as a young assistant joins Mannheim, revealing the same initial enthusiasm but also the same willingness to compromise, the same fastidiousness that had characterized Mannheim himself.

The battle is essentially that between a soulless capitalism and the needs and aspirations of the individual. Beyond that it is a debate about the nature of American values. According to the industrialist, Riker, "A man's duty is to go out and get what he wants. An idea like that made this country." The truth is that in this play an idea like that is shown to be unmaking the country and the prison becomes more than simply the setting of the play. It becomes an emblem of a society imprisoned by its own myths.

In *Tender is the Night* Fitzgerald chooses sexuality to express his sense of a world deformed at its core by the corrupting power of money. Incest, homosexuality, lesbianism are offered as images of a narcissistic, intransitive system. Hemingway draws on the same image in *To Have and Have Not*. In *The Great Disobedience* abortion, an illusory pregnancy, and homosexuality are offered as images of a world in which the generative impulse is dead. There seems, in other words, no future. As Caroline says, in accusing Riker of destroying those whose life he touches, "You've left my life bare as a tree is bare in a never-ending frost . . . remember the child who was never born!" Her husband ends up in a straitjacket, she in despair: "I don't believe in anything anymore." Mannheim is similarly desperate, feeling that there can be no solution, "just so long as one man is owned by another like a beast is owned." Even his profession now seems futile: "The time has come to stop playing around with neuroses and psychoses and the rest of the alphabet. I'm thinking that we'd better look to the first cause instead of helping to justify the crimes our great men commit. I'm thinking . . . we'd better start becoming doctors again." Somehow a new commitment is born, a new commitment dramatized in the familiar image of 1930s radicalism – man as Christ:

> I'm a strong man now. Strong, as though a new thing, a new blood is transfused into me. I feel that Victor wasn't entirely wrong. Like a lot of insane men his mind brushed away all the opaque reflections that attract us, and touched the central nerve. I feel . . . as though . . . something was actually born in here. A new son . . . the one they couldn't kill with Victor because things like this are not the property of a man. They belong to mankind. Long ago it was nailed to a cross, but it never died, perhaps because its conception lies in the constant struggle of men with masters of men. That is its immaculateness, its divorcement from the single father. . . there must be many men like this. There must be a new Jesus in tens of thousands walking the earth.

Miller has never since written this kind of clotted prose. The transubstantiation of liberal into radical seems to have tempted him to exchange controlled prose for an inflated rhetoric which this time is not itself offered for judgment. It is, as the judges detected, the weakest of the three plays which he produced as a student. He followed it, however, with a work which, though not produced for many years, was a powerful and accomplished drama. He began *The Golden Years* in 1939 and completed it in 1940; the typescript bears his Brooklyn address, 1350 East Third Street.

The Golden Years concerns the ravaging of Mexico by Cortes. Montezuma, King of the Aztecs, is pictured as insecure even in his absolute power, indeed, in part, because of his absolute power in that he is unsure what purpose it could be said to serve. Cortes, meanwhile, battles his way to the heart of the empire in search of gold, though in the name of the Christian God. The play explores the reason for Montezuma's capitulation before this adventurer who lacks even the sanction of the Spanish throne. It dramatizes the dilemma of a man who suspects he may have encountered his own fate and hence, mesmerized, paralyzed by the sheer certainty of the invader, surrenders himself and his people.

Written at a time when European powers had readily appeased Adolf Hitler, bemused and disabled by his effrontery and perhaps persuaded of his historical inevitability, it offers a comment on his own times as well as a study of power and its seductiveness. As he has reminded us, "Charles Lindberg went to Germany and came back to say that this was the wave of the future. They were neat, clean, and white. They knew how to deal with life."[3] Montezuma stared at Cortes and saw the future, too.

Miller speaks of *The Golden Years* as looking toward a "non-existent poetic theatre inspired by the Elizabethan models."[4] In fact there were other models closer to home in Maxwell Anderson's plays, while T. S. Eliot's *Murder in the Cathedral* received its first production at the hands of the Federal Theatre which Miller hoped would prove a home for his own play. Auden and Isherwood, likewise, believed in the possibility of a drama whose language transcended the urgencies of a world confronted by the prosaic realities of Depression at home and Fascism abroad. In fact 1930s writing abounded in the elevated language of an idealized socialism (as evidenced in the theatre by Clifford Odets, and in the novel by John Steinbeck), or simply the soft metaphysics of William Saroyan.

The Golden Years is not a verse drama. Its poetic language is functional, distinguishing a world structured on myth and symbol from one primarily dedicated to fact and engorged with the arrogance of power. To be sure Cortes pays lip service to the idea of transcendence, while Montezuma is as drenched in blood as the man who challenges him, but they are divided by more than joins them. For Cortes, religion is no more than cover for rapacity while Montezuma's power is in the service of a search for meaning which leads, through mere appearance, to the heart of what he takes to be truth, though he, too, yearns for the sense of significance and centrality which is one of the illusory gifts of power. That they are fatally illusioned, becoming each other's fate, is an irony which breaks both men, though only one comes to understand the extent of his betrayals.

Montezuma is a king who lives in fear. His seemingly unchallenged power, his conquests, his role as mediator with the gods, leave him uncertain as to his purpose, unsure of his destiny. Human sacrifice may appease the spirits, intercede with the gods, unlock the cipher of being, or it may mean nothing more than a gesture whose cruelty is not vitiated by a higher purpose. A threatened eclipse of the moon may indeed signal the end of time and indicate that he himself is the failed conclusion of history. He is thus afraid that meaning itself may be annihilated or that the futility of his own life may stand exposed, all his actions rendered devoid of purpose and he the agent of nothing more than his need for coherence. He is afraid, in other words, of inhabiting an absurd universe which will render his own life a nullity. Montezuma is mesmerized not simply by Cortes but by his own deepening despair. He looks for order and finds chaos. He is afraid, beyond anything, that there is no spine to experience, no shape to existence. Longing for significance, he is seduced by a myth which seems to offer him function and meaning if only through his surrender to a force which appears to have the sanction of history.

He seeks a force greater than himself so that he may prostrate himself before it and thus affirm it and his existence, discover true power through his obedience to authority. Implacable himself, he looks for a greater implacability in which he may lose himself and thus become an agent of the history in which he is no longer sure that he believes. Beyond this, he hopes that such a surrender may make him the acme of history and thus transform his status to that of deity. As Miller has remarked, "it was obvious that the invaders had to be gods because no ordinary humans could hope to defeat him. Paralyzed by his wish to placate the gods, and earn the approbation of heaven, he wanted to become a god, which was all that was left to him."[5]

The arrival of Cortes is, thus, less a challenge than an apotheosis, redemption for a man desperate to believe that he is more than a tyrant grown old, flourishing only on the desperation of others. For the first time he feels the ecstasy of surrender purged of its taint in so far as it is accommodated to myth, an acknowledgment of process, the fulfillment of prophecy, mere obedience to necessity. Urged to destroy Cortes he stays his hand, not out of fear but a respect for the sheer irrationality of the man, a suspicion that he may embody an unequivocal power to which he may submit and in which he may be subsumed. Cortes's arrogant claim to territory, his single-minded commitment to conquest, are the evidence for his significance. To destroy Cortes would be to destroy a threat which contains a hope.

Montezuma becomes an appeaser not because he fears he could not defeat Cortes but because he has no wish to do so. On one level they are close kin. Their instincts are imperial, their cruelty unqualified, because they serve some purpose beyond themselves. Both subordinate the world to an idea. Montezuma's weakness is to believe that his concept of honour is shared by a man for whom history, culture, faith, are so many trinkets to be rendered down in the crucible. Cortes is a pirate for whom theft is a sufficient reason for being. Montezuma wishes to believe anything but what his eyes reveal to him. If this man burns, destroys, ravages, it must be for a reason, as his own similar exploits have been, for only the gods and those who serve them have such a sanction. It never occurs to him that for Cortes the world exists only to be plundered. His claim to serve a god of love is invalidated by his actions. Montezuma makes no such claim. Quetzalcoatl and the other gods grow strong on blood and those sacrificed are presumed to be messengers, articulating hidden truths with their surrendered lives. Cortes peoples Mexico with corpses to feed his hunger for wealth. Montezuma does the same to feed his hunger for meaning.

On one level Cortes is a confidence trickster, distracting his victims with promises. He travels with a priest but the conversions which interest him are those of gold artifacts into ingots. His power, like that of all confidence tricksters, lies in his ability to make others believe that he has something worthwhile to offer. Adolf Hitler offered no less at Munich. Montezuma is vulnerable because he wants to believe. He is destroyed not by his credulity, which is secondary, but by his need to see in this challenge to his authority a destiny which will give meaning to his life. Uncertain in his own power, he is drawn to the certainty of Cortes as much as to the mythical role with which he endows him.

Miller has said that he finds an "optimistic undercurrent" in *The Golden Years* because there is "no real despair or defeat of the spirit."[6] Yet, in truth, the optimism is hard to find. The play ends with Montezuma dying and Cortes triumphant. The key, perhaps, lies in Montezuma's dying speech to Cortes: "When my people struck me, I was oppression in their eyes. Look on me, Conquistador; in my unmourned face see your face, and in my destiny, the destiny of all oppression that dares to dig its heel in the living heart of Mexico."[7] The debate is essentially over the logic of history. Montezuma's failure to resist will be redeemed in time by a more fundamental instinct to rebel against oppression. His death is exemplary and hence, in some sense, sacrificial. Ironically, his death generates the meaning which he has been seeking. He becomes what he believed the human sacrifices, which he had ordered, always to have been: a messenger.

For Miller, Cortes represented the "intensely organized energies" of Fascism, while Montezuma, for all his authoritarianism, stood for the wayward self-fixation which he saw as characterizing the democracies. Looking back, he sees *The Golden Years* as "struggling against passive acceptance of fate or even of defeat in life," as urging "action to control one's future."[8]

If Miller reacted against the temporizing of the European powers in the face of Hitler, he did so with the instincts of a revolutionary ("Why am I a revolutionary?" he asked himself in a diary entry dated 1941), as we read the play through our knowledge of the fate both of the Spanish empire and Hitler's imperial ambitions. On a deeper level, however, as his play *Broken Glass* was to show nearly fifty years later, the tension remains. There is no final triumph.

Even this early in his career, however, one central conviction is clear. In the words of Ernest Hemingway, a man can be destroyed but not defeated. As he was later to reject the theatre of the absurd, which seemed, to him, to express the futility of struggle, so, in 1939–40, he declined to accept the inevitability of appeasement and betrayal. At the centre of *The Golden Years*, as he himself has insisted, is an individual, Montezuma, whose role remains crucial. He is, in most ways, a product of his times, submitting as much to his sense of fate as to Cortes. Nonetheless, his final realization amounts to an insistence that history is not a juggernaut, out of control, a simple expression of irresistible force. It is a product of those who wish to see themselves as its victim. There is, in short, at the heart of *The Golden Years*, a surviving faith in the possibility of change and in the idea of the individual as an agent of change. And behind this, perhaps, is the notion that theatre itself, an individual creation requiring social form, may itself be an instrument for effecting that change.

As Miller admits, he was lavish in his use of actors, hoping to see his play produced by the Federal Theatre. When the Theatre was dissolved by act of Congress he sent it to the Group Theatre, who promptly lost it. It was finally produced, in 1987, at my urging, by BBC Radio for whom the apparently large cast and sounds of battle posed few problems. The success of this production led to a television version.

The Golden Years may appear to lack the theatricality of Peter Shaffer's *Royal Hunt of the Sun*, but in fact its theatrical potential is considerable, from the startling opening scene in which the moon is eclipsed, through to the operatic ending, with Montezuma facing his people in the moment of his own betrayal and disillusionment. The contrasting languages spoken by Montezuma and Cortes, the one lyrical, deeply metaphoric, the other bluntly prosaic and direct, express not only two different sensibilities but two different interpretations of experience. Here, as throughout his subsequent career, he found in the private dilemma of an individual the essence of a public concern, as he recognized the present as the price to be paid for the past. Later, in *The Crucible* and, forty years after that, in *Broken Glass*, he discovered in history the key to current dilemmas as well as a connection between ourselves and those from whose past failures we believe ourselves immune.

Miller followed *The Golden Years* with *The Half-Bridge* (1941–43), the only one of his plays to deal directly with the war. It has never been published or produced and is, perhaps, the weakest of his apprentice plays.

It concerns Mark Donegal, mate of a merchant ship, who is encouraged by a Nazi agent to use his ship for piracy and insurance fraud. Disillusioned by an America which seems to him to have betrayed its frontier past for a flaccid mediocrity, he is tempted. In common with many subsequent Miller protagonists he wants to leave his mark on the world but fails to ask himself what his life can amount to if that meaning isolates him from the very people who already grant him the significance for which he yearns. In the end it is not patriotism which deflects him but love, the love of a woman but also the love offered by his fellow shipmates. The half-bridge of the title is a reference to the incomplete life of anybody who fails to understand the necessity to open communication with others. His sense of a powerful absurdity governing human affairs is conquered, finally, by a new vision of human solidarity. The echoes of 1930s communalism are still apparent but, in common with the much revised *They Too Arise*, drained now of ideological content.

But if *The Half-Bridge* is of little more than academic interest Miller was now on the verge of launching his public career, for the following year his first Broadway play appeared. It was, however, a play with a history.

Some years ago Arthur Miller and I were idly turning over the contents of a box in the study of his Connecticut home when he came upon a bundle of pages tossed in a corner. The brittle paper was turning a scorched yellow-brown and beginning to crumble at the edges. Indeed there was a pollen-like dust between the pages as the wartime paper disintegrated. Several pages were heavily scored through and, judging by its eccentric numbering, much of the typescript was missing. Miller riffled through it, trying to make sense of the disorder. It was a novel, begun in 1940, and rejected by publishers. He had, he confessed, never quite got it right. In a quixotic gesture, he gave it to me. It is called *The Man Who Had All the Luck*.

It tells the story of a man, David, for whom everything turns out well and who thus believes that he has no hand in his own destiny. He is the beneficiary of chance, of coincidence, of, in short, luck. What seems missing from life is any sense of justice as an operative principle. The result is guilt and fear, guilt at what he feels is his unfair advantage, and fear of the ultimate fall which he is convinced must eventually come if the justice for which he looks, and in which, perversely, he wishes to believe, should finally operate. In contrast to him is another young man, Amos, who watches as his own hopes come to nothing. Others in this small community also have to live with disappointment. Overwhelmed by an absurdity which sends one man on to success and another spiraling down to failure, David first drifts into psychosis and then takes his own life. Death is the only reality he can embrace.

Unable to make the story work convincingly as a novel, Miller rewrote it as a play, publishing it in 1944 in a volume of new American writing, whose editor was prescient enough to include the work of other unknowns: Norman Mailer, Jane Bowles, and Ralph Ellison. In shrinking it from a 360-page novel he opted for a different story and a different style. It became a fable in which the accidents of fate are deliberately underscored, heightened, as the story moves from realistic psychological study to stylized exemplary tale. By the time it was produced, however, still further revisions had been made, the most crucial occurring to Miller as he sat on a Long Island beach. David and Amos became brothers. It was not simply that two parts of the play, which otherwise had been thematically but not psychologically linked, now came together, but that here, as in the later plays, abstract concerns could be earthed in living relationships. *All My Sons*, *Death of a Salesman*, and *The Price* all bear the marks of that afternoon on a Long Island beach.

If *The Man Who Had All the Luck* turned out to be an ironic title for a novel which failed to find a publisher, it was an equally ironic title for the play which opened at New York's Forrest Theatre in 1944, Miller's first ever professional production. It folded in four days. The failure, he later judged, was a consequence of a production which never found the style necessary to unlock its peculiar power. As he later remarked, "in a different theatrical time this play might well have stuck to the wall instead of oozing down."[9] But ooze down it did. The trauma was such that he decided to abandon the theatre. So it was that we came close to losing *Death of a Salesman*, *The Crucible*, *A View from the Bridge*, and all those plays which have made him and the American theatre so compelling for nearly half a century. He turned briefly back to the novel, in 1945 publishing his study of American anti-semitism, *Focus*. The theatre, though, would not be denied and he returned to it with *All My Sons* in 1947. It ran for 328 performances. Miller's career was launched.

The Man Who Had All the Luck was never quite forgotten, though, and in 1988 a successful staged reading in New York suddenly offered a clue to the play's inelegant nose-dive into obscurity. He recalled that the original production had been "lit in reassuring pink and rose" and offered as "a small town genre comedy."[10] He had been appalled at the time without knowing what could be done to rectify it. Now he came to see that as a fable it should create a distance between itself and its apparent realism. The coincidences, whereby fate apparently intrudes on David's behalf, should be "arrantly unapologetic." Character, while tangible, had to be subordinated to the "obsessive grip of a single idea."[11] ("I'd set out to write a kind of myth and . . . a myth pays most attention to the process of fate, as it works itself out, rather than to realistic character.")[12] And for one last time he considered whether his central character should live or die.

As he explained, in his introduction to the version published in 1989,

> The Man Who Had All the Luck tells me that in the midst of the collectivist Thirties I believed it decisive what an individual thinks and does about his life, regardless of overwhelming social forces . . . The play is after all attacking the evaluation of people by their success or failure and worse yet, denying the efficacy of property as a shield against psychological catastrophe . . . David Beeves in this play arrives as close as he can at a workable, conditional faith in the neutrality of the world's intention toward him.[13]

In 1989 that final version made its way into print and a forgotten play was reborn. If it proved a key work in Miller's development as a writer it had also touched a private and public nerve. There is, indeed, an autobiographical dimension to the story, and not simply because he derived an element of the plot from a story told to him by a relative of his first wife. It touched on something more personal.

It may seem odd that a young man yet to make his way in the professional theatre should write a play in which success seems a burden, but the fact is that, judged by the standards of the day, and of his family, he was a success. He was a graduate. Two of his plays had won awards at university and one a Theatre Guild Award. For several years he had been writing radio plays, even working with Orson Welles on one of them. But, as a playwright, who by definition worked with words, his success was inescapably a reproach to a father who was, effectively, illiterate. For all his admiration for his many qualities, in his heart he thought of his father as a failure and no son can make such a judgment without guilt. Can success anyway exist without the failure on which it depends for definition?

But it went further than that, for this was a culture in which success was a moral imperative, a natural birthright. Miller has said that in some ways the American dream is the fundamental theme of American writers and in the 1930s he had seen that dream collapse. As he remarked of The Man Who Had All the Luck, it "hardly seemed a Depression play," but "the obsessive terror of failure and guilt for success"[14] which it reflects had an immediate and real foundation. He had seen lives suddenly and arbitrarily ruined. Others, equally inexplicably, prospered. The logic that was presumed to connect effort to achievement seemed to have been surgically removed and that left a series of disturbing questions. Are we then not the authors of our fate? And, if not, who and what are we? His own father was ruined by the Wall Street Crash; a man to be admired became quite suddenly a man to be pitied, and pity can be as corrosive as guilt.

But there was another source for *The Man Who Had All the Luck*: the war. From the security and relative prosperity even of Depression America he had watched the European powers concede their destiny to a man whose assurance seemed to mesmerize those who confronted a power which increased with every success. Chamberlain and others seemed to invent an inevitability to which they could then submit. As later in his career, he was fascinated by those who refused to take their lives in their own hands. For, finally, a moral world requires the acknowledgment that we are the product of our actions. It is not that there is no injustice in the world, no inequity. It is not that there are no sudden changes in the economic and political realities which shape the world in which we live, but that within the circle of possibilities which we inhabit we are still responsible for what we do. Like the story of Job, of which it is a mirror image, *The Man Who Had All the Luck* is, Miller has confessed, essentially "an argument with God." The issue, he has explained, is "how much of our fate do we make and how much is accident?"

In the 1950s and 1960s Arthur Miller reacted against the theatre of the absurd precisely because it seemed to him complicit in the absurdity which it dramatized. So it is that in the end David Beeves has to confront himself, as so many of Miller's characters were at least to attempt to do. For either we are, as a character in *The Man Who Had All the Luck* insists, "a jellyfish. The tide goes in and the tide goes out. About what happens to him, a man has very little to say,"[15] or we are inventors of our own destiny, forced to acknowledge and accept responsibility for who we are and what we may be. For some the burden of that truth is all but insupportable; for others it is the key to a private and public meaning not preordained or dictated by circumstance but forged out of our encounter with the world and with ourselves.

NOTES

1 All quotations from unpublished texts are from typescripts held at the Harry Ransom Center of the University of Texas, or the Theatre Collection of the New York Public Library at Lincoln Center. In the context of this Companion detailed footnotes have been avoided.

2 Clifford Odets, *Golden Boy, Awake and Sing! The Big Knife* (Harmondsworth: Penguin, 1963), pp. 182–83.

3 Arthur Miller, interview with Christopher Bigsby, recorded at Arthur Miller's

house in Roxbury, Connecticut in summer 1995, for a series of four BBC radio programmes transmitted to mark his 80th birthday.

4 Arthur Miller, "Introduction," *The Golden Years* and *The Man Who Had All the Luck* (London: Methuen, 1989), p. 5.
5 Arthur Miller, interview with Christopher Bigsby, summer 1995.
6 Arthur Miller, "Introduction," *The Golden Years*, p. 6.
7 *The Golden Years*, p. 166.
8 Arthur Miller, "Introduction," *The Golden Years*, pp. 7–8.
9 Arthur Miller, interview with Christopher Bigsby, summer 1995.
10 Arthur Miller, "Introduction," *The Golden Years*, p. 6.
11 *Ibid.*
12 Christopher Bigsby (ed.), *Arthur Miller and Company* (London: Methuen, 1990).
13 Arthur Miller, "Introduction," *The Golden Years*, pp. 6–10.
14 Arthur Miller, interview with Christopher Bigsby, summer 1995.
15 *Ibid.*

4

STEVEN R. CENTOLA

All My Sons

Winner of the New York Drama Critics' Circle Award for best play of 1947, *All My Sons* is the work that launched Arthur Miller's long and distinguished career in the theatre. While few would argue that it is Miller's best or most important play, no one would dispute the fact that *All My Sons* deserves a special place in the playwright's canon because it constitutes his first major theatrical achievement, displays his extraordinary skill in handling dramatic form, and presages even better things yet to come from one of America's greatest dramatists.

The critical and commercial success of *All My Sons* marks a major turning point in Miller's career, for it came at a time when the young writer was struggling to establish his identity as a literary artist. Having won several awards for playwriting while he was enrolled in undergraduate school at the University of Michigan, Miller continued to develop the texts of stage plays even while supporting himself by working at odd jobs and successfully writing radio plays for the Columbia Workshop (CBS) and the Cavalcade of America (NBC) between the years 1938 and 1943. During the next two years, however, several events occurred that both challenged his commitment to playwriting and advanced his career as a writer. In 1944, Miller was asked to tour army training camps and gather information that could be used to supplement Ernie Pyle's script for the film *The Story of G. I. Joe.* Miller conducted many interviews both with new recruits and veteran soldiers and published the record of his conversations in a book of reportage entitled *Situation Normal.* In the same year, his dream of staging a Broadway production of one of his plays was realized when *The Man Who Had All the Luck* was produced at the Forrest Theater. Unfortunately, the play lasted only four performances and yielded mostly unfavorable reviews from his critics. Although Miller had better luck when *Focus,* his novel attacking anti-semitism in American society, was published in 1945, his disastrous experience with *The Man Who Had All the Luck* caused him to question his ability to write for the stage. He even decided to quit playwriting if he could not prove to himself with one last effort that he had the talent to write plays. Reflecting on his dissatisfaction with his achievement during the early phase of his career, Miller describes the ultimatum he gave himself:

> I was turning thirty then, the author of perhaps a dozen plays, none of which I could truly believe were finished. I had written many scenes, but not a play. A play, I saw then, was an organism of which I had fashioned only certain parts. The decision formed to write one more, and if it turned out to be unrealizable, I would go into another line of work.[1]

The play that resulted was *All My Sons*, and with its success and the subsequent acclaim won by both *Death of a Salesman* in 1949 and *The Crucible* in 1953, Miller secured his place as one of the leading dramatists to emerge from the post-World War II American theatre.

Miller's success with the dramatic form of *All My Sons*, ironically, had much to do with his failure with *The Man Who Had All the Luck*. According to Miller, one day while lying on the beach, he suddenly discovered how "a simple shift of relationships [in *The Man Who Had All the Luck*] . . . made at least two of the plays that followed possible, and a great deal else besides" (*Collected Plays*, pp. 14–15). What Miller realized was "that two of the characters, who had been friends in the previous drafts, were logically brothers and had the same father" (*Collected Plays*, p. 15). While this discovery could not help him save *The Man Who Had All the Luck* from its disaster, it did provide the basis for the drama in both *All My Sons* and *Death of a Salesman*. Miller explains:

> in writing of the father–son relationship and of the son's search for his relatedness there was a fullness of feeling I had never known before; a crescendo was struck with a force I could almost touch. The crux of *All My Sons*, which would not be written until nearly three years later, was formed; and the roots of *Death of a Salesman* were sprouted. (*Collected Plays*, p. 15)

Operating from this powerful sense of purpose, Miller found it easy to tell a story with a clear line of causation issuing from "the gradual and remorseless crush of factual and psychological conflict" (*Collected Plays*, p. 15). As he wrote *All My Sons*, he knew that the play would explore the way in which choices and behavior in the past impinge upon, shape, and even give rise to unforeseen and inescapable consequences in the future. For Miller discovered early on the structural principle that he would repeatedly return to as a playwright – a principle that he has aphoristically stated throughout his career by saying: "the structure of a play is always the story of how the birds came home to roost."[2] In *All My Sons*, Miller builds and reveals dramatic action that, by its very movement – by its creation, suspension, and resolution of tension; its inexorable rush toward tragic confrontation – proves that the past is always present and cannot be ignored, forgotten, or denied.

In its straightforward "revelation of process" (*Collected Plays*, p. 23), its linear progression of escalating crises building toward the explosive climax that in one shattering blow makes clear "the connections between the present and the past, between events and moral consequences, between the manifest and the hidden" (*Collected Plays*, p. 24), *All My Sons* exhibits the influence of one of Miller's acknowledged inspirations: Henrik Ibsen. Miller openly credits Ibsen with teaching him how a play could be built upon "a factual bedrock. A situation in his plays is never stated but revealed in terms of hard actions, irrevocable deeds; and sentiment is never confused with the action it conceals" (*Collected Plays*, p. 19). In *All My Sons*, Miller adopts Ibsen's technique of gradually "bringing the past into the present" (*Collected Plays*, p. 20), for one of the play's central themes "is the question of actions and consequences, and a way had to be found to throw a long line into the past in order to make that kind of connection viable" (*Collected Plays*, p. 20). But, like his Norwegian predecessor, Miller realized that "valid causation" (*Collected Plays*, p. 21) could only be achieved if the play conveys the complexity in life that transcends and belies a plot's tight lines and overt philosophical or social positions. *All My Sons* is indeed a tightly constructed play with ideas of importance, but the drama's success derives more from Miller's ability to capture the spirit and rhythm of a life not easily reducible to terse summary in a single assertion. In fact, one could even say that, despite its traditional form and adherence to the conventions of the realistic theatre, *All My Sons* resonates with ambiguity from the opening curtain to its powerful climactic close.

On its surface, the plot of *All My Sons* can easily be summarized. The play tells the story of a successful Mid-Western manufacturer of airplane parts who knowingly allows defective engines to be shipped to the United States Army during the Second World War. As a result, twenty-one American pilots die when the cracked cylinder heads cause their planes to malfunction and crash. Exonerated by the courts for his role in the catastrophe, Joe Keller, the play's central character, triumphantly returns to his community and futilely attempts to return to a life of normalcy, pretending the crime never occurred. The semblance of family harmony is maintained until his son, Chris, himself under pressure as his fiancée's brother forces him to acknowledge his own acquiescence, questions him about his role in the sordid business transaction. Chris, who had fought bravely in battle in the war and seen many of his troops perish under his command, has a different outlook from his father on the question of an individual's social responsibility. After several powerful scenes of intense debate about the individual's relation to society, Chris finally discloses his father's guilt and challenges him to accept responsibility for his actions. Until his son forces him to acknowledge his wrongdoing, Keller steadfastly maintains his innocence and justifies his anti-social behavior by proclaiming his right to keep the business from collapsing to ensure his family's survival. Ultimately, Chris succeeds in convincing Keller that he has an obligation to others in society as well. Keller belatedly realizes that his decisions have consequences and that his responsibilities extend beyond the family. Tortured by his guilt and unable to deal with his shame in his son's eyes, Keller tries to escape from his intolerable situation by putting a bullet in his head. The play ends with Chris facing with horror his own complicity in his father's self-destruction, and with Keller's death the play forcefully repudiates anti-social behavior that derives from the myth of privatism in American society.

While one could discuss this central theme in *All My Sons* exclusively in terms of its social context and its call for socially responsible behavior, reducing the play and Miller's treatment of this issue to these terms alone fails to do justice to its complexity and fascinating exploration of universally significant questions about the enigmatic nature of the self's relation to others. For as Christopher Bigsby accurately observes, while *All My Sons* is a play about our ability to connect with others and the world around us, it is also about more than our success or failure at achieving such a connection:

> this is also a play about betrayal, about fathers and sons, about America, about self-deceit, about self-righteousness, about egotism presented as idealism, about a fear of mortality, about guilt, about domestic life as evasion, about the space between appearance and reality, about the suspect nature of language, about denial, about repression, about a kind of despair finessed into hope, about money, about an existence resistant to our needs, about a wish for innocence when, as Miller was later to say in his autobiography, innocence kills, about a need for completion, about the gulf between the times we live in and the people we wish to believe ourselves to be, about the fragility of what we take to be reality, about time as enemy and time as moral force and so on . . .[3]

Ultimately, *All My Sons* is a play about both paradox and denial – or to state it more precisely, it is about a theme that Miller has described as "the paradox of denial."[4] In his autobiography, Miller discusses the circumstances that led to his systematic exploration of this theme while developing the character Maggie in *After the Fall*:

It was after returning from Germany that I began to feel committed to the new play, possibly because its theme – the paradox of denial – seemed so eminently the theme of Germany, and Germany's idealistically denied brutality emblematic of the human dilemma in our time . . . And so, bewildered and overwhelmed, she secretly came to side against herself, taking the world's part as its cynicism toward her ground down her brittle self-regard, until denial finally began its work, leaving her all but totally innocent of insight into her own collaboration as well as her blind blows of retaliation . . . The complex process of denial in the great world thus reflected in an individual seemed a wonderfully illuminating thematic center . . .

(*Timebends*, pp. 526–27)

While he may not have had the benefit of observing the Nuremberg Trials at the time he wrote *All My Sons*, he did witness the Second World War and was fully aware of the crimes against humanity evident in the Holocaust. Perhaps this background to the drama had as much to do with his writing a play about a guilty individual's betrayal of trust through war-profiteering crimes as the Nuremberg Trials and Germany's denial had later on his creation of *After the Fall*.

Beyond such speculation, however, other factors justify applying Miller's comments about Maggie and *After the Fall* to Joe Keller and *All My Sons*. Even though they differ stylistically, both plays are about choices and the paradox inherent in making choices. The paradox Miller describes in his Foreword to *After the Fall* is also evident in *All My Sons*:

there [is] . . . always the choice, always the conflict between his own needs and the desires and the impediments others put in his way. Always, and from the beginning, the panorama of human beings raising up in him and in each other the temptation of the final solution to the problem of being a self at all – the solution of obliterating whatever stands in the way, thus destroying what is loved as well.[5]

The crimes against society committed by Joe Keller derive from the same instinct for self-preservation and self-assertion that foster the adoption of a counterfeit innocence and the illusion of one's being a victim at the hands of others. Like Maggie, Keller prefers to see himself as a victim of others. Instead of acknowledging his complicity in the crime that sends unsuspecting pilots to their deaths, he lies about his involvement and denies his personal culpability so that he can preserve his false image of himself and maintain the illusion that he has regained his rightful place in society. Like Maggie, Keller denies his connection to the disaster because he blinds himself to the impulses that make him a danger to himself as well as to others. Keller cannot face what Miller calls "the murder in him, the sly and everlasting complicity with the forces of destruction" (Martin, *Theater*

Essays, p. 256). For this reason, Miller says, "Joe Keller's trouble, in a word, is not that he cannot tell right from wrong but that his cast of mind cannot admit that he, personally, has any viable connection with his world, his universe, or his society" (*Collected Plays*, p. 19). Hence, *All My Sons* "lays seige to . . . the fortress of unrelatedness" and shows why an individual's betrayal of trust and refusal to accept responsibility for others, if left uncensured by society, "can mean a jungle existence for all of us . . ." (*Collected Plays*, p. 19). Paradoxically, the very denial that is designed to protect him from prosecution and incarceration sets in motion the chain of events that lead to Keller's own self-imprisonment and self-imposed execution. Therefore, the paradox of denial in *All My Sons* is that not only does denial dehumanize, by nullifying the value of the social contract through the justification of indefensible anti-social acts, but it also intensifies the personal anguish and the irremediable alienation that plunge an individual into despair and bring about his tragic suicide.

Keller's anguish is in evidence throughout much of the play. He appears both "shamed" and "alarmed" early in Act One when his wife, Kate, reprimands him for telling children in the neighborhood that he has a jail hidden in his basement.[6] Defensively snapping, "What have I got to hide?" (*Collected Plays*, p. 74), Keller suggests not only that he begrudges Kate's condescending treatment of him, but also that he resents her veiled reminder that he does, indeed, have something to hide. The jail reference is repeated throughout the play to bring the past into the present and thereby strengthen the association between Keller's crime and his guilt. This motif underlines the fact that Keller's actions have consequences while also serving to illustrate the problem of setting oneself apart from and above the outer world. As though he were confined in a jail, Keller views the world as having "a forty-foot front . . . [that] ended at the building line" (p. 121). He denies his relation to society so that he can excuse unethical business practices that keep his manufacturing company fiscally sound and his family financially secure. So long as he acts to preserve the welfare of his family, Keller believes that anything he does can be justified. He convinces himself that his sole responsibility in life is to be successful so that he can support his wife and children. For Keller, "Nothin' is bigger" (p. 120) than the family.

Even the setting of the play is designed to reveal and comment on Keller's myopic world view. The entire play takes place in the *"back yard of the Keller home . . . The stage is hedged on right and left by tall, closely planted poplars which lend the yard a secluded atmosphere"* (p. 58). This scenic image successfully augments the stage action as gradual disclosures of family secrets and repressed feelings surface in the dialogue.

Miller skillfully works exposition into the plot that increases dramatic tension while simultaneously disclosing incriminating clues about Keller's guilt. For example, while reminiscing about his trial and the day he was released from prison, Keller describes himself parading in front of his neighbors after being exonerated and intentionally suffering their accusing stares while holding "a court paper in [his] pocket to prove" his innocence (p. 80). As George Deever, the embittered son of Keller's incarcerated partner, later tells the Keller family, the court paper really proves nothing since Keller won his trial on a technicality: the prosecution simply could not prove conclusively that Keller ordered his partner over the telephone to conceal the cracks and sell the faulty equipment. Nevertheless, by acting as if the court paper were proof of his innocence, Keller denies any connection to the crime and to the community whose trust he has violated. His denial of personal culpability shows not only his complete lack of remorse, but also his complete unwillingness to face the consequences of his actions. Paradoxically, by suggesting that only his possession of a court paper proves his innocence, Keller also unconsciously incriminates himself, for the audience knows that his innocence should derive solely from his awareness of the inaccuracy of the accusation against him. Keller's denial, therefore, has the opposite effect on his audience that it is designed to achieve.

Later, when Keller pleads with his son, Chris, to take his money and use it "without shame . . . with joy" (p. 87), Keller again unwittingly reveals his guilt. He knows that he has used unsavory means to build his fortune and that his son would have nothing to do with the family business if he knew that it prospered only because of the death of innocent pilots. Fearing that George Deever and his sister, Ann, will reveal the truth and turn Chris away from him, Keller tries to convince his son that the fortune earned is "good money, there's nothing wrong with that money" (p. 87). His insistence again produces unanticipated results. Instead of gaining Chris's confidence, Keller arouses his suspicion as Chris backs away from such unwanted suggestive conversation. The performance didascalia – "*a little frightened*" (p. 87) – that characterize Chris's apprehension over his father's unctuous appeal suggest that he is hesitant to understand too fully the implication of his father's entreaty. Like his father, Chris initially shows little interest in testing the strength of the bonds of family relationships with the uncomfortable truth.

When the truth about his role in the crime is finally revealed in Act Two, Keller tries to mitigate his guilt by portraying himself as the victim of forces beyond his control. He has convinced himself, and futilely tries to persuade Chris, that, given the limited choices available at the time, he made the best choice possible:

I'm in business, a man is in business; a hundred and twenty cracked, you're
out of business; you got a process, the process don't work you're out of
business; you don't know how to operate, your stuff is no good; they close
you up, they tear up your contracts, what the hell's it to them? You lay forty
years into a business and they knock you out in five minutes, what could I do,
let them take forty years, let them take my life away?   (p. 115)

Keller first tries to rationalize the crime by explaining that he only let the
defective machinery leave the shop because he hoped the parts would
perform satisfactorily. However, after Chris forces him to admit that he
knew the planes were likely to crash with the faulty engines, Keller justifies
his decision by pretending that it was consonant with the code of ethics
prevalent in American business transactions during the war:

Who worked for nothin' in that war? When they work for nothin', I'll work
for nothin'. Did they ship a gun or a truck outa Detroit before they got their
price? Is that clean? It's dollars and cents, nickels and dimes; war and peace,
it's nickels and dimes, what's clean? Half the Goddam country is gotta go if I
go!   (p. 125)

Instead of assuaging his guilt and restoring his son's lost respect and love,
Keller's denial of wrongdoing only serves to exacerbate the family crisis
and intensify his anguish and alienation.

Keller's crime is magnified in his son's eyes because he has all too
successfully manufactured the illusion that he is the infallible father figure.
By attempting to fulfill the inhuman demands of perfection that this
mythic, almost godlike, presence demands, Keller unwittingly sets himself
up for a fall. Like Miller's most popular father, Willy Loman in *Death of a
Salesman*, Keller never realizes that his effort to project and confirm in his
family's eyes his self-chosen image has contributed to his downfall. He
blinds himself to the truth because his role play is motivated by an
insecurity that comes from being "put out . . . [to] earn his keep" (p. 120)
when he was only ten years old. As Barry Gross points out, "There is no
zealot like a convert and there is probably no more devoted parent than a
neglected or an abandoned child."[7] Keller devotes himself to his family to
compensate for his childhood losses. However, instead of ensuring that the
problems of the past are not perpetually reenacted, his actions have the
obverse effect and cause a complete breakdown of the family unit.

One of the playwright's trademarks is his uncompromising honesty in the
investigation of the role each person plays in his own tragedy. Much of the
success of *All My Sons* has to do with Miller's complex vision of the
Kellers' shared guilt and complicity in the family's collapse. For Joe Keller
is not solely responsible for the Keller family's troubles. Like her husband,

Kate also lives in denial and resorts to lies and self-deception as a means of contending with her anguish and sorrow. Unable to accept the death of her elder son, Larry, in the war, Kate deludes herself into believing that he is still alive and will one day return home. To fortify her conviction, she adopts a blind faith in religion and obstinately argues that "God does not let a son be killed by his father" (*Collected Plays*, p. 114). Beyond all reason, she also succumbs to a superstitious reliance on astrology and maintains that Larry's horoscope contradicts everyone's suspicion that he died in the war. Kate prefers to believe that external forces – the stars – determine her son's destiny and not individual free choice. She futilely tries to deceive herself into believing that Larry could not deliberately crash his plane in a sincere effort to atone for his father's criminal act. However, when Ann Deever produces the incriminating letter from Larry that explains the motive for his suicide, Kate suffers no terrific shock. She has always known, while constantly denying, that Larry had died in the war.

Kate also plays a significant role in the cover-up of her husband's war-profiteering crime. Instead of encouraging him to face his responsibilities honestly, she protects him from prosecution by falsely verifying his lie. Ironically, however, her loyalty to her husband only serves to widen the gulf between them because their knowledge of their deception makes them feel uncomfortable in each other's presence. Both experience guilt and shame beneath the other's accusing stare. Therefore, by denying the facts and by conspiring to withhold the truth from their community, Joe and Kate Keller sentence themselves to a lonely and unhappy marriage.

Chris Keller is also responsible for his family's dilemma. The idealistic youth who energetically professes to detest dishonesty is as guilty as his parents of attempting to hide from reality. Though he persists in pushing his mother toward an acceptance of his brother's death, he does so for his own selfish reasons and not because he thinks it is in her best interest to be able to face reality. Likewise, even though he adopts a high moral tone and energetically indicts his father for his criminal irresponsibility, Chris knows that his words ring hollow because he has long suspected his father's guilt but deliberately avoided confronting the truth – again for purely selfish motives. At some level, Chris fears that, if he allows himself to see his father's human imperfections, he will also have to recognize his own limitations – and his experiences in the war make him dread that confrontation.

Having watched heroic young men under his command die selflessly in battle to save their comrades, Chris feels guilty for failing them and surviving the war. His guilt is the guilt of the survivor – the guilt, as Holga tells Quentin in *After the Fall*, that derives from knowing "no one is innocent they did not kill."[8] Chris desperately wants to escape from this guilt and the anguish it produces, so, when given the chance, he tries to find relief by disguising his disgust with himself as contempt for his father. His father becomes his scapegoat, and Chris casts all his own feelings of guilt and self-loathing onto his father in the hope that, by destroying his father, he can somehow expiate his own sins and escape from his own personal torment. It is hard, therefore, not to see and condemn the hypocrisy behind the zeal that leads to Keller's suicide. Miller effectively raises questions about Chris's real motives for bringing his father to justice and suggests that Chris's own denial at least partially accounts for his condemnation of his father.

A different sort of denial also helps to bring about his father's death. In a revealing comment, Chris tells his father why he is outraged by his socially irresponsible act: "*I* know you're no worse than most men but I thought you were better. I never saw you as a man. I saw you as my father" (*Collected Plays*, p. 125). By buying into the ideal father myth, Chris perpetuates the lie that his father is anything more than just a man. Such self-deception not only fosters Keller's illusions, but also paves the way for Chris's eventual, and inevitable, disillusionment. He demands the impossible – perfection from the imperfect – and inadvertently reinforces Keller's absurd conception of himself as above the law and his society. Paradoxically, when faced with the unmistakable proof that this unshakable image of his father has been nothing but an illusion, Chris unrealistically expects and demands the kind of noble gesture that is inconsistent with his father's badly flawed character. As Benjamin Nelson suggests, both father and son pay heavily for their denial: "Each man bears the burden of responsibility – Joe for casting himself in a role he cannot fulfill, and Chris for adamantly maintaining his adolescent adoration of an impossible idol – and each pays for the dichotomy between reality and the illusion he has fostered."[9]

Even minor characters in the play – Ann Deever, Jim Bayliss, and Sue Bayliss, specifically – demonstrate through their denial the adverse and oftentimes ironic effects of dishonest behavior. Like the Kellers, these characters withhold the truth from each other and themselves to sustain their illusions and protect their tenuous happiness. Ann Deever at least suspects Keller's guilt because of the letter she received from Larry before his suicide; however, she refrains from impeaching Keller until she feels compelled to do so in order to save her relationship with Chris. Her motives are selfish, governed primarily by a fundamental drive for self-preservation. Jim and Sue Bayliss also suspect Keller's guilt, yet they relinquish all sense of personal responsibility for ensuring that justice prevails. In fact, they continue to treat the Kellers as their best friends. Sue Bayliss even expresses admiration for Keller for pulling "a fast one to get out of jail" (*Collected Plays*, p. 94). Jim Bayliss goes one step further and tries to protect the Kellers from George Deever's hostile accusations and the family's ultimate confrontation over the truth. His interference, however, speaks loudly of his own insecurities and feeble effort to escape from reality. Jim tries to shield the family, particularly Chris, from the truth not only because he longs to protect them, but also because he needs to sustain the illusion of their perfection. He wants to keep alive the possibility for noble and decent behavior and believes the preservation of the Keller myth achieves this goal. Having already watched "The star of [his] honesty . . . go out," Jim knows he is lost "in the usual darkness" (p. 118). If he no longer has the illusory image of Chris's perfection to drive and inspire him, he will find it impossible "to remember the kind of man [he] wanted to be" (p. 118). Therefore, his denial has the same ironic impact as the self-deception and mendacity of the Keller family.

Even Larry's death shows the paradox of denial. His suicide is unmistakably a way of protesting and atoning for his father's crime. However, by choosing to die instead of returning home to bear the shame of his father's guilt, Larry fails to accept responsibility for bringing his father to justice for his crime. His death, like his father's eventual suicide, reflects an attempt to escape from the humiliation he would experience within his community. He dies to escape his anguish and therefore fails to transform guilt into responsibility. Only the nameless soldiers who die selflessly and valiantly in battle while fighting for the preservation of freedom and human dignity serve as a viable counterpart to the dishonorable and dishonored who walk the stage.

Particularly because of his treatment of the theme of the paradox of denial, Miller's play has a resonance that transcends its contemporary society and immediate situation. The catastrophe that affects the Keller family can occur anytime so long as people choose to embrace a counterfeit innocence that conceals their impulse to betray and dominate others. *All My Sons* proves that Miller's later indictment of Germany during the Nuremberg Trials in *After the Fall* can just as easily apply to any country which fosters illusions that elevate the native populace above the ostensibly menacing and inferior foreigners. In a country at war with an external threat, perhaps it is especially easy to succumb to such self-deception, and in that case, then, the background to *All My Sons* makes the play's drama that much more salient and relevant. In fact, one can even link the play to Miller's subsequent view of the phenomenon of the concentration camp as "the logical conclusion of contemporary life." Miller writes:

If you complain of people being shot down in the streets, of the absence of communication or social responsibility, of the rise of everyday violence which people have become accustomed to, and the dehumanization of feelings, then the ultimate development on an organized social level is the concentration camp. . . . The concentration camp is the final expression of human separateness and its ultimate consequence.[10]

In *All My Sons*, Miller shows how the impulse to betray and to deny responsibility for others, when left ungoverned, can run rampant and wreak havoc on the individual, his family, and his society – even, perhaps, civilization as a whole. The paradox of denial, therefore, is that the very defense mechanism that is employed to justify the rightness of a socially reprehensible act can ultimately become the exclusive means by which an individual self-destructs. The Kellers, and many of those around them, choose to blame everyone else for their dilemma, but only they are the authors of their destiny – and their failure to accept the tremendous burden of their freedom and responsibility is itself the cause of their personal tragedy.

NOTES

1 Arthur Miller, Introduction to *Arthur Miller's Collected Plays*, vol. I (New York: Viking Press, 1957), p. 16.

2 Arthur Miller, "The Shadows of the Gods," in Robert A. Martin (ed.), *The Theater Essays of Arthur Miller* (New York: Penguin Books, 1978), p. 179.

3 Christopher Bigsby, "A British View of an American Playwright," in Steven R. Centola (ed.), *The Achievement of Arthur Miller: New Essays* (Dallas: Contemporary Research Associates, 1995).

4 Arthur Miller, *Timebends* (New York: Grove Press, 1987), p. 526.

5 Arthur Miller, Foreword to *After the Fall*, in Martin (ed.), *The Theater Essays of Arthur Miller*, p. 257.

6 Arthur Miller, *All My Sons*, in *Arthur Miller's Collected Plays*, vol. I, p. 78.

7 Barry Gross, "*All My Sons* and the Larger Context," *Modern Drama* 18 (1975): 17.

8 Arthur Miller, *After the Fall*, in *Arthur Miller's Collected Plays*, vol. II (New York: Viking Press, 1981), p. 240.

9 Benjamin Nelson, *Arthur Miller: Portrait of a Playwright* (New York: David McKay, 1970), p. 88.

10 Olga Carlisle and Rose Styron, "Arthur Miller: An Interview," in Martin (ed.), *The Theater Essays of Arthur Miller*, p. 289.

5

MATTHEW C. ROUDANÉ

Death of a Salesman and the poetics of Arthur Miller

Death of a Salesman is a deceptively simple play. Its plot revolves around the last twenty-four hours in the life of Willy Loman, the hard-working sixty-three-year-old traveling salesman whose ideas of professional, public success jar with the realities of his private desires and modest accomplishments. Subtitled "Certain private conversations in two acts and a requiem," the play has a narrative which unwinds largely through Willy Loman's daydreams, private conversations revealing past family hopes and betrayals, and how those past experiences, commingled with entropic present circumstances, culminate in Willy's death. Realizing that in death he may provide for his family in ways he never could during his lifetime, Willy commits suicide, hoping that his insurance will grant Biff a "twenty-thousand-dollar"[1] deliverance, an extended period of grace. He hopes the insurance money will somehow expiate, or at least minimize, the guilt which he feels for his affair at the Standish Arms Hotel a lifetime ago. The simplicity of the play, however, quickly dissolves into filial ambiguity, civic paradox, and philosophic complexity.

Mythologizing America

Death of a Salesman presents a rich matrix of enabling fables that define the myth of the American dream. Indeed, most theatregoers assume, on an a priori level, that the principles Willy Loman values – initiative, hard work, family, freedom, consumerism, economic salvation, competition, the frontier, self-sufficiency, public recognition, personal fulfillment, and so on – animate American cultural poetics. The Founding Fathers, after all, predicated the US Constitution on the belief that every citizen possesses an inalienable right to the unfettered pursuit of the American Dream. No wonder Benjamin Franklin's practical 1757 essay on how to achieve Salvation, *The Way to Wealth* (whose title would have prompted Willy Loman to buy a copy), attracted the common working person. Although

Figure 1 Kate Reid, Dustin Hoffman, John Malkovich, and Stephen Lang in the 1984 New York production of *Death of a Salesman*, directed by Michael Rudman.

Willy Loman, inspired by a mythologized Dave Singleman and a desire to build a future for his boys through hard work, endorses such values, it is an endorsement foisted upon him less by personal choice than by a malevolent universe whose hostility mocks his every pursuit. Well-meaning yet lacking, a fatherless father, a salesman no longer capable of selling, Willy Loman can only cling to idyllic fables that baffle as they elude him. In the past, the ever talkative Willy has lived by "contacts" and "who you know and the smile on your face!" (*Death of a Salesman*, p. 86); in the present, Willy's talk reaches a Beckettian *de*crescendo, "Shhh!" (p. 136) being his last utterance before he speeds off to his suicide.

In its text and subtext, then, *Death of a Salesman* replicates a model of community and of citizenship to which most theatregoers – regardless of gender, race, nationality, or ideology – respond. The nature of that popular and intellectual response varies greatly, to be sure. The play embodies, for many, the *peripeteia*, *hamartia*, and *hubris* that Aristotle found essential for all great tragedies. For many feminist critics, on the other hand, the play stages "a nostalgic view of the plot of the universalized masculine protagonist of the Poetics";[2] it presents a grammar of space that marginalizes Linda Loman and, by extension, all women, who seem Othered, banished to the periphery of a patriarchal world. *Death of a Salesman*, the universalists counter, seems beyond philosophical limits or gendered subjectivity, and thus is a play to which all – social constructionists, Jungians, Marxists, poststructuralists, and so on – react. *Death of a Salesman* presents a constellation of conflicting views and warring narratives, and has become what Walter Benjamin would call a "cultural treasure." This explains its enduring appeal. Within a year of its premiere, *Death of a Salesman* was playing in every major city in the United States. As early as 1951 it was viewed by appreciative audiences in at least eleven countries abroad, including Great Britain, France, Israel, and Argentina. As Brenda Murphy observes, "since its premiere, there has never been a time when *Death of a Salesman* was not being performed somewhere in the world."[3]

This is not to imply that the play has received universal praise. For decades, artistic terrorists (to borrow Frank Zappa's term) masquerading as theatre reviewers, as well as serious scholars, have taken Miller to task. The charges are familiar. The play sentimentalizes experience. Its Hallmark Card flourish at the end dismantles the play's moral seriousness. The rhetoric of clichés diminishes its riposte. The play's protagonist is an unfit subject of tragedy, an unworthy man incapable of carrying the tragic burdens its author places on him. An implicit sexism somehow dates the play. And, among other charges, Miller in this play and in selected theatre essays presents a flawed essentialistic humanism. But the critical challenges, sometimes eloquently and convincingly argued, often seem much to do about little. The emotional impact of the play remains so strong that the response of most theatregoers, despite the occasional dissenting voice of some academics, has been overwhelmingly favourable for half a century.

Such praise comes from the notion that most in the audience relate to as they rebel against the Lomans. The adulterous father. The marginalized mother. Wayward children. A family's battles to pay bills. Unemployment. The child's quest. Spite. Loss. Felt but unexpressed love. Guilt and shame. Self-reliance. Theatregoers see themselves, their parents, or their children in the play. As David Mamet said to Miller after watching the play in 1984, "that is *my* story – not only did you write it about me, but *I could go up on stage right now and act it*."[4] A play concerning the most public of American myths, *Death of a Salesman* lays bare the private individual's sensibility, a sensibility neutralized by those very myths. Dustin Hoffman revealed that after he read the play at the age of sixteen, he "had a kind of small breakdown for about two weeks." Hoffman, who read Bernard's lines in a 1966 record version of the play and then played Willy in the celebrated 1984 Broadhurst Theater revival in New York, says of Miller: "He's my artistic father."[5] In an era when many scholars question precisely what constitutes American essentialism, most theatregoers still regard *Death of a Salesman* as the quintessential American play.

But the play also transcends its own American heritage and claims to American essentialism. As C. W. E. Bigsby suggests, the play has "had no difficulty finding an international audience, often being produced in countries whose own myths are radically different, where, indeed, the salesman is an alien and exotic breed . . . Certainly, no country seems to have been baffled by a play in which an individual creates his own fate while believing himself to be an agent of social process. No audience seems to have had difficulty in responding to the story of a man distracted from human necessities by public myths."[6] Many audience members watching the 1950 Vienna production wept, as did the Chinese audiences after seeing the 1983 Beijing run. The play "has been played before a native audience in a small Arctic village with the same villagers returning night after night to witness the performance in a language they did not understand."[7]

Death of a Salesman continues to engage audiences on an international level, not only because it traverses intercultural borders, but also because it brings audiences back to the edges of prehistory itself. Postmodern in texture, reifying a world in which experience is "always ready" for the Lomans, the play gains its theatrical power from ancient echoes, its Hellenic mixture of pity and fear stirring primal emotions. Miller himself believes that

> it's a well-told, paradoxical story. It seems to catch the paradoxes of being alive in a technological civilization. In one way or another, different kinds of people, different classes of people apparently feel that they're *in* the play . . . It seems to have more or less the same effect everywhere there is a dominating technology. Although it's also popular in places where life is far more pretechnological. Maybe it involves some of the most rudimentary elements in the civilizing process: family cohesion, death and dying, parricide, rebirth, and so on. The elements, I guess, are rather fundamental. People *feel* these themes no matter where they are.[8]

Audiences feel such themes because, despite the play's modernity, tribal undercurrents animate the narrative. Although critics have long questioned Miller's conception of tragedy, and understandably so, the playwright nonetheless places in useful perspective his views regarding the tragic textures of *Death of a Salesman*. In Willy Loman, Miller writes in "Tragedy and the Common Man" (1949), "we are in the presence of a character who is ready to lay down his life, if need be, to secure one thing – his sense of personal dignity." Despite the deep irony of his life choices, Willy Loman represents, for many, the commonplace "individual attempting to gain his 'rightful' position in his society"; in "his willingness to throw all he has into the contest, the battle to secure his rightful place in his world," Willy's struggle defines his Sispheian heroism.[9] Audiences experience, in other words, the afterwash of the tragic.

The set and the stage directions

Miller underpins the tragic power of the play through the wonderfully multivalent set and setting. When theatregoers settled into their seats at the packed Morosco Theatre on opening night in 1949 and waited for the play to begin, they heard the melody of a flute. The aural dissolves (like Willy's dreams) to the visual as the curtain rises and the salesman's skeletal house comes into focus. Elia Kazan and Miller worked meticulously with Jo Mielziner, who developed the set, and Eddie Kook, the lighting engineer. Miller provides one of the best-known opening stage directions in American drama, directions on which Kazan, Mielziner, and Kook based their collaborative efforts. Functioning as a kind of prose-poem, the initial stage directions prefigure many of the play's major dynamics.

The stage directions function in at least two important ways. First, they delineate the spatial and physical machinery of the play, including the basic layout of props, the importance of the forestage, the use of such kinesic devices as music and lighting, and, above all, the centrality of the salesman's house. Mielziner filled the stage with realistic props: a kitchen table with three chairs, a small refrigerator, telephone, wastebasket, stairs, three beds, an athletic trophy, and a chest of drawers. But these realistic props were placed within a highly expressionistic set. No solid walls separated Willy and Linda's bedroom, situated slightly elevated and stage right from the kitchen, or the boys' bedroom, located on the second floor, from the kitchen. Instead of a solid roof, only gabled rafters angling upwards, silhouetting a roof line, were used. The back of each room had walls of sorts, but they were translucent backdrops. Since no walls separated the rooms, characters were not necessarily confined spatially or, in the daydream sequences, temporally. When the action occurs in time present, for instance, the actors observe the imaginary wall-lines. But, Miller's stage directions indicate, *"in the scenes of the past these boundaries are broken, and characters enter or leave a room by stepping 'through' a wall onto the forestage"* (*Death of a Salesman*, p. 12).

Audiences gazed at another backdrop behind the house, which featured two trees and images of towering buildings. During Willy's daydreams about the past, Mielziner bathed the stage in a soft amber light, its golden hues suggesting the glory of a past in which the Lomans' neighborhood was filled with grass, trees with green leaves, and a beautiful horizon. The past was a time of freshly painted cars, homes, and soaring hopes. Biff proudly donned his golden football uniform before adoring fans. It was a time when Linda smiled easily. The idealism and happiness of the past have been leeched from the Lomans' present, however. Now, Linda enamels herself with her *"iron repression"* (p. 12). Often during the present scenes, lights from the rear cover the stage with an ominous reddish orange glow. These lighting gradations permit the spatial, the temporal, and the thematic to inhabit the stage simultaneously, and in ways that perfectly suggest the interiority of the characters. The shifts in lighting, if subtly done, not only make for a spatial fluidity, but also register through direct sensory experience the cohering of social, psychic, and actual time.

A particularly foreboding scene illustrates Miller's dramaturgy. The menacing gas heater, located behind a translucent backdrop, visually seems to come alive at the end of Act One. The time is in the present as Biff enters that darkened kitchen, lights a cigarette, and walks downstage into *"a golden pool of light"* (p. 68). At the same time Willy and Linda are in their bedroom, reminiscing about the charisma Biff exuded in high school; Willy says that his son was

> Like a young god. Hercules – something like that. And the sun, the sun all around him. Remember how he waved to me? Right up from the field, with the representatives of three colleges standing by? And the buyers I brought, and the cheers when he came out – Loman, Loman, Loman! God Almighty, he'll be great yet. A star like that, magnificent, can never fade away!   (p. 68)

When Willy utters the "never fade away" lines, however, Kook slowly dimmed the lights that were pointed at Willy, a haunting visual intimation that Linda is helping her husband to bed for the last time. Miller's stage direction accentuates the effect as the *"gas heater begins to glow through the kitchen wall, near the stairs, a blue flame beneath red coils"* (p. 68). Moments later a horrified Biff discovers the rubber tubing Willy hides behind the gas heater. Visually, such stage atmosphere makes for brilliant theatrics. With props, lighting, body movement, and language operating contrapuntally, Miller draws the audience into the Lomans' holy storm.

The initial stage directions function in a second important way. They foreground, through metaphor, many of the play's deeper ambiguities and conflicts. The flute music sounds *"small and fine, telling of grass and trees and the horizon"* (p. 11). The music holds important past references for Willy: his father made and sold flutes as a traveling salesman; through a kind of free associative pattern, the music reveals something of Willy's past desires and dreams, when all things seemed possible to him. Once the music fades, the stage directions concentrate on the house itself, a *"small, fragile-seeming home,"* a home dwarfed by the *"solid vault of apartment houses"* (p. 11). The vault allusion, whether referring ironically to a site of banking, investing, and finance, or to a site of entombment, entrapment, a place of no exit, clearly draws attention to the fragility of the Loman home. Miller creates a trope for the decline of the natural world. Towering apartments, radiating *"an angry glow of orange"* (p. 11), surround the home, allowing only a minimal amount of blue light from the sky to fall upon their property. Later, Willy fondly reminisces about lilacs, wisteria, peonies, and daffodils. He tries to plant seeds, impossible though such an effort to reconnect himself with the organic rhythms of the universe proves to be. The plight of the Lomans, then, finds its parallels in the architecture and urban space of their home. In text and performances, Miller insists on maintaining the drama's essential contrariety: *"An air of the dream clings to the place, a dream rising out of reality"* (p. 11), though reality ensures that Willy never fulfills his dreams, and his dreams never fully square with reality. Miller juxtaposes an imploding urban landscape of time present – "Smell the stink from that apartment house!" (p. 18) – with Willy's longings for a pastoral landscape, one necessarily reconstructed only in time past.

Images of the fall, falling, and the fallen

Miller's stage directions provide insight into what Kazan (and Stanislavsky before him) calls the characters' spines, or their fundamental nature. When Willy enters carrying two large valises, symbolically filled with sixty-odd years of Willy's existence, he *"thankfully lets his burdens down"* (p. 12). His physical and spiritual exhaustion obvious, Willy *"hears but is not aware of"* the flute music. Joseph Hirsch's original poster used in advertizing the play in New York City in some ways visually prepared audiences for a troubling image of a troubled salesman: Willy's rear view is pictured, his slumping shoulders outlined through his business suit. Head bowed, dress hat on, he carries his sample cases, the image of an exhausted if not defeated man. Miller heightens our sense of Willy's physical and spiritual depletion by selectively fading the lights on him.

Miller presents no fewer than twenty-five scenes in which Willy's body language and dialogue create images of the fall, the falling, or the fallen. While Charley repeatedly asks his neighbor if he is ever going to grow *up*, Willy usually appears *"beaten down"* (p. 65). Willy often seeks relief by collapsing into a chair, where he *"lies back, exhausted"* (p. 67). He also sits down in a chair after Howard fires him. Indeed, Miller places special emphasis on the chair in Howard's office: he felt that "the chair must become alive, quite as though his old boss were in it as he addresses him." Mielziner and Kook "once worked an entire afternoon lighting a chair," Miller reports, and, in performance, the result was a highly effective expressionistic moment, one in which, "rather than being lit, the chair subtly seemed to begin emanating light."[10] During the restaurant scene he "*tries to get to his feet*" several times as Biff, "*agonized, holds Willy down*" in his chair (*Death of a Salesman*, p. 112).

Miller fills the daydream scene in Boston with images of a fall, moving from the chair at Frank's Chop House to the bed in the Standish Arms. In the Volker Schlöndorff version (1985), Willy (played by Dustin Hoffman) and the Woman (played by Linda Kozlowski, resplendent with Marilyn Monroesque hair and body) embrace as they *fall* in a slow motion sequence into bed. After hearing Biff's knocking on the door, she pleads, "Willy, Willy, are you going to get up, get up, get up, get up?" (p. 114) while the audience watches a man in the process of falling down, down, down, down. After Biff discovers his father with the Woman, Willy, "*getting down beside Biff*" (p. 120), explains his loneliness. A shattered Biff exits while "*Willy is left on the floor on his knees*" (p. 121); as Willy's mind returns to the present, he remains huddled down against the toilet, abandoned by his sons. During his famous "Spite, spite is the word of your undoing!" speech, Willy is "*sinking into a chair at the table, with full accusation*" (p. 130). Willy's verbal scattershots, increasingly detached from deeds, reinforce his impotence: he snaps his fingers while giving Biff orders, but his directives are ignored. Biff blots out his father. Willy insists that Linda throw away her worn stockings, but, unknown to Willy, she keeps them.

Miller also reinforces the falling and fallen imagery through the dialogue. When Willy begs his boss for a salary, we hear that he once averaged, in 1928, a salary of a hundred and seventy dollars per week; now he begs for sixty-five, then fifty per week, the regressive monetary requests paralleling Willy's downward spiral. From Biff's running *down* eleven flights of stairs to his realization that he was not a salesman with Oliver but merely a shipping clerk; from Biff's idolizing his father to calling him a "phony little fake!" (p. 121); from Linda's announcement that she will cook a big family breakfast to her throwing the flowers to the floor, images which suggest fallen hopes and expectations dominate the text. Fittingly, at the funeral, Linda "*lays down the flowers, kneels, and sits back on her heels. All stare down at the grave*" (p. 136). The sound of loud, frenzied music lowers to the "*soft pulsation of a single cello string*" (p. 136). In a case of the watchers watching the watchers watch, the audience and the Loman family remember stories of Dave Singleman's massive funeral and cannot help but compare it to Willy's sparsely attended burial ceremony. From page to stage, Miller meticulously structures *Death of a Salesman* upon a cluster of retrogressive images, images that correspond directly with the Lomans' fall.

Family backgrounds

Miller worked assiduously to create the Lomans' fall. Although written in about six weeks in 1948, *Death of a Salesman* had a long gestation period. Some years after the first production of the play, Miller discovered a college notebook he used as a student at the University of Michigan in the 1930s. Miller had "totally forgotten that ten years earlier I had begun a play in college about a salesman and his family but had abandoned it" (*Timebends*, p. 129). Further, Miller recalls his teenage encounters with his "two pioneer uncles," Manny Newman and Lee Balsam (*Timebends*, p. 121). From them he sought advice about carpentry, a trade that would become a life-long vocation for the playwright. Working with Uncle Balsam on a porch design as a teenager, Miller writes that this "was my first experience with the fevers of construction, and I could not fall asleep for anticipation of tomorrow; and it was exactly the same one cold April in 1948 when I built a ten-by-twelve studio near my first house in Connecticut where I intended to write a play about a salesman" (*Timebends*, p. 121). The relative dynamics of carpentry and the stagecrafting of *Death of a Salesman* would be strong. In each, planning, interconnections, and designs are crucial, while in the case of carpentry Arthur Miller has written that "the idea of creating a new shadow on the earth has never lost its fascination" (*Timebends*, p. 121). While Miller's studio would cast a private shadow, a work space for the individual artist, the end-product, *Death of a Salesman*, cast a very long public shadow.

The impact of his uncles ultimately had less to do with carpentry, however, and much more to do with *Death of a Salesman*. Both were salesmen. Tellingly enough, Miller regarded Uncle Manny and Uncle Lee, like Ben and Willy's father, as pioneering men. It was Manny Newman, especially, who entranced Miller for years, and whose contradictions shaped Miller's conception of Willy Loman and his family. Miller's recollection of the Newman home, for example, parallels the Lomans'. "There was a shadowy darkness in their [the Newmans'] house, a scent of sex and dream, of lies and invention, and above all of contradictions and surprise" (*Timebends*, p. 122). Admitting that his memories of the Newman household were the product of a teenage experience, Miller still remembers "the lure and mystery with which my mind unaccountably surrounded the Newmans. I could never approach their little house without the expectation that something extraordinary was about to happen in there, some sexual lewdness, perhaps, or an amazing revelation of some other kind." Their house "was dank with sexuality" and "was secretly obsessed, as though they were obscenely involved with one another – a fantasy of mine, of course" (*Timebends*, p. 124). No wonder the Loman house is a home in whose structure linger secret obsessions.[11]

One of Manny Newman's sons, Abby, told Miller, "'He wanted a business for us. So we could all work together . . . A business for the boys'" (*Timebends*, p. 130).[12] For the playwright, who had now been thinking about writing *Death of a Salesman* for ten years, this revelation was a galvanizing moment. Miller would interfold the family business motif throughout *Death of a Salesman*. Early in the play, for instance, Willy hopes that "Someday I'll have my own business" (*Death of a Salesman*, p. 30), and after his young boys volunteer to help, Willy marvels, "Oh, won't that be something! Me comin' into the Boston stores with you boys carryin' my bags. What a sensation!" (p. 31) Late in the play, Stanley, the waiter at Frank's Chop House, learns that Happy and Biff might be "going into business together" (p. 100). In repartee encoded with layers of rich ironies, Stanley replies, "Great! That's the best for you. Because a family business, you know what I mean? – that's the best." He quickly adds, "'Cause what's the difference? Somebody steals? It's in the family. Know what I mean?" (p. 100). Stanley is wrong.

Although the Lomans never go into business together, they discover that there is a huge difference. From Happy's stealing other executives' fiancées to Biff's stealing the high school football, the box full of basketballs, the lumber and cement from the neighborhood, the suit in Kansas City, and Bill Oliver's fountain pen, the question of stealing deepens to encompass not only social crimes but fundamental private issues: the stealing of one's very identity, the loss of the self, the abrogation of responsibility. Inheritors of Willy's sins from the past, Happy and Biff find themselves fated to perpetuate the values instilled by their father in the present and future. Biff and Happy are flawed extensions of Willy and Linda, the genetic lineage carried on with devastating efficiency and symmetry. For throughout Miller presents characters who carry within them modern versions of an Aristotelian fatal flaw, the moral fissure, the *hubris*, that foretells their tragedy. Willy trains his sons well. Minor errors must be heaped upon larger sins, extending a terrible replicating process and ensuring that a tragic parental heritage will be passed on to all descendants. For each character, there is no escape from this family's tabooed ancestral history. Biff, especially, feels the tragic inevitability of his biological and spiritual fate. Problems of guilt and innocence haunt him, as do the relations between private life and social processes.

So one of the central problems Miller embeds in the script is that, though the Lomans know they have transgressed social law in their petty thievery and personal deceits, they seldom take the necessary first steps toward self-disclosure and, more significantly, self-knowledge. For the Lomans, Truth kills. Until the last twenty-four hours in Willy's life, neither Biff nor anyone else faces facts. The Real has long been devalued, deformed, defleshed. Illusion and its relation to familial bonds and the larger (in Rousseau's sense of the term) social contract have been conveniently twisted into the appearance of Truth. In brief, the Lomans remain co-conspirators, master builders of their illusory world.

Even Linda, who knows that "only the shallowness of the water" (p. 59) saved Willy from suicide the year before, and that Willy has "been trying to kill himself" (p. 58) recently, contributes to the truth–illusion matrix. If Linda casts herself as supportive wife, she is also a complex figure who plays a central role within the family dynamics. This became more apparent when Miller directed the play in Beijing, where he emphasized Linda's centrality. She was "'in action,'" Miller says. "She's not just sitting around. She's the one who knows from the beginning of the play that Willy's trying to kill himself. She's got the vital information." He pinpoints Linda's predicament, one underscoring the impossibility of her life: "Linda sustains the illusion because that's the only way Willy can be sustained. At the same time any cure or change is impossible in Willy. Ironically, she's helping to guarantee that Willy will never recover from his illusion. She has to support it; she has no alternative, given his nature and hers."[13] Hence Linda each morning takes the rubber pipe from the hot water heater – only to replace it each night when Willy returns home. "Ashamed," fearful that she might "insult him" (*Death of a Salesman*, p. 60), and not knowing how to deal with such a stubborn husband, Linda weds herself to an illusory world. To deny the crisis is to live, perhaps, another day. Illusions appear so suffused within the psychodynamics and vocabulary of the family that the Lomans, we realize, have slipped years ago into a psychotic denial, hoping all along that outer events will somehow right themselves – and their lives. Nothing could be further from the truth. Minutes before Willy kills himself, Biff screams to his father, "We never told the truth for ten minutes in this house!" – an insight immediately confirmed in Happy's lie: "We always told the truth!" (p. 131).

It would be misleading to claim that Manny Newman was the sole model for Willy Loman. Miller drew on multiple models and incidents, both fictional and historical. While "making preliminary sketches of scenes and ideas for a salesman play," Miller decided on the name Loman. "'Loman,'" Miller reports, "had the sound of reality, of someone who had actually lived, even if I had never known anyone by that name" (*Timebends*,

p. 177). But one cold winter afternoon, while walking to the subway in New York City, the playwright noticed a film that was currently showing, one that had influenced his own aesthetic imagination years earlier. The film was Fritz Lang's *The Testament of Dr. Mabuse*. A key character's name in the film: Lohmann. Miller also provides a corrective to two generations of those scholars who reduced Willy's surname to a too obvious allusion. "In later years I found it discouraging to observe the confidence with which some commentators of *Death of a Salesman* smirked at the heavy-handed symbolism of 'Low-man.' What the name really meant to me was a terror-stricken man calling into the void for help that will never come" (*Timebends*, p. 179).

Surely there were many sources for Willy and the other characters. Miller drew upon his literary forebears as well as his own personal experiences during the Great Depression, which he has often called a moral catastrophe. Desperate American salesmen trying to fuel the Dynamo fascinated him. In Manny Newman's salesman friend, Miller saw the contours of hopeless heroism:

> Like any traveling salesman, he had to my mind a kind of intrepid valor that withstood the inevitable putdowns, the scoreless attempts to sell. In a sense, these men lived like artists, like actors whose product is first of all themselves, forever imagining triumphs in a world that either ignores them or denies their presence altogether. But just often enough to keep the game going one of them makes it and swings to the moon on a thread of dreams unwinding out of himself. (*Timebends*, p. 127)

In Manny Newman, Miller located similar patterns. After a chance meeting at the Colonial Theatre in Boston, Miller saw Manny, who had just watched *All My Sons*. He was weeping. "I could see his grim hotel room behind him, the long trip up from New York in his little car, the hopeless hope of the day's business" (*Timebends*, p. 131).

Toward a new poetics

The influence of Miller's encounters with family and cinema had yet a deeper influence on *Death of a Salesman*. More than merely providing a model of character development, Manny Newman inspired Miller to theatricalize plot and narrative in wholly new forms. When Miller called out to Manny in the lobby of the Colonial Theatre, a distracted Manny ignored Miller's greeting and simply replied, "'Buddy is doing very well'" (*Timebends*, pp. 130–31). The lack of transition between Miller's "'Manny!'" and Manny's reference to Buddy, his eldest son who Miller describes in Biff-like terms, triggered the possibility of a new dramatic method. The absence of conversational transition, Miller writes,

> stuck in my mind; it was a signal to me of the new form that until now I had only tentatively imagined could exist. I had not the slightest idea of writing about a salesman then, totally absorbed as I was in my present production. But how wonderful, I thought, to do a play without transitions at all, dialogue that would simply leap from bone to bone of a skeleton that would not for an instant cease being added to, an organism as strictly economic as a leaf, as trim as an ant. (*Timebends*, p. 131)

Animating the transitions would be Miller's daring use of time. *Death of a Salesman*, after all, ignores the linear, chronocentric unfolding of time. To be sure, the action takes place during the last twenty-four hours of Willy's life, but the drama privileges the time of Willy's inner awareness. Time filters through daydreams. Miller conflates time. And it is a time that measures the intensity of felt experience, not the monotony of nine-to-five routines. In *Timebends*, Miller describes his intention to write

> a play that would do to an audience what Manny had done to me in our surprising meeting – cut through time like a knife through a layer cake or a road through a mountain revealing its geologic layers, and instead of one incident in one time-frame succeeding another, display past and present concurrently, with neither one ever coming to a stop.
>
> The past, I saw, is a formality, merely a dimmer present, for everything we are is at every moment alive in us. How fantastic a play would be that did not still the mind's simultaneity, did not allow a man to "forget" and turned him to see present through past and past through present, a form that in itself, quite apart from its content and meaning, would be inescapable as a psychological process and as a collecting point for all that his life in society had poured into him. This little man walking into the street had all my youth inside him, it seemed. And I suppose because I was more conscious than he, I had in some sense already created him. (*Timebends*, p. 131)

Miller wanted, to borrow Tom Wolfe's metaphor from *The Right Stuff*, to push the envelope, to reinvent the nature of theatricality itself. He wanted a play whose very ontology would be even more inventive than that achieved by some of his American predecessors, such as O'Neill in the early sea plays, in *The Hairy Ape* and *The Emperor Jones*, or Elmer Rice in *The Adding Machine*, works that challenged the prevailing American realistic theatre. Miller wanted to formulate a dramatic structure that would allow the play textually and theatrically to capture the simultaneity of the human mind as that mind registers outer experience through its own inner subjectivity.

Furthermore, Miller was not satisfied with merely drawing upon his uncles, other salesmen, and such notable portraits of American salesmen as seen in O'Neill's *Marco Millions* and *The Iceman Cometh*, or, in a more general sense, the plight of the American worker as reflected in Clifford Odets's *Awake and Sing!* and *Waiting for Lefty*. This hardly implies that Miller strays from social commitment. Indeed, more than any American playwright, Miller embeds a moral optimism and social seriousness in every play. This was as true for the earlier plays, from *The Golden Years* and *All My Sons* through *The Price* and *The American Clock*, as it is for his work in the 1990s, *The Ride Down Mount Morgan, The Last Yankee*, and *Broken Glass*. Such key theatre essays as "Tragedy and the Common Man" (1949), Introduction to *Collected Plays* (1957), and "About Theatre Language" (1994) highlight the civic function of Miller's artistry. He is an ethicist. His entire theatre stands as a critique of the *republica*. But in *Death of a Salesman* he wanted to refurbish the presentation of his moral and social commitment in a new form.

Miller sought nothing less than a new poetics. The notion of creating a sense of simultaneity, a dramatic process by which he could bend time, became increasingly important. He had worked carefully to achieve the success of the realistic *All My Sons*, which in 1994 he identified as his "most Ibsen-influenced play."[14] Yet even as he was beginning to enjoy the economic freedoms and entitlements from royalties generated by his first Broadway success, Miller tested new possibilities. As he put it, "*All My Sons* had exhausted my lifelong interest in the Greco–Ibsen form" (*Timebends*, p. 144). This seems to be a curious remark for a thirty-two-year-old with only two Broadway productions to his credit, but it clearly indicates that his artistic instincts prompted dramaturgic revolution. He came of age as a young dramatist when "we thought it [the realism of Broadway] the perfect style for an unchallenging, simpleminded linear middle-class conformist view of life."[15] Even today some directors and audiences have difficulty when the playwright strays too far from mimesis. "They can't stand a metaphor," Miller told the editor of this volume:

> Metaphor is dangerous, ambiguous; it leaves people slightly mystified and the conscience of the American theatre is that of an intelligent business man. He is a realistic, intelligent, even sensitive person, but he ain't interested in metaphors. He wants to know who's on first and this has made for a very strong realistic tradition, not just in the theatre but in the novel, the movies, and so on. But as soon as you begin to stretch that into a metaphoric area, they get uneasy.[16]

And so, during his apprenticeship years, Miller grappled with the social power and aesthetic limitations of realism. "My own first playwriting attempt was purely mimetic, a realistic play about my own family . . . I came out of the thirties unsure whether there could be a viable counterform to the realism around me."[17] Miller felt that "the problem with *All My Sons* was not that it was too realistic but that it left too little space and time for the wordless darkness that underlies all verbal truth" (*Timebends*, p. 144). For *Death of a Salesman*, photographic realism simply could not reflect the interior subjectivity he was seeking. He needed a play that exteriorized the "logic of the imagination."[18] One key to the greatness of *Death of a Salesman*, therefore, concerns its dramatic form as that form refracts the time of Willy Loman's experience.[19]

A poetic language

Just as Miller searched for a unique dramatic form and use of time, so he sought out a unique grammar of expression. He needed a language that would expose, in theatrical and psychological terms, the inside of Willy's head. Above all, he wanted a language that would present the simultaneity of Willy's thought processes and daydreams. A child of American dramatic realism, a playwright influenced by the social theories and dramatic practices of the eminently realistic Henrik Ibsen, Miller felt compelled to reformulate language in *Death of a Salesman*. Although Joseph A. Hynes claims the play's language seems highly sentimental,[20] and Harold Bloom that while "Miller is by no means a bad writer . . . he is scarcely an eloquent master of language,"[21] the playwright may be viewed as one of the most gifted and radical sculptors of language in American drama.

Interestingly, Tennessee Williams, not Ibsen or Shaw, liberated Miller. After Kazan took Miller to see *A Streetcar Named Desire* in New Haven, he was inspired to work even more precisely with his language. Seeing *Streetcar* "strengthened" Miller. It was a play that opened "one specific door," one that did not deal so much with "the story or characters or direction, but [with] words and their liberation, [with] the joy of the writer in writing them, the radiant eloquence of its composition, [that] moved me more than all its pathos. It formed a bridge . . . to the whole tradition of unashamed word-joy . . . we had . . . turned our backs on" (*Timebends*, p. 182). The beneficiary of this word-joy would be Willy Loman.

> With *Streetcar*, Tennessee has printed a license to speak at full throat, and it helped strengthen me as I turned to Willy Loman, a salesman always full of words, and better yet, a man who could never cease trying, like Adam, to name himself and the world's wonders. I had known all along that this play

could not be encompassed by conventional realism, and for one integral reason: in Willy the past was as alive as what was happening at the moment, sometimes even crashing in to completely overwhelm his mind. I wanted precisely the same fluidity in the form, and now it was clear to me that this must be primarily verbal. The language would of course have to be recognizably his to begin with, but it seemed possible now to infiltrate it with a kind of superconsciousness. (*Timebends*, p. 182)

If Williams formed a bridge, whose foundation was the word, Miller suddenly crossed this creative bridge more confidently and entered fresh imaginative terrain. As in *After the Fall* and *The Ride Down Mount Morgan*, Miller sought in *Death of a Salesman* the verbal equivalents for his characters' troubled inner selves, a search that led him away from the realism of Ibsen, O'Casey, (the later) O'Neill, Odets, and Hellman and toward a new dramatic expression. He was also enormously attracted by what Williams called the "plastic theater."[22] The use of lights, music, sets, and other nonverbal expressions that would complement the textual version of the play became central kinesic forces in production. This willingness to open up his theatre to more than a merely language-grounded realism allowed Miller to create a lyric drama, a more poetic theatre, a more interiorized realism. Stage symbol, scenic image, body language were to assume important roles, roles accentuating the conflicts that the Lomans articulated to audiences through language.

Death of a Salesman works because of its linguistic simplicity. Miller had discovered his verbal *métier*. For, on one level, the play is exceedingly realistic, its language wrested from the American idiolect of clichés, its characters instantly recognizable to any theatregoer, its intertextual and extratheatrical references derived from the stuff of American popular culture of the day. References to Studebakers and Chevvys, Ebbets Field and Red Grange, B. F. Goodrich and Thomas Edison immediately established personal correspondences and cultural signifiers for each member of the audience. Surely the irony of Biff, captain and quarterback of the *All-Scholastic* (my emphasis) Championship Team of the City of New York, failing math and never graduating touched the nerve of parents whose sons were (whether they liked it or not) inculcated with athletics in the United States. World War II now over, it was time once again to release the furies on the gridiron. Adonises always beat Anemics.

Yet for all its linguistic simplicity, Miller interfolds a voracious repartee throughout *Death of a Salesman*. Miller's is a militant script. Nor is such voracity limited to Willy; all the characters have absorbed an assertive or even violent vocabulary. Willy hopes his boys can "lick the civilized world" (*Death of a Salesman*, p. 64), though Biff screams, "screw the business world!" (p. 61).Willy threatens to "whip" Biff, though he brags to Ben that his boys would "go into the jaws of hell for me" (p. 52). Biff claims that Willy "always wiped the floor with" Linda (p. 55), and Howard says to Willy, "If I had a spot I'd slam you right in" (p. 80). The infantile Happy brags that he "can outbox, outrun, and outlift anybody in that store" and resents the fact that he has "to take orders from those common, petty sons-of-bitches" (p. 24); he also wonders if he has "an overdeveloped sense of competition" (p. 25) and, near the end of Act Two, orders from the restaurant giant lobsters "with the claws" (p. 99), a fitting dinner for a man who, leering at Miss Forsythe, blathers, "I got radar or something" (p. 100). Only Happy, staring at his father's grave, could utter such banalities as "I'm staying right in this city, and I'm gonna beat this racket! . . . [Willy] fought it out here, and this is where I'm gonna win it for him" (pp. 138–39). In Boston, the Woman refers to herself as a football, one who has just been booted out of an illicit affair with Willy (pp. 119–20). Willy reflects in his last daydream, ". . . and when you hit, hit low, and hit hard" (p. 135), a reflection meant for Biff but which actually foreshadows his own suicide moments later. The ever-supportive Linda turns acerbic after her boys abandon Willy at the restaurant. She lambastes Happy and his "lousy rotten whores!" (p. 124) and orders Biff to clean up the scattered flowers she has just knocked to the floor: "Pick up this stuff, I'm not your maid any more. Pick it up, you bum, you!" (p. 124). Miller even anthropomorphizes some consumer objects through vigorous language: "That goddam Studebaker! [it's . . .] on its last legs." The refrigerator consumes belts "like a goddam maniac" (p. 73). And Howard's dictaphone, a symbolic reminder of how far Willy lags behind his own technological era, talks to Willy, who has no idea of how to turn off the newfangled invention. The taped voice of Howard's son spinning out of control foregrounds, of course, Willy's own life, which is spinning out of control. After all, Willy does not fit in with the industrialized world; he is more at home in a pastoral world, one in which he can use his hands to build a porch or plant seeds in a garden.

Miller's vigorous repartee – the rapidity and intensity with which actors deliver their lines – gains theatrical momentum through its imagistic referents. These are death-saturated dialogues. Willy launches the tragic trajectory of the play at the very start when admitting, "I'm tired to the death" (p. 13), which becomes a haunting monody throughout the play: "I'm so tired" (p. 68), he says to Linda at the end of Act One. Miller extends the death motif when a rested Willy opens Act Two by saying he slept "like a dead one" (p. 71), and Willy repeats the refrain minutes later when confiding to Howard, "I'm just a little tired" (p. 80). In a comment prefiguring his own demise, Willy wishes Howard's father, Frank, the best in the grave – "may he rest in peace" (p. 80). Linda knows that Willy's old friends are "all dead, retired" (p. 57). Schoolchildren "nearly died laughing!" at Biff's Birnbaum imitation (p. 118). Miller describes the music that has "*died away*" (p. 88). As the play reaches its climax, Biff utters, "Forget I'm alive" (p. 129) and Willy tells his son, "Then hang yourself! For spite, hang yourself!" (p. 132).

Death allusions permeate the script. Willy complains that builders "massacred the neighborhod" (p. 17). He boasts he "knocked 'em cold in Providence, slaughtered 'em in Boston" (p. 33), and that he will "knock 'em dead next week" (p. 36). Charley says, "My New England man comes back and he's bleedin', they murdered him up there" (p. 51); Willy calls business "murderous" p. 51). Although Bernard's language, in its reasoned cadences, plays counterpoint to the Lomans' outbursts, his most revealing lines describe Biff's return from Boston, the half-hour fist-fight they had, and how they kept "punching each other down the cellar, and crying right through it. I've often thought of how strange it was that I knew he'd given up his life" (p. 94). Near the end of Act Two, Willy says to Biff, "You're trying to put a knife in me – don't think I don't know what you're doing!" (p. 130). Images of fire abound, too. Not surprisingly, Willy is right when he talks about the woods burning. From the angry glow of orange to the Woman thinking there is a fire in the hotel, from the fire-engine red Chevy to Willy's being fired, from Biff's burning his sneaker in the furnace to his pleas that his father burn his phony dream, Miller's language suggests conflagration.

Despite whatever (anti)heroic attributes we ascribe to Willy, he is a figure savagely divided against himself. He emerges as a competitive man whose vision of entrepreneurial spirit, which has devolved into a series of self-deceiving gestures, too often fuels pride. He is a man who contradicts himself. However, given Willy's *physis* (what the ancient Greeks by the time of Sophocles conceived of as one's authentic nature), it could not have been otherwise. At all costs, Willy must leave his thumbprint on the world.[23] He must constantly name and re-name himself. Forever doomed to linger in the margins, Willy locates his essential self within the epicenter of the business world: "Go to Filene's, go to the Hub, go to Slattery's, Boston. Call out the name Willy Loman and see what happens! Big shot!" (*Death of a Salesman*, p. 62). But his pride descends to arrogance, and from arrogance to ignorance, an ignorance fostered by a competitive American business work ethic. Hence *Death of a Salesman*, many critics suggest, is a critique of a capitalist society that brutalizes the unsuccessful. In Marxist terms, Willy completes the brutalization process by reducing himself to a commodity, an object, a thing, which enables him to make the greatest and last sale of his entire professional life: the sale of his very existence for the insurance payment. The play exposes, for the ideologue, the inadequacies of a bourgeois America. This at least was the dominant view expressed by critics after the play's successful runs at the Pushkin Theatre in Leningrad and the Vakhtangov Theatre in Moscow during the summer of 1959. Since the Cold War was in full force, such a response seems predictable enough. However, while the sociopolitical textures of the play undeniably manifest themselves throughout, *Death of a Salesman* gains its power from other sources.

Death of a Salesman goes well beyond the level of oversimplified social protest (and a play to be used in the service of a particular ideology) because it concerns the fundamental practical and metaphysical question: what does it mean to be fulfilled in one's very existence? This question underpins the play's greatness, reinforces its philosophic largeness. For in Miller's cosmology, Willy Loman is much more than a neurotic malady, or, as Biff argues, "a hard-working drummer who landed in the ash can like all the rest of them!" (p. 132). Unquestionably the allure of wealth and fulfillment entice Willy Loman to dream, and to die. But a felt poignancy filled the Morosco Theatre on 10 February 1949 when Lee J. Cobb as Willy confides to Howard:

> We've got quite a little streak of self-reliance in our family. I thought I'd go out with my older brother and try to locate him, and maybe settle in the North with the old man. And I was almost decided to go, when I met a salesman in the Parker House. His name was Dave Singleman. And he was eighty-four years old, and he'd drummed merchandise in thirty-one states. And old Dave, he'd go up to his room, y'understand, put on his green velvet slippers – I'll never forget – and pick up his phone and call the buyers, and without ever leaving his room, at the age of eighty-four, he made his living. And when I saw that, I realized that selling was the greatest career a man could want.
>
> (p. 81)

No matter that Howard will fire Willy momentarily, or that Willy, like Dave Singleman, will soon die "the death of a salesman" (p. 81). For many, Willy Loman's aspirations have a ring of truth to them, grounded though they may be in a romanticized vision of an American Dream, one that ultimately certifies death.

Willy invites the audience to enter "the inside of his head," the original working title of the play. In effect, the audience becomes privy to the crisis within Willy and to the philosophic complexity of *Death of a Salesman*. Thus when Willy continues, " 'Cause what could be more satisfying than to be able to go, at the age of eighty-four, into twenty or thirty different cities, and pick up a phone, and be remembered and loved and helped by so many different people?" (p. 81), he confirms what Linda knows. "So attention must be paid. He's not to be allowed to fall into his grave like an old dog. Attention, attention must be finally paid to such a person" (p. 56). Willy Loman's real condition lies in his insecurity in the universe, his profound sense of being unfulfilled, and in his inability to observe his own emotional speed limits. No question Willy exaggerates, cheats, and lies, charges which he is ill equipped to refute but well suited to deny. But when he screams to Biff, "I am not a dime a dozen! I am Willy Loman, and you are Biff Loman!" (p. 132), is he not laying claim, not only to his dignity and individual worth but also to every person's worthiness?

Undoubtedly Willy suffers from O'Neillean "pipe dreams," or Ibsenesque "vital lies." When convenient, or necessary, Willy confers upon illusions the status of objective reality. Yet he, in a sense, tragically knows at least part of himself. In telling rare occasions he locates his demythicized self without the rhetorical gallantries that mask his inadequacies. He admits that he is foolish to look at and that he babbles too much; he acknowledges that he feels temporary about himself. Strange thoughts bother him. He asks the grown Bernard for advice. Adding to Willy's paradoxical nature are those moments in which he mixes self-disclosure with external fact: "You'll [Happy] retire me for life on seventy goddam dollars a week? And your women and your car and your apartment, and you'll retire me for life! Christ's sake, I couldn't get past Yonkers today! Where are you guys, where are you? The woods are burning! I can't drive a car!" (p. 41). Miller occasionally bestows upon Willy a capacity for self-knowledge within the marketplace, as evident during the scene in Howard's office: "I put thirty-four years into this firm, Howard, and now I can't pay my insurance! You can't eat the orange and throw the peel away – a man is not a piece of fruit!" (p. 82). Willy knows America is no isocracy in which all people have equal power. Adding to Willy's tragic stature are those singular moments when he honestly assesses his overall predicament, as seen, for instance, when he meets his sons in the restaurant: "I'm not interested in stories about the past or any crap of that kind because the woods are burning, boys, you understand? There's a big blaze going on all around. I was fired today" (p. 107). Such insights make Willy more than a misfit or an oversimplified Everyman. Rather, they enhance his tragic stature precisely because they reveal to the audience Willy's capacity to distinguish reality from chimera; that the majority of his other remarks make such distinctions less clear only adds to the sense of tragic loss. Thus audiences find in Willy traces of the past tragic figures who populated the stages of Shaw, Ibsen, and Shakespeare and, backtracking to the primal origins of Western dramatic heritage, of Sophocles and Euripides. This is why Arthur Miller, I believe, is to the second half of twentieth-century American drama what Eugene O'Neill was to the first half: our supreme tragedian.

Coda

Half a century later, the significance of *Death of a Salesman* has only increased. As Miller remarks, "People tell me that *Death of a Salesman* is more pertinent now than then. The suppression of the individual by placing him below the imperious needs of society or technology seems to have manufactured more Willys in the world. But again, it is far more primitive than that. Like many myths and classical dramas, it is a story about violence within a family."[24]

If we live in a world which, indeed, manufactures more Willys, it is easy to understand why theatregoers today continue to be moved the way 1949 audiences were. From an ecological point of view, Willy's ravings about overpopulation, builders massacring elms to construct apartment complexes, and "Bricks and windows, windows and bricks" (*Death of a Salesman*, p. 17) resonate for twenty-first century audiences in London, Beijing, and any major city in the United States. From an economic perspective, Willy's struggles to pay the mortgage and, above all, his insurance, resonate for theatregoers who themselves increasingly feel the financial pressures exacted upon them by an increasingly capitalist, or at least Westernized, world. On a domestic level, global audiences respond to the play's exploration of the primal family unit and the way in which Miller presents the dynamics of the relationship between husband and wife, and parents and children. In a country where social security is more a lie of the mind than political fact, Willy's being fired after working thirty-four years with the firm annihilates Emersonian notions of self-reliance. Willy exists in a world that increasingly detaches itself from him, reminding him daily of his own insignificance. Whether driving 700 miles only to be denied a sale or meeting his sons for dinner only to be abandoned by them, Willy knows that he will reap more profits in one masterstroke – his suicide – than in all the sales he closed in a lifetime. As he points out to Ben, "Does it take more guts to stand here the rest of my life ringing up a zero?" (p. 126). Willy, exhausted after dealing with feelings of innocence and guilt, protection and betrayal, and celebration and loss, reasons "you end up worth more dead than alive" (p. 98). The Lomans, in sum, have become inextricably linked to various enabling American mythologies – and pathologies. This is precisely why *Death of a Salesman* outlines the collective and essentially moral anxieties of a nation as those anxieties, occupying the interstice of the Real and the Illusion, affect the individual.[25]

The funeral scene confirms Willy's ultimate fall. If the Requiem provides a sense of closure for Willy and for the audience, the surviving Lomans continue voicing their competing narratives. Happy blathers on, pointlessly. Biff, despite heroic efforts to face facts, still carries on an Oedipal resistance to his father. Willy, he insists, bought into the wrong dreams and did not know himself. Were the play to end with Biff's lines, maybe "the secret we and Miller thereby deny is that we hate Willy because he represents everything we want to deny about ourselves."[26] But Miller doesn't end the play there, and I am not convinced he allows us to hate Willy. Charley's important "nobody dast blame this man" speech, perhaps, places Willy's fate in a broader social and philosophical context. Charley refers to the utter precariousness of human existence when that life comes face to face with emptiness. Questions of hate, spite, and so on continue to reverberate, but as distant echoes. Willy was, indeed, riding out there on a smile and a shoeshine, without a spiritual insurance policy that would have allowed his dreams to exist in equipoise with reality. Since he lived most of his life on the fault lines of the "earthquake" to which Charley refers (*Death of a Salesman*, p. 138), he could only survive with the hopeless hope of "a salesman" who's "got to dream, boy" (p. 138). If intellectually such a reading seems forced, it makes perfect sense theatrically. And, for Miller and most theatregoers, this is all that matters.

Despite the carnivalesque world of the Lomans, Miller provides a resolution of sorts. This resolution may be best understood in the context of the playwright's intellectual position, which reveals itself through his moral optimism. From *The Golden Years* through *Broken Glass*, Miller's poetics emphasize the primacy of the individual's social duty and the importance of familial love. Implicit in all the major plays is Miller's belief in the unifying force of love that creates the possibility for social revolt in the *polis* and personal insight within the family. These essentializing forces, which elude the Lomans, only increase the play's sense of tragic loss. The poetics of Arthur Miller are informed with a sense of charity and love which the Lomans can never adequately express. This is why Linda, sobbing quietly as the curtain falls, can only contemplate what could, or should, have been.

NOTES

1 Arthur Miller, *Death of a Salesman* (New York: Viking Press, 1976), p. 17.
2 Linda Kintz, "The Sociosymbolic Work of Family in *Death of a Salesman*," in Matthew C. Roudané (ed.), *Approaches to Teaching Miller's Death of a*

Salesman (New York: The Modern Language Association of America, 1995), p. 106. See also in this same volume Susan Harris Smith, "Contextualizing *Death of a Salesman* as an American Play," pp. 27–32, and Janet N. Balakian, "Beyond the Male Locker Room: *Death of a Salesman* from a Feminist Perspective," pp. 115–24. For other useful essays debating feminist issues in the play, see Charlotte Canning, "Is This Play About Women?: A Feminist Reading of *Death of a Salesman*," in Steven R. Centola, *The Achievement of Arthur Miller* (Dallas: Contemporary Research Associates, 1995), pp. 69–76; Gayle Austin, "The Exchange of Women and Male Homosocial Desire in Arthur Miller's *Death of a Salesman* and Lillian Hellman's *Another Part of the Forest*," in June Schlueter (ed.), *Feminist Rereadings of Modern American Drama* (Rutherford, NJ: Farleigh Dickinson University Press, 1989), pp. 59–66; and Kay Stanton, "Women and the American Dream of *Death of a Salesman*," in *Feminist Rereadings*, pp. 67–102.

3 Brenda Murphy, *Miller: Death of a Salesman* (Cambridge: Cambridge University Press, 1995), p. 70.

4 "David Mamet," in Christopher Bigsby (ed.), *Arthur Miller and Company* (London: Methuen, 1990), p. 64.

5 "Dustin Hoffman," in Bigsby, *Arthur Miller and Company*, pp. 70–71.

6 Christopher Bigsby, *Modern American Drama, 1945–1990* (Cambridge: Cambridge University Press, 1992), p. 89.

7 Murphy, *Miller: Death of a Salesman*, p. 106.

8 Matthew C. Roudané, "An Interview with Arthur Miller," in Roudané (ed.), *Conversations with Arthur Miller* (Jackson: University Press of Mississippi, 1987), pp. 360–61.

9 Arthur Miller, "Tragedy and the Common Man," *New York Times*, 27 February 1949, section II, pp. 1, 3.

10 Arthur Miller, *Timebends* (New York: Grove Press, 1987), p. 190.

11 The physiological and psychological correspondences linking Manny Newman and Willy Loman seem equally compelling. "Manny Newman was cute and ugly, a Pan risen out of the earth, a bantam with a lisp, sunken brown eyes, a lumpy, pendulous nose, dark brown skin, and gnarled arms," Miller recalls (*Timebends*, p. 122). Physiologically, traces of Manny may be found in Willy, who confides to Linda that he is foolish-looking. F. H. Stewarts, a salesman, mockingly calls Willy a walrus. More importantly, Manny was also, like Willy, "a competitor, at all times, in all things, and at every moment" (*Timebends*, p. 122).

Although Miller only spent a few hours with Manny Newman during his lifetime, he nonetheless proved to be one of the pivotal figures upon whom Miller based Willy Loman. In describing Newman, Miller could very well be talking about Willy: "he was so absurd, so completely isolated from the ordinary laws of gravity, so elaborate in his fantastic inventions, and despite his ugliness so lyrically in love with fame and fortune and their inevitable descent on his family, that he possessed my imagination until I knew more or less precisely how he would react to any sign or word or idea" (*Timebends*, p. 123).

The coalescence of fiction and fact reaches its most poignant expression through the emotion of a profound sadness both Willy and Manny shared. During that fateful night in Boston, the Woman says to Willy, "You are the saddest, self-centredest soul I ever did see-saw" (*Death of a Salesman*, p. 116). Of Manny Newman Miller would write, "his unpredictable manipulations of fact freed my mind to lope and skip among fantasies of my own, but always underneath was the river of his sadness" (*Timebends*, p. 123). And director Elia Kazan, after reading a working draft of the script in 1948, telephoned Miller and in an "alarmingly somber" voice said, "My God, it's so sad" (*Timebends*, p. 185). Sadness, however, must be masked at all costs. Appearance counts. Hence there was a "competitiveness that drugged" Manny Newman's mind (*Timebends*, p. 124), the same competitive personality that would energize as it immobilized Willy Loman. Caught in a naturalistic world that reduces him to an insignificant speck in the universe, Willy and his soaring inner spirits are tempered by an outer deterministic environment: "There's more people! That's what's ruining this country! Population is getting out of control. The competition is maddening!" (*Death of a Salesman*, pp. 17–18). It was Manny Newman's and Willy Loman's "romance of hope" (*Timebends*, p. 126), then, that would partially define the trajectory of their lives.

12 Miller's conversation with Manny Newman's son was also a galvanizing, revelatory moment because it helped the playwright clarify the contradictory nature of Willy Loman. When he heard that Manny wanted "a business for the boys," Miller realized that this conventional, mundane wish was a shot of "electricity that switched all the random iron filings in my mind in one direction. A hopelessly distracted Manny was transformed into a man with purpose: he had been trying to make a gift that would crown all those striving years; all those lies he told, all his imaginings and crazy exaggerations, even the almost military discipline he had laid on his boys, were in this instant given form and point. To be sure, a business expressed his own egotism, but love, too" (*Timebends*, p. 130). Miller's reminiscence of Manny Newman found its theatrical corollary within Willy Loman; here Miller describes the Real, his uncle, but what follows even more accurately externalizes the fictional Willy Loman: "That homely, ridiculous little man had after all never ceased to struggle for a certain victory, the only kind open to him in this society – selling to achieve his lost self as a man with his name and his sons' names on a business of his own" (*Timebends*, p. 130).

Miller acknowledges that another salesman, a friend of his uncle, "was more vivid to me than even Manny." This salesman, unmarried and fitted with a wooden leg, differed in temperament from Manny Newman, his "reflective air" giving rise to an observation that arrested Miller. "'You've changed, haven't you?' he said. 'You've gotten serious.'" For a young man soon to turn craft into art, the salesman's observation gave Miller "the dignity of a history of my own," and, more importantly, the courage to follow artistic instincts within a meritocracy that valorizes a business as sacrament, ethic and ethos. "If ever I knew that salesman's name I forgot it long ago, but not his few interested words that helped crack the shell of suffocating subjectivity surrounding my existence" (*Timebends*, pp. 126–27).

13 Roudané, "Interview," p. 370.

14 Arthur Miller, "Ibsen and the Drama of Today," in James McFarland (ed.), *The Cambridge Companion to Ibsen* (Cambridge: Cambridge University Press, 1994), p. 232.

15 Arthur Miller, "About Theatre Language," in Miller, *The Last Yankee* (New York: Penguin, 1994), p. 81.
16 Unpublished interview with Arthur Miller, conducted by Christopher Bigsby, 1994.
17 Miller, "About Theatre Language," pp. 81, 84.
18 Bigsby, *Modern American Drama*, p. 90.
19 Miller elaborates on the use of form and time in the play:

> The form of *Death of a Salesman* was an attempt, as much as anything else, to convey the bending of time. There are two or three sorts of time in that play. One is social time; one is psychic time, the way we remember things; and the third is the sense of time created by the play and shared by the audience. When I directed *Salesman* in China, which was the first time I had attempted to direct it from scratch, I became aware all over again that the play is taking place in the Greek unity of twenty-four hours; and yet, it is dealing with material that goes back probably twenty-five years. And it almost goes forward through Ben, who is dead. So *time* was an obsession for me at the moment, and I wanted a way of presenting it so that it became the *fiber* of the play, rather than being something that somebody comments about. In fact, there is very little comment verbally in *Salesman* about time. I also wanted a form that could sustain in itself the way we deal with crises, which is not to deal with them. After all, there is a lot of comedy in *Salesman*; people forget it because it is so dark by the end of the play. But if you stand behind the audience you hear a lot of laughter. It's a deadly ironical laughter most of the time, but it *is* a species of laughter. The comedy is really a way for Willy and others to put off the evil day, which is the thing we all do. I wanted that to *happen* and not be something talked *about*. I wanted the feeling to come across rather than a set of speeches about how we delay dealing with issues. I wanted a play, that is, that had almost a biological life of its own. It would be as incontrovertible as the musculature of the human body. Everything connecting with everything else, all of it working according to plan. No excesses. Nothing explaining itself; all of it simply inevitable, as one structure, as one corpus. All of those feelings of a society falling to pieces which I had, still have, of being unable to deal with it, which we all know now. All of this, however, presented not with speeches in *Salesman*, but by putting together pieces of Willy's life, so that what we were deducing about it was the speech; what we were making of it was the moral of it; what it was doing to us rather than a romantic speech about facing death and living a fruitless life. All of these elements and many more went into the form of *Death of a Salesman*. All this could never have been contained in the form of *All My Sons*. (Roudané, "Interview," pp. 363–64)

20 Joseph A. Hynes, "'Attention, Attention Must Be Paid . . . ,'" *College English* 23 (1962): 576.
21 Harold Bloom, "Introduction," in Bloom (ed.), *Modern Critical Interpretations: Arthur Miller's Death of a Salesman* (New York: Chelsea House, 1988), p. 1.
22 Tennessee Williams, "Production Notes," *The Glass Menagerie*, in *The Theatre of Tennessee Williams*, vol. 1 (New York: New Directions, 1971), pp. 131–34.

23 For an informative discussion linking Arthur Miller, Willy Loman, and the function of art, see Bigsby's interview with Miller in *Arthur Miller and Company*, p. 233.

24 Roudané, "Interview," p. 361.

25 For excellent discussions of the public/private dialectic in Miller, see C. W. E. Bigsby, *A Critical Introduction to Twentieth-Century American Drama*, vol. II (Cambridge: Cambridge University Press, 1984), pp. 135–248; Bigsby, *Modern American Drama*, pp. 72–125; Bigsby, "Introduction to the Revised Edition," *The Portable Arthur Miller* (New York: Penguin, 1995), pp. xxv–xli; Robert A. Martin, "Arthur Miller: Public Issues, Private Tensions," in Matthew C. Roudané (ed.), *Public Issues, Private Tensions: Contemporary American Drama* (New York: AMS Press, 1993), pp. 65–75; Martin, "The Nature of Tragedy in Arthur Miller's *Death of a Salesman*," *South Atlantic Review* 61 (1996): 97–106; Bernard F. Dukore, *Death of a Salesman and The Crucible: Text and Performance* (London: Macmillan, 1989), pp. 16–20, 33–39, 45–56; Thomas P. Adler, *American Drama, 1940–1960: A Critical History* (New York: Twayne, 1994), pp. 62–83; June Schlueter and James K. Flanagan, *Arthur Miller* (New York: Frederick Ungar, 1987), pp. 56–66; Janet N. Balakian, "*Salesman*: Private Tensions Raised to a Poetic Social Level," in Centola, *The Achievement of Arthur Miller*, pp. 59–68; *Platform Papers: 7. Arthur Miller* (London: Royal National Theatre, 1995), pp. 3–36; and Matthew C. Roudané, "Arthur Miller and His Influence on Contemporary American Drama," *American Drama* 6 (1996): 1–13.

26 Walter A. Davis, *Get the Guests: Psychoanalysis, Modern American Drama, and the Audience* (Madison: University of Wisconsin Press, 1994), p. 144.

6

THOMAS P. ADLER

Conscience and community in *An Enemy of the People* and *The Crucible*

"It's all clear to me now, finally at this late hour. They had their script. I had mine. Theirs: 'Confess, lie, and you'll live.'"

Tema Nason, *Ethel [Rosenberg]: The Fictional Autobiography* (1990)

When the Wooster Group, one of the more controversial of the experimental theatrical troupes active during the 1970s and 1980s, incorporated segments of *The Crucible* (1953) into their performance piece entitled *LSD (. . . Just the High Points . . .)* (1984), Arthur Miller's threat of legal action eventually forced the project to be withdrawn from the stage. Even though the excerpts included from Miller's work were reduced first from forty-five minutes to twenty-five minutes and then later to ten minutes – and that recited virtually in gibberish – the dramatist objected on the grounds that such a treatment might be regarded as a parody, which violated his initial intention, rather than an homage, and so might somehow preclude a serious New York revival of his play. Not only does Miller's action provide a fascinating case study in the ongoing debate over who "owns" or maintains interpretive authority over the written text when it becomes a performance text – the author or the director – it also evidences what might seem a peculiar paradox. As David Savran notes, "By insisting on his own interpretation, Miller has, ironically, aligned himself with the very forces that *The Crucible* condemns, those authorities who exercise their power arrogantly and arbitrarily to ensure their own continued political and cultural dominion."[1] The creators of *LSD* had, in fact, signaled this in their greatly reduced version by uttering "accidental lines" from Miller's work which were then "silenced by the buzzer" in order to demonstrate the "enforced suppression" (*Wooster*, p. 193) that their performance piece, itself concerned with victimization and cultural oppression, experienced because of the playwright's objections. Yet, in 1961, Miller had raised not the least demur when Bernard Stambler reproduced much of his dramatic text verbatim in the libretto to his and composer Robert Ward's operatic version (which went on to win the Pulitzer Prize for Music).

An additional irony presents itself in that, immediately before writing *The Crucible*, Miller, in adapting *An Enemy of the People* (1950), had subjected Ibsen's 1882 play to his own interpretation. As Gerald Rabkin comments, Miller himself "*has* changed textuality by not hesitating to revise his dramatic texts *after* initial production . . . and he was not constrained by the playwright's intentionality in his version of Ibsen's *An Enemy of the People*, which eliminated all unsympathetic ambiguity from [Dr. Thomas] Stockmann's character."[2] Essentially, Miller removes what he saw as potentially a protofascist strain in Stockmann's espousal of an evolving aristocracy of leaders with broad powers to mould community standards. In his autobiography, *Timebends*, Miller justifies his alteration of Ibsen's original by remarking upon the discomfort he "felt with one or two of its implications. Though Dr. Stockmann fights admirably for absolute license to tell society the truth, he goes on to imply the existence of an unspecified elite that can prescribe what people are to believe," concluding that it "is indefensible in a democratic society, albeit the normal practice, to ascribe superior prescience to a self-elected group."[3]

Apart from the shadings in the protagonist's character and Miller's introduction of more colloquial language, the alterations between original and adaptation might be accounted minimal; perhaps the most significant, given the political climate of the 1950s in which he wrote, is the addition of a speech by Stockmann's brother Peter, the town's mayor, which suggests how, sensing some internal threat to its stability, even a democracy might rationalize the adoption of totalitarian tactics in the name of preserving security and avoiding revolution: "Now, God knows, in ordinary times I'd agree a hundred percent with anybody's right to say anything. But these are not ordinary times" (*An Enemy of the People*, p. 89). In the Preface to his adaptation of *An Enemy of the People* – which he terms "a new translation into spoken English" (p. 12) and which lasted originally for only thirty-six performances – Miller isolates those qualities that to his way of thinking make Ibsen "really pertinent today," chief among them being "his insistence, his utter conviction, that he is going to say what he has to say, and that the audience, by God, is going to listen," and his belief in the dramatist's "right to entertain with his brains as well as his heart," that is, "the stage [as] *the* place for ideas" (pp. 7–8). Regardless of whether this accurately articulates Ibsen's characteristic contribution, *Enemy* is very much in the nature of a dramatized debate. The question it poses is: what is the nature of good government, and, when, if ever, does adherence to abstract principles, either in support of or in revolt against a lawfully constituted government, become an extreme that cannot be tolerated if individual rights and the community are to be protected?

The bureaucrats in power in this Norwegian town, led by Peter Stockmann, define an authoritarian, hierarchical, homogeneous ideal, in which the individual remains subordinate to the state, tolerance extends only to non-dissenters of like mind, and basic rights, such as free speech, can be abrogated at will or whim for expediency's sake, all in the name of maintaining indispensable "moral authority." The radical challenge to this theory of government comes from Dr. Thomas Stockmann, who envisions a more representative society in which those outside the traditional governing class are somehow brought within the net, in order that their "ability, self-respect, and intelligence" can be nurtured. To make his point about an ideal form of participatory democracy – a kind of Deweyan deliberative community – in which an enlightened electorate is empowered by the very act of its participation, the doctor dons the mayor's hat, his "official insignia," that can, unlike a crown, be worn by whomever the people choose. At this point, he thinks they will unquestioningly support his self-assumed mission of purifying the town's fetid waters, which are symbolic of a deeper "pestilence" of intolerance and suppression rotting the society.

In *The Quintessence of Ibsenism*, G. B. Shaw not only pinpointed as Ibsen's chief structural innovation the introduction of "discussion" into the drama, but delineated as foremost in Ibsen's agenda the destruction of ideals, that is, of those lies that prevent one's living in and accepting unadorned reality. In fact, the progress of numerous Shavian protagonists as various as Major Barbara and St. Joan is an emphatically educative one similar to the pattern he had detected at work in Ibsen: from idealism or illusion, through disillusionment, to reality. The doctor in *Enemy*, with his credo of "blow[ing] up every lie we live by" (*An Enemy of the People*, p. 66), gives ample proof of this Shavian art of destroying ideals, most startlingly of the notion that "the majority is always right." Perhaps following the lead of John Stuart Mill, who proclaimed in *On Liberty* (1859) that "No government, by a democracy or a numerous aristocracy, either in its political acts or in the opinions, qualities, and tone of mind, ever did or could rise above mediocrity, except in so far as the Many have let themselves by guided (which in their best times they have always done) by the counsels and influence of a more highly gifted and instructed One or Few,"[4] Thomas Stockmann asserts that, in fact, "the majority is always wrong" (*An Enemy of the People*, p. 94). Since majority rule results in a leveled-down, lowest common denominator of "meatheads," the enlightened "*one* must know" the truth – and by implication lead – "before many can" (p. 95). So Stockmann, branded a "criminal" and a "traitor" by the majority, must become at least a gadfly if not a revolutionist.

Although Miller leaves the basic tenet underlying the doctor's actions unchallenged, he does (as Rabkin noted) present a less flawed Stockmann than Ibsen. In both works, the idealistic doctor naively believes that people will always go with the truth, even when doing so threatens their material well-being; and so when he reveals that the town's medicinal baths feed on polluted springs, he confidently expects they will be rebuilt using tax dollars. Yet, though he might leave a patient half-bandaged while he runs off to make his case, or rant about having the walls scrubbed to remove the moral filth after Peter's visit, or mistakenly think the townspeople will confer upon him sainthood for carrying on his crusade, Miller's protagonist is never quite so "muddleheaded" as Ibsen portrayed him as being. For Miller has deliberately removed certain tendencies that he feared would be found racist by his audiences – such as an intimation about eugenics and biological engineering to breed a superior governing class – arguing that it would be "inconceivable" for Ibsen ever to have intended that to be the case. Rather, again like Mill, Ibsen argues for " 'the aristocracy of character, of will, of mind – that alone can free us' " (p. 10).

Miller's Stockmann, nevertheless, is still generously over-endowed with a messiah complex. He embraces as a form of solitary martyrdom the designation "enemy of the people" (Miller's mob, in fact, is even darker than Ibsen's and linked more nearly with the American public of the Cold War fifties), and his missionary zeal perhaps verges on madness. Along with specifically likening himself to Galileo, the doctor identifies himself with Christ; the bribes that he is offered if he will compromise his position seem akin to Satan's temptations of Jesus in the wilderness. In response to the townspeople "crucifying their hero," he will gather around himself a "school of twelve" disciples – in this instance, young people with free and independent minds – whom he and his daughter Petra, who with her sincerely espoused doctrine of work represents the hope for the future, will instruct. And, like Christ, he is betrayed, both by his brother/enemy (à la Cain and Abel) as well as by the representative of the liberal press. Undoubtedly alluding to his own fellow liberals who buckled under to outside pressure, Miller condemns the unprincipled editor Hovstad, who ultimately temporizes and sells out for financial security, because he "DIDN'T DARE." Very handily, Miller can find in Ibsen's original text a profoundly ironic commentary on the contemporary political situation of paranoia and persecution when Dr. Stockmann muses about "go[ing] to America" where "the spirit must be bigger" and "at least there must be more room to hide" (p. 101).

The lessened ambiguity in Miller's handling of Dr. Stockmann may be linked to another facet of Ibsen's writing that his literary descendant could well have pointed to, and assuredly found congenial: an antithetical mode of thinking. In *Enemy* this is configured as an absolute opposition between society and the individual, the majority and the minority, power and truth. The tendency to privilege one side of the binary over the other results not only in didacticism but in what some would construe as dogmatism. This makes for a moral system that is generally more Manichaean than nuanced in nature. Miller, while insisting vehemently on the individual's "need, if not holy right, to resist the pressure to conform" to society (*Timebends*, p. 324) – which would appear to signal a totally relativistic or pluralistic perspective – still remains a moral absolutist. As he writes in his preface to *Enemy*, "At rock bottom, then, the play is concerned with the inviolability of objective truth" (*An Enemy of the People*, p. 9). What Miller, in fact, found most perplexing and frightening about the late forties and early fifties "was not only the rise of 'McCarthyism' . . . but something which seemed much more weird and mysterious. It was the fact that a political, objective, knowledgeable campaign from the far Right was capable of creating not only a terror, but a new subjective reality, a veritable mystique which was gradually assuming even a holy resonance."[5] What seems most to have disturbed him, then, was a confusion of the relative with the absolute, so that "subjective reality" could be foisted off as "objective truth."

Although it initially ran for only 197 performances when it opened on Broadway, *The Crucible* has become Miller's most frequently produced play. (At this writing, a new film version starring Daniel Day-Lewis and Winona Ryder is before the cameras in Massachusetts.) Since increasingly most audiences will no longer remember the particular sociopolitical situation of anti-Communism that reached its apogee in the House Un-American Activities Committee hearings, Miller has made the claim that "if I hadn't written *The Crucible* that period would be unregistered in our literature on any popular level," and that it continues to be the work that he "feel[s] proudest" of "because I made something lasting out of a violent but brief turmoil."[6] Partial proof of that "lasting" quality might be found, Miller muses, in the appeal the work exerts at times of political upheaval, when audiences around the world seem to have taken it to heart as "either a warning of tyranny on the way or a reminder of tyranny just past" (*Timebends*, p. 348). Yet from Miller's personal perspective as a writer, that tumultuous period in America's history – which saw him being denied a passport in 1954 to travel to the play's Brussels premiere and being found

Figure 2 Clare Holman in *The Crucible*, the Royal National Theatre, London.

in contempt of Congress in 1957 (though never imprisoned) for his refusal to incriminate friends by naming names of Communist sympathizers – evidences a phenomenon every bit as troubling as the demand for ideological purity: a deep-seated fear of the artist's power and influence. As Miller would formulate it in his autobiography years later, "The overwhelmingly significant truth, I thought, as I still do, was the artist-hating brutality of the Committee and its envy of its victims' power to attract public attention and to make big money at it besides" (*Timebends*, p. 242).

In *An Enemy of the People*, the literal text which is read, and which to Miller's way of thinking passes the test of "objective truth," is comprised of the scientific report that Dr. Stockmann receives through the mails that confirms the fact of bacterial pollution and that he then shares with the public authorities and the Norwegian press, expecting them to receive its evidence unquestioningly and move to the same conclusion as he has about an ethically appropriate course of action. In Puritan New England, as C. W. E. Bigsby provocatively suggests, those wielding religious and political power claim to possess an authorized text requiring "a singular reading of the world, a reality constituted by those who claim to possess or interpret the Word."[7] In fact, to study the witch trials themselves necessarily "becomes," as Bernard Rosenthal claims, "a textual problem – one of narration, of weighing competing narratives against each other for their reliability."[8] To a large extent, this proves true of Miller's play as well, for in *The Crucible* there are several texts that are "read" and either interpreted or misinterpreted. First, the playwright himself reads and finds an analogy between two historical texts: that of Salem at the time of the witch-hunt in 1692; and that of America in the McCarthy era of the 1950s. Abigail, as we shall see, likewise reads the "text" of the Puritan community and its believers, just as both she and Elizabeth will turn the body of John Proctor – its gestures, its expressions – into a text to be read; if Abigail, for example, finds love and loneliness in his face and interprets his "blush" as evidence of continuing sexual temptation, Elizabeth interprets it as shame and embarrassment over his character flaw.

Although Miller begins his "Note on the Historical Accuracy" of *The Crucible* by stating emphatically "This play is not history" (*Collected Plays*, p. 224), it most definitely constitutes a reading *of* history, with the playwright explicitly rendering his personal interpretation in the narrative interludes – available to readers of the text but not to audiences in the theatre – that he intersperses within the dialogue. In these, he not only expresses his value judgments upon the Puritan community, but also establishes the lineage for those strains he finds still alive in the America of his time. Employing the mythic opposition between civilization and the wilderness, he pictures a society on the edge of a "virgin forest [that] was the Devil's last preserve and home to marauding Indian tribes"; its "parochial snobbery" over their moral destiny – the conviction "that they held in their steady hands the candle that would light the world" – exacerbated by (as Paul Boyer and Stephen Nissenbaum have confirmed)[9] dissension over religious leadership, property rights, economic change, sexual repression, and the movement "toward greater individual freedom," all of which helped fuel persecution of the Other as a way to forestall a fractious dissolution. The Puritan theocracy, in short, had to be built upon an ideology of "exclusion and prohibition" in order to survive (*Collected Plays*, p. 228). Those who felt the least rebellion against the Establishment were almost forced, then, to channel their own guilt into accusations demonizing the Other. Several commentators have suggested that when Miller comes to set up the conflict between the Puritan theocracy and the authority of individual conscience in *The Crucible*, he might be distorting aspects of the former in order unswervingly to espouse the latter. E. Miller Budick, for instance, points to the "moral arrogance" of what she designates as "Miller's own narrator" in dredging up "his Puritan forbears' ethical deficiencies," while Edmund Morgan believes that the dramatist has set up Puritanism as a straw man or escape hatch that allows audiences to transfer their own moral inadequacies to its "benighted and outworn creed."[10]

One inheritance from Puritanism, Miller suggests, is the continuing application of religious categories to political actions, so that the nation is seen as having a "mission." Another is categorizing things in terms of "diametrically opposed absolutes," so that "a political policy is equated with moral right, and opposition to it with diabolical malevolence." As a consequence, "in America, any man who is not reactionary in his views is open to the charge of alliance with the Red hell" (*Collected Plays*, p. 249). If, in Salem, Miller discerned at work a "cleansing" through a "projection of one's own vileness onto others in order to wipe it out with their blood," in 1950s America he sadly found "a public rite of contrition . . . an obligatory kowtow before the state, the century's only credible god" (*Time-bends*, pp. 337, 395). So the McCarthy hearings, "profoundly ritualistic" in themselves, become, in Miller's reading of the two historical periods, "a surreal spiritual transaction that connected Washington to Salem." The analogy at the base of Miller's political allegory has, however, not gone unquestioned, particularly by those who would argue that whereas there really never had been any witches in Salem, there most assuredly were Communists to be ferreted out. For his part Miller replied that anyone denying the existence of witches in 1692 would have been guaranteed a short life.

The first significant prop that Miller introduces into his play is a stack of books. When the Reverend Hale, summoned from Beverly to Salem to help in the initial investigation of witchcraft, enters, he comes onto the stage carrying several "heavy" tomes on demonology "weighted [down] with authority." He goes on to describe their contents: "Here is all the invisible world, caught, defined, and calculated. In these books the Devil stands stripped of all his brute disguises. Here are all your familiar spirits – your incubi and succubi; your witches that go by land, by air, and by sea; your wizards of the night and of the day" (*Collected Plays*, p. 253). To argue that specters inhabiting an "invisible world" can be scrutinized and measured as if they were subject to sensory perception appears somewhat akin to Lear's error that qualitative emotions can be quantified and precisely verbalized, or Othello's misguided demand for the "ocular proof" of one's honor or dishonor. By the play's last act, a chastened and much less assured Hale concludes "we cannot read His [God's] will" (p. 320). As James Martine notices, Hale appears without his books when he ministers to the condemned in jail,[11] although he now preaches – perhaps as a salve to the guilt he feels concerning his responsibility for those already executed – that it would be preferable to lie, to confess to witchery, and live rather than to die a martyr's death, since for him "life" is an absolute value, superseding even morality. Among the other authorities, Judge Danforth will admit that "witchcraft is *ipso facto*, on its face and by its very nature, an invisible crime, is it not? Therefore, who may possibly be witness to it?" (*Collected Plays*, p. 297) – though that gives him no pause in investigating and condemning solely on the basis of spectral evidence. As Reverend Parris reemphasizes, "We are here, Your Honor, precisely to discover what no one has ever seen" (p. 300).

Versions of the word "see," in fact, recur frequently in the play, keeping before the audience this question of seeing the unseen, of reading or misreading the evidence. The workings of this verbal patterning become clear almost from the play's opening moments, as the townspeople claim to see not only things visible to the eye but spectral appearances as well. If Parris can claim to have seen one of the girls "naked" in the woods during Tituba's ceremony, another will claim to have seen his daughter Betty "fly." Only the wise old Rebecca Nurse, who has "seen" children's games before, can discern how such happenings can be accommodated to reasonable explanation: the girls are going through "their silly seasons, and when it comes on them they will run the Devil bowlegged keeping up with their mischief" (p. 247). By the end of Act One, fearful, to the point of hysteria, of being punished for transgressing religious and social codes in the forest, and subject to the power of suggestion, Abigail and Betty let forth a veritable crescendo of accusations which links together the notion of seeing with the naming of a half-dozen accused, as each girl claims in a frenzied sort of litany that she "saw" so-and-so with the Devil. It takes Giles Corey, who will be pressed to death, and John Proctor, hanged for witchcraft, to break the chain and refuse to name names – as Miller and others, like his fellow playwright Lillian Hellman, refused to do when called to testify before the Congressional committee.

Proctor, from early on, challenges authority that coerces through terror, saying he "likes not its smell" (p. 246) – being particularly galled by the contemptuous way the Reverend Parris exercises his domination through fire-and-brimstone threats and through materialistic showiness in golden candlesticks that seem to Proctor almost idolatrous; in short, he "sees no light of God" (p. 273) shining through Parris's actions, which he finds deeply disturbing since the tenets of Puritanism posit an outward sign of inward grace. If the authorities, both religious and civil, insist on their ability to perceive and interpret the unseen, Abigail, in "reading" the Puritan community, claims a universal disjunction between the visible and the invisible, the seen and the unseen. Pointing to her seduction by John Proctor in words perhaps intended to evoke the biblical tree of the knowledge of good and evil in the Garden, she exclaims: "John Proctor . . . took me from my sleep and put knowledge in my heart. I never knew what pretense Salem was. I never knew the lying lessons I was taught by all these Christian women with their covenanted men! And now you bid me tear the light out of my eyes?" (p. 241). Essentially, then, these outwardly god-fearing and self-righteous people recall for her the "whited sepulchers" of scripture. The word "pretense," in the sense of falsity or lie, also ramifies (like the word "see") throughout the play, beginning with Abigail's early confession that what was reputed to be witchcraft "were sport," later echoed by Mary Warren's "it were pretense" but redefined in the eyes of Proctor and his supporters as "fraud."

In an additional scene that Miller inserted between Acts One and Two late in the initial Broadway run (but that most critics, like Gerald Weales, judge "not an obligatory scene, either dramatically or thematically"[12]), the playwright clarifies both Abigail's motives and the reasons why she sees the adultery as a positive act from the point of view of her own psychological development. Since it is perhaps the most self-revelatory of Abigail's speeches, casting her in a somewhat more sympathetic light, it bears glossing for what it adds to the verbal motif of "pretense": "It were a fire you walked me through, and all my ignorance was burned away . . . I used to weep for my sins when the wind lifted up my skirts; and blushed for shame because some old Rebecca called me loose. And then you burned my ignorance away. As bare as some December tree I saw them all – walking like saints to church, running to feed the sick, and hyprocrites in their hearts!" (*The Crucible: Text and Criticism*, p. 150). The "fire" of their passion becomes for her, then, the crucible that she claims effected her growth from ignorance to experience, just as the trial will be the crucible that burns Proctor down to his essential elements. If the repressive and closed Puritan society somehow made her conclude that her sexual stirrings were shameful and peculiar to herself alone, Abigail discovered in the sexual act that these were normal and universal human feelings, that if she was depraved, then underneath they were all depraved, only acting as if they were among the elect whom God had saved. To lie – to appear on the surface to be what one is not (the Shakespearean motif of "seems" vs. "is" appears applicable here) – is perhaps the greatest among the sins, and her appointed mission in life becomes to reveal this flaw.

Although one impetus behind both *An Enemy of the People* and *The Crucible* would seem to be a challenge to a hegemonic world order that demonizes the other, the outsider who rebels, some recent criticism cogently demonstrates that, in his handling of the women characters in the later play, Miller falls prey, however unwittingly, to some of the very same patriarchal attitudes he appears to be criticizing. Wendy Schissel, for example, argues not only that Tituba, Parris's black slave from Barbados, has been made a scapegoat, but that Miller has objectified Abigail and Elizabeth by casting them as "extremes of female sexuality – sultriness and frigidity, respectively – which test a man's body, endanger his spirit, and threaten his 'natural' dominance or needs"; consequently, the text "reinforces stereotypes of *femme fatales* and cold-unforgiving wives" in order to cater to men's "vicarious enjoyment [of] a cathartic male character who has enacted their sexual and political fantasies."[13] John, in truth, does tend to blame the victim of his lust for seducing him, quick to openly name Abigail as "whore" rather than himself as "adulterer"; and if it is Elizabeth who ultimately verbalizes the judgment upon herself as "cold," John has intimated at this rationalization for his betrayal all along. The Establishment itself criminalizes sexual desire, reading the women's bodies as the source of sin and shame; feminine power is interpreted as dangerous in the eyes of a "Puritanism [that] transforms risky sexuality into witchcraft."[14] The first women accused of witchcraft exist on the margins of a society where class strata and property holdings were increasingly noticed. And Tituba refuses to be bound by the restrictive Puritan interpretation of the Devil, reading him in the more expansive role of trickster and source of community vibrancy: "Devil, him be pleasureman in Barbados, him be singin' and dancin' in Barbados . . . you riles him up 'round here . . . but in Barbados he be just as sweet" (*Collected Plays*, p. 313). As Ann Scarboro remarks, apart from the too easy one-dimensionality of Tituba's characterization, complete with pidgin English, Miller does grant "her a subtle power by making her a critic of the Puritans' devil."[15]

Miller found the germ for the adulterous relationship in what seemed to him a peculiar reference in the trial records to the Proctors' servant girl having been expelled from the house; to make it more theatrically viable, he raised Abigail's age from eleven to seventeen, at the same time lowering Proctor's from the sixties to the thirties. Even so, several commentators have doubted Miller's success at making the adultery integral to the larger plot and the development of his protagonist's character. Yet Miller focuses on it almost from the beginning, and it becomes a central motivation for the characters. Although John claims that any "promise" made to Abigail was purely an animal act, that they "touched" momentarily in a physical way without any deeper commitment, Abigail insists that he desires her still and is hypocritical in continuing to "bend" to Elizabeth and act out of duty to her. Unsuccessful in supplanting Elizabeth in Proctor's hearth and heart, a vindictive Abigail will wreak vengeance on her by naming her as a witch in hope of finally displacing her. John's guilt over the brief affair, his seeing the sexual sin as an indication of utter depravity, his unwillingness to forgive himself, and his need to be punished are what drive much of the later action. When he decides, in the almost Shakespearean cadences that close Act Two, to reveal his lechery publicly, he exalts that now all "our old pretense will be ripped away" – both the lies about witchcraft and any mask of personal godliness – so that "we are only what we always were, but naked now" (*Collected Plays*, p. 284). Whereas Abigail centers his "goodness" in his bringing her out of innocence into experience, John sees a larger social role and responsibility, arguing that to fail to bring the community out of ignorance, that is, out of its self-imposed condition of blindness to what is ripping it apart, would be the greatest sin and a failure truly worthy of damnation.

Elizabeth is set apart from all the play's other major characters in that she is the only one who understands, from the very beginning, that however much she may be able to read the physiognomy of the body as text, she cannot read another's heart – in fact, must not presume to read the heart of the other. If it perhaps will always remain true that she can never totally forget John's adultery, neither, however, will she judge, instructing her husband that "the magistrate sits in your heart" (p. 265). Though she "sees" evidence of John's continued interest in Abigail (his being in a room alone with her, his hesitancy in revealing their adultery, his failure to revoke the promise made in bed), she knows that judgment, like forgiveness, must come from the self. That the only goodness which counts is interior to the individual is forcefully brought home when Elizabeth redefines the nature of her own goodness, so that it coincides not with others' interpretation of it but rather with the dictates of her own heart. Under questioning by Hale as to whether she believes in the existence of witches and the minister's utter shock when she answers no, she insists on the priority of her knowledge of her own moral character rather than others' reading of it: "I cannot think the Devil may own a woman's soul, Mr. Hale, when she keeps an upright way, as I have. I am a good woman, I know it; and if you believe I may do only good work in the world, and yet be secretly bound to Satan, then I must tell you sir, I do not believe it" (p. 276). Her husband situates Elizabeth's goodness in her inability to lie, which would seem to set her completely apart from the hypocritical Puritan community as defined by Abigail.

Yet in that moment of greatest tension, when asked in court under oath whether John is the lecher he has already, without her knowledge, confessed himself to being in order to save her, she does lie out of love, not just to protect his honor but to validate her belief that only the individual can "read" and then name his or her own good or evil. Is to lie in this instance, then, not an act of love? Is the refusal to specify the guilt of others, to name names (whether in Salem in the 1690s or in America in the

1950s) not an act of love? Her lie is not, as Schissel worries it might be interpreted, an "act of betrayal," nor evidence of her as "schemer" ("Re(dis)covering the Witches," p. 468), but arises instead from moral conviction. Even though her confession of herself as a "cold wife" who prompted John's lechery seems an overly-judgmental act of self-limitation, it cannot subjectively be faulted for, as she says, "I have read my heart" (*Collected Plays*, p. 323). Her doubt, nevertheless, that she was ever worthy to *be loved* by John, which apparently resulted in a less than total giving of self, is perhaps on the personal level analogous to the larger Puritan conviction of depravity, a fettering belief in one's unworthiness to be saved. Elizabeth's refusal finally to sit in judgment upon the other, though John might initially interpret it as an indication of emotional distance, sets her apart from other Miller protagonists such as Chris Keller in *All My Sons* and Biff Loman in *Death of a Salesman*. In each case, they do judge the father and find him wanting, not in the abstract but for having failed to fulfill their expectations as a moral exemplar. When the fathers act on that accusation by committing suicide, then the surviving sons must live on with their guilt over having brought the father, however justifiably, to the bar of judgment.

In the play's final act, John Proctor makes a series of decisions, some of them reversing earlier ones, manifesting the existential nature of Miller's *Crucible*. When John had first confessed to his sin of lechery, he did so both to alleviate his guilt and to save his wife's life, since he trusted that the Court would see the vindictiveness at the base of Abigail's charges. Now it would, he rationalizes, given his "private" sin, be more "honest" (that is, a closer approximation of outer and inner) to lie and live. When he signs the confession to being in the devil's company, he does so not only because he deems himself unworthy to die a saint's death, for to do so would be (in a culmination of that verbal pattern) a "pretense," but also because, perceiving an apparent discrepancy between their moral character and his, he refuses to falsely name and incriminate others. Yet only moments later, John tears up his confession when he realizes that the text will be made public and taken as evidence that he claims others to be in Satan's power, thus blackening their good names. Furthermore, he destroys the written "lie" because, though it would save his life, it would ruin both his own good name and that of his children. For the notion of one's name assumes a talismanic power in Miller: an outward sign of an inner integrity. Proctor must judge and answer only to himself: human conscience is the final authority, autonomous in all things. Even the law must, in fact, be violated when it comes into conflict with the dictates of a rightly formed conscience. Miller himself identifies the "real and inner theme" of *The Crucible* as "the handing over of conscience to another, be it woman, the state, or a terror, and the realization that with conscience goes the person, the soul immortal, and the name" (*Collected Plays*, p. 47).

So Proctor finally does what Elizabeth has been goading him into doing all along: whereas before others had appropriated his identity and (re)constructed it according to their own agenda, now he takes charge of his destiny and in that moment discovers his identity. Perceiving a threat to his "sense of personal dignity," he "evaluates himself justly," to use Miller's phrases from his essay "Tragedy and the Common Man." Freed from excessive emphasis on human imperfection and redeemed by having placed others outside himself first, John is defined not by the "shame" that Hale (mis)reads in the act; rather, as Elizabeth affirms, "He have his goodness now" (*Collected Plays*, p. 329), which can never be taken from him. As Miller understands his protagonist's conflict, Proctor is "a man who is confronted with the opportunity, the possibility of negating himself, of calling true what he knows is half-truth . . . he's being asked by the court to condemn himself to a spiritual death. He can't finally do it. He dies a physical death, but he gains his soul, so to speak, he becomes his rebellion" (Roudané, *Conversations*, p. 158). So ultimately John can unhesitatingly mount the gibbet like the other scapegoat/saints in this community, the text of whose iconic bodies can now be read as martyrs to the tyranny of a patriarchal system that has come unhinged. Like every man who "need[s] to leave a thumbprint somewhere in the world" (*Collected Plays*, p. 29), he can now inscribe his name justly in the family and in the society – in short, on the text that is history. Elizabeth stands listening to the drum rolls of the executioners, bathed in light from " the new sun," reading the text rightly across the ages, as she had always done.

NOTES

Since *An Enemy of the People* is not included in the *Collected Plays*, page references are to the Penguin edition (New York, 1977). Also, the additional scene Miller wrote for *The Crucible* does not appear in the standard edition; it can be found as an Appendix to the play in Gerald Weales (ed.), *The Crucible: Text and Criticism* (New York: Penguin, 1977), pp. 148–52.

1 David Savran, *The Wooster Group, 1975–1985: Breaking the Rules* (Ann Arbor: UMI Research Press, 1986), p. 219.

2 Gerald Rabkin, "Is There a Text on This Stage?: Theatre/Authorship/Interpretation," *Performing Arts Journal* 26/27 (1985): 158.

3 Arthur Miller, *Timebends* (New York: Grove Press, 1987), pp. 323–24.

4 John Stuart Mill, *On Liberty*, ed. David Spitz (New York: Norton, 1975), pp. 62–63.

5 *Arthur Miller's Collected Plays*, vol. 1 (New York: Viking Press, 1957).

6 In Matthew C. Roudané (ed.), *Conversations with Arthur Miller* (Jackson: University Press of Mississippi, 1987), pp. 179, 360.

7 C. W. E. Bigsby, *Modern American Drama, 1945–1990* (Cambridge: Cambridge University Press, 1992), p. 96.

8 Bernard Rosenthal, *Salem Story: Reading the Witch Trials of 1692* (Cambridge: Cambridge University Press, 1993), p. 27

9 Paul Boyer and Stephen Nissenbaum, *Salem Possessed: The Social Origins of Witchcraft* (Cambridge, MA: Harvard University Press, 1974).

10 E. Miller Budick, "History and Other Spectres in Arthur Miller's *The Crucible*," *Modern Drama* 28.4 (1985): 538; Edmund S. Morgan, "Arthur Miller's *The Crucible* and the Salem Witch Trials: A Historian's View," in John M. Wallace (ed.), *The Golden and Brazen World: Papers in Literature and History 1650–1800* (Berkeley: University of California Press, 1985), p. 187.

11 James J. Martine, *The Crucible: Politics, Property, and Pretense* (New York, Twayne, 1993), p. 30.

12 Gerald Weales (ed.), *The Crucible: Text and Criticism*, p. 154.

13 Wendy Schissel, "Re(dis)covering the Witches in Arthur Miller's *The Crucible*: A Feminist Reading," *Modern Drama* 37.3 (1994): 464, 461.

14 Iska Alter, "Betrayal and Blessedness: Explorations of Feminine Power in *The Crucible, A View from the Bridge*, and *After the Fall*," in June Schlueter (ed.), *Feminist Rereadings of Modern American Drama* (Rutherford, NJ: Farleigh Dickinson University Press, 1989), p. 123.

15 Ann Scarboro, "Afterword" to Maryse Conde, *I, Tituba, Black Witch of Salem*, trans. Richard Philcox (New York: Ballantine, 1994), p. 222.

7

ALBERT WERTHEIM

A View from the Bridge

First performed as a one-act play in 1955, Arthur Miller's *A View from the Bridge* was later rewritten and restaged as a full-length, two-act play. Miller's Introduction to the second version comments on both the expansion of the play and its source. Of the latter, Miller remarks: "I had known the story of *A View from the Bridge* for a long time. A water-front worker who had known Eddie's prototype told it to me. I had never thought to make a play of it because it was too complete, there was nothing I could add."[1] In *Timebends*, his autobiography, Miller speaks at length of his interest in the Brooklyn waterfront and of his relationship with Vincent James "Vinny" Longhi, whom he describes as "a new member of the bar with political ambitions."[2] Longhi and Longhi's friend, Mitch Berenson, sought out Miller to help them make known and keep alive the work of Pete Panto, a young longshoreman who had earned a gangland execution for attempting to foment a revolt against the union leadership of Joseph Ryan, the corrupt and probably Mafia-affiliated then head of the International Longshoremen's Association (ILA). With Longhi and Berenson as his cicerones, Miller entered the dark, dangerous, corrupt world of Red Hook, the largely Italian, Brooklyn waterfront neighborhood. From this experience and from a Longhi anecdote the story and atmosphere of *A View from the Bridge* seem to have been born:

> In the course of time Longhi mentioned a story he'd recently heard of a longshoreman who had ratted to the Immigration Bureau on two brothers, his own relatives, who were living illegally in his very home, in order to break an engagement between one of them and his niece. The squealer was disgraced, and no one knew where he had gone off to, and some whispered that he had been murdered by one of the brothers. But the story went past me; I was still searching for a handle on Pete Panto. (*Timebends*, p. 152)

That was 1947. The one-act version of *A View from the Bridge* emerged eight years later.

No work of literature has one unique point of origin. It tends, rather, to emerge from a complexity of events, influences and feelings. So, too, there is a background for *A View from the Bridge* more complex than Longhi's anecdote. And some of that complex background is remarkably valuable for providing new insights into both Miller's play and the parlous political times during which it was conceived and written. Clearly Longhi and Berenson not merely provided the anecdote that gave rise to *A View from the Bridge* but led the playwright into the cavernous inferno of Red Hook (and indirectly to Hollywood). Miller himself remarks that he was brought "into what had become for me a dangerous and mysterious world at the water's edge that drama and literature had never touched":

> Now, looking back, I see how volcanic this decision was for me. Out of it would come a movie script (never to be produced); a play, *A View from the Bridge*; and a trip to Hollywood, where I would meet an unknown young actress, Marilyn Monroe, and at the same time come into direct collision with the subterranean machine that enforced political blacklisting and the ideological disciplining of film writers, actors, and directors. (*Timebends*, p. 149)

Looking back to that period in his life from a forty-year distance, Miller, in *Timebends*, vividly recreates a sinister, chilling portrait of the New York docks complete with mobsters, local dictators like Tony (brother of the notorious Albert) Anastasia, graft, dissenters like Pete Panto being dropped with cement weights from a pier, and rigged union elections. What Miller found was a longshore world that smacked of a Hollywood celluloid gangster script complete with plum parts for the likes of Edward G. Robinson, Humphrey Bogart, Richard Widmark, or Jimmy Cagney. And Hollywood is just where Miller eventually took his material.

The raw truths and the raw life of the Red Hook waterfront had their origins in Italy; and Miller leapt at the opportunity to go to Italy, guided by Longhi and Berenson. It turned out to be a memorable trip, "a trip," Miller writes, "whose echoes would inform much of my life to come" (*Timebends*, p. 153). Their travels in southern Italy led Miller, Longhi, and Berenson to Calabria and to Palermo, home for many Brooklyn dockworkers. When in *A View from the Bridge*, Marco and Rodolpho speak of their town in Sicily, Miller knew first hand what he had his characters describe. In Palermo, moreover, the threesome came to meet and know one of the celebrated principals in the drama of twentieth-century American crime: Lucky Luciano. In short, Miller's knowledge of the Red Hook piers rife with gangsterism and corrupt and mob-run unions, was complemented in Italy with a first-hand look at the Brooklyn waterfront's Sicilian background and origins. His understanding and outrage were funneled into a new dramatic work, a screenplay, *The Hook*, whose name suggests at once the affectionate appellation for Red Hook, the hook or crane used on the docks to lift heavy goods, and of course the more metaphorical uses of the word as a trap or snare.

Miller's initial curiosity about the Brooklyn waterfront came from seeing graffiti that asked, *"Dove Pete Panto?"* ("Where is Pete Panto?") the brave young dockworker who had dared to challenge the corrupt ILA leadership and had died for his daring. *The Hook* was to be a tribute to Panto and a blow to waterfront gangsterism. And what better vehicle than the movies, which, unlike a Broadway play, could send its message quickly to millions of Americans like Panto's co-workers, to the corrupt unions, and to members of Congress and crime commissions? Miller showed a version of his script to his friend, Elia Kazan, who had directed Miller's hit play *Death of a Salesman* and who was at that time trying to move his career away from Broadway and toward Hollywood. Kazan quickly saw the potential of Miller's filmscript and agreed to help prepare *The Hook* for a movie studio and to direct it. In spring 1950, Kazan and Miller boarded a train headed for Los Angeles to show the script to the studio moguls and to work on it further. They knew, however, that *The Hook*'s anti-union subject matter and muckraking tone might make the filmscript problematic for some studios. They were right; but eventually Harry Cohn, President of Columbia Pictures, bought the script.

Hollywood for Miller was clearly a major growth experience. There, of course, he was to meet Marilyn Monroe; there he was to discover that West Coast sensuality of which Clifford Odets was to write in *The Big Knife* and which Nathaniel West had earlier satirized in *The Day of the Locust*; and there he was to meet head-on the new American beast that was one part film studio, one part Cold Warfare, and one part mobsters masquerading as patriots. In Hollywood, Miller and Kazan worked diligently on *The Hook* and sold it to Columbia Pictures; but before the film could be made, Harry Cohn suddenly announced that it had to be vetted by a "labor relations man." It did after all deal with unions. In *Timebends*, Miller recalls his astonishment when Cohn informed him that he was having the script checked not by a film professional, not by the Columbia Pictures script or marketing department, but by a union official and by the FBI (p. 305).

In his autobiography, *A Life*, Elia Kazan vividly describes how Cohn arranged for a meeting with Roy Brewer, the head of the International Alliance of the Theatrical and Stage Employees, the American Federation of Labor stagehands union.[3] Brewer had read the script and decided that what was needed was an anti-Communist angle. The union official suddenly turned play doctor proposed that Marty, the main character in

The Hook, should rebuff a reporter from a Communist newspaper because, Brewer maintained, "The racketeers are much less a menace to labor than the Communists" (*A Life*, pp. 410–11). Suddenly, Kazan recalls, the film-script was in jeopardy:

> As we left the meeting, Art and I didn't know if we had an agreement or not. I wondered about Cohn's reaction. It had been a dreadful scene. A man we'd never met, who had nothing to do with the artistic values of our script, seemed to believe he had the power to decide whether or not we could go ahead with the film. We felt humiliated. (*A Life*, p. 412)

Miller recalls the events somewhat differently, saying that Kazan telephoned him to say that

> Cohn wanted some changes; if I agreed, the film would be doable, he said. The main one was that the bad guys in the story, the union crooks and their gangster protectors, should be Communists . . . Roy Brewer, the head of all the Hollywood unions, had been brought into the matter – by the FBI, presumably; he had read the script and said flatly that it was all a lie, that he was a personal friend of Joe Ryan, head of the International Longshoremen's Association, and that none of the practices I described took place on the piers. Finally, he informed Cohn that if the film was made he would pull all the projectionists across the country out on strike so that it could never be shown. The FBI, moreover, regarded it as a very dangerous story that might cause big trouble on the nation's waterfronts. (*Timebends*, p. 308)

Miller withdrew the script. The studio's reply came in the form of an accusatory telegram: "ITS INTERESTING HOW THE MINUTE WE TRY TO MAKE THE SCRIPT PRO-AMERICAN YOU PULLOUT. HARRY COHN" (*Timebends*, p. 308). With these events and those words, Miller found himself drawn headlong into the late 1940s and 1950s American political maelstrom generated by the investigations of the House Un-American Activities Committee (HUAC). Not so long after the demise of *The Hook*, both Kazan and Miller found themselves facing the HUAC tribunal and being asked to name names of colleagues with Communist affiliations.

The Hook is a script characteristic of the Arthur Miller who had recently written *All My Sons* and *Death of a Salesman*. Like Joe Keller and Willy Loman, Marty in *The Hook* is a man who is not educated enough to see larger issues but must come to his realizations through the pain of personal experience; and again like Joe and Willy, Marty never totally understands what happens to him or what he achieves.

But Miller's focus in *The Hook* is not so much on Marty as it is on waterfront corruption and graft, and upon the consequent reduction of human beings to animals. From the opening shots and dialogue in the filmscript, the audience gets brief portraits of Farragut, the corrupt union delegate; Rocky, the manager of the rackets and of the despicable hiring practices on the docks;[4] Louis, the union President; and Mr. Haenkel, the dock owner who wants to maximize his profits by having the longshoremen work double time instead of overtime. The film movingly depicts the "shape-up," the process whereby men are hired for the day's unloading of a freighter. Rocky cynically and mockingly flings two counters (i.e. tokens indicating those hired for work) to a mob of job-hungry workers who scuffle for the counters like animals fighting for a piece of flesh.[5] The brutality of the scene is underlined when, in the course of a work speed-up, a crane is made to dump its contents of steel bars, killing Barney, an intransigent dockworker (*The Hook*, pp. 10–11). These are powerfully dramatic moments that will be pillaged and will resurface some years later in the Budd Schulberg–Elia Kazan screenplay, *On the Waterfront*.

Awakened and energized by his friend Barney's death, Marty initiates a personal crusade against the union bosses and corruption of the pier. Forced to leave the docks, he takes a job working as a bookie for Rocky, thus trading one corruption for another. As Marty's understanding grows and as Miller's film develops, Marty breaks free from Rocky and takes an increasingly bold stand against the dockside despots, the mobsters and racketeers who preside unchallenged over life and labor in Red Hook and along the New York waterfront. By the conclusion of the film, Marty makes a heroic bid for the union presidency, dangerously challenging the incumbent Louis, who is thoroughly in the hands of mobster kingpin Jack Uptown. The dockworkers seem to find their voice through Marty, and it would seem that Marty can win the election. A frightened Louis fixes the election by stuffing the ballot box, but even when the falsely added votes are subtracted, it becomes clear that Marty would still not have won, because fear of losing their jobs made the men lose their courage and rectitude at the ballot box. When Louis attempts to appease Marty and bring him back into line by offering him the position of union delegate, the oldest dockworker, Old Dominick, exclaims in his broken Italian–English, "No Delegate! Marty, he's lie! The men no want no crook! The men no want racketeer! No!" (*The Hook*, p. 172). And the film concludes with Marty turning his back on the offer and walking toward the audience flanked by the other men.

The above description of *The Hook* clearly reveals Miller as an apt student of Odets and as heir to the Odets mantle. Miller's filmscript can easily be viewed as *Waiting for Lefty* fifteen years later, fleshed out as a full-length drama and bearing a rich patina of Odet's agitprop style. But Odets was writing during the depths of the Depression and Miller during the first surges of HUAC and Senator Joseph McCarthy. Odets's powerful drama moved millions whereas Miller's equally powerful script regrettably was never filmed and never published. To this day, *The Hook*, which represents the culmination of so much that formed Miller as a writer, is little known and lamentably either unmentioned or glossed over by those who write about Miller's work.

Whatever innocence Kazan and Miller may have had about HUAC before going to Hollywood, they must quickly have lost it when *The Hook* died. Kazan's autobiography protests, perhaps too strongly and pointedly, that Miller lacked the courage to fight for *The Hook* (*A Life*, pp. 414–15) and that Kazan himself would have fought on high-mindedly for the script. Kazan, furthermore, filled with self-justification, goes on to say that he decided to make a clean breast of his own Communist past affiliations to Darryl Zanuck (*A Life*, p. 415) and to Cohn. The latter replied, "You're just a goodhearted whore like me. We'll find something else to do together" (*A Life*, p. 414), and later had Kazan as his house guest while *On the Waterfront* was being edited (*A Life*, p. 410). Despite the patriotic indignation toward Communism with which *A Life* abounds, it is clear that Kazan is a pragmatist and a survivor. Miller, by contrast, seems to have channeled his indignation toward the demise of *The Hook* and toward HUAC and the McCarthy hearings into *The Crucible*.

In April 1952, Kazan was subpoenaed by HUAC. Encouraged by Darryl Zanuck to do so (*A Life*, p. 455), he named names when he appeared before that committee. Kazan's autobiography again resounds with self-justification and resentment when he speaks of erstwhile friends (*A Life*, pp. 468–72) who, after his HUAC testimony, branded him a Judas.[6] Among those friends was Arthur Miller, who, Kazan recounts, cut him dead (*A Life*, p. 461). Four years later, Miller was himself summoned before HUAC, refusing to reveal the identity of colleagues with prior or present Communist Party affiliations.

In treating Kazan's HUAC testimony and its aftermath, *A Life* is a curious amalgam of self-righteous indignation, knee-jerk anti-Communist sloganeering, and self-congratulation about his success despite being reviled. Those elements seem as well to color events that led to the making of the film *On the Waterfront*. After the HUAC hearings, Kazan sought out the friendship of author Budd Schulberg, who had also been called before HUAC, had named names and was subsequently ostracized from the company of old friends:

> Budd had testified as I had, been reviled by many of his old companions as I'd been. His closest friend had stopped talking to him as Miller had shunned me.

Now the "progressives" had us both on their shit list. As we talked that first night in New Hope, there was an immediate warm sympathy between us. We became brothers. (*A Life*, p. 487)

The script of *The Hook* having been abandoned by Miller, Kazan and Schulberg teamed up to create a new New York waterfront screenplay that would essentially endorse and benefit from the wave of American Cold War anti-Communism. At the same time, it would both exonerate and celebrate Kazan's and Schulberg's HUAC testimonies.

In making their new screenplay, *On the Waterfront*, Schulberg and Kazan turned away from the Red Hook docks of Brooklyn and looked across the water to their mirror image in Hoboken. There they heard the story of another Pete Panto, Tony Mike DiVincenzo, who, subpoenaed by the Waterfront Crime Commission, had fingered the racketeers and mobsters who ruled the Hoboken piers. To Kazan the parallel between DiVincenzo and himself was immediately and poignantly clear:

He was called a rat, a squealer and stoolie. He was ostracized, then threatened . . . I doubt that Budd was affected personally as I was by the parallel of Tony's story. His reaction to the loss of certain friends was not as bitter as my own; he had not experienced their blackballing as frequently and intensely as I had in the neighborhood known as Broadway . . . But I did see Tony Mike's story as my own, and that connection did lend the tone of irrefutable anger to the scenes I photographed and to my work with actors.
(*A Life*, pp. 499, 500)

Kazan makes a facile equation between alleged Communists and felonious mobsters, dramatizing his own ostracism while ignoring the subsequent entertainment industry blackballing of those he fingered as Communists and fellow travelers. And it is in this spirit of self-exoneration that, two years after Kazan's HUAC testimony, *On the Waterfront* (1954) seems to have been made.

The Schulberg–Kazan screenplay owes a good deal to *The Hook*. As a crane with steel bars is made to dump its load, killing a querulous worker in the latter, so a cargo sling loaded with cases of whiskey is made to release its contents, killing the querulous Kayo Nolan in the former.[7] Farragut, Rocky, and Jack Uptown in *The Hook* are essentially revived in *On the Waterfront* as Big Mac, Charley Malloy, and Johnny Friendly. And Miller's moving scene in which the longshoremen in their "shape-up" scramble like animals for the counters thrown into the crowd also finds its way into the Schulberg–Kazan script (*On the Waterfront*, pp. 30–32).

At the same time, it is important to acknowledge that *On the Waterfront* is a far more powerful script than *The Hook*. Miller's Marty is a character who finds his truth in a Red Hook world of mixed loyalties and blurred moralities. When Marty's friends desert him at the ballot box, a Miller aware of the complexities of human motivations eschews the too easy path of allowing the heroic stand of one person instantly to reform the others around him. That is Miller's way, one reminiscent of the uneasy ending of *All My Sons* and of the equivocal "Requiem" of *Death of a Salesman*. It is not the black and white way life was presented by Hollywood in the 1950s. The Schulberg–Kazan film, by contrast, makes the distinctions between the forces of good and evil as pellucid as they are in a medieval morality play; and when Terry Doyle (Marlon Brando) makes his solo heroic stand against the mob, the film dazzlingly presents sudden mass conversion. The concluding stage direction reads, "Longshoremen by the hundreds march into the pier behind Terry like a conquering army" (*On the Waterfront*, p. 140). Some of the difference between *The Hook* and *On the Waterfront* again becomes clear when one realizes that the ending of *On the Waterfront* owes much to the ending of *The Hook*, in which Miller has a final shot of "Marty walking, silent, Old Dominick beside him, and the Gang near him . . . Walking toward us, his face elated, determined, serious . . . and as he walks the crowd of men behind him thickens as they will pour out of the hall. And it keeps thickening, widening . . . FADE OUT" (*The Hook*, p. 173). For Kazan and Schulberg, Terry Malloy's triumph is an unequivocal, pat, feel good, Hollywood ending. Marty's triumph, however, is compromised by the recognition that his moment of glory will be among his last, for the racketeers will not let him live long.

The Hook, in short, was a script clouded with moral dilemma and one squarely about a corrupt labor union, a script that looked back to Odets. *On the Waterfront*, steeped in the politics of the 1950s, was, by contrast, a film in which the moral issues were clear and one that required little sophistication from moviegoers to perceive the Cold War political agenda sharply visible beneath the film's gossamer labor union and dockside facade. Yet it was precisely its anti-Communist contemporaneity and easy distinction between good and evil that infused new vitality into Miller's seemingly anachronistic 1930s labor union issues, made the film so popular in its day, and helped to canonize it as an American film classic.

Arthur Miller was not to be called before HUAC until 1956. Before that, however, he had addressed the new American witch-hunting in *The Crucible* (1953) and the issue of naming names in *A View from the Bridge* (1955). In the latter, he returned to the Brooklyn waterfront of *The Hook* but, unlike Kazan, chose not to re-explore corrupt unions. Instead he staged a tragedy based on mixed loyalties, conflicting emotions, and a central character, Eddie Carbone, caught in the gaps between tribal and codified laws. Perhaps in response to *On the Waterfront*, perhaps to work out his own complicated feelings toward Kazan and others who named names in their HUAC testimonies, Miller returned to Red Hook in 1955 in order to write a tragedy that would probe the psychological and dramatic dimensions of the informer who "ratted" on his illegal alien relatives, the anecdote Longhi had related to Miller in 1947.

The Brooklyn Bridge resonates with meaning for two of America's finest poets, Walt Whitman and Hart Crane. It does so no less for America's premier playwright. Overshadowing the Red Hook docks, the Roeblings' structural masterpiece becomes for Miller a symbol of a span between disparate civilizations. It stretches from ethnic Brooklyn neighborhoods filled with laborers, foreign-accented immigrants and the children of those immigrants to the cosmopolitan, urbane, Manhattan area settled by New York's original Dutch colonists, now populated by bankers and financiers, and serving as the point of origin for America's connection to an international world. It stretches as well from a Brooklyn of social taboos, of family and clan allegiances imported from the Old Country, to Manhattan's City Hall and courts, to a social contract in the New World regulated by codified laws and government institutions. The bridge between cultures is not merely there in the symbol of the Brooklyn Bridge but there as well anthropomorphized in the on-stage figure of Alfieri, the immigrant-son lawyer who practices in Red Hook and tries to explain American legal statutes to men like Eddie Carbone, reared in the traditions of Sicilian family and tribal loyalties, imperatives, and taboos.

As Miller shows him and in keeping with the play's title, Eddie is an unsophisticated dockworker trying to bridge and accommodate disparate and not always conscious psychological feelings. Pushed by the pressures brought to bear in the plot, he wrestles tragically with very human ambivalences. On the one hand, he harbors strong, appropriate, protective paternal feelings toward Catherine, his wife's orphaned niece whom he and his wife, Beatrice, have raised. Yet at the same time, those feelings, situated as they are on the extreme edge of the paternal or avuncular, threaten to spill over into taboo sexual desire. Miller makes this powerfully clear when, for example, he shows Eddie's pleasure as Catherine lights his cigar. This is an action of warm and innocent affection between niece and uncle, but of course it is also one laden with blatant sexual and phallic meaning, which can seem heavy-handed in the printed text but which is enormously effective in the theatre, especially if the actor playing Eddie can convey the doubleness of the moment. Symptomatic of Eddie's sexual ambivalence is his sexual withdrawal from his wife, Beatrice, with whom he has not had coital relations in three months. Beatrice and the audience understand, as

Eddie does not, the connection between the cessation of conjugal relations and the transference of Eddie's erotic feelings to Catherine. Much of the power of Eddie as a tragic figure is that, unlike a Shakespearean hero, he is neither a reflective nor an articulate character. He himself does not quite understand what is happening to him. Incapable of speaking openly about sexuality, he is nonetheless racked by his failed masculinity, his impotence in the marriage bed. He is beset by incestuous passion, a love that dare not speak its name, a love he cannot, dare not recognize. Beatrice intuitively senses what is happening to Eddie. Alfieri and the audience, endowed with elementary Freudian literacy, understand it more clearly. But Eddie's ignorance or willed ignorance creates a dramatic irony and complexity central to the tragic richness of the play.

When Beatrice's cousins, Marco and Rodolpho, arrive from Italy, Eddie's ambivalences intensify. The swarthy, laconic, married, Marco, with his wrestler's build, fits the socially acceptable Sicilian virile stereotype; but his brother, Rodolpho, challenges the stereotype at every turn. Blond, effusive, single, lithe of gait, skilled in sewing and singing, he gives Eddie "the heeby-jeebies" (*A View from the Bridge*, p. 30). Eddie's homophobia becomes intensified and increasingly articulated as Catherine and Rodolpho take more than a cousinly interest in one another. The other characters see Rodolpho's physical and personal eccentricities as charming. Eddie says denigratingly that they are obvious indicators of Rodolpho's homosexual effeminacy. Paradoxically, then, Eddie sees Rodolpho at once as both homosexual and heterosexual adversary who threatens in either case to take Catherine from him. Eddie suspects, furthermore – and perhaps not with total misperception – that Rodolpho is attracted to Catherine because she can be his ticket to American citizenship. Given Eddie's own ambivalent feelings toward Catherine, he wishes on the one hand, as a responsible uncle would, to protect his niece, a mere inexperienced and naive *girl*, from marrying a homosexual who merely wishes to exploit her to gain citizenship. On the other hand, he fabricates an image of Rodolpho as a sexually "abnormal" and ruthlessly pragmatic exploiter in order to disable a rival lover for the desirable *woman* that the incest taboo will never allow Eddie himself to possess. Beatrice blurts out the awful truth at a climactic moment late in the play, "You want somethin' else, Eddie, and you can never have her!" (p. 83).

Eddie's fiction that Catherine is a virginal madonna figure or mere child in need of his protection is shattered when he surprises a post-coital Catherine and Rodolpho. Eddie is likewise confronted with incontrovertible proof of Rodolpho's masculinity and heterosexuality, as well as with the recognition that he has lost Catherine to her illegal alien cousin. Until this point in the play, Eddie has suppressed his erotic desire for his niece, sublimating his passion into the acceptable behavior of a concerned parent. When Catherine acknowledges the sexual *rite de passage* she has just undergone, "Eddie, I'm not gonna be a baby any more!" (p. 63), Eddie's suppressed desires, jealousy, and anger well forth and *"He reaches out suddenly, draws her to him, and as she strives to free herself he kisses her on the mouth."* Stunningly replacing his usual avuncular kiss with the taboo kiss of a lover, Eddie throws Catherine's lost virginity in her face. Simultaneously, of course, he releases an unmistakably powerful sexual drive that is given increased dramatic force for the audience by what has been previously revealed about Eddie's conjugal abstinence.

When a stunned Rodolpho reacts to Eddie's sexually charged kiss by pleading his honorable intentions and exclaiming that he wants Catherine for his wife, Eddie verbally attacks the young man for his effeminacy: "What are you gonna be? Show me!" and *"pins his arms, laughing, and suddenly kisses him"* (p. 63). The moment is fraught with dramatic tension and extraordinary ambivalence. It is hardly as simple as Eddie's enacting the other love that dare not speak its name, a homoerotic attraction to Rodolpho.[8] Mastered by forces he does not fully comprehend, Eddie kisses Rodolpho in a desperate act to castrate the young man, prove that Rodolpho is queer, and thereby challenge the validity of the heterosexual act that has moments before taken place. It is, moreover, possible that for Eddie kissing Rodolpho, though a taboo act, is made acceptable as a last-ditch attempt to reveal Catherine's lover for what he is. One might also speculate that the kissing of Rodolpho is meant to draw attention from the kissing of Catherine and from a discovery of a love more unacceptable than love for another man. Who, Eddie no doubt thinks, would ever accuse him, a manly longshoreman strong in approved homosocial bonding, of homosexuality? He is, however, open to accusations of unnatural incestuous feelings, so these need to be securely closeted. Indeed, veiled accusations have already been implicit in Beatrice's comments and in the interchange between Eddie and Alfieri:

> ALFIERI: She wants to get married, Eddie. She can't marry you, can she?
> EDDIE: *furiously*: What're you talkin' about, marry me! I don't know what
> the hell you're talkin' about. (pp. 46–47)

The two successive kisses are partially meant to destroy Catherine and Rodolpho's union, but they also bespeak Eddie's incestuous and perhaps homosexual passions. What is important here is precisely that the full meaning of those kisses is not totally clear to Eddie, Catherine, Rodolpho, or the audience. The characters and the audience find themselves at an intersection of passions and motives, on a bridge between conscious and unconscious acts, between acceptable and unacceptable behaviors.

Again fraught with mixed motives and mastered by passions he does not truly comprehend, Eddie names the names of Marco and Rodolpho to the Immigration Bureau. In doing so, he breaks the unwritten laws of the clan but complies with the written laws of the land. Once more, he acts, from one point of view, as a concerned parent making a final gesture to save his child from a disastrous marriage; and from another point of view, he takes the revenge of a spurned lover who cannot allow his rival to possess the woman who has rejected him. Pushed to the extremities, furthermore, he breaks the taboo of informing to frantically closet the more terrible taboo of incest.

Drawing on the figure of Rocky in *The Hook*, who is also concerned about his name in the Red Hook community (*The Hook*, p. 119), Miller has Eddie Carbone want to retrieve his good name from Marco. He wants an affirmation that he has acted in Catherine's best interests, that Rodolpho is morally and sexually feckless, and that he himself should not become a neighborhood pariah. Yet when Eddie screams, "I want my name, Marco" (*A View from the Bridge*, p. 84), the real answer to his demand should be something of the order of "incestuous swine." Only Beatrice comes close to saying that. The tragic pity we feel for Eddie, a pity for which Alfieri gives the cues, comes from the realization that Eddie is a man of powerful passions and a man who never quite understands those passions. Moreover, his phallic maleness channeled into a taboo lust he cannot acknowledge, turns in on him, tragically undoes him, and his knife does likewise. The stage directions read "*Eddie lunges with the knife. Marco grabs his arm, turning the blade inward and pressing it home . . . and Eddie, the knife still in his hand, falls to his knees before Marco. The two women support him for a moment, calling his name again and again*" (p. 85). Eddie is never fully aware of who he is, what motivates him and others, or what his name should be. In keening "Eddie," the women are no more able than Miller's protagonist himself to give a name to the inchoate constellation of feelings and drives he embodies.

An intersection of conscious and unconscious motives and passions creates a tangled skein that nonetheless relentlessly draws Eddie, Catherine, Rodolpho, and Beatrice into its tragic weave. It is this which sets *A View from the Bridge* significantly apart from *The Hook* and from Schulberg and Kazan's *On the Waterfront*. It is easy and not altogether wrong to say that in *On the Waterfront* and *A View from the Bridge* Kazan and Miller respectively return to their initial joint venture, *The Hook*; Kazan doing so to create a scenario justifying naming names to HUAC, and Miller retorting with one condemning his central character for the same thing. C. W. E.

Bigsby comes close to the truth when he writes, "It has been said that Miller wrote this play to denounce the informer, as Elia Kazan went on to make the movie, *On the Waterfront*, which justified the informer. Whatever the truth of that the force of the play lies elsewhere."[9] Indeed, the force of *A View from the Bridge* does lie elsewhere; and it has much to do with Miller's decision to eschew the black and white portraits derived from 1930s agitprop theatre that marked *The Hook* as a theatrical descendant of *Waiting for Lefty* and to forego as well the morality play, good and evil, portraits of *On the Waterfront*.

As its very title suggests, Miller's play is about being between extremes, about disparate loyalties and mixed motives, about tribal versus codified law, about acceptable and unacceptable sexual behaviors. *The Hook* and *On the Waterfront* simplify, *A View from the Bridge* problematizes. In this way, *A View from the Bridge* marks Miller's significant development as a writer after *The Hook*. Miller's play is very much other than a rejoinder in kind to *On the Waterfront*. It is to Miller's credit as both a playwright and a human being that, as *A View from the Bridge* reveals, he came to see HUAC informers not as archetypal or caricature villains or the situation as one of easily recognizable right and wrong distinctions. The moving, sympathetic portrait of Eddie Carbone allows Miller to acknowledge and to make his audience understand that those who named names at the HUAC hearings were men like Kazan whose actions stemmed from a constellation of motives, some conscionable, some damnable. Miller's play raises questions, moreover, about how much Kazan may have acted out of unrealized jealousy of others; out of resentment for losing Marilyn Monroe, who had been his sexual partner on several occasions as Kazan's *A Life* too frequently reminds us, to Miller, whom Kazan characterizes as his less virile friend; out of a psychological need to act out a masculine, patriotic stance;[10] and out of the need to protect himself.

Is Eddie, is Kazan, are HUAC informers to be condemned as villains or to be viewed with pity and fear as tragic characters? Does not Rodolpho woo Catherine out of sincere love yet also with a recognition that marrying her will give him US citizenship? Disparate motives coexist. Likewise, a man like Kazan might well testify before HUAC motivated by an immigrant's sincere love of his adopted country and still be motivated, too, by a knowledge that naming names, heeding Zanuck's advice, will enable him to escape blacklisting in Hollywood and survive as a successful film director. To see *A View from the Bridge* in the context of its time and in the context of *The Hook* and *On the Waterfront*, is to see Miller's profound and admirable ability to understand the mixed motives of his friends who named names. He can admire, condemn, and forgive them even as the audience comes, like Miller's mouthpiece Alfieri, to understand, admire, condemn, and forgive Eddie Carbone.

Miller's experiences on the waterfront and his subsequent trip to Italy, the writing of *The Hook* and the reasons for its rejection by the Hollywood studio, the HUAC hearings and the condemnation of Kazan and others who named names, Kazan's self-righteous self-defense projected in *On the Waterfront*, Miller's ability to vent his anger toward the new American witch-hunts in *The Crucible*, all seem to form a concatenation of events and experiences that led Miller to *A View from the Bridge* and to a new, generous attitude toward what HUAC wrought.[11] Miller seems to learn and pass on to his audience the realization that to view from the bridge is to achieve the understanding one gains from tragedy. One learns to see the frailty of human beings with pity and fear rather than to deem them angels or villains.

NOTES

1 Arthur Miller, *A View from the Bridge* (New York: Viking Press, 1960), p. vii.
2 Arthur Miller, *Timebends* (New York: Grove Press, 1987), p. 148.
3 Elia Kazan, *A Life* (New York: Alfred A. Knopf, 1988), pp. 410–11.
4 There is an impressive congruence between Rocky and the portrait of Tony Anastasia in *Timebends*, pp. 152–53.
5 Arthur Miller, *The Hook: A Play for the Screen* (MCA Ltd., no date), pp. 7–8. The text used for this study is the one at the Lilly Library, Indiana University.
6 See also Victor S. Navasky, *Naming Names* (New York: Viking Press, 1980), pp. 199–206.
7 Budd Schulberg, *On the Waterfront: A Screenplay* (Carbondale and Edwardsville: Southern Illinois University Press, 1980), pp. 30–32.
8 See David Savran, *Communists, Cowboys, and Queers* (Minneapolis and London: University of Minnesota Press, 1992), pp. 41–42.
9 C. W. E. Bigsby, *Modern American Drama, 1945–1990* (Cambridge: Cambridge University Press, 1992), p. 103.
10 In *A Life*, pp. 32–34, Kazan reveals that at the age of 14 he had mumps, which destroyed one of his testicles. This, he says, "affected my whole life" (p. 32); and it does seem that this admittedly traumatic loss may well have influenced his subsequent sexual voracity and his persistent need to prove his manliness. One wonders whether Miller, who had known Kazan so intimately, knew this, and whether it had an impact on Miller's characterization of Eddie as someone who needs to prove his masculinity and sexuality, yet whose sexuality is in question by virtue of his long absence from Beatrice's bed.
11 Perhaps that new attitude created enough of a *rapprochement* between Miller and Kazan so that in 1964 Kazan could direct Miller's *After the Fall*. The character of Mickey, the informer, in that play seems rather clearly based on Kazan. One can only wonder whether, when Kazan agreed to direct the play, Miller felt some sweet revenge and whether Kazan undertook the direction in a spirit of atonement or masochism.

8

JANET N. BALAKIAN

The Holocaust, the Depression, and McCarthyism: Miller in the sixties

In some ways Miller seemed out of synch with the sixties. Rather than writing about Vietnam or civil rights, he chose to look back to the Depression in *The Price*, the Holocaust in *After the Fall* and *Incident at Vichy*, McCarthyism and the Depression in *After the Fall*. Yet all three plays also explore the problem of denial, and to Miller this was the central issue of the moment. Denial, after all, lay behind the American attitude toward race, and it facilitated the waging of an immoral war in south-east Asia. There is certainly no evidence that he abstracted himself from the political realities of the decade. Quite the contrary. He became actively involved in the anti-war movement. Yale, the University of Michigan, and even West Point invited him to speak about the war. He had not, however, forgotten about McCarthyism, warning students, at a University of Michigan teach-in, that the FBI, who, he claimed, was sitting among them, would hold them accountable for their actions and even ask them to condemn their present passions in the future. He nevertheless applauded the student protest, calling it "the essential risk of living."[1] Moreover, he consoled students by telling them that even if their movement did not end in victory, "it should not be the occasion for disillusion, because we must go on groping from one illusion of virtue to another" (*Timebends*, p. 100). Yet he noted a contrast between the personal nature of the student revolt of the sixties and the more altruistic radicalism of the thirties, the decade that would always be his moral and political touchstone.

> This was not the symbolic ideological rhetoric of another time when Hitlerism, however threatening, was very far away and few people really believed the United States would enter a new European war . . . They were not saving somebody else, and that was the difference between them and their fathers in the thirties, when with all the poverty and dislocation of life it still took a leap of the imagination for a student to be radicalized. The ticket to radicalization in the sixties was the draft card in the wallet.
>
> (*Timebends*, pp. 100–01)

In another sense, however, Miller saw a similarity between the sixties and the thirties. In both, "the alienated had the prophecy but not the power" (*Timebends*, p. 101). Further, he likened the teach-ins of the sixties to the Crash of 1929 in that both exposed corruption in high places (*Timebends*, p. 102). Lying in bed in the Michigan Union, where he had spent his first night at college thirty years before, he "wondered how many times a country could be disowned by a vital and intelligent sector of its youth before something broke, something deep inside its structure that could never be repaired again . . . Is this the way America grows, or is this the way she slowly dies?" (*Timebends*, pp. 102–03). As in the forties and fifties, he saw democracy threatened.

A liberal to the core, Miller was a Eugene McCarthy delegate to the 1968 Democratic Party National Convention in Chicago. But he never had much hope that the convention would really allow the pacifists to separate the Democrats from support of the Vietnam War. When it became obvious that Humphrey would be the presidential nominee, without promising to end the war, however, Miller thought the time had come to unify the Robert Kennedy and Eugene McCarthy factions in order to strengthen the challenge to Humphrey and to influence future policy (*Timebends*, p. 546). Thus, he drafted a statement freeing the many delegates pledged to Gene McCarthy to vote as they wished.

Not only did Miller participate in sit-ins at the University of Michigan and in the Democratic Convention, but he also became politically involved in the international scene. His life-long commitment to protecting the liberties of writers made him a natural president of PEN in 1965. He also petitioned the Soviet government to lift the ban on Alexander Solzhenitsyn's works. Despite this political activity, however, Miller felt the lack of any genuine moral vision, any transcendent idea. "I could find no refreshing current of history such as I had imagined touching in the thirties and forties, only a moral stagnation" (*Timebends*, p. 553). Beyond that, he doubted the ability of the theatre to address the enormity of Vietnam and, after a hostile critical response to *After the Fall*, he even momentarily lost the desire to write.

Not only did his obsession with the Depression, Fascism, and McCarthyism seem, to many, to be anachronistic in a decade so full of its own turbulence, but, to some extent, so did his dramaturgy. Beckett and Pinter were powerful presences, and for some critics the absurd seemed to have superceded other forms both theatrically and philosophically. It was not a path that Miller could take. As he told me,

> When people tend to celebrate the meaningless, it ends up with fascism. When they get too comfortable with the inevitable defeat of human hope . . .

I smell dictatorship around the corner; probably because I was born into the era when it was not an exaggeration to think that the hopeless could maybe turn out the lights on everything and kill you for being a Jew or a skeptic.[2]

For Miller, Vietnam did potentially change the nature of the dramatic problem. He had seriously "begun to question whether a play that gradually unveiled a submerged theme could ever be written again" (*Timebends*, p. 548). Convinced that America was refusing to face its national self-deception, he felt that such denial was all that remained to reveal (*Timebends*, p. 548). Despite this, his most successful play of the 1960s, *The Price*, is one in which the past is slowly unveiled. Nonetheless, if he seemed out of step with the dramatic current of the sixties, it was not because of an inherent conservatism but because he remained dedicated to exploring the psyches of characters whose actions had consequences. He continued to believe that private and public histories were a key to present realities.

In England, Tom Stoppard was interested in the dramatic possibilities of multiple levels of reality and shifting identities;[3] Miller, in *The Price* and *After the Fall*, was more concerned with their philosophical and moral implications. While Harold Pinter rejected the notion that events can be verified (Brockett and Findlay, *Century of Innovation*, p. 627), each of Miller's plays in the sixties affirms that there is a truth to be known, if we struggle to find it. In 1964, however, Miller was much less interested in the current theatrical scene than he was in the Nazi trials in Frankfurt, Germany, for which he was the special commentator for *The New York Herald Tribune*. He wrote an impassioned article attempting to "reinstate an understanding in the public mind of the dynamics of Fascism."[4] The trials sharpened his viewpoint about guilt and responsibility, prominent themes in both his 1964 plays, *After the Fall* and its companion piece, *Incident at Vichy*. In *After the Fall*, the protagonist, Quentin, measures his domestic and professional responsibilities against the backdrop of a concentration camp watchtower. A lawyer, Quentin has come to see life as a law case that he must plead before an empty bench with no judge and no verdict. In effect, the play is an odyssey of individual anguish, a "trial of a man by his own conscience, his own values, his own deeds." The play's action, consisting of freely associated but highly selected memories, takes place in Quentin's mind. He speaks to a Listener, presumably seated just offstage, and reviews major events of his life as each is dramatized on the gray landscape of the set. All of the characters remain onstage throughout Quentin's confession, each activated in turn by the narrative. The Listener, who could be a psychoanalyst, or close friend, is, according to Miller,

Figure 3 Jason Robards Jr. and Barbara Loden in *After the Fall*, the Lincoln Center Repertory Company, 1964, directed by Elia Kazan.

Quentin himself "turned at the edge of the abyss to look at his experience, his nature and his time."[5] On the verge of marrying for the third time, he feels the need to examine the reason for his previous failed marriages, especially his relationship with Maggie, a young woman who becomes a leading singer–performer, who critics and audiences of the original production insisted on seeing as a version of Miller's own second wife, Marilyn Monroe. But Quentin is not only concerned with the personal experience of betrayal. History itself offers similar evidence, and history is as much the subject of *After the Fall* as private failures, history in terms of the Holocaust but also in terms of the McCarthy witch-hunt of the fifties. Indeed, one of the characters, Mickey, is summoned before the House Un-American Activities Committee and invited to betray his friends.

The image of the concentration camp pervades the play, and Quentin sees it not only as a metaphor for the Holocaust, but also for McCarthyism, and for his own guilt about betraying others who depend on him. When asked why he chose to use a concentration camp in *After the Fall*, Miller explained: "I have always felt that concentration camps, though they're a phenomenon of totalitarian states, are also the logical conclusion of contemporary life . . . In this play the question is, what is there between people that is indestructible? The concentration camp is the final expression of human separateness and its ultimate consequence. It is organized abandonment" (Roudané, *Conversations*, p. 108). For Miller, as for many post-war Jewish–American novelists, the Holocaust is the modern equivalent of the Fall, the relentless reality of evil. Perhaps that is why it took Miller twenty years to begin addressing this kind of darkness.

Upon returning from the Frankfurt trials, Miller realized that "the theme of survivor guilt was emerging from [the] gargantuan manuscript," which was *After the Fall* (*Timebends*, p. 520). But, along with survivor guilt, *After the Fall* also addresses the question of "idealistically denied brutality," which was relevant not only to German history but to America's role in Vietnam and, beyond that, to a contemporary human dilemma: our tendency "to deaden our connections, and hence our psyches, to those actions we found it difficult to justify" (*Timebends*, p. 520). The problem of denial first arose for Miller when he was struggling to write a play about the atom bomb; indeed, the above quotation comes from a passage in Miller's autobiography in which he recounts a meeting with Oppenheimer, "father" of the bomb. As he wrote a play in blank verse about an Oppenheimer-like character preparing to signal the fateful test explosion of the first experimental weapon, it occurred to him that guilt of this kind might be something we fabricate to deny our real responsibilities, provoking pain without the humiliation of contrition, thereby weakening the need to change our lives (*Timebends*, p. 521). It became clear to him, suddenly, why Camus' *The Fall*, which he had planned to adapt as a screenplay in the early sixties, but which more importantly became the novel that inspired *After the Fall*, had left him dissatisfied. As Miller saw it, the unstated question posed in Camus' novel was not how to live with a bad conscience – that was merely guilt – but how to find out why one went to another's rescue only to collaborate in his defeat. Where *The Fall* is the book of an observer, he wanted to write about the participant in such a catastrophe, a defendant, appearing before the court of his own conscience, who gradually comes to understand his collaboration in his own moral failure. The result was *After the Fall*.

Quentin's quest, which is the substance of the play and which determines its form, is to understand his own life and the reasons for the betrayals that have characterized that life and the lives of all those he encounters. His search belongs to a tradition of tragic protagonists – Hamlet, Oedipus, and Othello – who also "drive to make life real by conquering denial, the secret thrust of tragedy" (*Timebends*, p. 519). But the play poses the problem of how to engage the tragic in our secular world where human history does not move from the Garden of Eden to the crucifix, but from Eden to the Holocaust. As Quentin says, "My disaster really began when I looked up one day and the bench was empty. No judge in sight."[6] But if God is dead, Christian mythology still provides an enabling metaphor. Miller grapples with the chaos of contemporary experience by way of the myth of the Fall much as Faulkner uses original sin, Joyce the Homeric tradition, and Eliot the story of the grail. In Miller's vision, the Holocaust, McCarthyism, and the Depression become the twentieth-century correlatives for the Fall.

In addition to grappling with the horror of the Holocaust, however, *After the Fall* was also a bold dramaturgic experiment for Miller, and it was one facilitated by the new Lincoln Center for the Performing Arts, under Robert Whitehead and Elia Kazan (Roudané, *Conversations*, p. 68). The Lincoln Center set-up enabled Miller to read his unfinished script to the actors and then to revise and rewrite during rehearsals, a luxury that Broadway could never afford. In fact, it affected the play's ultimate form, which revealed itself to Miller as he wrote it over the course of two years in much the same way as Quentin discovers himself as he recalls his past through the process of the play. We watch Quentin's life openly evolve and take form before our eyes as though we were eavesdropping on a psycho-analytic session. The play's dramatic structure likewise operates by a kind of free association as apparently unrelated incidents are brought together to generate a new meaning. The play itself is a metaphor, but its process is also metaphorical. In a 1964 interview Miller explained this process:

> It's the biggest sweep of embrace that I've ever taken . . . It involves a new form. The play is a continuous stream of meaning. It's not built on what happens next in terms of the usual continuity of a tale – but upon what naked meaning grows out of the one before. And the movement expands from meaning to meaning, openly . . . The way a mind would go in quest of a meaning, the way a new river cuts its bed, seeking the path to contain its force. And sometimes it stumbles and loses its way, only to find its way back. But all of it in the open, before your eyes, creating its own form . . . If I were writing this play for Broadway, I would be spiritually discouraged . . . It requires everybody to do what I did, which is to stretch inwardly and outwardly toward an image larger than life. (Roudané, *Conversations*, p. 69)

Accordingly, actors are required to perform both realistically and in a stylized manner as they enact scenes from Quentin's memory, memories that link domestic betrayal, McCarthyism, and the Holocaust, but that also constitute fragments of a meaning which will only emerge through juxtaposition, through sudden and unlooked-for assonances. The play's free-flowing form enables the action to shuttle from private to public, from past to present with such speed that at moments the memories have the simultaneity of a musical chord.

The scene in which Miller moves us from a subway platform to the crash of surf at Atlantic City offers a good example of this technique, as personal and political betrayal are welded together. Atlantic City was the destination of Quentin's family when they abandoned him for the day as a child. It is also the place where Maggie and Quentin's relationship will end bitterly and where he will enact his vengeance on both wife and mother. Meaning leaps across this temporal gap.

In *After the Fall*, betrayal is both personal and political. Quentin proclaims that no one can be innocent after the Holocaust, that while his brothers died in the camps, they also built them. On a domestic level, Quentin's mother had been betrayed by her father when he forced her to marry rather than pursue her college education. Her husband in turn had been betrayed by his mother when she insisted that he stop his education in order to work. Betrayal has a political dimension when Mickey asks permission to reveal Lou's name before the House Un-American Activities Committee, which would destroy his career. It also has a personal dimension as wives betray husbands and husbands wives. A world that demands survival lends itself more to deceit than to love. Ironically, it is this knowledge that enables Quentin to commit himself to Holga, the woman who finally redeems him at the end of the play, because she shares his understanding. What she has seen in the Holocaust, he has seen in his personal and professional life. Having grappled with his past and accepted his complicity, he is at last able to embrace life and move on. Thus, the play celebrates human will, and, ultimately, a flawed love, as the real redeemer, while formally and thematically identifying memory as the path to responsibility. The past, Quentin announces, is holy.

Miller, then, fuses McCarthyism, the Holocaust, and domestic betrayal in *After the Fall*. For those who saw too great a disproportion between mass murder and adultery, Miller responded by saying, "you've got to begin somewhere. Otherwise the larger social evil becomes simply something spinning in space. It has no human root at all, which is a very common thing to believe."[7] Indeed, Miller's power as a playwright derives precisely from his ability to make cataclysmic social issues personal and concrete.

After the Fall is a confessional play. Miller, however, wanted his character to confront his history by reenacting it rather than describing it in the third person. For this reason he responded positively to Marcello Mastroianni who played Quentin in Zeffirelli's 1966 production in Rome because "he seemed to be trying to puzzle out what was happening to him while still regarding himself from a certain distance." When the play was staged in India, the director told Miller that it had required no adaptation because "in the old Indian plays the god comes forth and re-enacts his incarnations" (*Timebends*, pp. 535–36). Formally speaking, that is what happens in the play. But to achieve this effect, Miller needed to break down still further the walls of realistic theatre.

In Italy Zeffirelli managed to capture the artistic conception of *After the Fall* better than did the New York production. He created the suggestion of the inside of Quentin's head by constructing a stage of steel frames which gave the impression that one was looking into the back of a bellows camera. Actors could enter through openings in these covers and make their entrances and exits on the stage at any depth. In addition, pneumatic lifts silently and invisibly raised the actors so that they could appear and disappear instantaneously. In fact, Zeffirelli created an image suggesting that the action was, indeed, happening inside a man's head (Roudané, *Conversations*, p. 108).

The 1990 British production, directed by Michael Blakemore, used a visual image suggested by Miller, who on visiting the Greek Theatre, Epidaurus, saw a flight of steps that led down to a cave shaped to resemble a vortex, at the end of which were the remains of ashes. The theory was that it had been used to minister to mental distress: the sufferer would be left inside the cave, which would then be closed while he contemplated by firelight the spiral twisting around him. This constituted an apt image for *After the Fall*, which traces the protagonist's character from a profound doubt about his own life and human nature, to a cautious, but sturdy hope.[8]

In the New York production, however, the stage had been open and round, making it impossible for characters to appear and disappear (Roudané, *Conversations*, p. 108). The inappropriate staging seems emblematic of America's persistent difficulty in understanding Miller as a non-realistic playwright. Certainly, critics had difficulty grasping his strategy, though it was one he had used in *Death of a Salesman* in 1949. In 1969 Walter Kerr thought it preposterous to "imagine that head expanding until it has encompassed the stage and all the people on it, until it contains the whole visible universe." He also found the play problematic because Quentin provided our only point of view.[9]

British critics, usually more receptive to Miller's work, had similar problems with the play. Dennis Welland saw the form of *After the Fall* as essentially that of a dramatic monologue interspersed by representations of past events.[10] Welland further argued that Quentin's constant presence on stage makes him obtrusive and static (Welland, *Miller: the Playwright*, p. 90). But the "psychic time" that dictates the structure of each scene shifts so quickly from one memory to the next that the play never has time to become static. In fact, Miller had learned the cinematic technique of swift transitions, a sudden bringing together of disparate images, and economy of story-telling, from writing the screenplay for *The Misfits* in 1961.[11] And, because time bends so quickly in *After the Fall*, he is able to engage more issues, both public and private, than in any of his other plays.

But *The Misfits* was not only an important formal predecessor to *After the Fall*: it presented the same anguished search for permanence in a world of flux that Miller depicts in the play. *After the Fall*, however, goes further than Reno to locate lost innocence. His Old Testament sensibility forces him to see a flawed human nature that has its roots in Genesis. As he puts it, "where choice begins, Paradise ends, Innocence ends, for what is Paradise but the absence of any need to choose this action?"[12] The struggle resulting from this imperative to choice consists of two alternatives: to express our unbridled inner compulsions, "pleading unawareness as a virtue and a defense," or to pacify our destructive impulses (Martin, *Theater Essays*, p. 255). As he continued to write, he was less able to attribute moral collapse to materialism and capitalism than he was to see human nature as the cause of such a collapse. Accordingly, C. W. E. Bigsby points out that the Holocaust challenged Miller's liberal philosophy and theatrical strategy, which placed the self and its struggle with determinism at the heart of his concern. In Miller's early plays, characters focus the meaning of their lives on their names, but the concentration camp annihilates the name and the individual. Therefore, the process of *After the Fall* is designed to restore to the individual a sense of control, to reassert a moral responsibility (Bigsby, *Introduction to Twentieth-Century American Drama*, p. 215). In a 1984 interview Miller discussed his later plays within the context of the Declaration of Independence, the Constitution, and the Bill of Rights, in which "the power is in the people – literally, not metaphysically" (Roudané, *Conversations*, p. 327). So it is that when Quentin asks Holga how she became so full of hope after enduring the Holocaust, she says, "it's a mistake to ever look for hope outside one's self" (*After the Fall*, p. 21). Indeed, it is precisely this emphasis on the individual which led him to write a play set within one individual's head. If the thirties influenced Miller's early sympathy for human solidarity through socialism, Fascism and then McCarthyism quickly annihilated it.

The companion piece to *After the Fall*, *Incident at Vichy*, embodies Miller's most critical and analytic response to Fascism and to the Holocaust. It dramatizes a daily occurrence in 1942: the systematic rounding-up of suspected Jews by the Vichy government as it submitted to German racial laws. On this particular morning, eight men and a boy have been shuttled into a detention center and lined up on a bench, none of them sure why.

Figure 4 Hal Holbrook and Joseph Wiseman in *Incident at Vichy*, New York, 1964.

The play records the suspicions, misgivings, self-assurances, and delusions of those who know their identity papers are false but refuse to acquiesce to the death camp (Schlueter and Flanagan, *Arthur Miller*, p. 102).

June Schlueter compares the characters in *Incident at Vichy* to Beckett's archetypal pair in *Waiting for Godot*; they talk while they wait in the detention space, creating as a defense the illusion of their significance. The abducted people of Miller's play are trapped in a situation from which there is no exit, yet they continue to pretend that freedom will come. As the prisoners wait to be summoned individually into the adjacent room, where the identity check takes place, they try to replace despair with hope, even as it becomes increasingly clear that there is none (Schlueter and Flanagan, *Arthur Miller*, p. 102).

The play is an emphatic call for responsibility and for an acceptance of our complicity with evil. Its linear dramatic structure, however, is strikingly different from the free-flowing, stream of consciousness style of his other Holocaust plays, *After the Fall* and *Playing for Time*. Whereas Miller had defined a moral configuration through the psyche of an individual man in *After the Fall*, and later through a woman in *Playing for Time*, with flashbacks and soliloquies, in *Vichy* he moved from the private landscape of Quentin's mind to the historical forum of Vichy France during the Nazi occupation. *Incident at Vichy* is based on historical fact, and for a writer obsessed with history, memory, and the moral consequences of human behavior, the story, told to him by a former psychoanalyst, was a natural Miller play. Indeed, the London production brought home to him the fragility of memory and history when he had to remind the actors who the Nazi SS were (*Timebends*, p. 540). The psychoanalyst, who Miller knew, had been picked up in Vichy France with false papers during the war and saved by a man he had never seen before. This unknown man, a gentile, had substituted himself in a line of suspects waiting to have their papers and penises inspected in a hunt for Jews. The second historical root to the play lay closer to home. Prince Josef von Schwarzenberg, senior surviving member of an ancient Austrian noble line, and a close friend of Miller's wife, Inge Morath, had "declined" to cooperate with the Nazis and suffered for it during the war. He became the source for Von Berg, the prince in *Vichy*, who steps in to take the place of a condemned man. Miller was fascinated by Josef von Schwarzenberg because he embodied a self-sacrificing moral integrity in the face of Fascism.

In his Sartrean reading of the play, Lawrence Lowenthal discounts Robert Brustein's argument that Miller's characters are simply "types" or "public speakers with a symbolic role." He sees them rather as dynamic, fluid, undetermined beings, "freedoms caught in a trap." We know nothing about them, aside from their professions, until they reveal themselves through their choices, which often prove to be surprising. They are all faced with undeniable limits, but within these limits they are always free to act. The Jew can resist or submit; the German can murder or rebel. Indeed, the structural movement of the play is existential in that the pressure to choose – to defy or cooperate with the Nazis – becomes inevitable.[13] The only solution to the plague that Miller depicts is responsible and free human action; *Incident at Vichy* affirms that we cannot flee from commitment and responsibility into determinism.

Critics failed to understand the "choral," metaphoric, and non-realistic fabric of *Vichy*. Fortunately, Harold Clurman, Miller's long-time friend and creator of The Group Theatre, who directed the play, understood that Miller was not only writing about the immorality associated with Vichy, France, during the war, but about evil writ large. Accordingly, he advised Boris Aronson to design a metaphoric set. Miller articulated his wider concern in a 1964 interview with Barbara Gelb in *The New York Times*:

> The occasion of the play is the occupation of France but it's about today. It concerns the question of insight – of seeing in ourselves the capacity for collaboration with the evil one condemns. It is a question that exists for all of us – what, for example, is the responsibility of each of us for allowing the slums of Harlem to exist? Some perfectly exemplary citizens, considerate of their families and friends, contributing to charities and so forth, are directly profiting from conditions like that.[14]

He sees the atrocity of Nazism as part of an ubiquitous social injustice, and in this play he translates that belief into an archetypal situation. We watch a group of people who confront the possibility and, indeed, the inevitability, of death. Each devises his own strategy, relies on his own ideological conviction. Bayard, the electrician, is wholeheartedly a Marxist who believes that business exploits the working class. Lebeau, the painter, places his faith in the imagination as, in his art, he prefers invention to an absurd and horrific reality; Monceau, the actor, insists that a simulated confidence will sustain them. Prince Von Berg gives his life coherence by believing that individual responsibility can redeem an amoral world; Leduc, the psychoanalyst and cynic, distrusts Von Berg's idealism, believing that all people are fundamentally amoral.

As always Miller is interested in private action which has public significance, and that explains why Von Berg became a hero representative of the sixties:

> That faceless, unknown man would pop up in my mind when I read about the people in Queens refusing to call the police while a woman was being stabbed to death on the street outside their windows. He would form himself in the air when I listened to delinquent boys whose many different distortions of character seemed to spring from a common want of human solidarity. Friends troubled by having to do things they disapproved of brought him to mind, people for whom the very concept of choosing their actions was a long forgotten thing. Wherever I felt the seemingly implacable tide of human drift and the withering of will, in myself and in others, this faceless person came to mind. And he appears most clearly and imperatively amid the jumble of emotions surrounding the Negro in this country, and the whole unsettled moral problem of the destruction of the Jews in Europe.[15]

For Miller, the horror of the Holocaust, like the mania of McCarthyism, is not confined to the past, since our present contains that past. As early as 1945, in his novel *Focus*, he was telling us that racial discrimination stems from ignorance and was placing moral responsibility on the individual.

Like his 1985 Holocaust play, *Playing for Time*, *Incident at Vichy* struggles with the paradox of an ostensibly civilized country committing genocide, of free individuals apparently willing to surrender their freedom to authority. As he remarked in the context of the Frankfurt trials, "Some 6,000 SS men did duty in Auschwitz during its four years of operation, and not one is known to have refused to do what he was told . . . [The Germans] are being called on to be free, to rebel in their spirit against the age-old respect for authority which has plagued their history" ("Our Guilt for the World's Evil"). C. W. E. Bigsby (in *Introduction to Twentieth-Century American Drama*) points out, however, that in *Incident at Vichy* the characters are their roles, even though the play argues against the process which encourages people to see themselves and others as symbols. In effect, reductivism is at risk of becoming both subject and methodology.

The confrontation between Leduc and Von Berg constitutes the heart of the play's conflict. Feeling spiteful toward his wife because he was getting medicine for her toothache when he was picked up by the Nazis, Leduc wants Von Berg to tell her that he will be sent to the furnaces. Von Berg resists, and from his reaction it becomes clear that he has the greater compassion and moral responsibility. While Leduc is disturbed by the fact that Von Berg keeps "finding these little shreds of hope,"[16] he is really bitter that Von Berg will escape being murdered simply because he is a gentile. Von Berg asks, "but if one gives up one's ideals . . . what . . . is left?" It is a scene in which, once again, Miller grapples with the problem of the survivor, he who inevitably profits from the death of the Jews merely by having survived. *Incident at Vichy* searches for the act that transcends self-interest in a postlapsarian world. Leduc thus regards Von Berg's attempted suicide as meaningless because, as he later observes, what matters is responsibility, not guilt. Once again, too, Miller characteristically intertwines private and public tensions: Leduc's marital strife is bound up with the Nazi occupation of Vichy, while Leduc sees his own heart of darkness in the context of this larger nihilism. His broken marriage is a metaphor for the moral crack in a supposedly civilized country. Trust, love, and faith have been breached on both personal and political levels, and all of Europe throbs like his wife's aching tooth. Leduc tries to make amends for his failed marriage by retracting his impulse to avenge himself on his wife, but the fact that he knows he will die undercuts his effort to redeem his relationship.

If *Incident at Vichy* demonstrates Miller's ability to build a play on debate, it also exemplifies his powerful use of symbolic action. When the Professor calls the Old Jew to come into his office, he pulls at his bundle of feathers until it rips open. This idea came from a Czech film that moved Miller. *The Shop on Main Street* was set in a town in Bohemia where all the Jews are rounded up for their death without knowing their fate. They are told to bring a few belongings with them, and, once they have left, there is a shot of the town square with feathers blowing around. For Miller, the birds' plumage represents bedding, a refugee's only possible property, and it is therefore a metaphor for uprooted domesticity. As he observed, "once they're released, you can't capture them any more. And there's a pathetic quality to that: the fact that the old guy's clutching what to our minds would be a practically valueless bag of nothing, of air. It's his identity, though" (Roudané, *Conversations*, p. 358). While some critics, like Steven Centola, have identified the feathers with ineffectual religions and value systems that make one take a passive or resigned posture in the face of persecution, Miller argues that the Old Jew has transcended religious systems: "he's got one foot in heaven. He knows that this is the ancient persecutor, the face of hell, that comes in every generation, and this is his turn with him . . . And he's praying against it . . . he's got . . . one eye on God, who's reaching out His hands to him" (Roudané, *Conversations*, p. 358). Although Miller claims that the Old Jew's eyes are watching God, there is a strong sense in *Vichy*, as in all of Miller's dramatic worlds, that this is a Godless universe. His characters must find something sacred within themselves in order to overcome oppression. Moreover, Miller poignantly juxtaposes that symbol of uprooted domesticity with the sinister Nazi laughter. Those bursts of amoral laughter punctuate the entire play, reminding us that everything that the characters say, as they wait to be examined, is responsive to the Nazi occupation.

In the play's canvas of isolated debates, the concluding scene is especially forensic. It becomes a seminar on responsibility. When Von Berg tells his friend Leduc that he would like to be able to leave, Leduc responds:

> It is not you I am angry with. In one part of my mind it is not even this Nazi. I am only angry that I should have been born before the day when man has accepted his own nature; that he is not reasonable, that he is full of murder, that his ideals are only the little tax he pays for the right to hate and kill with a clear conscience. (*Incident at Vichy*, p. 48)

Like *After the Fall*, *Incident at Vichy* grapples with the need to accept our complicity with evil. Leduc insists that marginalizing the other is a fact of life:

Jew is only the name we give to that stranger, that agony we cannot feel, that death we look at like a cold abstraction. Each man has his Jew; the black, the yellow, the white, it is the other. And the Jews have their Jews. And now, now above all, you must see that you have yours – the man whose death leaves you relieved that you are not him, despite your decency. And that is why there is nothing and will be nothing – until you face your own complicity with this . . . your own humanity. (p. 48)

Leduc reminds Von Berg that his cousin, Baron Kessler, had helped remove all the Jewish doctors from medical school, a fact that Von Berg has tried to forget. He tells him, "It's not your guilt I want, it's your responsibility." The opened door at the end of this scene provides Von Berg's chance to answer his own question, to salvage whatever humanity he can, to thrust his pass to freedom into Leduc's hands.

Critics argue that *Incident at Vichy* is too didactic and that Miller presents an unambiguous moral world, but the final moment of the play is full of ambivalence. The Major turns to Von Berg with murderous fury in his face but only half-raises his weapon. Light begins to dim as four new prisoners appear, rapidly herded in by the detectives, who glance about at the ceiling, the walls, the feathers on the floor, and the two motionless men. The light fades on the new captives and lingers for a moment on the Major and Von Berg, who stand there, "forever incomprehensible to one another, looking into each other's eyes" (p. 51). Miller prevents the play from becoming overly melodramatic by undercutting the final redemptive note with the arrival of the new prisoners. Moreover, Leduc's acceptance of Von Berg's pass to freedom precludes a simply affirmative ending because he chooses survival at the expense of Von Berg's life.

Von Berg's decision, nonetheless, is affirmative, and for Miller the war created the need to reassert liberal ideals as a moral imperative. Thus, character becomes not just a feature of plot, but the subject of his work. As C. W. E. Bigsby points out (in *Introduction to Twentieth-Century American Drama*), if the individual were to be responsible for his actions, he had to be granted the autonomy and social significance that were denied by the absurdists, the Marxists, and by the events of the war which destroyed individualism and idealism. Miller's emphasis on individual action has everything to do with his concept of tragedy. *Incident at Vichy* is like Miller's earlier tragic plays in that it is about Von Berg's inability to walk away from the central conflict, and therefore, about his tragic existence. Indeed, the play is part of a tradition of tragedy in which the tragic hero illuminated "the hidden scheme of existence", either by breaking one of its laws, or by proving a moral world at the cost of his own life. As Miller has made clear, tragedies are about the consequence of a character's total compulsion to evaluate himself justly.

Incident at Vichy does have limitations because only Leduc and Von Berg evolve as characters. The play's brevity, however, does not limit its depth: confining the play to a simple room of detention intensifies the action. The circumscribed room becomes a metaphor for the constrictions placed upon the individual will in much the way that the towering apartment buildings in *Death of a Salesman* encroach on Willy Loman, the courtroom stifles John Proctor, and the concentration camp looms over the dramatic worlds of *After the Fall* and *Playing for Time*. They are emblems of the tension between the self and society, between an insistence on identity and an acknowledgment of the limitations of that identity.

Enoch Brater has argued that the emotional truth of Miller's later protagonists matters less than his earlier ones because he sacrifices their emotional truth to their allegorical utility,[17] but this was also true of the characters in Miller's early fable, *The Man Who Had All the Luck*. The later Miller characters, however, seem to see themselves more self-consciously in terms of history and metaphysics, and *Incident at Vichy* marks the beginning of that phase. Despite what some critics perceive as the one-dimensional characters, the play spoke with sufficient emotional power to cause it to be banned from the Soviet stage for nineteen years. During the anti-Jewish convulsion in the late sixties, it was the first of Miller's works to be so banned. When Miller annoyed the Soviets with protests against their treatment of writers and their anti-Semitism, they closed down Volchek's production of the play. Not until 1987, and Gorbachev's liberalization of the Soviet Union, was it allowed on the Soviet stage. French producers, meanwhile, relinquished rights to the play for fear of resentment at the implication of French collaboration with Nazi anti-semitism. And when Pierre Cardin finally produced it in Paris in the eighties, it received bitter reviews (*Timebends*, p. 540). Clearly, Miller's plays function as an accurate barometer for world politics.

The Price picks up the issues of free will and responsibility that were at the heart of *After the Fall* and *Incident at Vichy*. Contrary to Robert Brustein's and Kenneth Tynan's complaint that Miller was writing an apolitical play in the midst of political turbulence, Miller saw the issues of illusion and denial in *The Price* in the context of the sixties. For him the sixties were a time when we were once again looking outside ourselves for salvation from ourselves; both the play and life were telling him that we were doomed to perpetuate our illusions because truth was too costly to face (*Timebends*, p. 542). While Miller claims that his play reflects the

Figure 5   Bob Peck, Alan MacNaughtan, and David Calder in *The Price*, The Young Vic, London, 1990.

sixties, illusion, denial, and betrayal have been his concerns throughout his career.

The play takes place in the attic of a Manhattan brownstone. Ten rooms of furniture and personal belongings of the Franz family have been stored there for years. Because the building is scheduled for demolition, Victor Franz, a policeman, and his wife, Esther, have returned to "this physical and emotional stockpile" (Schlueter and Flanagan, *Arthur Miller*, p. 110) to negotiate a sale with Solomon, an old furniture dealer. Though Walter Franz, a surgeon, does not join his brother until the second act, he is, by inference, already a character in Act One, when Victor and Esther reveal that the brothers' professional lives have resulted from opposite decisions made in response to their father. When their father was driven into financial and psychological destitution by the stock-market crash of 1929, the self-sacrificing Victor forfeited college and became a cop, while the self-interested Walter pursued a medical career (Schlueter and Flanagan, *Arthur Miller*, p. 110).

The two brothers participate in a moral fencing match in which Walter reveals a fact that he is convinced will change Victor's assessment of the past: their father was not bankrupt after all; he had saved several thousand dollars. Some critics maintain that Victor had never known about the money, and that if he had, he might not have chosen to become a cop. On the contrary, although Victor feels disappointed about his life's achievements in middle age, he seems to have known about the money, but chose to spend twenty-eight years on the police force anyway because of love and moral responsibility.

Victor and Walter think they have "achieved . . . indifference to the betrayals of the past that maturity confers. But it all comes back; the old angry symbols evoke the old emotions of injustice, and they part unreconciled" (*Timebends*, p. 542). Victor apparently represents the moral vision since he is the brother who sacrificed his career to stand by his father. His career as a cop represents his commitment to justice, but it has also cost him the price of a medical career. Walter seems self-interested, having abandoned his father in order to go to medical school. Yet he has paid his own price for his ambition. He returns to the old Manhattan brownstone in an attempt to settle with his conscience by offering his brother money and a job in the hospital. When Victor refuses to be bought, Walter attributes his reaction to vindictiveness. In the process of debating the price of their parents' old furniture, they really evaluate the price they have both paid for the decisions they have made in their lives. In effect, Victor and Walter are Biff and Happy Loman twenty years later, the idealist and the materialist.

Miller saw the conflict between the two brothers as representative of the sixties and early seventies, when "the whole question arose in the States as to whether any kind of life was possible that wasn't totally self-serving, totally cynical" (Bigsby, *Introduction to Twentieth-Century American Drama*, p. 148). The play demands a careful balance between the brothers. As Miller explains,

> If you extend their characteristics into the world, you see that neither one of them could run the world. The things that can be done by Walter, full of daring, selfishness, power lust and inventiveness, are not the things the other one can do, which is to stick to a job that needs to be done, stay by the hearth and see to it that the fire doesn't go out. The price each pays for being what he is is what this is about.
> (Roudané, *Conversations*, p. 196)

Walter and Victor gradually strip away each other's illusions and rationalizations about the past as their old Manhattan brownstone is about to be torn down, like a cherry orchard. We weigh the evidence of the past as the brothers talk, but, unlike a detective story, *The Price* is about two equally valid ways of proceeding with life. By the sixties Miller's vision had become more complex. The moral remedies of the thirties no longer apply, and a greater ambiguity is apparent. The play leads us to react against Walter, and then slowly reveals Victor's culpability. We come to understand the role that self-deception has played in his perception of himself and the world. As Miller puts it, "the satisfaction is the perception of the tension. It's not solved and life isn't. It can't be solved. It's a play without any candy" (Roudané, *Conversations*, p. 329). Walter claims that he warned Victor not to allow their father to exploit him; Victor insists, "I made no choice. The icebox was empty!"[18]

Walter maintains that he wished to lend Victor money; Victor insists that "We do what we want to do, don't we?" (*The Price*, p. 97). The fact is, though, that Victor was fully aware that his sacrifice was unnecessary in a material sense, that his father was not the victim he wished to present him as being. As his brother insists, "It's a fantasy. Your father was penniless and your brother a son of a bitch and you play no part at all. You knew he had money" (p. 104). Victor can only retort, "I don't know what I knew!" (p. 105) and then plead that "He loved me . . . He just didn't want to end up on the grass! It's not that you don't love somebody, it's that you've got to survive . . . We do what we have to do" (p. 107). He has moved from arguing that actions spring from desire to saying that circumstances determine actions. This is what Miller calls a "biological morality" (Balakian, "Conversation," p. 158), meaning by that that our actions spring from our need to survive. Victor's decision to forego his career and stay with his father was thus his attempt to restore his father's belief in human solidarity, which his marriage and the Depression had shattered. But Walter confronts him with the brutal fact that nothing ever fell apart, that they were brought up to lead lives of Darwinian necessity. Moreover, betrayal, not trust, defined their family.

> Were we really brought up to believe in one another? We were brought up to succeed . . . Why else would he respect me so and not you? . . . Was there ever any love here? When he needed her, she vomited. And when you needed him, he laughed. What was unbearable is not that it all fell apart, it was that there was never anything here. *(The Price*, p. 109)

Walter is convinced that Victor had invented a fiction of their lives in order to justify his life and make it bearable:

> We invent ourselves, Vic, to wipe out what we know. You invent a life of self-sacrifice . . . but what never existed here cannot be upheld. You were not upholding something, you were denying what you knew they were. And denying yourself. And that's all that is standing between us now – an illusion. That I kicked them in the face and you must uphold them against me . . . there was nothing here to betray. I am not your enemy. It is all an illusion and

if you could walk through it, we could meet . . . It was only two seemingly
different roads out of the same trap.   (p. 110)

The Price is fundamentally about shattering illusions. But even when Victor
takes responsibility for his decision to help his father, he reveals that his life
has evolved in a way he had never predicted. He confesses to Solomon:

> it's that you've got to make decisions before you know what's involved, but
> you're stuck with the results anyway . . . I figured I'd go on the Force
> temporarily, just to get us through the Depression, then go back to school.
> But the war came, we had the kid, and you turn around and you've racked up
> fifteen years on the pension. And what you started out to do is a million miles
> away . . . We always agreed, we stay out of the rat race . . . But . . . it all ends
> up she wants, she wants. And I can't really blame her – there's just no respect
> for anything but money.   (p. 48)

Miller has said that in The Price he was interested in "the structuring of
experience," or paradox, what happens when our actions create results that
we never intended. Here, financial demands have dictated the course of
Victor's life. Once again, Miller is fascinated by how the economy shapes a
character's fate, just as he was in All My Sons, Death of a Salesman, and
The American Clock. The Depression left a permanent scar on his imagination. Walter chooses to deal with economic imperatives differently from his
brother.

The conflict between brothers and between fathers and sons continues to
be paradigmatic for Miller. He sees the fratricidal enigma in the context of
Cain and Abel. Once again, the father incorporates power and a moral law
which he has either broken or fallen prey to. Even the two-act structure
reinforces the division of the two brothers, both acts of which are divided
into two parts. Act One is Victor's act; Act Two, Walter's. And Solomon,
the namesake of the biblical king who demonstrated his wisdom by
presiding over the division of a child, presides over both brothers and both
acts, like a chorus and moral arbiter.

Miller cast Solomon as a Jew because he is a survivor. He is also the
source of the play's humor, a vaudeville act (Bigsby, Introduction to
Twentieth-Century American Drama, p. 149). Despite his daughter's
suicide and multiple divorces, he continues to believe in life. His decision
to take on this furniture deal infuses him with fresh blood, gives him a
new lease on life, a new "possibility." For Solomon, life is "a viewpoint."
"It's a mental world," he exclaims, comparing marrying at seventy-five to
secondhand furniture. He is also aware of living at a time when
permanent values are distrusted. As he explains of the Franz's dining-
room table:

> If it wouldn't break there is no more possibilities. . . . A man sits down to such a table he knows not only he's married, he's got to stay married – there is no more possibilities . . . What is the key word today? Disposable. The more you can throw it away the more it's beautiful. The car, the furniture, the wife, the children – everything has to be disposable. Because you see the main thing today – is shopping.
>
> (*The Price*, p. 41)

Miller's characters are always in a race with things that rust, and the Crash made impermanence and the betrayal of the American system a relentless fact. In opposition to this fear, Solomon's profession depends on trust (Bigsby, *Introduction to Twentieth-Century American Drama*, p. 114). Like Victor, the cop, he "picks up the pieces" of life's chaos, but like Walter he also knows that the world runs on greed and competition. He lends the play its special humor, humor that derives from his tragic experience. Solomon's cosmic acceptance of the betrayals of time helps Victor come to terms with his past. Moreover, Solomon has the last laugh because he knows that the brothers cannot exorcise their father's influence on them.[19] His laughter at the end is, in one sense, his joy at being almost ninety and back in business again. But it could also be an echo of the sardonic laughter of their father. Miller has left the ending ambiguous.

Grounded in a material world, *The Price*, like most of Miller's plays, probes social and psychological rationalizations to discover an existential ethic. Victor, like Quentin, learns to take his destiny in his hands when he stops indicting others. As C. W. E. Bigsby says, "the price to pay for reconstructing meaning and purpose is the death of innocence and accepting responsibility for actions. The price for ignoring this challenge is greater, the destruction of human relations – the price paid by Walter and Victor."[20] Renée Winegarten asserts that here for the first time Miller appears to be implying that there may be something equivocal and limited about the notion that we are our brother's keeper.[21] But betrayal is as brutal a fact in this play as it is in nearly everything Miller has written. As he has told me, "the fluctuating moral consequences of a given human nature are really what all my plays are about" (Balakian, "Conversation," p. 158). *The Price* highlights the paradox of Miller's world view, which is at once deterministic and existential as he explores the tension between the given and the willed. Earlier in his career Miller said, "I'm under no illusions that people really invent themselves. They do to a degree, but they're working with a social matrix."[22] *The Price*, however, insists that we have more control over our fate than we are readily willing to admit. Perhaps that is the reason it was so well received in 1968, a time when many Americans felt that we were denying our arrogant role in Vietnam and needed to take responsibility for it. More likely, however, the play's popularity stemmed from the fact that audiences could easily connect with Walter's and Victor's conflict, and that they felt at home in the comfortable and accessible world of Ibsenesque realism.

In the sixties, then, although Miller was actively involved in protesting the Vietnam War, in serving as a delegate to the Democratic Party National Convention, and in protecting the rights of writers as president of PEN, he continued to write about the Depression, the Holocaust, and McCarthyism. For him, they represented the same breach of faith and denial that American involvement in Vietnam and racism revealed. Miller's moral pulse beat too strongly for him to write absurdist plays, or to join the experimental and avant-garde theatre movements of the sixties. *After the Fall, Incident at Vichy*, and *The Price* all affirm the need for individual responsibility and for our acknowledgment of personal and political truths. His dramatic method shifted from the psycho-history of *After the Fall*, to the realism of *Incident at Vichy* and *The Price*. But whatever the style of presentation, Miller's plays assume an underlying rational structure to existence, demonstrate the pressure of the past on the present to which it is causally connected. In the sixties, Miller continued to write social plays, examining the way society shapes and breaks the psyche. He persisted in creating what he calls a poetic theatre, one that fuses social and psychological conflicts in one symbolic act, though that fusion perhaps seems less subtle in *After the Fall* and in *Incident at Vichy* than it does in *The Price*. He also remained committed to exploring the implications of human nature. Indeed, Miller's Old Testament sensibility always drove him back to the mythic Fall in Genesis, for which the Depression, the Holocaust, and McCarthyism became his twentieth-century correlatives.

Ultimately, however, each play celebrates human will: in *Incident at Vichy*, Von Berg sacrifices his life for a Jew; in *After the Fall*, Quentin, having confronted personal and historical demons, embraces a new wife and begins his life with a renewed sense of self; in *The Price*, Victor and Walter acknowledge their responsibility for their decisions. In his celebration of the self as sole redeemer, Miller is, perhaps, a quintessentially American writer. But his emphasis on the flawed self places him in a rather different context. Perhaps Miller's tragic sensibility made him a more appropriate playwright for the sixties than those who wrote for the various avant-garde companies. For him denial was the besetting sin and a confrontation with the past a moral necessity as well as a key to present failures. Avant-garde groups apotheosised the present moment, acknowledging the past only at the level of myth. Arthur Miller, however, shaped by the Greeks and by Ibsen, felt compelled to explore a character's connection with his past and thereby his union with a larger destiny. In Miller's plays of the sixties, as in all of his work, the birds come home to roost, and one's character determines one's fate.

NOTES

1 Arthur Miller, *Timebends* (New York: Grove Press, 1987), p. 100.

2 Jan Balakian, "A Conversation with Arthur Miller," *Michigan Quarterly Review* 29.2 (1990): 158.

3 Oscar G. Brockett and Robert R. Findlay, *Century of Innovation: A History of European and American Theatre and Drama Since 1870* (Englewood Cliffs: Prentice-Hall, 1973), p. 632.

4 Matthew C. Roudané (ed.), *Conversations with Arthur Miller* (Jackson: University Press of Mississippi, 1987), p. 28.

5 June Schlueter and James K. Flanagan, *Arthur Miller* (New York: Frederick Ungar, 1987), p. 92.

6 Arthur Miller, *After the Fall* (New York: Viking Press, 1964), p. 3.

7 C. W. E. Bisgby, *A Critical Introduction to Twentieth-Century American Drama*, vol. 11 (Cambridge: Cambridge University Press, 1984), p. 215.

8 Christopher Bigsby (ed.), *Arthur Miller and Company* (London: Methuen, 1990), p. 142.

9 James J. Martine (ed.), *Critical Essays on Arthur Miller* (Boston: G. K. Hall, 1979), p. 122.

10 Dennis Welland, *Miller: the Playwright*, 3rd edn. (London and New York: Methuen, 1985), p. 90.

11 Edward Murray, "Arthur Miller – *Death of a Salesman, The Misfits*, and *After the Fall*," in *The Cinematic Imagination* (New York: Frederick Ungar, 1972), p. 156.

12 Robert A. Martin (ed.), *The Theater Essays of Arthur Miller* (New York: Viking Press, 1978), p. 255.

13 Lawrence D. Lowenthal, "Arthur Miller's Incident at Vichy: A Sartrean Interpretation," in Martine (ed.), *Critical Essays on Arthur Miller*, pp. 143–54.

14 Barbara Gelb, "Question: 'Am I My Brother's Keeper?,'" *The New York Times*, 29 November 1964, section 2, pp. 1–3. Collected in Roudané (ed.), *Conversations with Arthur Miller*, pp. 78–82.

15 Arthur Miller, "Our Guilt for the World's Evil," *The New York Times Magazine*, 3 January 1965, pp. 10–11, 48.

16 Arthur Miller, *Incident at Vichy* (New York: Dramatists Play Service, Inc., 1964).

17 Enoch Brater, "Ethics and Ethnicity in the Plays of Arthur Miller," in Sarah Blacher Cohen (ed.), *From Hester Street to Hollywood: The Jewish–American Stage and Screen* (Bloomington: Indiana University Press, 1983), p. 123.

18 Arthur Miller, *The Price* (New York: Penguin, 1985), p. 92.

19 Ralph Tyler, "Arthur Miller Says The Time is Right for *The Price*," *The New York Times*, 17 June 1979, section 2, p. 1, 6D.

20 C. W. E. Bisgby, "What Price Arthur Miller? An Analysis of *The Price*," in Martine (ed.), *Critical Essays on Arthur Miller*, p. 163.

21 Renée Winegarten, "The World of Arthur Miller," *The Jewish Quarterly* 17.62 (1969).
22 Arthur Miller, "On Social Plays," in Martin (ed.), *The Theater Essays of Arthur Miller*, pp. 51–69.

9

WILLIAM W. DEMASTES

Miller's 1970s "power" plays

The 1970s was a decade of nearly devastating turmoil for the United States from which in many ways it is still recovering. The American incursion into Cambodia leading to the bloody protests at Kent State University, the withdrawal from Vietnam after years of divisive protest at home, South Vietnam's eventual collapse, Watergate, and the resignation of a president under disgrace all shook the very foundation of a United States that was anything but united.

Miller created three works for the stage in the seventies that confronted and expanded upon the cultural divisiveness so prevalent then and still present today. *The Creation of the World and Other Business* and *The American Clock* each offered reflections on the issue of authenticating existence by assuming individual and collective responsibility for our various internal failures. These two plays, written in the early seventies, work well with the hard-hitting and existentially disturbing play, *The Archbishop's Ceiling* (written in 1977 but only to receive its final, revised form in 1984), which confronts the questionable effects of our attempts to exercise that authenticity in a world that has lost moral control of its own destiny. Two plays present an ideal, and one puts the ideal into direct confrontation with the real, all three adding up to a serious debate on how that ideal can survive and affect the shifting reality it encounters. Interestingly, none of them directly confronts actual issues afflicting 1970s America, such as Vietnam or Watergate; rather, they move into somewhat unexpected realms in their search for cures to those immediate contemporary ills. The result is that they speak to us even today, unencumbered by any dated address to 1970s particulars.

The Creation of the World and Other Business presents a new "mythology" whose design is to redirect humanity's attention away from the sources of its most fundamental failings. In this play, Miller has produced his own interpretation of Genesis, creating a work that has been called religious parody and a comic-strip reworking of creation. The play includes the creation of Eve, the Fall, and the Cain and Abel story, hardly material at first sight suitable for the comic treatment Miller chooses to give it. The humor primarily derives from various anachronistic insertions, including comments by characters which sound more like seventies-style conversations in Central Park than momentous exchanges made in Eden. God, Adam, and the rest "converse" without epic trappings and notably without any sense of awe or reverence. The 1972 New York production highlighted the broad humor of the text and included such iconic effects as Michelangelo poses designed not to reflect majesty but to beg a comforting laughter of recognition.

Perhaps confusing at first, Miller's attempts to demythologize and localize the events were efforts at placing the significance of his biblical rewrite on a contemporary footing. Much like various efforts by Shaw to demythologize and modernize cultural icons in, for example, *Caesar and Cleopatra* and *Saint Joan*, Miller has given his mythic figures a flesh-and-blood reality, God and Lucifer included. The effect is that Miller interprets the creation of Eve, the Fall, and the Cain and Abel story as present and ongoing acts. The play, C. W. E. Bigsby suggests, "is a consciously naive attempt to trace human imperfection to its source by unwinding the process of history and myth."[1] Is it possible, Miller seems to ask, that although we cannot return to Eden, we may be able to confront our past, mythic and actual, and thereby transform our possibilities?

The Creation of the World is not a lost masterpiece,[2] but it is a play worthy of close attention since it crystallizes persistent concerns Miller has had and suggests future directions he would take, the play's uncharacteristic tone notwithstanding. In appearance, at least, this play seems entirely out of place in the Miller canon, but as Miller himself observed, "There are reverberations of all my plays in this one. It's wry, but with an underlying earnestness."[3]

The earnest intent begins with Miller's reinterpretation of God and Lucifer. God and Lucifer, he reminds us – as if once again we have forgotten – must be identified for what they represent, forces of good and evil we have invariably confused and conflated. The play opens with a telling confession on God's part: "Actually, Adam – and I know this won't shake your confidence – but now and then I do something and, quite frankly, it's only afterwards that I discover the reasons . . . In fact, that is probably why I feel such a special closeness to you: you sprang out of my instinct rather than some design."[4] Miller intends his God to be a learning God and the world's design to be an organically evolving one involving crucial human input. Miller's God is omnipotent – capable of great acts of creation *and* destruction – but while he is a moral God, he is not fully omniscient or prescient. Rather, he is a God of evaluation and reaction rather than a proactive being confidently in control of his creation. Lucifer, on the other hand, carries the early parts of the play, an attractive figure who tantalizes both an indecisive God and a naive humanity with numerous tempting offers. The struggle between God and Lucifer is played out in the human arena where the victor is ultimately selected by human judges.

Lucifer's seeming selflessness expresses an evil not easily identifiable as such. It is nonconfrontational, and it feeds on the longings of those he hopes to entrap, offering what is naively desired for a fee that seems hardly to be missed. Far from a catastrophe, Lucifer sees the Fall as an opportunity for him to join forces with God. Rather than allowing the new, postlapsarian sense of universal differentiation (of "good" and "evil") to dichotomize into oppositional good/God and evil/Lucifer, Lucifer suggests the two stand together: "You immaculate on Your throne, absolute good, and I beside You, perfectly evil. Father and son, the two inseparable buddies" (*The Creation of the World*, p. 400). The reason, Lucifer adds, is that "[w]ithout absolute righteousness there can never be a war! We will flummox the generals! Father, you are a handshake away from a second Paradise!" (p. 401). The seemingly virtuous, certainly non-evil appearance of the proposal – to avoid war, greed, and senseless slaughter – is an ideal to be sought, but the means to the end must be more scrupulously evaluated. Lucifer essentially argues a postlapsarian leveling of goodness in a way similar to God's prelapsarian world of innocence, where nothing rises above or falls below anything else. If the prelapsarian world was one without human responsibility – turning humans into mere babes in the woods – so, too, would Lucifer's postlapsarian Eden deny to humans a consciousness of, or even need for, responsible behavior, returning them to mere mindless worshipers of the powers above them. At first glance, the reward of peace seems worth the price of surrendering responsibility.

God, however, comes to an increased understanding that, in the now postlapsarian world, responsibility/power/control must be shared, not with Lucifer but with his humans, and that there must be a standard by which to measure behavior. God essentially bows out of the decision-making process and grants his human beings the choice between personal control and attendant responsibility or mindless capitulation to guiltless pleasures. God ultimately resists Lucifer's attempts to create a mindless world of simple pleasure, but he also resists the urge to destroy Lucifer. Good and evil must remain clearly distinguishable categories of choice. God asserts: "Where evil begins, I end. When good loves evil, it is no longer good, and if God could love the devil, then God has died" (p. 402). Creating a world of idle comfort entails sacrificing moral responsibility. It is an option, tantalizing though it might be, that God rejects, but he leaves the final choice open for his human creations. The critical question to follow is: will humans do the same?

Miller's Genesis speaks directly to the problems of a contemporary world in which it appears we have chosen Lucifer over God since Lucifer offers much of what we at least intuitively desire. And what he offers seems far from what we conceive of as evil. He does not ask that we murder, rape, or pillage; he only asks that we enjoy ourselves and in return simply relinquish personal responsibility and control. We give him power, and he gives us pleasure. It is not a matter of choosing between God's or Lucifer's power but of choosing between God's "gift" of personal choice and responsibility and Lucifer's offer to relieve us of that burden in exchange for "the easy life." Evil has assumed a cloak of respectability in Miller's myth. Furthermore, God's gift has dire consequences whereas Lucifer's offer appears to have none. Reviewing God's world, Lucifer observes: "Everything I see throws up the same irrational lesson. The hungriest bird sings best. What a system! That deprivation should make music" (p. 404). Suffering is indeed part of God's world: without the bad there can be no good. Lucifer wants to obliterate the distinction thereby eliminating any need for God, or at least for what he represents.

But in the play it becomes apparent that human beings are not equipped for such a world of non-responsible amorality. These first humans grow to need distinctions between good and evil in their lives and a sense of justice to explain their complex world. Though they initially accept Lucifer's amorality, the fruits of that acceptance are eventually revealed to be non-sustaining. Good and evil must exist as categorical realities, and with them must go a sense of order amid the disorder and vitality of life humans long to enjoy. In fact, Lucifer's world of empty leisure becomes something of a hell itself, created by Lucifer for himself and not for his would-be minions.

Following Abel's murder, Eve pleads to God for justice. She cannot accept Lucifer's amoral world. God's reply offers the contrasting, sobering vision to Lucifer's option:

> Only if the eye of God opens in the heart of every man; only if each himself will choose the way of life, not death. For otherwise you go as beasts, locked up in the darkness of their nature. *Slight pause.* I saw that Cain was pious, yet in him I saw envy too. And so I thought – if Cain was so enraged that he lift his hand against his brother, but then, remembering his love for Abel and for me, [could he] even in his fury lay down his arms? (p. 441)

God's gift is not an amoral world of comfort, and it is certainly not a world of undifferentiated good – which would, of course, appear no different from an amoral one. Rather his world is one of continuous choice between good and evil, and human beings have been provided with the tools to develop greater or lesser abilities to distinguish between the two. Ultimately, it is our choices that make our world because he has given that choice to us. God continues to provide us with the option to choose, and so we are never fully trapped/doomed/condemned by our past.

Miller's argument seems to be one wherein Lucifer's tantalizing vision is that of a false prophet/god, but it is a vision we have collectively fallen victim to throughout history (and prehistory). It is a lesson to be relearned because humanity continually forgets it, confusing goodness with comfort. The consequence is a mechanistic God, at least for the moment disengaged, apparently awaiting a new direction from his human creations before he reemerges. This abstract, mythic argument relates well to the world of the 1970s (and after). Miller argues that Lucifer's "siren calls" ultimately lead to our continued misery, a misery signaled by a growing sense of moral emptiness even amid material comforts stemming from a "progressive" world view. Watergate and Vietnam perhaps have their origin in amoral assertions of this prevailing sense of permissiveness. Comfort and freedom from universal responsibility/guilt, naively desired, are the roots of doom.

While Miller's efforts to highlight the virtues of Godlike selfless compassion/responsibility over those of Lucifer-like egoistic pleasure/guiltlessness may not have succeeded on the stage in *The Creation of the World*, the cosmology propounded is nonetheless powerful. The play may or may not be seen as an apology for Judeo-Christianity, but it is certainly a dramatization of the moral issues implicit in a viable social contract, relevant to Jew, Christian, agnostic, or atheist. It offers a new cosmology for a world in need of fundamental reevaluation, a world in which mankind in general and the individual in particular assume responsibility for their actions and for their world.

Miller idealized his conceptions in *The Creation of the World*, but in *The Archbishop's Ceiling* those idealizations are put to hard tests. Lucifer has taken control of the world, in part literally in the form of Eastern European tyranny, but also more pervasively (and sinisterly) in the form of multiple buy-outs of human conscience. What becomes problematic for Miller is the very real proposition that the enemy has been internalized, colluding with us in our own destruction in ways almost impossible to distinguish from our more noble urges, efforts, and instincts.

The Archbishop's Ceiling is set in the capital city of an Eastern Bloc country (in interviews, Miller identifies it as Czechoslovakia) about an hour's flight from Paris. Adrian, an American novelist, makes a surprise visit to his literary friends in that city, a visit that is Adrian's poorly disguised attempt to gain material for his novel-in-progress, an attempt to capture the ambiguities and uncertainties of living under totalitarian control.

Adrian meets his old friend Maya, a poet who has given up her poetry and accepted a position as a non-political talk-show host for the state-run radio. Her erstwhile lover/protector is Marcus, a former dissident who has become an unofficial host for foreign literary figures in his country. Sigmund is a somewhat younger artist than Marcus and so never struggled against the past regime, but he has come up from his peasant roots to confront the current regime, demonstrating great literary talent and winning the adoration of his countrymen.

By everyone's admission, the current regime is more lenient, granting privileges and conveniences unavailable in the past. In return, it expects compliance. Sigmund, however, refuses, writing subversive letters to foreign journals and secretly composing what appears to be a literary masterpiece assaulting that regime, the only copy of which has just been confiscated.

This group of four (plus a Danish *ingénue* picked up by the womanizing Marcus) meets in Marcus's government-allocated apartment, the former residence of the country's archbishop, a large, though rundown, formerly opulent set of rooms. Of the living room (the play's stage), the text observes: "*The ceiling is first seen: in high relief the Four Winds, cheeks swelling, and cherubim, darkened unevenly by soot and age.*"[5] In this ceiling, oppressively and dominatingly overseeing the play's action, is presumed to be a concealed microphone allowing the state to overhear all. Presumption here is important because at no point in the play do we have any verification. Miller's use of the microphone is ingenious, serving the play at various levels. At one level, the microphone represents the violation of privacy instituted by the totalitarian regime. Beyond this literal level, the insertion of this microphone into the ceiling's soot-covered relief is an invasion of Lucifer into God's former domain and the manifestation of the thing that has come to replace the moral world that the archbishop's ceiling once represented. In both cases, it is the manifestation of the "other" to be resisted. Seen thus, the play could seem little more than a simple allegorical tale of good subdued by evil that belies the complexities evident in the contemporary world.

Miller moves beyond this oppositional schematization, however, by having the alleged microphone work upon its victims at a subtle psychological level. Its presence discourages authentic, genuine human communication and encourages a behavior which at the least mimics acquiescence. Because everyone in the room assumes that the state hears what they say, they never fully reveal themselves but "perform" for their unseen audience.

Beyond that, however, the play moves to a level which is somewhat less invasive as the microphone becomes an external manifestation of a more universal internal human process that in many ways has little to do with the microphone in the ceiling, whose force becomes metaphorical. Each character in fact "performs" before numerous self-planted microphones which nonetheless exercise some coercive power. Simply put, the omnipresent ear of God, sited in the original ceiling decorations, has been replaced by the multiple ears of Lucifer, represented literally by the totalitarian state but also figuratively by countless compromising temptations placed before us as idols to pray before, or at least to perform before. If we perform properly before them, we are rewarded accordingly. And our performances appear hardly ever activated by a desire for selfless good. In fact, even when we do perform disinterestedly, the problem of self-delusion remains a troubling possibility. Benevolent action often covers a desire for selfish reward.

Miller creates a very complex web in *The Archbishop's Ceiling*, one in which reality itself is not only muddied by totalitarian willful illusion but also by unconscious delusion and outright lies. Truth is the ultimate victim. Indeed, with truth and reality under such pressure, it becomes difficult to establish their status. Miller has created, as Bigsby notes, "a metaphysical anxiety in the play which moves Miller closer to Beckett and Pinter than ever before."[6] This far-reaching work, in fact, touches upon much of what Miller had previously confronted in his earlier works. June Schlueter and James K. Flanagan observe:

> A sophisticated foray into the epistemological nature of reality and of art, the play combines and extends the private illusions of a Joe Keller or a Willy Loman and the public myths that control our lives in *The Crucible* and *Incident at Vichy*. Miller's measure of truth, which ultimately is incapable of discriminating between the fictive and the real, is the world–stage metaphor.[7]

The audience for this world–stage – the various literal and metaphorical microphones – dictates how we behave. And if we begin by shrewdly attempting to separate our authentic selves from our performance selves, these pervasive conditions of performance eventually break down our abilities to distinguish the two. As Miller himself has put it, "one learns to *include the bug* in the baggage of one's mind, in the calculus of one's plans and expectations, and this is not without effect."[8] The effect is loss of a coherent identity. How, exactly, can authentic behavior be determined in a world that has become a stage for inauthentic performance, each character adopting various personae which play for particular rewards in a world where apparent disinterest and self-sacrifice are the best disguise of all? Ethics/morality have been replaced by a metatheatrical utilitarianism.

That the play best finds its setting in the Eastern Bloc seems apparent. But as Miller observes, we must recall that in the 1970s, when the play was written, "[t]he White House was bugged, businesses were bugging competitors to defeat their strategies, and Watergate and the publication of the Pentagon Papers . . . demonstrated that the Soviets had little to teach American presidents about domestic espionage."[9] While Miller speaks here on the political level, he adds that eventually "the real issue change[s] from a purely political one to the question of what effect this surveillance was having on the minds of people who had to live under such ceilings, on whichever side of the Cold War line they happened to be."[10] Eventually, this continual warring on the human psyche evolves a mindset that sees the bugs' omnipresence as an actual good. Miller reports a conversation with an Eastern Bloc writing colleague: "What you people in the West don't understand is that we are not a competitive society and we don't wish to be. We want the government to protect us, that is what government is for."[11] The ostensible enemy becomes the protector; lines of resistance between good and evil become almost irreparably blurred because what we gain often appears an equitable trade-off for what we lose. The result is that we welcome a life where we live in an amoral world bereft of personal responsibility for our actions and even for our well-being. Miller's play lowers us into this seemingly alien world only to have us realize that in many ways it is *our* world, a world our naive idealism leaves us ill equipped to cope with even as we resist the charge that we are in that world. We have grown so used to the multiple invasions – forcing us to perform for the government, our employer, even our friends and lovers – that we have lost sight of its destructive grind on our beings.

The naive American of the play, Adrian, ineffectually casts about, seeking certainty in what he observes in this alien Eastern world. His various statements are fraught with declarations of certainty, for example, concerning the loyalty and/or good intentions of everyone among his circle of friends. But the declarations become increasingly more revealing of Adrian's growing self-doubt as they evolve into desperate declarations of hope rather than certainty. Do these friends like each other, trust each other? Are they even friends? Is what is spoken to be believed, or is all an act intended for the state microphone, or for some other microphone? Is anything other than an act? What is reality? Adrian sees that he is lost in this world. What he does not realize is that his Western world begs the same questions; now that he has seen the betrayals of the East from the objective position of an outsider, he can perhaps begin to see the West (and himself) with the same eyes. Does he write for some sort of moral good or because it gets him fame? Does he like his friends as friends or as subject matter for his novels? Is he a friend or just acting like one for personal gain? Coming to a realization that life itself is a creative fiction, he seems ultimately to dispense with his passion to write and turns more completely to search for an authenticating path of existence for himself, freed of the simplifications under which he formerly operated. Initially, being cast into such a world and being conscious of its ambiguities hardly seems to bring him closer to escape from that world. At best, it appears that the awareness opens his eyes to the compromises forced upon us all as we struggle to negotiate our ways through life.

Marcus is a man more completely part of the East *and* West (he operates comfortably on both sides of the Iron Curtain) and so is more fully aware of the facts of his own various performance personae. Marcus's sense of ambiguity is more self-conscious, and he is apparently more certain of the results of his performances and more willing to accommodate the various microphones he confronts. He feels pride that his past inflexible activism (which landed him in prison) has helped to create a more flexible regime. But he currently performs various tasks for the new regime in return for comfort and limited liberties, to the point that he fears further activism (by anyone) will result in a return to the oppressive past and, perhaps more importantly, to a loss of his personal gains. This concern may be legitimate, but does this interest in maintaining the *status quo* make him a supporter of the government and a betrayer of his ideals of true freedom? Is some freedom not better than no freedom? By answering in the affirmative, he feels compelled to use his friendship with Sigmund to stifle his younger colleague's dissident behavior, a sure sign of betrayal in favor of his own limited comforts. But, then again, is this purely self-interest? After all, other fellow countrymen are benefiting from the more lenient regime, too. Is his a real effort to prevent catastrophe and a return to the past? Furthermore, is he a true friend trying to prevent Sigmund from self-destruction? In a case of clear ambiguity, all responses are in part accurate and in part false.

Marcus is perhaps the most complex and easily the most enigmatic of the characters in the play. He relays a piece of autobiography to Adrian which illustrates a certain historical adaptability to the world he has become so much a part of. After World War II, Marcus attempted to emigrate to America. While he was aboard ship, his country fell into Communist hands, and he was denied admission to America as a result, suspected of being a Communist spy. Upon his return to his homeland, he was arrested for being an American spy. In such a world, survival requires compromise, and the tool is adaptive performance skills. Accepting what is offered and paying for it through small betrayals of both sides – neither police nor dissidents should upset the balance – is perhaps not as evil as at first it may appear. But the price is far more than a compromise of ideals. The price becomes the "self." There appears no longer to be a *real* Marcus distinguishable from the various performance Marcuses, a problem Adrian begins to realize about himself.

Sigmund's rebellious tendencies initially signal that he is the one authentic character in the play, and to a degree he is. He seems to perform only for the good of his country. But his whole existence as an artist and dissident is ironically tied to his government, his ultimate and only real audience; this audience in turn makes the Sigmund performer attractive to his compatriots on the streets. He becomes their hero *because* of the state. He becomes nothing if he leaves his country and his government's resistance to his work. And he becomes nothing as well if the police state ceases to exist. Ironically, Sigmund feels a mixture of joy and despair when his manuscript is released from state confiscation, signal of his partial victory over the state but also of a withering symbiotic relationship where the host state may no longer be strong enough to support its dissident parasites. Sigmund's performances require the totalitarian audience. As Maya points out, Sigmund regularly taunts the state with minor acts of defiance merely to assure himself of its continued surveillance of his actions. As a dissenter, he would sink into obscurity without his object of dissent, evidenced by his unwillingness to flee the country. Though this unwillingness to flee could be perceived as a selfless act, Miller nonetheless presents enough ambiguity to call into question even the reality and authenticity of his play's key dissenter.

The play ends on what appears to be a note of despair, given that it offers no real, or at least no obvious, hope for escape. We can't even determine where right is, where truth lies, or where reality is grounded. Operating in this world necessitates an uncomfortably multivalent compromise wherein relative goodness and badness are the best we can hope for, where ideal behavior is impossible or at least unidentifiable (which amounts to the same thing). The easy bivalent (simple black/white–right/wrong) assessments are impossible, and the slippery surfaces of multivalent realities require sophisticated footing of a kind that Americans (if not also Europeans) have not fully developed.

If Adrian needs to grow up in this world, perhaps Miller is suggesting a need for America as a whole to grow up as well. Answers are not as simple as they once appeared to be. Maybe working with the devil, learning to operate in Lucifer's world, is the only option we have before us. Maybe, as Bigsby suggests, America must grow to accept such European perspectives as those put forth by Beckett and Pinter. But recall that Bigsby suggests only that Miller comes *close* to Pinter and Beckett in this work. Perhaps amid this anguished, reluctant realization, we can still long for the apparently impossible, namely for an overturning of Lucifer's dominion and a (re)construction of a world more fully predicated on a sense of moral responsibility involving truly disinterested actions benefiting our fellows via a fully rounded sense of social commitment.

This appeal to the "impossible" may in fact be the appeal Miller is making. After all, even the qualified resistance to the totalitarian microphone has had the effect of wearing the regime down to mere bullying and idle threats where once it exacted severe punishments for disobedience. Marcus and Sigmund have both contributed to this weakening, even as they seem in many ways to help validate and even to sustain the regime. If the slow process has worn this totalitarian microphone down, then perhaps other microphones can be made to meet similar fates, though they are even more universally ingrained than the totalitarian oppressor. If this is Miller's point, he clearly differs from Beckett or Pinter, providing a uniquely American spin on the existential endgames these other artists have presented. After all, Miller's omnipresent microphones are not ontological constants as Beckett's Godot (or no-Godot) is; their existence relies on human complicity, demonstrating a changeable reality which can therefore at least theoretically be eliminated or adjusted in ways that Beckett's ominous, rock-solid reality cannot. Realizing one's own entrapment, as Adrian has, may actually be a first step to assuming personal responsibility and working to alter a seemingly unalterable order. If the microphone can be removed, perhaps the archbishop's ceiling can be restored, perhaps Lucifer/comfort can be replaced by an awaiting God/morality. Miller depicts the process as more complex than he had apparently formerly recognized, but it is not necessarily an impossible task. Accepting a European sense of complexity, Miller nevertheless offers a grain of American optimism.

Miller returns to the American scene with *The American Clock*, but for him the landscape has changed. America can no longer see itself as "fixable" by simply repairing damaged cogs in the machine and willing a return to a simpler past. The image itself must be changed. Fine-tuning American governmental or corporate structures to make them work as they should is no longer sufficient.

The American Clock, set in the 1920s and 1930s, offers us a collective and clear picture of our contemporary dilemma in ways which are perhaps more effective than a work set in the contemporary period. The choice of material becomes metaphorically significant. The play initially depicts a rich and comfortable country kneeling "to a golden calf in a blanket of red, white, and blue,"[12] as one character observes. That world is shattered by the Great Depression, yet amid the ensuing suffering the entire American population seems content to await a return to prosperity without evaluating the roots of its insubstantiality. What needs to occur, that populace seems to conclude, is for someone or something to return us to that old order. Ironically, it is World War II which brings the country out of the Depression, which sets things right. This war is all the more tragic because it allows a 1940s return to the 1920s – with only minor adjustments – rather than forcing the country to address the roots of a flawed vision that lingers through the 1970s and beyond. Miller seems to be warning that even today America is foolheartedly waiting for a renewed prosperity – a return to past solutions – to obliterate the memory of the catastrophes of the late 1960s and 1970s. And with the renewed prosperity will come an attendant reestablishment of faith in comfort. It seems, however, that Miller hopes America can awaken to a need for more fundamental revisioning.

In his autobiography, *Timebends*, Miller observes of *The Archbishop's Ceiling* and *The American Clock*:

> Both were hard-minded attempts to grasp what I felt life in the seventies had all but lost – a unified concept of human beings, the intimate psychological side joined with the social–political. To put it another way, I wanted to set us in our history by revealing a line to measure from. In *Clock* it was the objective facts of social collapse; in *Archbishop*, the bedrock circumstances of real liberty.[13]

Looking closely at his work in the 1970s, Miller quite significantly asks whether we have reached a stage of general, universal apathy where nothing matters but moral mediocrity, radical self-interest, and simple comfort. Miller suggests that if humanity can accept responsibility for its actions and develop a sense of accountability, then perhaps we can construct for ourselves an adjusted postmodern vision which can reinsert a sense of right action into our world.

The Fall resulted in our no longer being able to hear the voices of nature's creatures amid the din of personal ego. Our continued fall (via the first fratricide) resulted in losing our contact with the voice of God and "performing" instead before false idols promising only personal gain. We can reverse the process by dismantling our bonds to ego and striving to recapture our ability to "converse" with nature, responsibly to engage it rather than to seek personal gain from it. Miller's art continues to be a constructive art amid a cult of cynical deconstruction. As he puts it, referring to the 1970s in particular (though still a relevant point today), "We had come to prize and celebrate in our art disconnection for its own sake, but this was not at all the same as tearing apart the givens of experience in order to recreate a fresh unity that would inform us newly about our lives."[14] If we see Miller as naive, it is because he chooses to be naive amid such counterproductive sophistication. At very least, his work continues to offer hope in a world overburdened with despair.

NOTES

1 C. W. E. Bigsby, *A Critical Introduction to Twentieth-Century American Drama*, vol. II (Cambridge: Cambridge University Press, 1984), p. 318.

2 The Broadway production was a critical failure, closed within a month, and lost $250,000. The reasons for the failure are varied, among them were criticisms of Miller's colloquialized tone and other unacceptable choices of portrayal. For assessments assaulting Miller's decisions, see, for example, reviews by Stanley Kauffman (*New Republic*, 23 and 30 December 1972, p. 26), Clive Barnes (*The New York Times*, 1 December 1972, p. 28), and Richard Watts (*The New York Post*, 1 December 1972).

3 Quoted in Samuel G. Freedman, "Miller Tries a New Form for an Old Play," *The New York Times* (23 October 1983), section H, p. 5.

4 Arthur Miller, *The Creation of the World and Other Business*, in *Arthur Miller's Collected Plays*, vol. II (New York: Viking Press, 1981), p. 379. Subsequent references will be cited in the text.

5 Arthur Miller, *The Archbishop's Ceiling*, in *The Archbishop's Ceiling and The American Clock: Two Plays* (New York: Grove Press, 1989), p. 3.

6 Bigsby, *A Critical Introduction*, p. 237.

7 June Schlueter and James K. Flanagan, *Arthur Miller* (New York: Frederick Ungar, 1987), p. 125.

8 Arthur Miller, "Conditions of Freedom: Two Plays of the Seventies," in *The Archbishop's Ceiling and The American Clock: Two Plays*, p. ix.

9 *Ibid.*, p. viii.

10 *Ibid.*, pp. viii–ix.

11 *Ibid.*, p. xi.

12 Arthur Miller, *The American Clock*, in *The Archbishop's Ceiling and The American Clock: Two Plays* (New York: Grove Press, 1989), p. 107.

13 Arthur Miller, *Timebends* (New York: Grove Press, 1987), p. 587.

14 *Ibid.*

10

JUNE SCHLUETER

Miller in the eighties

Personally, the 1980s were stable years for Arthur Miller. Sixty-five when the decade began, Miller had long since established himself as a, if not the, major figure in the American theatre. Having returned to playwriting in 1964 with *After the Fall*, a play that may well have helped him come to terms with his first two marriages and the suicide of his second wife, Marilyn Monroe, the Miller of the 1980s shared a comfortable life in Roxbury, Connecticut, with his third wife, Inge Morath, a professional photographer who co-produced three handsome travel accounts with her husband: *In Russia* (1969), *In the Country* (1977), and *Chinese Encounters* (1979).[1]

Miller had purchased the Roxbury farm during his marriage to Monroe, but he seldom used the residence until he married Morath. By the 1980s, the couple had raised a daughter there and sent the young Rebecca to Yale. Miller, who, like Willy Loman, longed to work with his hands, found the eighteenth-century frame house a hospitable setting for his hobby, which, since the age of six, was carpentry. Relaxed in his Roxbury home (and only moderately disrupted by a 1983 fire that claimed a portion of it, including his best books), Miller dedicated many hours to drafting and redrafting the copious manuscripts of the last thirty years. In the 1980s, colleagues and interviewers reported that the gentleman farmer/carpenter/writer/husband/father was personally content.

Politically, however, Miller was still restless. In the 1980s, the man who had challenged the House Un-American Activities Committee in the McCarthy era and been outspoken in his support of social causes remained an active and consistent voice for human rights and freedom of speech. In 1980, for example, he signed a letter with other American Jews protesting the Begin government's expansion of settlements on the West Bank and joined several other writers, including Edward Albee, John Updike, and Bernard Malamud, in a letter of support for the Polish Solidarity movement. On 12 March 1984, he published a *New York Times* piece objecting to mandated school prayer, arguing that, given the potential for misuse, there was little political wisdom in buttressing civil authority with religion (Khomeini was his example). In 1985, on behalf of the International PEN Club, he traveled to Istanbul with Harold Pinter to lend solidarity to Turkish writers, artists, and political prisoners, following that country's 1980 military coup. At the US Embassy, he offered an after-dinner speech to an Ambassador already indignant over the sharp criticism offered by Pinter, suggesting he saw no signs of Western democracy in Turkey. Later that year, he protested an immigration law that denied permanent residence to certain artists. In his introduction to the paperback edition of *Focus* (1985), a novel first published in 1945, Miller deplored the resurgence of the anti-Semitic mind, which was evidencing its resilience not only in the form of hostility in Asian countries – Thailand and Cambodia, for example – to strangers in their lands. In 1986, Miller, along with other American and Soviet writers, traveled to Vilnius, Lithuania, for a cultural exchange that needed first to set aside ideological defenses. A year later, he and fifteen American and European writers and scientists convened in Russia and met with Mikhail Gorbachev, who noted that the Soviet people were beginning to think in new ways. Actively engaged in defending the rights of writers at least since the 1960s, when he was president of PEN, Miller joined Toni Morrison, Norman Mailer, Allen Ginsberg, and others in a 1988 reading of the works of imprisoned writers around the world at the United Nations Parish in New York. Seldom silent on issues that challenged his own public values, Miller responded to the Tiananmen Square repression by telling the story of the father of Ying Ruocheng, who had played Willy Loman in the Beijing production of *Death of a Salesman*: having refused to issue a statement supporting the Chinese official action, the man was relieved of his responsibility as Vice-Minister of Culture.

Professionally, Miller continued to enjoy warm receptions in regional theatres across the country. Notable revivals of *Death of a Salesman* included those staged by Steppenwolf Theater Co. (Chicago, 1980), Actors Theatre of Louisville (1987), and the Los Angeles Theatre Center (1989). Along the fringes of New York, there were revivals of *The Price* at the Philadelphia Drama Guild (1985) and the George Street Playhouse (New Brunswick, NJ, 1985), of *The Crucible* at Trinity Repertory (Providence, 1986), and of *A View from the Bridge* (1982), *All My Sons* (1986), and *The Crucible* (1989) at the Long Wharf Theatre (New Haven), not to mention a revival of Robert Ward's operatic version of *The Crucible* by New York's Juilliard Opera Center in 1988.

The academic community also continued to recognize Miller's achievements. With Cao Yu, China's most respected dramatist, the playwright was invited to present a program on "Theater in Modern China" at Columbia University in 1980. In 1983, New York University honored him with the Elmer Holmes Bobst Award in Drama. In 1984, Miller and his wife were given honorary degrees from the University of Hartford. And in 1988, Miller joined other invited playwrights – Tom Stoppard, August Wilson, Athol Fugard, and Tina Howe – in a symposium on "The Challenge of Writing for the Theater Today," sponsored by the First New York International Festival of the Arts and hosted by the Graduate Center of The City University of New York.

Nonetheless, as the decade progressed, he became increasingly unhappy with the American theatre, and especially with New York's Broadway. He acknowledged those who would argue that Broadway was not the measure of American theatre and that the United States was rich in regional theatre, but he returned to a statement he had made in 1955: "The American theatre is five blocks long, by about one and a half blocks wide."[2] In the 1980s, Miller frequently expressed his disillusionment with this powerful strip of commercial theatre, which, over the years, had become less inclined to encourage his writing. On the one hand, he tried to protect the institution, protesting a 1982 attempt on the part of Broadway producers to limit dramatists' earnings and working vigorously (though unsuccessfully) to save two Broadway theatres from demolition. On the other, he resisted the commercial theatre's changing character, which increasingly excluded the serious playwright. In a 1988 essay for *US News and World Report*, he confessed that he had "gotten too tired to scream about the situation any more," having expressed dissatisfaction with New York's commercial theatre since 1952.[3]

Ironically, vintage Miller proved more successful in the 1980s in Broadway revivals than in those that appeared on New York's off- or off-off-Broadway stages.

The Jewish Repertory Theater's staging in 1983 of *Up from Paradise*, for example, a musical version of *The Creation of the World and Other Business* (1972), which Miller had read in a concert version at the Whitney Museum two years earlier, faced Frank Rich's indictment: this is "casual, warm-spirited and innocuous musical chalk talk," not "as far removed from *Creation of the World* as one might wish." Commenting on Stanley Silverman's music, Rich scoffed, "the score often sounds like liturgical fragments that God had the good sense to eliminate from His sanctified repertory."[4]

Playhouse 91's revival of *After the Fall*, with Frank Langella as Quentin and Dianne Wiest as Maggie, had only a short run, from October to December 1984. The play had not been revived since its original staging twenty years earlier, which had prompted Robert Brustein to dismiss it as "a shameless piece of tabloid gossip, an act of exhibitionism which makes us all voyeurs."[5] The suggestion then was that Miller was exploiting the private life of Marilyn Monroe, whose sexuality and suicide he chronicles. The eighties revival – perhaps because Americans had adjusted to the loss of their sex queen, perhaps because Wiest bore little resemblance to Marilyn – brought no such response. This time, the critics saw the play either as "tortuous rhetoric . . . full of circumlocutions, portentous questions, and conundrums" (Rich)[6] or as a specimen of the kind of piece "in which a muddled and banal individual psychology gobbles up history and politics" (Erika Munk).[7]

On Broadway, however, the critical response to Miller *redoux* was respectful. In 1983, the Ambassador Theater became home to a revival of *A View from the Bridge*, with Tony LoBianco as Eddie Carbone. In a sense, this production of *A View from the Bridge* was a Broadway premiere. The one-act version of the play had appeared on Broadway in 1955 with *A Memory of Two Mondays*, receiving mixed reviews and running for nineteen weeks. In 1956, Peter Brook had staged the first production of the two-act version in London, with Anthony Quayle playing Eddie Carbone; banned by the censor, the play was immensely popular. Off-Broadway's Sheridan Square Playhouse had revived the two-act play in 1965, but it was eighteen years before director Arvin Brown brought the play to Broadway, after a run the previous year at the Long Wharf. Though the 1983 New York reception was uneven, with critics alternately praising and condemning Miller's work – Clive Barnes comparing it to Greek tragedy,[8] John Simon calling it "pretentious melodrama"[9] – critics (Simon excepted) uniformly recognized the power embodied in the Eddie Carbone role and celebrated LoBianco's performance (for which he won a Tony).

Arvin Brown's production of *All My Sons*, which similarly was mounted at the Long Wharf prior to its New York revival, opened at the John Golden Theatre in 1987, winning a Tony for the best revival that year. Here, too, the critics realized the force of Miller's characterization, praising Richard Kiley for his portrayal of Joe Keller and (in the case of Frank Rich) wishing that Joyce Ebert's performance as the family matriarch "matched Mr. Miller's writing." Both Rich and Don Nelson (of the *Daily News*) spoke of the play's contemporary relevance: at the time of its revival, reports of corruption in industry and in government as well as on Wall Street were almost daily fare and the term "cover-up" had acquired special force.[10]

The return of *All My Sons* to Broadway was preceded by a television version of the play, aired in Public Television's American Playhouse series.

Directed by Jack O'Brien, the production featured James Whitmore as Keller, Michael Learned as Kate, and Aidan Quinn as their son. John J. O'Connor's review for the *New York Times* was admiring, noting that, in this play about the dark corners of a Norman Rockwell magazine cover, "the passion holds."[11]

For Miller – and for Broadway – the triumph of the decade came when the Broadhurst Theater reintroduced *Death of a Salesman* in 1984, with Dustin Hoffman as Willy Loman. George C. Scott had imitated the inimitable in 1975 at The Circle in the Square when he took on the role following Lee J. Cobb's 1949 portrayal, which had become nearly iconographic. But no Broadway stage had hosted another Willy Loman until 1984, when Hoffman, a "skinny little sucked-out shell of a man," challenged the "rumpled hulk" of the indelible Cobb.[12] A seasoned method actor of enormous versatility, Hoffman, along with the remarkable John Malkovich as Biff, captured the public. Within three days of its opening, the box office had realized more than $3,000,000 in ticket receipts.

The critics warmly received the production and catalogued the play's enduring strengths. Eileen Blumenthal applauded *Salesman*'s "substantial power" and "the deep compassion at its center."[13] Douglas Watt admitted that "the power and compassion of Miller's masterpiece are still capable of moving us deeply . . ."[14] And Benedict Nightingale endorsed Willy Loman as "a protagonist who will continue to move and fascinate audiences as long as American drama exists."[15]

Miller's popularity was buttressed the following year when twenty-five million people watched *Death of a Salesman* on CBS television. In a CBS interview with Miller, Forrest Sawyer recognized in *Death of a Salesman* a "voice that cuts across time, continents, and cultures": the formula so simply identified – yet so painfully realized – of a classic. Indeed, in the 1980s, *Salesman* saw productions in Sydney (1982), Amsterdam (1982), Tokyo (1984), Manchester, England (1986), and Birmingham, England (1988).

The most pointed affirmation of the play's broad cultural appeal came in 1984 with the production in Beijing. Miller's eight-week journal,[16] covering six weeks of rehearsal, records how each Chinese actor grew into his or her role and how playwright and cast came to understand the commonality that was manifest even in two cultures so apparently different as those of China and the United States.

The rehearsal process was one of discovery, with actors regularly seeking explanations for their characters' behavior and, finally, coming to realize that Chinese audiences would have much in common with Miller's characters. As Zhu Lin, the actress playing Linda, remarked, "their lives are like Willy's," to which Ying Ruocheng, the actor playing Willy, added, "They have no hopes of becoming rich or famous themselves, they are ordinary men and women. But this gap in the play – this generation gap – they can identify with, it is absolutely Chinese."[17] Miller's description of Willy during the first week of rehearsal may just as readily apply to Miller himself: "He is the walking believer, the bearer of a flame whose going-out would leave us flat, with merely what the past has given us. He is forever signaling to a future that he cannot describe and will not live to see, but he is in love with it all the same."[18]

During the 1980s, Miller wrote actively, his major dramatic undertaking a sprawling draft of *The Ride Down Mount Morgan*, which was to see its initial production and publication, in deeply edited form, in London in 1991. He also produced a full-length play, *The American Clock* (1980); rewrote *The Archbishop's Ceiling*, first staged at the Kennedy Center in Washington, DC in 1977 and remounted, in revised form, in Cleveland in 1984; wrote several short plays, two of which – *Elegy for a Lady* and *Some Kind of Love Story* – premiered at the Long Wharf Theatre in New Haven (1982) and appeared in double bills entitled *Two by A.M.* in New York (1982) and *Two-Way Mirror* in London (1989), another two – *I Can't Remember Anything* and *Clara* – appearing in a double bill called *Danger: Memory!* at New York's Lincoln Center (1987) and London's Hampstead Theatre (1988). In 1980, *Playing for Time*, a screenplay based on a book by Fania Fenelon, was televised on CBS; in 1985, it was staged at the Studio Theatre, Washington, DC. By the end of the decade, Miller had completed a screenplay, *Everybody Wins*, which would appear in 1990. He also published a book-length account of the *Salesman* production in Beijing (1984). And, to the delight of scholars who yearned to know more about Miller's life, and the dismay of those who had hoped to write the biography, he published the autobiographical *Timebends: A Life* (1987).

The American Clock had a somewhat unusual production history before it reached Broadway's Biltmore Theater in November 1980. Earlier that year, it had previewed at the Harold Clurman Theater on 42nd Street, premiered at the Sopoleto Festival, in Charleston, South Carolina, then moved to the Mechanic Theater in Baltimore and, finally, to the Biltmore, where, despite its many tryouts, it was a commercial and critical flop, closing after twelve performances. As Barnes's review suggested, "This *Clock* Is a Bit Off."[19] Barnes's judgment was endorsed by Douglas Watt, who noted that "*The American Clock*, trying to tick away the past, simply doesn't work. The parts don't mesh."[20] Rich added his clever lament: "It's a bitter loss for the theatre that *The American Clock* has arrived on Broadway unwound."[21] Much of the problem may have been, as Rich pointed out, that between Charleston and New York, Miller rewrote the script, attempting to contain some of its sprawl but ignoring the play's structural problems and introducing sentimentality and too many unsubtle touches.

Like *After the Fall*, the play relies heavily on autobiographical material. Set in the Depression, when Miller's father lost his considerable financial resources, *The American Clock* flips through the mental album of a man whose early family life still obsesses him. Inspired by Studs Terkel's *Hard Times*, this disjointed memory play recreates one family's experience of a devastating moment in American economic history. But, as Jack Kroll remarks in his *Newsweek* review, "*The American Clock* never finds an effective dramatic shape; it's part play, part chronicle, but mostly it's Miller's last evocation of the images and people that have haunted him more than any others in his life."[22]

Miller's canvas is broad, his backdrop an impression of United States geography, suggesting the extent of this great American calamity, which the play's narrator, Lee Baum, ranks as one of the two truly national disasters: unlike World Wars I and II, Vietnam, or the Revolution, the Great Depression – and the Civil War – touched everyone. The intimate portrait of the Baum family, with father Moe and mother Rose at its head, appears against a national mural of some thirty-five sketched-in incidental victims, from the farmlands of middle America to the streets and gutters of New York.

Lee recalls the story of Henry, the Iowa farmer who was shamed into reclaiming his farm for a dollar and into a near lynching of a judge who moved east in search of a job. He remembers the young Sidney, who is urged by his mother to pledge himself to the landlady's thirteen-year-old daughter in exchange for free rent, and the Mississippi butcher who, though paid by the government to distribute meat, handed out maggots instead. In the Mid-West, he met an unpaid sheriff who gave his radio to a black man in exchange for chicken dinners to impress his second cousin, who might get him a paying job. And in New York he met a man with a Gramercy Park address begging for food. The seventy-year-old Robertson, who shares the story-telling with Lee, talks of how he warned people to bail out of the stockmarket but to no avail. The shoeshine man, Clarence, who had forty-five dollars cash to his name, had purchased one hundred thousand dollars worth of stock ten dollars at a time, but he would not believe the man who carried thirty thousand dollars in his shoes.

Lee recalls his childhood relief at withdrawing his twelve dollars from the bank just before it collapsed, and his disillusionment at having the bike he bought with the cash stolen. He remembers the drama he and his father staged for the Welfare Office so Lee could be eligible for the WPA. And, with special poignancy, he tells of how his mother gave him her diamond bracelet to pawn.

Miller uses fine brush strokes in creating Rose, who, accustomed to Park Avenue living, must move to Brooklyn and, finally, sell even her beloved piano. Played by Miller's sister, Joan Copeland, in the Broadway production, the character, though impressionistic, offers the narrator's one sustained personal memory, repeatedly suggesting the relationship between mother and son that persists beyond Lee's childhood and Rose's death.

Following the Broadway production, Miller continued to revise the play. *The American Clock* reached its final form in 1984, when it was performed at the Mark Taper Forum in Los Angeles. That version found its way to Britain's National Theatre two years later, with a subtitle, "A Vaudeville," reflecting the production style that Peter Wood, with Miller's endorsement, brought to the play. In his introduction to the Grove Press edition (1989), Miller expresses his satisfaction with the Wood production, which featured a jazz band, songs from the thirties, and a music hall spotlight. Miller particularly praised the treatment of Ted Quinn, a champion of democracy, an opponent of monopolies, and president-designee of General Electric. In Wood's production, Quinn delivered his speeches while tap dancing; when the phone rings and Quinn must decide whether to answer it as president of the company or repudiate the position, he places the receiver on the stage floor and dances away. The playwright was also fond of the treatment of Rose and her piano: the actress sat at the piano, hands poised above the keyboard, as the pianist in the band played thirties music.

Miller's hope in writing *The American Clock* was to recreate the national and personal fact and feel of the Depression: to "give some sense of life as we lived it when the clock was ticking every day."[23] For him, Wood's music-hall style established a tone that enabled the play to sustain a balance between the epic and the intimate.

The Grove Press edition of *The American Clock* also includes *The Archbishop's Ceiling*, which, like *The American Clock*, Miller revised, in fact restoring the text to its original form before changes were made for the 1977 production at the Kennedy Center in Washington DC. It was restaged in 1984 at the Bolton Theatre in Cleveland and in 1988 at the Huntington Theatre in Boston, but it has yet to find a home on the New York stage. The Bristol Old Vic mounted a production in 1985, and in 1986 the Royal Shakespeare Company staged it in The Pit at the Barbican, with Michael Billington calling it a "complex, gritty, intellectually teasing play."[24] Its

1984 publication by Methuen marked the first time that a British text of a Miller play had preceded the American. Indeed, the moment expressed a cultural difference that had been developing for some time: even as the American critics were complaining that Miller's recent work did not match his earlier achievement, British critics were developing a deep appreciation for Miller's plays and a growing respect for their sophistication.

The eighties saw revivals in England of much vintage Miller, most notably Bill Bryden's staging of *The Crucible* at the Comedy Theatre in London in 1981; Gregory Hertsov's mounting of *Death of a Salesman* at the Royal Exchange Theatre, Manchester, in 1986, and Michael Meacham's at the Birmingham Repertory Theatre in 1988; David Thacker's Young Vic productions of *The Crucible* in 1986 and *An Enemy of the People* in 1989; Peter Wood's staging of *The American Clock* at the National in 1986; Alan Ayckbourn's revival of *A View from the Bridge* at the National in 1987; and Barry Kyle's RSC production of *The Crucible* in 1989. In addition, BBC Radio broadcast *The Price* in 1989, with Richard Dreyfuss as Victor and Timothy West as Gregory Solomon. At the end of the decade, Thacker was planning a seventy-fifth birthday celebration for Miller, which would include a revival of *The Price* at the Young Vic (1990) and of *The Crucible* at the National (1990). In 1991, Britain was to preempt America once again in the publication and production of *The Ride Down Mount Morgan*. In 1989, through the efforts of C. W. E. Bigsby, Britain formalized its affection for Miller by establishing The Arthur Miller Centre for American Studies at the University of East Anglia.

The difference between the American reception of Miller and the British held for Miller's new short plays as well. In America, *Elegy for a Lady* and *Some Kind of Love Story*, both spare, two-character pieces, did not live beyond New Haven, where they ran for six weeks in 1982 to sold-out houses at the Long Wharf, only to be characterized by Rich as an "experiment in esthetic simplicity by a writer who's prone to thinking big."[25] By contrast, Thacker's staging at The Young Vic in London in 1989, with Helen Mirren and Bob Peck, was warmly received. Both plays are evocative pieces which, while portraying the tender side of human experience, extended Miller's preoccupation with the nature of the real. Miller's prefatory note speaks of them as

> passionate voyages through the masks of illusion to an ultimate reality. In *Some Kind of Love Story* it is social reality and the corruption of justice which a delusionary woman both conceals and unveils. The search in *Elegy for a Lady* is for the shape and meaning of a sexual relationship that is being brought to a close by a lover's probable death. In both the unreal is an agony to be striven against and, at the same time, accepted as life's condition.[26]

Elegy for a Lady takes place in a boutique, where an older man is searching for a present for his thirty-year-old lover, who is about to die. The two characters are the Man and the Proprietress, who offers not only gift suggestions but compassion and support. With the Proprietress's help, the Man decides that what he wants most to say is "thank you." He settles, finally, on an antique watch, prompted not by some cruel impulse to remind his lover of her mortality but by the Proprietress's gentle suggestion that his lover "wants to make it stay exactly as it is . . . forever."[27]

The question of what to give sustains the dramatic action, but *Elegy for a Lady* subtly and suggestively questions more. Clearly the Man does not know for certain whether his lover is dying. He knows she is scheduled for surgery on the twenty-eighth of the month, that she has a tumor she says was diagnosed as benign, and that she has been in emotional pain. Often she would not answer her phone, and when she did she would sometimes leave the phone for as long as two minutes and, occasionally, allow a sob to interrupt the conversation. The Man has constructed a reality that may or may not be true. In his conversation with the Proprietress, he shapes and reshapes his story, trying to define the nature of his relationship with the dying woman and to understand his own feelings about her and about himself. The Proprietress's suggestions, not of gifts but of feelings, help him to create an understanding of how the woman he loves might feel about her own impending death, if indeed she is dying, and how he is responding to the coming loss. Gently, the Proprietress urges him into an acceptance of his recent exclusion from his lover's life, as the audience understands that the elegy may not be for the death of the lady but for the death of the Man.

If the circumstantial truth is elusive, however, the emotional truth is clear, endorsed by yet another teasing question about the Proprietress. When the Man comes to understand that his quest may be a meditation on a loss having nothing to do with cancer claiming his lady, the Proprietress "embraces him, her body pressed to his, an immense longing in it and a sense of a last embrace." The Proprietress may be the woman, the meeting their farewell. As the Man takes the watch and chain, a gift from the Proprietress to him, she remarks, "You never said her name." The Man, starting to smile, responds, "You never said yours. (*Slight pause*) Thank you. Thank you . . . very much."[28]

Some Kind of Love Story, the unpolished of these two dramatic gems, creates a different tone, preferring fast-moving, vulgar dialogue between a detective and a whore, but it explores the same issues as its companion piece. Former lovers Angela and Tom meet one night to discuss the Felix Epstein case, which Tom has been trying to crack for five years. Angela, he is convinced, has privileged information and holds the key to the innocent Felix's release from prison. But Angela will not tell.

The elusive quality of the truth rests not only in Tom's inability to extract information from Angela but also in Angela's schizophrenia: the former prostitute, now wife to a man who beats her, suffers from multiple personality syndrome. She moves quickly in and out of alternate identities, thinking at times she is Emily, an eight-year-old girl, Leontine, a house whore, and Renata, a respectable upper-class lady. Although Tom recognizes each of her masks, he is never sure when he is seeing the naked self, never certain whether to trust what Angela says. Yet his love for her prompts him to believe even what he cannot confirm: though he does not at first see the squad car that Angela insists is parked below, he trusts his feelings that she is telling the truth.

The play proceeds as a kind of detective story, with Tom O'Toole devoting his energies to freeing Felix from prison. On this occasion, Angela has summoned him to her apartment out of fear for her life, and she is prepared to tell him at least something of what she knows. The details implicate the city's political guardians in drugs and in conspiracy to conceal murder and suggestively implicate a network of criminals that could undermine the law enforcement of the country's major cities. But they also include confession of sexual involvement with at least three of the case's principals, not to mention the detective. Tom's key witness carries little credibility, only a biased ability to interpret, and more reason to lie than to reveal. Yet after five years of silence, she provides Tom with the clues he needs to pursue his cause. If reality is elusive in *Elegy for a Lady*, it is equally so here, where access to the truth depends on a schizophrenic.

Four years after the staging of *Two by A.M.* in New York, a second double-bill by Miller appeared at Lincoln Center's Mitzi E. Newhouse Theater. *Danger: Memory!*, a pair of one-acters entitled *I Can't Remember Anything* and *Clara*, were received by New Yorkers as mere footnotes to Miller's playwriting career. In England, by contrast, where the double bill was staged in 1988 under Jack Gold's direction, reviewers were sympathetic to the political force of both plays: Andrew Hislop, for example, judged them "powerful dramas subtly crafted by a master playwright."[29]

I Can't Remember Anything, a two-hander in which aging friends remember and forget their pasts, renews in its male character, Leo, Miller's irrepressible social voice. Recalling his commitment to Communist causes, Leo now arranges to donate his organs to Yale–New Haven Hospital as a final protest against the American mendacity that his companion, Leonora, somewhat perfunctorily deplores. Leo's reviews of the past are only occasionally encouraged by Leonora, who prefers to remember as little as possible, seeking amnesia in alcohol. The conversation that constitutes this brief, autumnal play moves through memories and present failings, settling always on the decay of American life. Though Leo energetically recalls the past and Leonora energetically represses it, the two share a sense of loss that gives this nostalgic piece its poignant flavor.

The companion piece, *Clara*, is also about memory, though on its surface it is a detective story. Following the decapitation of his daughter Clara, who has devoted her life to social causes, Albert Kroll tries to recall and to repress the patches of his and her past that might give Detective Lieutenant Fine a clue to the identity of the murderer. That reconstruction of personal history, however, might also provide an explanation for Clara's vulnerability and ultimately attach moral responsibility for the murder to her father. Thus, recovering details of Kroll's liberal activism becomes a painstaking process for the detective, a painful one for Kroll. Through three mental encounters with his young daughter, Kroll comes to understand that, as beneficiary of his social idealism, Clara has failed to proceed with caution in her work with rehabilitating criminals, one of whom is Fine's prime suspect. Kroll's acceptance of moral culpability might seem mere self-reproach, but it is of a piece with the Miller of *After the Fall* and *Incident at Vichy* and even with Miller's earliest work. For with Joe Keller, Kroll comes to understand that the tentacles of responsibility are everywhere.

The persistent question of moral responsibility had formed the basis as well of the 1980 television play, *Playing for Time*. Fania Fenelon, the principal character, survives the Auschwitz concentration camp through participating in an orchestra that entertains German officers. Fenelon "plays for time," learning to use her position to advantage, often alienating her women colleagues. Miller contrasts Fania with Marianne, who, weakened by fear, prostitutes herself to the Germans. Vanessa Redgrave and Jane Alexander both received Emmy Awards for their performances, the teleplay won an Outstanding Drama Special Award, and Miller earned an Emmy.

Indeed, even *The Golden Years*, the radio play written in 1939 and broadcast, for the first time, by BBC Radio 3 in 1987, stands as testimony to the continuity of Miller's thought. A treatment of the conflict between Montezuma and Cortes, the play alludes to a Europe in the face of Hitler and, in Bigsby's description, is also "a poetic debate over the fallibility of the human race whose evil cannot be expunged by its equal desire for transcendence."[30] And *The Man Who Had All the Luck* (1944), revived at the Bristol Old Vic in 1986 under the direction of Paul Unwin, stands as yet another example of Miller's insistent agenda: in that play, the tyranny of Hitler serves as backdrop to the comfort and success of David Beeves.

Miller's major literary achievement in the 1980s was *Timebends: A Life*, a 600-page memoir that is rich in detail but selective chronologically. Miller spends teasingly little space on his recent life in *Timebends*: few events from the 1980s – or from his long and happy marriage to Inge Morath – find their way into its pages. Instead, much of the book recalls Miller's early years in Brooklyn and the terrible but stimulating fifties, where his energies were invested in negotiating professional, personal, and political terrors and pleasures. These were the years of post-*Salesman* fame and recognition, of marriage to a "donating," suicidal woman who was America's sex queen; of Joe McCarthy, the blacklist, and the House Un-American Activities Committee.

When Miller recalls those years and his own behavior, one realizes how central they are to the moral essay of his life and understands the non-linear shape of the book. One might read this autobiography with index in hand, following each of the entries on, say, Marilyn Monroe or Willy Loman. But its richness resides in reading successively the seemingly random recollection of events that one man's memory and purpose have connected. Individually, each narrative presents a snapshot that expands and deepens as it yields to a sequential thought. Through its segues and its interruptions, *Timebends* enables Miller to linger over those moments that he sees as definitive in the making – and the presentation – of self. This self-portrait at seventy-two validates the dozens of dramatic characters that have emanated from the same moral center that presents itself here with dignity and insistence.

The publication of the Miller autobiography brought a flurry of largely laudatory reviews. The review excerpts assembled by Grove Press for its *New York Times* advertisement[31] is suggestive of the general response: Liz Smith's judgment was that "Miller raises autobiographical writing to the level of genius" (*Daily News*), Jay Parini expressed his belief that "*Timebends* may be among the great books of our day" (*USA Today*), Roger Shattuck characterized the book as "a work of genuine literary craftsmanship and social exploration" (*New York Times Book Review*, front page), and Peter Ackroyd declared, "This is autobiography as art" (*The Times* [London]).

Ackroyd's commentary on the book reflects the historical moment in the reception of Miller, whose work, at that point, was underappreciated in New York. Claiming that Miller's "quintessential American" identity was an illusion, Ackroyd offered the opinion that Miller

is quite out of place in the United States – not because of his erstwhile Marxism or the diagnoses of American ills in his drama, but because he is a man of traditional values in a nation with no real faith in tradition, a moralist in a society that avoids serious moral debate, a classical tragedian in a culture that relies upon the more obvious charms of show business. This is the autobiography of a playwright in the wrong country.[32]

American reviewers less ready to dissociate themselves from the elder statesman of the American theatre commented on the digressive, sometimes attenuated, and often disconnected narrative structure, with alternating expressions of annoyance and admiration; all recalled the courage that characterized Miller's political life and the often confused searching that characterized the personal. Christopher Lehmann-Haupt, writing for the *New York Times*, best expressed readers' simultaneous satisfaction with what Miller said and dissatisfaction with what he did not by looking to the future to resolve "the puzzles posed by this large and powerful auto-biography." Only then, he suggested, will we "finally know if this time was bent or whole."[33]

In 1981, Viking published *Collected Plays, Volume II*,[34] containing *The Misfits, After the Fall, Incident at Vichy, The Price, The Creation of the World and Other Business*, and *Playing for Time*. In the introduction to that volume, Miller takes exception to critics' typecasting him as a "realistic" playwright, noting that no play since *All My Sons* has followed a strict linear, cause-and-effect line. Indeed, no careful reader of Miller's work should need to be persuaded that the playwright's professional career is a record of theatrical experiment and risk. Typically, Miller's plays explore the landscape of the mind, with its diversions and its uncertainties, with as much precision as they do the social context that gives unity to the canon. In his treatment of both content and form, Miller has, in fact, been fascinated with the fluid line between the fictive and the real – and with how to treat that division in dramatic form. As the playwright rather modestly remarks, "The truth is that I have never been able to settle upon a single useful style."[35]

Whatever the measure of Miller's work, it is evident that critics in the US have not responded charitably to the newer plays. Gerald Weales's review of the earlier version of *The Archbishop's Ceiling*, performed at the Kennedy Center, might summarize their response: "I will settle for the playwright of earlier days. Come home, Arthur Miller, and rediscover the American Maya."[36] In England, by contrast, where Miller is widely honored, his reputation has grown. Noticing the difference and trying to explain it, Michael Billington, writing for *The Guardian*, offers the following cultural critique:

[Miller] retains to this day . . . the liberal's faith in human perfectibility. But, for all the quintessential American-ness of his themes, he has the European dramatist's belief in the need to ask daunting questions rather than provide comforting answers. In the end, that to me is what makes him such a fascinating writer: he remains totally anchored in American life while challenging almost all of the values and beliefs that make the society tick. He is the late twentieth century's most eloquent critic of the devalued American dream.[37]

The frequency with which Miller's plays were produced in the 1980s in New York, in regional theatres, in major European and Asian cities, and on university stages testifies to Miller's remarkably constant reputation and catholic appeal. The new plays of the 1980s – *The American Clock*, *The Archbishop's Ceiling*, and four one-acters – extend his career-long inquiry into the persistence of moral choice and deepen his increasingly sophisticated testing of the line between truth and fiction. Though undervalued in America, the plays of the 1980s secure Miller's place as elder statesman of English-language theatre.

NOTES

1 Arthur Miller, with Inge Morath, *In Russia* (New York: Viking Press, 1969); *In the Country* (New York: Viking Press, 1977); and *Chinese Encounters* (New York: Farrar, Straus, and Giroux, 1979). In addition, Morath's *Portraits* (New York: Aperture, 1986), a photographic tribute to artists and writers, contains an introduction by Miller.
2 Arthur Miller, "The American Theater," *Holiday* 17 (1955): 90; reprinted in Robert A. Martin (ed.), *The Theater Essays of Arthur Miller* (New York: Viking Press, 1978), p. 31.
3 *US News and World Report*, 11 January 1988, p. 55.
4 Frank Rich, "Stage: Miller's *Up From Paradise*," *The New York Times*, 16 October 1983.
5 Robert Brustein, "Arthur Miller's Mea Culpa," *New Republic* 150 (8 February 1964), p. 27.
6 Frank Rich, "Theater: *After the Fall* Is Revived," *The New York Times*, 5 October 1984.
7 Erika Munk, "Men's Business," *Village Voice*, 16 October 1984.
8 Clive Barnes, "Miller's Powerful *Bridge* Finally Makes It to Broadway," *The New York Post*, 4 February 1983.
9 John Simon, "The Miller's Stale," *New York*, 21 February 1983.
10 Frank Rich, "Theater: Richard Kiley in Miller's *All My Sons*," *The New York Times*, 23 April 1987, p. C22; Don Nelsen, "A Question of Deception," *The New York Daily News*, 21 April 1987, p. 1.
11 John J. O'Connor, "Arthur Miller's *All My Sons*, on 13," *The New York Times*, 19 January 1987, p. C16.
12 Jack Kroll, "Hoffman's Blazing Salesman," *Newsweek*, 9 April 1984.
13 Eileen Blumenthal, "Liked, but Not Well Liked," *Village Voice*, 10 April 1984.

14 Douglas Watt, *Death of a Salesman* Powerful," *The New York Daily News*, as reprinted in Easton (PA) *Express*, 13 May 1984.
15 Benedict Nightingale, "*Salesman* Demonstrates Its Enduring Strengths," *The New York Times*, 8 April 1984.
16 Arthur Miller, *Salesman in Beijing* (New York: Viking Press, 1984), p. 245.
17 *Ibid.*, pp. 131–32.
18 *Ibid.*, p. 49.
19 Clive Barnes, "This *Clock* Is a Bit Off," *The New York Post*, 21 November 1980.
20 Douglas Watt, "*American Clock* Ticks Away at Past," *The New York Daily News*, 21 November 1980.
21 Frank Rich, "Play: Miller's *American Clock*," *The New York Times*, 21 November 1980.
22 Jack Kroll, "After the Fall," *Newsweek*, 1 December 1980.
23 Arthur Miller, Introduction to *The Archbishop's Ceiling and The American Clock* (New York: Grove Press, 1989), p. xiv.
24 See Christopher Bigsby, *File on Miller* (London: Methuen, 1987), p. 51. Billington was responding to the revised version. In the original play, performed at the Kennedy Center, Washington, DC, in 1977, Sigmund is the protagonist, his letter to the United Nations the focus of attention; Adrian is excused from sexual involvement with Maya; and there is a critic present named Martin. A number of plot details also changed in the published version.
25 Frank Rich, "Stage: 2 By Arthur Miller," *The New York Times*, 10 November 1982.
26 Arthur Miller, "Author's Note," in *Two-Way Mirror: A Double Bill* (London: Methuen, 1984).
27 Arthur Miller, *Elegy for a Lady*, in *Two-Way Mirror: A Double Bill*, p. 20.
28 *Ibid.*, p. 21.
29 Andrew Hislop, "The Experience of History," *TLS*, 15–21 April 1988, p. 424.
30 See Bigsby, *File on Miller*, p. 12.
31 *The New York Times*, 9 December 1987, p. C31.
32 Peter Ackroyd, "A Serious Man of Plays," *The Times* (London), 5 November 1987, books section, p. 1.
33 Christopher Lehmann-Haupt, "Books of the Times," *The New York Times*, 2 November 1987, p. C22.
34 Arthur Miller, *Collected Plays, Volume II* (New York: Viking Press, 1981; London: Secker and Warburg, 1981).
35 *Ibid.*, p. 2.
36 Gerald Weales, "Come Home to Maya: The Stage," *Commonweal*, 8 July 1977, p. 432. The reference to Maya connects with Weales's comment that "*maya* means the power to create illusions."
37 See Christopher Bigsby (ed.), *Arthur Miller and Company* (London: Methuen, 1990), p. 189.

II

CHRISTOPHER BIGSBY

Miller in the nineties

In 1990 Arthur Miller was seventy-five years old. He might have been forgiven for settling into a cosy retirement. Henrik Ibsen wrote his last play at seventy-one while Samuel Beckett produced little after he was sixty. His public career had already lasted forty-six years, longer than those of Chekhov, Strindberg, Brecht, O'Neill, or Williams. Yet the 1990s proved his most prolific period since the 1960s. By the middle of the decade he had written three new plays, a film script for *The Crucible*, which began shooting in late 1995, and a novella published as *Homely Girl*, in the United States, and *Plain Girl*, in the United Kingdom. He continued to monitor the political situation, writing articles to *The New York Times*, supporting censored and imprisoned writers and traveling widely. He was, in other words, what he had been for the previous five decades, an active participant in theatrical, political, and social life.

He began the decade with a new play. In 1991 he opened *The Ride Down Mount Morgan* in London, a choice in part determined by the director's availability but in part by a deepening despair over Broadway's decline and in particular the determining power of money, whether that related to production costs or the unwillingness of actors to desert Hollywood for New York.

Nor were the circumstances of production entirely remote from the concerns of a play which was in part a response to what Miller saw as the collapse of values in 1980s America, a sense that self-interest and self-concern had triumphed over social responsibility. *The Ride Down Mount Morgan*, comic, farcical, but, he insisted, "riding all the time over a tragic tide,"[1] like so many of his other plays was a portrait of his times.

The Ride Down Mount Morgan concerns a man, Lyman Felt, who crashes in a snow storm while driving down a mountainside. Two women rush to his hospital bedside, both believing themselves to be his wife. In fact he has been bigamously married for nine years, using the same name but maintaining two quite distinct personalities, as though testing the nature of

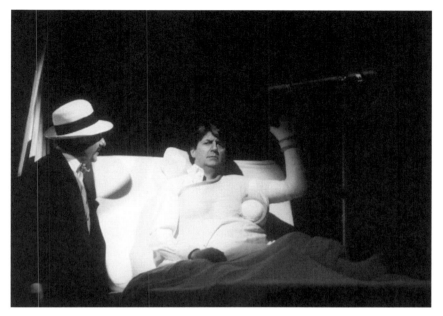

Figure 6 Tom Conti and Harry Landis in the first production of *The Ride Down Mount Morgan*, Wyndham's Theatre, London, 1991.

identity. Set largely in a hospital ward, the play nonetheless moves in time and space as Lyman's memory and fantasy conjure scenes from the past or generate scenarios in the present.

In his twenties Lyman Felt had been a writer before changing direction and establishing an immensely successful and socially responsible insurance company. There came a moment, however, when he ceased to believe in the logic of his life and began to feel that it was possible for him to have everything he wanted, in emotional and sexual terms. Suddenly convinced that there is no transcendent purpose and no ultimate moral sanction he comes to believe that everything is possible in a society which has elevated self-interest over social concern. An affair is thus transformed into a bigamous marriage, a furtive liaison into what seem to him to be two relationships equally fulfilling to all concerned. Such a decision, he feels, is both more honest and satisfying, for although it involves deceit of others it becomes an authentic act in so far as it purges him of guilt and his marriages of the banality of habit. Now he feels he can commit himself to both women and thus remove barriers which had previously damaged his relationships. Free of guilt he lives on an adrenaline high which is itself a denial of the stasis which he fears, a stasis which is itself, perhaps, a reminder of mortality. But more recently the purpose of such an existence seems less clear to him and it is possible that the "accident" may itself have been contrived in order to provoke the confrontation he believes himself to fear. As he discovers in his ride down Mount Morgan, the removal of barriers may lead to disaster.

There are echoes of his early plays. The two sides of Lyman's character, poetic and materialist, idealistic and pragmatic, reflect a similar division between the brothers in *Death of a Salesman* and *The Price*, contained here within a single personality. And as in those plays this ambivalence reflects contending interpretations of the American experience, forged, as it was, out of a blend of spiritual need and material endeavor. The concern with betrayal, meanwhile, has been a virtual leitmotif of his work. As Lyman observes, "A man can be faithful to himself or to other people – but not to both. At least not happily. We all know this, but it's immoral to admit it – the first law of life is betrayal; why else did those Rabbis pick Cain and Abel to open the Bible? . . . We're all ego . . . ego plus an occasional prayer."[2]

"The point of the exercise," Miller has said, "is to investigate some of the qualities and meanings of truthfulness and deception." Beyond that, however, it is to explore the nature of ethical choice in a world from which the sanction of religion and ideology have been withdrawn at a time when the liberal consensus has lost all substance.

Lyman no longer believes, as once he did, that there is a moral spine to experience. He recalls the entirely arbitrary circumstances of his first encounter with his wife, turning, as it did, on mere chance, and finds that he can no longer recognize "the moral purpose of the universe" (*Mount Morgan*, p. 22). Beyond that he cannot sustain the notion of an integral self: "a man is a fourteen-room house – in the bedroom he's asleep with his intelligent wife, in the living room he's rolling around with some bareass girl, in the library he's paying his taxes, in the yard he's raising tomatoes, and in the cellar he's making a bomb to blow it all up" (*Mount Morgan*, p. 22). In the circumstances there seems to be no coherent self, no moral core to identity, and hence no purpose in restraint. The only arbiter is an imperial self whose presumptive rights go unchallenged by faith or conviction. Suddenly he feels free to contradict himself. The Lyman married to Theo is afraid of flying; the Lyman married to Leah is a pilot. One fears speed; the other embraces it. Character is no longer a given, a defining trap, simply a field of possibility. But in a relativistic world what values are there? What is the rock on which he, or the society which he represents, can stand? What, except the desires of the individual?

For Miller, Lyman is

a man of high integrity but no values . . . a very typical figure in our world now . . . It is a paradox. He is intent on not suppressing his instinctual life, on living fully in every way possible. There is his integrity. He will confront the worst about himself and then proceed from there . . . He manages to convince himself, and I believe some part of the audience, that there is a higher value than other people and that value is the psychic survival of the individual. That is the dilemma. The play has no solution to it . . . But it is laid out in front of us.

The issues are not time-bound but there is little doubt that Miller was responding to his sense of the direction in which America was moving in the 1970s and 1980s. A reference to Nixon's election was replaced by one to Reagan's. Lyman is, Miller insists, "the quintessential Eighties Man, the man who has everything, but there's no end to his appetite."

Lyman, however, is not a simple hedonist. The real force which motivates him, which sends him on his frantic accumulation of experience, is a fear of death. The play takes place when he is one year short of the age at which his father had died, a father who appears in the play carrying a length of black cloth, like a shroud, with which he tries to cover his son. The fact of death is a reminder that meaning is provisional and his own efforts absurd. Material success is insufficient. Like Camus's Caligula he presses possibility to extremes, trying to find meaning on the edge. An incident on safari in Africa convinces him that he can confront his self-doubts and purge his sense of guilt. It is a false epiphany, a self-justifying revelation which he believes absolves him of responsibility for his life, confusing, as he does, guilt with responsibility, the latter having been rendered redundant by the fact of mortality and the collapse of communal values. For Lyman the world becomes no more than a blur. Only his personal needs and satisfactions remain in sharp focus.

Lyman's character changes with his wives. In that sense he reflects back to them their own characters. The irony is that he becomes lost, no more than a series of reflections. The play ends with a moment of simplicity as his nurse recalls a banal but curiously affecting moment with her family. When Miller speaks of Lyman "falling into his life" it would seem to be this that he is referring to.

Structurally, the play is reminiscent of *After the Fall*. A man, at a moment of crisis, summons the past in an attempt to understand and confront himself. Past and present are refracted through the sensibility of the protagonist. Once again we are inside the head of a central character whose memories, fantasies, and actions become the substance of the drama. This, incidentally, is a justification for women characters who never become much more than aspects of his needs and fears. What might otherwise seem reductive portraits thus stand as further evidence of the state of mind of a man for whom the world exists to serve the self.

The Ride Down Mount Morgan presents director and actors with problems. The situation is close to farce: the tone is for the most part comic. Yet there is an underlying concern with moral value. It is a delicate balancing act. Much the same could be said of the central character. Lyman is something more than the easy charm he exudes or the detachment which his role as commentator/participant implies. He has convinced himself of his own probity and of the genuine nature of his feelings toward both his wives. Tom Conti, who played the part in the first production, never quite managed this, opting for simple charm, a decision which lowered the stakes in a play which offers more than the wry irony he settled for. More successful were the actresses who did find a style which enabled them to balance fantasy and reality, although, since they are never allowed autonomy, we are not permitted to make a judgment about their characters and the degree to which they provoke or are complicit in Lyman's actions.

For Miller, the play is

> an attempt to investigate the immense contradictions of the human animal. It is also an attempt to look at man's limitless capacity for self-deception and for integrity. This character is terrible, he is ghastly, but he does create, for example, a very socially responsible corporation. He works himself up from nothing to being chief executive of an immense insurance company, which has very progressive, liberal, policies towards minorities. He has a lot of terrific qualities. He has also got an immense appetite for life, for women, for everything. So he is a kind of Faustian character and, like our civilization, he is capable of enormous construction and destruction. I have just let it fall as it is. The play does not condemn him particularly; it simply leaves him standing to one side of himself, trying to find himself.

Lyman's appetite for life, his disregard for moral constraints, is the other side of his success as a businessman. However, the very act of self-analysis which his "accident" precipitates suggests the survival of that former self, the writer. His ability literally to step out of himself (the plaster cast in which he is encased and which restrains him on his hospital bed is so contrived that the actor can slip out of it and appear to stand beside himself) is evidence that his life is not unexamined. In speaking of *The Price*, in which one brother appears to be ruthless and the other a self-sacrificing idealist (a contrast more apparent than real), Miller remarked that any society needs a combination of such qualities if it is to survive. The same seems true here. It is not that Lyman's bigamy stands justified, or that

Figure 7 Margot Leicester and Helen Burns in the first production of *The Last Yankee*,
The Young Vic, London, 1993.

Miller has developed a liking for Faust, but that Lyman's wayward energy, his testing of boundaries, however misdirected, reveals one end of the human spectrum, the other end of which is represented either by the poet or by the stolid but affecting humanity of the nurse. Miller's remark that his only hope "is to end up with the right regrets," suggests the extent to which Lyman does, perhaps, learn from his plunge down a mountainside into his own disordered self.

Another moral education lies at the heart of his second 1990s play, *The Last Yankee*, in which two marriages are each placed under strain by the differing needs and perceptions of those who once thought they shared so much. Spaces have opened up and into these spaces have spilled anxieties, suspicions, and perhaps even contempt. Accusation, guilt, self-doubt have clogged the arteries of affection. Miller has said that marriage is a case of mutual forgiveness, and the need and desire for that is strong here, but it does battle with other instincts: those for self-justification and self-preservation. These are characters who cannot get the taste of failure out of their mouths while far from certain as to why it seems so significant. Some contract seems to have been broken, some common agreement as to what binds individual to individual and each to his or her society.

The Last Yankee is set in a state mental hospital where three women are suffering from clinical depression. One, Patricia, is the wife of Leroy Hamilton, a carpenter she accuses of lacking those qualities required to survive in a competitive world. A second, Karen, is almost a mirror image. Her husband, Mr. Frick, is a model of success, a driven man whose businesses dominate the local economy. Both women seem to have been broken by the failure of experience to match their needs and aspirations. The third woman remains motionless on a bed, unnamed and unnoticed. The women are in recoil from life, disappointed and bewildered. Their husbands wait, one patiently, the other not, anxious that their wives should be returned to a normality which they have themselves not questioned.

Patricia, like her brothers, has absorbed what F. Scott Fitzgerald, in *Tender is the Night*, called the lies told to children at the doors of log cabins. A family of immigrants, they believed in the inevitability and necessity of success and though success comes their way – one wins the All New England Golf Tournament, the other a silver medal in the Olympic Games for pole vault – it falls short of what they expect. The brothers commit suicide. Patricia, too, sees life as a competition in which her husband refuses to participate. The keynote of her life is disappointment, a word which echoes in the text and which becomes both a symptom for and an explanation of the depression from which she and so many others suffer. She had won the county beauty pageant when she was nineteen. The rest of her life seems an anticlimax. Her retreat to the mental hospital is her equivalent of her brothers' suicides.

Patricia is drawn to religion as a solution to her sense of despair, albeit a vaguely focused and contaminated religion. Indeed that contamination underscores the material dimension of America's spiritual ideal. The minister she admires boasts of the Pontiac Grand Am given to him by his parishioners, an echo of Puritanism's links with capitalism. Indeed this apparently slight play manages to offer itself as a metaphor of American experience, an image of that dream of perfection and its inevitable failure.

Behind the clinical depression from which Patricia and the other women suffer is that other Depression which haunts Miller's plays, for what they see in their own apparent decline, their failure to realize the promises which America made, is the collapse of a dream which is intimately connected with their sense of themselves. As Miller has said, speaking of *The Last Yankee*, "We live in fear of falling, fear of losing status. At the present moment it is the first generation doing worse than their parents." We are not that far from the world of *Death of a Salesman*, in which Willy Loman is obsessed with failure because his life, and those of his sons, fails to match the mythical success which he believes to be the sole justification for existence. His real failure, and Patricia's, is more fundamental. It is a failure to acknowledge and to offer love, a failure to see that lives are justified and identity affirmed not by material success, by competitive ruthlessness or personal charm, but by exhibiting a commitment to others and to the self built out of something more substantial than mere appearance. Yet what is true of Willy Loman, and here of Patricia, is also true of Frick, who is successful in all ways except those which really matter. Like Willy he has been so concerned to chase the chimera of success that he has remained blind not only to the needs of others but to a love which might have redeemed him from his relentless pursuit of meaning. He *is* Frick's lumber supplies. He is defined by what he owns.

Leroy, the last Yankee, by contrast, Miller explains, "is somebody who has stepped off the train. He is not running after the brass ring any more. His wife is on that train. She can't see happiness unless it is accompanied by economic success . . . He does not have an unearned income. She feels he has disserved himself and her by failing in that respect." Leroy is a descendent of Alexander Hamilton who, despite his role in developing the Constitution, is recalled for his suspicion of the "common people" and his defense of those with position and money. It is not Frick alone who is struck by the irony. Leroy is a carpenter, a craftsman, who lacks the aggressive qualities and competitive instincts of a society on the make. He is Biff Loman forty years on. And yet he, too, has his genuine human failures. After twenty years he still cannot grasp the nature of his wife's illness nor recognize the legitimacy of her claim that his other-worldliness has a price. He is also caught in his own contradictions. While urging her to "trust" he is himself instinctively distrustful of others. He is as wary of other people and as self-contained, in his own way, as Frick. He claims an unconcern for his family heritage and bafflement that he should be expected to behave in accord with his family ancestry, only immediately to invoke the same expectation of a fellow workman who he suspects of stealing his tools. Patricia may be the one consigned to a hospital but he is not without his insecurities and flaws.

This irony is even more apparent in the case of Frick who has plainly driven his wife to despair. Self-absorbed and intolerant, he is baffled by his wife's condition because he barely registers her existence. And yet, beneath the casual bigotry which he displays and the impatience and embarrass-ment which he feels at his wife's bizarre behavior, there is a residual commitment.

The Last Yankee is more concerned with redemption than despair, though the hope is tentative. We are, in effect, offered three possibilities. Patricia leaves the institution and the implication is that some healing process has taken place. In some ways her twenty-year sleep of the spirit is an echo of Rip Van Winkle's twenty-year sleep in the New England hills. She wakes at the end to discover that she may have misread experience, that the world may not be as she saw it and that America's promises may have been more subtle than she supposed. Karen does not leave. Her fate is in the balance. There is, however, a third possibility. A patient lies catatonic throughout the play, never really stirring, and, indeed, the play ends not with the departure of Leroy and Patricia but with "The PATIENT on the bed [who] remains motionless. A stillness envelops the whole stage, immobility seems eternal. End."[3] My experience of watching the play is that audiences want the play to end with the exit of Patricia and Leroy. Unsurprisingly, they applaud their exit and I have seen the lighting faded at that moment. If the stage directions are followed, however, the effect is very different, indeed disturbingly so. The silence switches attention from those who leave to the one who remains. The play ends not with movement but stasis.

At its heart, though, is a conviction which was equally at the centre of *After the Fall*. As Leroy says to Patricia: "We are in this world and you're going to have to find some way to love it!" (*The Last Yankee*, p. 32). She has to stop becoming in order to be. Like Maggie, in *After the Fall*, she has to realize that she is holding her life in her own hands and cease to live provisionally. Willy Loman had felt temporary because he was never content to accept what he was. Patricia's task is to accept both herself and her husband for what they are. *The Last Yankee* is a plea not for resignation but acceptance.

America was born out of a belief in perfection. It was a new start for mankind. Here error would be purged and a new Jerusalem built. It follows that the burden of a failed utopia falls on those who feel they have not realized its promise. To fail here is to acknowledge some deep flaw in the self, for responsibility cannot lie with a society whose promise of happiness and possibility are its reason for being. Here a sense of failure reaches right down into the self, threatening to fracture it along the fault lines of human imperfection. And where the individual feels at odds with national myths embraced as private truths a kind of madness wells up, the psyche threatening to shatter as you would split a log for the fire. So, Willy Loman (*Death of a Salesman*), Eddie Carbone (*A View from the Bridge*), Maggie (*After the Fall*), Angela (*Some Kind of Love Story*), and now Patricia and Karen in *The Last Yankee*, tread a boundary line not so much between sanity and insanity as between two different worlds, that of myth and that of reality, that of desire and that of fact.

All four characters in *The Last Yankee* have a sense of insufficiency, of disappointment. The world is not what they took it for nor they what they might have been. Like so many Miller characters before them they know that something is wrong, that the spine of their lives has, indeed, been damaged. Something has been lost. A faith has been breached. They suspect that they have been betrayed or that they are themselves guilty of betrayal. Yet this is not a play about defeat. There is still a dance to be danced. If there are indeed those overwhelmed by the pressures of private and public experience there are also those who may find a way of embracing those experiences.

In the 1930s F. Scott Fitzgerald wrote an essay called "The Crack Up." In it he drew a parallel between the psychological and emotional collapse of an individual and that of the country which, as the Depression deepened, seemed to have lost all sense of meaning. Its old myths no longer seemed operative. The promises contained in its social contract, which had offered happiness along with material well-being, had been broken. The task which lay ahead was the reconstruction of the self and the reinvention of a nation. Miller has spoken of that same period, and of our own times which echo it, in much the same terms, insisting on the need to identify and embrace those fundamental truths which exist to one side of the American dream. A fellow New Englander, Henry David Thoreau, once recalled standing barefoot in a pond and wiggling his toes down through the mud to the granite beneath. It was an image of the struggle to discover those bedrock realities on which a life may be built. Miller's plays have had that concern. *The Last Yankee* is no exception and here, as earlier, those realities have to do not with public reputations, material possessions, or social roles, nor even with their willful refusal, but with the urgent need to restore that charity which is perhaps the key to the meaning which his characters seek.

Fitzgerald once wrote in his notebook that he spoke with the authority of failure and Ernest Hemingway with the authority of success and that, as a result, they could never sit across the same table again. The task of the characters in *The Last Yankee* is not merely to sit across the table from one another but also to acknowledge the inadequacy of those words which can only divide and those values and myths which can only demean.

The Last Yankee is a chamber piece, a play for four voices. It is a kind of dance, a sad gavotte in which, for much of the time, the characters circle one another, maintaining their distance, unsure that they can dance to the same tune. There is, however, another tune, another dance. Karen's tentative and pathetic tap dance is her first attempt to recover pride, while Patricia and Leroy move together again, as they had before, in an attempt to reconstitute the rhythm of their lives, a rhythm broken by destructive myths and ambitions at odds with their needs.

That theme, of broken relationships and a damaged society, also proved central to his next work, a play which looked back in time but which bore directly on a disturbing present.

In November 1938, a Polish Jew, Hershel Grynaspen, assassinated the third secretary of the German Embassy in Paris. The Nazi government used this as an excuse for an explosion of violence against Jews in which synagogues, houses, and stores were destroyed and individuals attacked. This was Kristallnacht. It was a clear indication of what was to follow. The world watched and the world did nothing.

In 1939 Arthur Miller sat down and began *The Golden Years*, a play in which he tried to understand the paralyzing, mesmeric effect of such violence. The play was lost for decades, only resurfacing and receiving its first performance in 1987. Perhaps it stirred a memory, for another image had stayed with him from that time.

Fifty years ago he heard of a woman who had suddenly lost the use of her legs. The doctors could find no physical reason for this nor could they propose any treatment which would cure her condition. It was an incident and an image which fascinated him and on several occasions he considered using it but "couldn't find a way in." One other memory accompanied it. The woman's husband always dressed in black, "as if he were in mourning for his life." Fifty years on the two images came together in a play which, in an early form, was to have been called *The Man in Black*.

Broken Glass is set in Brooklyn, late in November 1938, a few days after Kristallnacht. America itself, still in the grip of the Depression, and, in Miller's words, "in deep spiritual disorganization," scarcely seems to absorb the news. Sylvia Gellburg, however, does and loses the use of her legs, though whether because of that or something else remains unclear, at least for the present. The fact is that she has other problems which center on her husband, a successful businessman who feels ambiguously about his Jewish identity and deeply insecure about his sexuality.

Sylvia's fate is in the hands of a doctor, an idealist who is as fallible as most idealists. What is at stake, however, is not just Sylvia's health but the survival of all the play's characters as they struggle to make sense of the radical shifts which seem to be occurring in private and public life.

Is it possible that someone should be physically affected by outside events? Since writing the play Miller himself has stumbled on the fact that there was indeed an unusual amount of physical paralysis among Jews in America while recent evidence points to a high incidence of hysterical blindness among Cambodian women following the horrors perpetrated by the Khmer Rouge in Cambodia. But *Broken Glass* is not docu-drama and Miller does not write thesis plays. Instead he offers an image of that paralysis of the spirit which is a fact of personal lives as much as of

Figure 8 Arthur Miller in rehearsal with Margot Leicester and Henry Goodman for *Broken Glass*, the Royal National Theatre, 1994.

national policy. The characters in this play wrestle above all with their own private demons. Faced with painful truths they have chosen denial but there comes a moment when protective strategy becomes the source of disabling pain.

The Gellburgs live at a time when prejudice is not only a product of Europe. For Miller, "America was dense with anti-Semitism. Especially New York." They live at a time, too, when the Depression offers a reminder of the fragility of a social world which can collapse overnight. Suddenly civility, moral assurance, myths of progress and individual integrity, seem deeply compromised. In his words "the social contract was being torn up in America while in Europe the fascists were destroying the underlying web of obligations that keep society in place." When the ground moves beneath your feet no wonder the equilibrium is profoundly disturbed. And what is true on a public level is no less true on a private one.

Phillip absorbs the contempt he feels around him, measuring himself by the standards of others. His success is real enough, even if it is built on a fact which he would rather not acknowledge, namely that his company, perhaps ironically entitled Guarantee and Trust, assigns him the function of dispossessing people of their property and hence their hopes. But that success is drained of meaning when his private life is infected with an irony which is all but unbearable. Gellburg loves his wife, but what can that mean when love cannot express itself and when, one day, it comes up against a sudden mystery which threatens his sense of reality?

His wife, Sylvia, who has settled for half and accommodated to disappointment, can no longer bear living a routine existence. Private and public events push her to a point of crisis. Her one hope now seems to lie with a doctor, Harry Hyman, who is described by Miller as a "scientific idealist." His idealism consists of his commitment to the community where he lives and to the sustaining of life rather than mere existence. But he himself has an appetite for life which makes him vulnerable to his own passions even as it draws others to him. In the past lie adulterous affairs which make his wife ever watchful for new signs of betrayal. Yet he can captivate her as easily as his female patients by the very vitality which he exudes and by his ability to conjure fictions, dreams, out of the air.

He is committed to curing Sylvia but she represents danger to him as he represents hope to her. Is it possible for him to rescue her from the quicksand without sinking himself? And what is her husband to think as he watches another man reach out a hand to the woman he loves but who he is seemingly incapable of saving? A good deal more than glass is broken in this play. Society is at odds with itself; individual relationships are fractured. In Miller's words, *Broken Glass* is concerned with "a public concern and a private neurosis." The task is "to find that juncture where they actually meet." On one level they meet in the mind of a woman shocked into paralysis. To understand the cause of her distress may thus be to understand, too, something of that greater failure of charity, of love, which it shadows.

These days marriages are disposable. Pay some money and they go away. Miller's plays have always been based on a simple question: "what happens when you can't walk away?" In the 1930s the options were fewer. Love could shrivel and die or be damaged, then, just as fast as today but a neat interment seemed more difficult to accomplish. Instead, people put their lives on hold and found a way to get by. Resignation was seen as a virtue. But resignation kills as surely on a personal level as, we were to learn, in the 1930s, it did on a political one.

Some knew that better than others. To be Jewish was to know that the sky could fall in. As Miller has remarked, for him, as a Jew, the world can end. This, however, is no longer privileged information. You do not have to listen particularly attentively to hear the sound of stars hitting the gutter, of glass shattering on the sidewalk, in Sarajevo or the Sudan. Besides, violence, betrayals, a sudden withdrawal of love and its replacement with indifference, are hardly the exclusive preserve of social life. They are the small change of personal experience. They are what destroy the spirit. *Broken Glass* is thus a play which simultaneously explores the sometimes dangerous and sometimes redeeming compromises of personal life and the wider issues which make the world we inhabit such a terrifying and sometimes such a hopeful place.

Is it possible, though, that there is a further connection here, namely that between ourselves and those who so denied their humanity in the 1930s and 1940s and do so again in the ethnic conflicts of the 1990s? Miller's answer is clear: "In each of us, whether recognized or not, is that same bloody ethnic nationalism. This is not coming from the moon. This is coming from us. And we have not come close to even confronting this thing. All the patriotism and the ethnic nationalism is knocking on the door and it's as dangerous as it ever was." Our bewildered inaction in the face of this is as lethal now as it was once before. Speaking in 1995, when war was still being waged in the former Yugoslavia, he insisted that, "it is the paralysis which could destroy the world . . . The idea of being paralyzed in the face of forces we don't understand is the mark of our times, perhaps of all times. Yugoslavia is the ultimate paralysis." Yet, being Miller, he is not willing to give up. The characters in *Broken Glass* are "trying to see their way out of the tomb." You could say the same of Miller's play. As he has observed, "I like to think it is art that gives us a glimpse of the situation." It may be that "all art can do is offer a counter image. It can't stop neo-Nazis," but "theatre can reach out to touch people and bring them together. So long as you have theatre you have a society."

It would be comfortable if *Broken Glass* could be contained by its historical moment, a time capsule to be opened so that we can for a moment breathe the dank air of another time, wonder at the passions of another age. It would be comfortable, but untrue. Not merely do those joined by love still discover what strangers they can become, but, around the world, what we have taken to be the solid foundations of civilization continue to crack and crumble. An event which shook Miller in 1937 was the bombing, by the Fascists, of the Spanish town of Guernica. In 1994, people in Sarajevo were blown apart by gunners on a hillside for no better reason than that they could be. As Miller said, even as rehearsals for his play were underway: "they are sitting there blowing the hell out of that town and we're all sitting here saying 'tch! tch! isn't that terrible.' They blew up sixteen children and did you see anybody pause on his way to lunch? That's what this play's about." That, and much more.

To Miller we are not will-less observers of our own lives nor is history anything but a construction of men and women who either abdicate or accept their responsibility. The greatest betrayal lies in the conviction that we are powerless to intervene in our own fate. That moral and political paralysis, he insists, "could destroy the world."

The 1990s were only four years old when *Broken Glass* was staged and already Arthur Miller had produced three new plays. Today, at the age of eighty-two he is as prolific, as witty, and profound as at any time in his career. He continues to deal not in what he once disparagingly called "sidewalk realism" but in metaphor. *Broken Glass* is one such example. Like all metaphors it gains its power from the fact that it is rooted in the real, but its resonance from the proliferating meanings which echo in the mind long after the final light has faded in the theatre.

If there is a central theme to Arthur Miller's work it is a concern for what he has called a "common longing for meaning." His characters are all caught at moments in their lives when what they fear above everything is that there shall have been no purpose to their existence. If they look to the past, as they do in virtually everything he has written, it is because they are searching for some structure of meaning, a key to random experiences and an explanation for a profound sense of failure, anxiety, and betrayal. If he is thought of as a social playwright, and he is patently that, his sense that all public issues are rooted in a fallible human nature is the basis for plays which never sacrifice character to idea.

In *The Ride Down Mount Morgan*, *The Last Yankee* and, now, *Broken Glass* he has chosen to address, with humor and passion, the state of society and the nature of human values. Who else is there, in this final decade of the millennium, who could say as much? In any other profession Miller would have retired long since. It is not going to happen. As he himself has said: "I couldn't retire. It would be like cutting my heart out. Why would I do that?"

NOTES

1 Arthur Miller in interview with the author. Subsequent quotations are from this interview unless otherwise indicated.
2 Arthur Miller, *The Ride Down Mount Morgan* (London: Warner Chappell Plays, 1995), pp. 61–62.
3 Arthur Miller, *The Last Yankee* (London: Methuen Drama, 1993), p. 38.

12

R. BARTON PALMER

Arthur Miller and the cinema

Since his first Broadway success, commercial filmmakers have shown great interest in the works, especially the plays, of Arthur Miller. An impressive number of cinematic versions, intended for both theatrical and televisual release, have been produced. As I write this piece, a second film of *The Crucible*, for which the playwright himself wrote the screenplay, is in production, indicating the lasting appeal, especially of his early plays, to filmmakers. Such enthusiasm is neither surprising nor exceptional. Driven by a need for quality material with proven popularity, the cinema is eager to produce screen versions of the writings of successful authors, a group of which Miller is one of the most distinguished current members.

The resulting films pose a difficult, if interesting problem for the critic. On the one hand, they belong indirectly to the *oeuvre* of the original author; they are versions of his works and thus merit attention in a book such as the present one. On the other, the films of Miller's works belong primarily to another medium that has reproduced and even reconstructed them for its own purposes. As a result, the connection of the film to its source is sometimes unimportant for either the filmmaker or his spectators. Not that Miller himself would be especially eager in every case to claim these films as his own. If, in his maturity, he has become interested in writing for the screen, during his early career he remained, with the notable exception of *The Misfits*, rather indifferent to what Hollywood or other filmmakers made from his work.

Arthur Miller and Hollywood

This indifference explains, but only in part, the relatively insignificant contribution of Miller to the cinema during the years of his greatest Broadway successes. In this chapter we will look to cinema, especially Hollywood history, for a more complete understanding of why one of the postwar era's most important playwrights had so little influence on postwar filmmaking.

Exploiting a trend that began in earnest during the war, Hollywood in the fifties often turned to Broadway plays as source material. Faced with continuing financial difficulties, producers hoped to repeat the commercial and critical success of such earlier films as *The Little Foxes* (William Wyler, 1941) and *Watch on the Rhine* (Herman Shumlin, 1943), both based on Broadway hits by Lillian Hellman (full reference to film titles, with the US version either first or second [in the case of foreign language productions], will be followed by the director's name and year of release in the country of origin). Why, then, did Arthur Miller, arguably the greatest postwar playwright, enjoy so little success in the domestic cinema? Why were the plays of Tennessee Williams, for example, much more often produced by Hollywood – and usually with greater critical acclaim and more financial profit? Why was one of Miller's most praised and admired works – *The Crucible* – ignored by Hollywood but filmed in France? Why was even this film a critical and commercial failure? Also produced in France (where it had achieved phenomenal popularity on the stage), *A View from the Bridge* was only a marginal success, despite the stewardship of a director – Sidney Lumet – who seemed ideal for the project. Why? Even *The Misfits*, Miller's only significant foray into the Hollywood entertainment cinema, made in close collaboration with both a director sympathetic to his sensibilities and a leading lady (Marilyn Monroe, then Mrs. Miller) close to his heart, did disappointingly at the box office, garnered largely negative reviews, and subsequently has been ignored by film scholars.

The answer to all these questions is not that Miller's sophisticated literary and dramatic approaches made his plays unsuitable for screen production. Hollywood in the fifties, there is no doubt, was interested in and capable of transforming even serious Broadway plays into screen hits. Miller's greatest triumphs were achieved on Broadway during an era in cinematic history when authors like Tennessee Williams and William Inge furnished the texts for films that were among the most acclaimed and financially successful: *A Streetcar Named Desire* (Elia Kazan, 1951), *Baby Doll* (Elia Kazan, 1956), *Cat on a Hot Tin Roof* (Richard Brooks, 1958), *Picnic* (Joshua Logan, 1955), and *Bus Stop* (Joshua Logan, 1956), to name only a few of the most obvious examples. More than any other decade of Hollywood history, the fifties witnessed an outpouring of successful theatrical adaptations, many based on the more literary Broadway successes that, with their "adult" materials, would have never made it to the screen in earlier periods because of the puritanical Production Code, now challenged by daring directors and producers. The evolution of the adult film during the period is heavily influenced by Broadway; in fact, the screen version of *Streetcar* begins the trend, which is then extended by many notable stage-based productions, such as *The Children's Hour* (William Wyler, 1961, with Lillian Hellman adapting her own play) and *A Hatful of Rain* (Fred Zinnemann, 1957, with Alfred Hayes co-adapting his own play).

Fifties Hollywood cinema is also, if not dominated, at least heavily populated by the brighter creative lights of Broadway; the result was, if only in part, an impressive literary cinema. Of the first five films cited above, four were directed by men who built a career in the two media, who reached the height of their profession, and went further, precisely because they worked in Hollywood and on Broadway. *Picnic*'s production was designed by Jo Mielziner, whose ingenious stagecraft and fruitful collaboration with Elia Kazan on both Williams and Miller projects contributed much to the innovative and effective look of the fifties American stage. The only non-Broadway director of the first group, Richard Brooks, more or less specialized in adapting prestigious literary properties; he counts among his screen credits versions of works by Tennessee Williams, Fyodor Dostoevsky, Joseph Conrad, Truman Capote, and Sinclair Lewis. As the last two films mentioned above show, even old-time Hollywood professionals like William Wyler and Fred Zinnemann often turned to the American stage for material.

In short, Hollywood at this time was eager to produce screen versions of Broadway plays and would borrow, as appropriate, the creative work force with the knowledge and expertise to proceed in a sophisticated fashion with them. Thus Miller's minimal success with commercial filmmaking cannot be explained by any supposed incompatibility between the theatre and cinema of the era. Nor, as we shall see, is it the case that Miller's works for the most part were unsuited to the cinema, either because of their formal features or themes.

The remainder of this chapter will develop explanations for Miller's relative lack of success with *All My Sons* (Irving Reis, 1948), *Death of a Salesman* (Laslo Benedek, 1951), *The Misfits* (John Huston, 1961), and *Vu du Pont (A View from the Bridge)* (Sidney Lumet, 1961). Only a very brief comment is called for on *Les Sorcières de Salem* (Raymond Rouleau, 1957), which, as Miller has pointed out, is not "*The Crucible*, but a version of it."[1] I will for reasons of space ignore aspects of Miller's career that are more or less relevant to such an inquiry: his work as a screenwriter on projects other than *The Misfits*, particularly as an uncredited contributor to *The Story of G.I. Joe* (William A. Wellman, 1945) and as the featured adaptor of *Playing for Time* (Daniel Mann, 1980), the acclaimed television movie devoted to Fania Fenelon, Holocaust survivor; the many radio plays he wrote and produced during the early part of his career (proof that he could appeal to a broadly popular audience); the numerous fine television productions of his plays, in the US and abroad, with which Miller was sometimes directly involved; the outstanding television film of *Salesman*, based on a much acclaimed New York revival, that was directed by Volker Schlöndorff and has, through video release, reached a very wide audience. Such omissions, one hopes, will be compensated for by close attention to the initial screen versions of the major plays upon which Miller's reputation, at least in the United States, has come to rest.

All My Sons and film noir

During its classic period (1930–65), the Hollywood film industry was committed to an intense production program designed to fill and refill the seats in the nation's theatres. Changing their programs twice a week, these theatres, especially the first-run houses in urban centers upon which the industry heavily depended, needed some one hundred and four main features a year to exhibit. In these circumstances, producers understandably were eager to purchase "pre-sold" properties: novels, short stories, and plays with a proven popularity that might transfer easily to the screen. Such properties were usually handled in one of two ways: either they were absorbed into an already existing series or genre, whose popularity would further increase the film's likelihood of success; or they were produced as "themselves," as prestige pictures that would testify to Hollywood's concern with art and draw viewers interested in re-creations of famous literary monuments. Not surprisingly, *Death of a Salesman*, perhaps the single best known play to come from postwar Broadway, was produced as itself, even though it did not receive the prestige picture treatment.

In contrast, *All My Sons*, despite its long run on Broadway and several awards for excellence, never achieved the same recognition with the general American public. Miller himself remained then largely unknown, at least outside theatre circles. In fact, the film version's original advertising trailer never mentions Miller's play; instead it emphasizes the starring roles of Edward G. Robinson and Burt Lancaster as a father and son who disagree and violently conflict. Similarly, the credits bill Robinson and Lancaster first in large letters, only later and briefly to note, in much smaller type, that the film is based on a prize-winning play by Arthur Miller.

This evidence indicates what an examination of the film and its context of production confirms: that *All My Sons* was intended as a genre piece and star vehicle for Burt Lancaster and, especially, Edward G. Robinson, a production that would interestingly – and profitably – recycle the character-izations that had made them popular. In fact, Robinson was one of the biggest box office draws in the immediate postwar era, enjoying a renais-sance in popularity that can be traced to a conscious change of screen image. At the beginning of his career, his snarling incarnation of the conscienceless thug Rico Bandello in *Little Caesar* (Mervyn Le Roy, 1931) led to many similar parts as criminal heavies, perhaps most memorably as Wolf Larsen in *The Sea Wolf* (Michael Curtiz, 1941). During the war years, however, Robinson switched to a new character type: the respectable bourgeois who is either a pillar of stern morality, e.g., the memorable Barton Keyes, a tireless insurance investigator, in *Double Indemnity* (Billy Wilder, 1944), or is drawn into crime when some baser instinct or moral flaw overwhelms his outwardly conformist sensibility.

It is as the respectable bourgeois gone wrong that Robinson gives his most memorable and acclaimed performances in the middle and late forties: perhaps the best of these is his role as a timid petty bank officer who escapes his overbearing wife only to be betrayed by a manipulative prostitute, whom he then murders in despair (*Scarlet Street* [Fritz Lang, 1945]). These characters share much in common with Miller's Joe Keller, especially as Robinson interprets him. Robinson even recycled his charac-terization of Keller the year after working on the Miller project in his portrayal of banking magnate Gino Monetti in *House of Strangers* (Joseph L. Mankiewicz, 1949), a film derived from the archly Oedipal novel by Jerome Wiedman with a title that could easily have been used for Miller's play: *I'll Never Go There Again*. The film bears a striking resemblance to *All My Sons*. Monetti has worked for years to build up a business that would constitute the legacy to his three sons, but then it is revealed that his financial success is based on a series of illegal practices. Trusting the bank's assets to his sons, Gino is betrayed: only Max, the oldest, works in his defense, and he is sent to prison on false charges engineered by one of his brothers.

For whatever cultural reasons, the flawed father who has done his best to achieve the American dream only to be rejected by the son(s) he hoped would be his inheritor(s) is a popular figure in films of the period, not just those starring Robinson. For example, a more melodramatic handling of the same character is to be found in *Edward, My Son* (George Cukor, 1949), based on the Robert Morley play; here the narrative is more confessional and moralistic, less noir, structured by the reminiscence of a father, ruthlessly successful in business (played by Spencer Tracy), about a son, now dead, whom he misunderstood and mistreated.

Like Robinson, Burt Lancaster saw his screen persona in the postwar era defined by a series of roles in films that portrayed the failure of the American dream, not its fulfillment. At the beginning of his career Lancaster was cast in parts that ironically juxtaposed an imposing physical presence (with its suggestion of repressed violence) to the character's inability to escape those who would manipulate and use him. Typical is his screen debut as the doomed Ole Anderson in Robert Siodmak's 1946 version of Hemingway's *The Killers*. Lancaster plays a boxer who is used and discarded by a gangster and a *femme fatale*; the film's most famous sequence pictures a resigned and impotent Lancaster silently awaiting the hired guns hastening to assassinate him.

The screen personae of both Robinson and Lancaster at the time *All My Sons* was produced were thus ideally suited to screenwriter Chester Erskine's reconception of Miller's drama: as the encounter, relentlessly emotional and intense, between a father whose desire for financial success has led him to commit a horrible crime and a son whose urge toward independence has been continually thwarted by a reflexive attachment to the deceptively respectable surface of family pieties.

The films mentioned above form an important part of a larger movement within postwar Hollywood production that was aptly termed film noir, or "dark film," by French critics of the period. Film noir begins in the forties with grim, often amoral adaptations of hard-boiled detective fiction (e.g., *The Maltese Falcon* [John Huston, 1941], *The Big Sleep* [Howard Hawks, 1946], and *The Postman Always Rings Twice* [Tay Garnett, 1946], screen versions of pulp novels by Dashiell Hammett, Raymond Chandler, and James M. Cain respectively). But the closing years of the decade witnessed a change in focus for this series. Many later noir films forsake an underworld of professional criminals and the socially marginalized for the middle-class family home in crisis, a setting traditionally reserved for another Hollywood type, the melodrama. In the manner of melodrama, these films are usually set in comfortable, respectable surroundings and project some prospect of future happiness for the younger generation. However, they are more centrally unmelodramatic (hence noir) in revealing the unsolvable problems of a nuclear family undermined by generational conflicts, long-buried deceptions, frustrated urges, or unadmitted hostilities.

Like Miller's play, these later noir productions generally stage a conflict between collective family values and individual desire that leads directly to disaster. For example, in *The Pitfall* (André de Toth, 1948), a hard-working family man, bored with the daily grind at home and the office, has a fling with a imprisoned embezzler's girlfriend, only to endanger first his marriage and then the safety of his wife and child. Sometimes films noirs have explicitly political agendas: *The Prowler* (Joseph Losey, 1950), for example, traces the temporarily successful plot of an upwardly mobile policeman to steal the wife and possessions of a rich man. Because it works simultaneously on familial and political levels, Miller's play offered material ideal for a production in this series.

Producer/writer Chester Erskine clearly intended for *All My Sons* to be a film noir with political overtones. His selection as director of Irving Reis, a rather undistinguished journeyman, is otherwise hard to explain. The most important success enjoyed by Reis prior to his work on the film version of Miller's play was in *Crack-Up* (1946). This film noir traces the workings of a sinister plot to discredit an expert on art forgeries who has uncovered a conspiracy to substitute fakes for the most important paintings in the New York Metropolitan Museum. Erskine himself was interested in both noir fiction and film. One of his unpublished short stories later became the basis for *Angel Face* (Otto Preminger, 1953), a tale of star-crossed lovers whose murderous intrigues end in a righteous and quite moral suicide; he also produced and wrote *Witness to Murder* (Roy Rowland, 1954), in which a woman, falsely accused of criminal harassment, is confined to a mental hospital, only, upon her release, to confront and indict her accuser. These narratives offer themes and incidents similar to those in both Miller's and Erskine's versions of *All My Sons*.

While the play text of *All My Sons* offered screenwriter/producer and director the materials they needed to produce a film noir, these needed to be made more commercial. Miller's social realism offers a dramatic situation that builds, in the Ibsen manner, slowly, indirectly, but inevitably toward the fateful and conclusive confrontation between Keller and his son. Furthermore, that conflict is set within a complex familial and social fabric that inflects and symbolically enriches it. In other words, the minor characters do not merely provide "reality effects," thereby endowing the central dramatic conflict with an aura of verisimilitude. Even the cursory examination of their lives that the play affords reveals interesting parallels and contrasts to the main action.

For example, Jim Bayliss's friendship with Kate Keller – emphasized particularly at the beginning of Act Three – suggests an instability of desire behind the facade of bourgeois respectability, an instability whose presence is deepened by Jim's confession that he had in the past deserted his wife for a time. This episode made him face up to losing his "star of honesty." Chris, he believes, is going through the same experience and will eventually accept the fallen state of the adult world. However Jim's prediction is inaccurate; Chris takes a moral stand he forces his father to share. Furthermore, Jim's presence in the Keller household during the long night of Chris's angry absence dramatically suggests the patriarch's loss of power and position. Joe immediately sends Jim away when he finds him in the kitchen with his wife.

Miller uses George Deever in much the same way. The disgruntled son of Keller's imprisoned former partner returns to his old neighborhood and the Keller house to prevent Ann's marriage to Chris, which he thinks would be yet another victory of Keller manipulativeness – and immorality – over his kin. The motherly warmth of Kate Keller, who treats him like a son and even tempts him with the prospect of a beautiful sexual partner, distracts George from his anger. Kate reintegrates the young man into her family, a bond he soon afterward abruptly rejects when Joe "forgets" about the illness that caused his absence from the office on the day the defective parts were shipped. This mini-drama interrupts and delays the very actions that are soon to bring Chris to share George's point of view – a process of revelation that George's recognition mirrors, ironically, of course, because the "truth" for George means that his father is innocent and that he must ask the old man's forgiveness, not the other way around.

In such ways, the apparent randomness, indirection, and "realistic" complexity of the dramatic fabric conceal an inner melodramatic core, a realm of transcendent meaning that motivates and justifies the presence of every character, every detail. Poetic justice, the operative principle of melodramatic narrative, transforms what appears to be unlikeliness and coincidence. The device of the letter, often criticized as melodramatic, is in fact deeply so. Its existence and introduction at this point into all the characters' lives makes good dramatic sense; and it is also metaphysically appropriate, in so far as it confirms the transcendent principles of collective responsibility Chris takes pains to enunciate.

Unlike a melodrama, however, the revelation of the truth does not permit a restoration of the family. The recognition of Chris and Larry that the community of the nation takes precedence over family ties and loyalties is forced upon Keller by his reading of the letter, which contains a truth that forces him to his death, and this in turn releases Chris from bondage to his parents' world. From a larger perspective, Keller's suicide comments negatively on the American success ethic with its ruthless pursuit of self-interest. Like film noir and the hard-boiled fiction that precedes it, Miller's *All My Sons* uncovers and delineates the dark side of American culture, the ruthlessness and crime beneath the respectable surface.

In conformity with Hollywood narrative principles, Erskine's script simplifies the play's dramatic texture by focusing more obviously on the central conflict while emphasizing the underlying melodramatic elements from the outset. The film thus lacks the play's complex tonality and subtlety of structure (particularly with regard to the secondary characters), but is otherwise generally faithful to Miller's conception. For example, the interesting role of Jim Bayliss is reduced and simplified. Two further examples will readily illustrate the process of adaptation.

In the film, the tensions between Joe and Chris – as well as the love they share for one another – are introduced immediately and clearly. Instead of a complex scene of which the interaction between father and son is only part, Erskine develops the central dramatic issues starkly and unambiguously. The opening sequence of the film shows Chris exiting the family home past Joe, who is raking leaves. The conversation between father and son reveals Chris's desire for a new life if his parents cannot accept the marriage he plans to Ann. Chris's impulse toward independence expresses itself in action; he walks toward his car in order to pick up Ann, constantly interrupted by his father who, conceding the son's desire for his own life, must admit that he doesn't know him very well. The scene ends with Chris driving off to get Ann, an image that rhymes with the film's conclusion where it is Kate who speeds the now united couple on their way toward marriage, exhorting them to "live." The conception of Erskine and Reis here simplifies the defining social fabric of the relationship between Keller and his son. But this *scène à deux* is true to Miller's larger intentions, not just literally but also symbolically, because the film discovers a visual and strictly cinematic correlative for Chris's desire to separate from his family. Erskine and Reis also here obey the narrative imperative of Hollywood film, the drive of the mass cultural text to identify its story-telling goal quickly and unambiguously. In short, what worked on stage works in the film as well.

The film's version of George's recognition is similarly successful. Convinced by the warmth of Kate's welcome and swayed to some degree by Keller's argument that his father would never take responsibility for errors or misjudgments, George decides to stay for dinner. The scene shifts from the house's exterior to its interior – once again a telling visual correlative of George's reintegration within the Keller family. The seating around a huge table images the restored togetherness of the various characters; ironically it is during dinner that Joe's "forgetfulness" about his illness that fateful day is revealed. George recognizes the truth, moves to the porch, and asks Ann to go away with him. Ann agrees and steps off the porch with George, thus motivating Chris to visit Mr. Deever so that he can discover the truth. Here is yet another move away from the family home that indexes its moral and epistemological bankruptcy. Chris must seek out the other father, who has been physically weakened but spiritually strengthened by his fall from grace, in order to learn the truth about his own.

Death of a Salesman and the postwar social problem film

I have spent considerable time discussing Reis's *All My Sons* because the film is undoubtedly the most successful one made from a Miller work. The reasons for that success prove fairly easy to identify: (1) the theme, dramatic structure, and social realist style of Miller's play could not only be accommodated by Hollywood, but fit into a larger textual pattern – the film noir series – then very popular on the screen (a happy coincidence of highbrow and middlebrow tastes); (2) Miller's main characters were natural roles for two of Hollywood's brightest stars, both of whom played well with an ensemble cast of professionals; (3) the underlying melodramatic elements of the play text could be profitably emphasized in the film version. *All My Sons* was a success if not a sensation with critics and viewers. It remained relatively faithful to Miller's text, even though, ironically, faithfulness was not an issue in either production or marketing.

Death of a Salesman offered Hollywood an even more successful play with much the same materials: a generational conflict between father and son, an understated if profoundly affecting critique of the American dream, and clear, effective dramatic encounters undisrupted by Miller's experiments with objectifying the main character's inner life. Like Joe Keller, Willy Loman finally fails to achieve the success promised to the industrious middle-class patriarch who dedicates himself to supporting his family. Like Joe Keller, Willy Loman is responsible in part, through his own blindness and culpability, for destroying his most valued human connection: the relationship with a favored and adored son. Here was material that could be adapted to fit either or both of two then popular series: bourgeois film noir or the social problem film, a developing Hollywood trend heavily influenced by the American exhibition successes of key Italian neo-realist releases such as *Bicycle Thief* (Vittorio de Sica, 1948). Early fifties social problem films were the serious, realist, "other" to the dominant series of the era. Spectacular blockbusters, featuring casts of thousands, with exotic settings photographed in living Technicolor and in one of the newfangled wide-screen processes such as Cinemascope, offered escape and fantasy rather than a confrontation with contemporary discontents.

The social problem films, however, were also commercialized entertainment. In fact, conditions within the industry made it profitable for the studios to contract with independent producers who had made a reputation with small-budget black and white features on socially "relevant" subjects. The apogee of that trend was reached with *Marty* (Delbert Mann, 1954), based on a teleplay by Paddy Chayefsky, who is one of a group of writers whose acclaimed scripts for television were turned into feature films in the realist series, Rod Serling being perhaps the most famous of the group. Though produced on a shoestring budget without the usual Hollywood glamorization, *Marty* was a huge financial and critical success, making back its investment several times over and garnering the Grand Prix at Cannes as well as the Best Picture Academy Award. *Marty* was the only small black and white picture of the era to achieve this kind of popularity, but such films were generally profitable even in the early fifties.

Perhaps the most famous of the independent producers who mined this area of popular taste was Stanley Kramer, an educated man (New York University) with left-wing politics who made a name for himself in the late forties with a series of financially successful small black and white features. Teamed with the politically like-minded Sam Katz and Carl Foreman (eventually blacklisted for his leftist associations), Kramer achieved a breakthrough success with *Home of the Brave* (Mark Robson, 1949), based on the hit play by Arthur Laurents about anti-semitism in the armed forces. Collaborating on the screenwriting with Foreman, Kramer daringly changed the film's focus to racism, substituting a black soldier for the play's Jew. Like the other social problem films of the late forties, *Home of the Brave* struck a popular chord with an audience conditioned by wartime filmmaking to admire "message" pictures. The film made its makers a great deal of money, started a trend of liberal-minded "race" movies, and convinced Columbia to sign Kramer to an unusual contract: in five years he was to produce thirty low-budget features in the expectation that these would turn a good profit.

Characteristically, Kramer collaborated with directors who felt a social commitment to meaningful filmmaking and were left of center in their politics. He produced several films with Edward Dmytryk, who was black-listed for Communist sympathies, briefly exiled, and finally reinstated with the industry after recanting. Kramer and Foreman also worked with Fred Zinnemann, somewhat more successfully, on realist small pictures such as *The Men* (1950).

Having purchased the film rights to *Death of a Salesman*, Kramer was apparently indecisive about how to proceed – or so we can infer from his treatment of the material. Miller's play was far too famous and acclaimed a property, even in 1950 before it gained classic status, to be much changed for the screen. And yet Miller's modernist dramatization of Willy Loman's consciousness, his "objective" staging of Willy's involuntary forays into the past, called for an expressionist stylization and theatricality that ran counter to Kramer's solidly realist sensibility.

In fact, Kramer was probably initially attracted to the understated political themes in *Death of a Salesman*; although this would alter the complexity of Miller's conception, a screen version could construct Willy as a pure victim of social circumstances that crush him but permit the final gesture of self-annihilation, which could be presented as a kind of victory for the common man. Willy, then, would be more typical than aberrant, undone less by psychopathology than an economic system that uses him up and then heartlessly discards him. Such handling of the material would anchor Miller's drama in a realistically evoked contemporary America. Kramer may have been inclined to adapt the material in this fashion. Both *Home of the Brave* and *The Men*, Kramer's biggest successes before taking on this project, offer protagonists of this type: a black soldier (James Edwards) ironically "wounded" by prejudice and not enemy fire who learns to walk again by acknowledging and expressing his anger at whites; a white soldier (Marlon Brando) paralyzed in battle who, through the love of a good woman, learns to overcome the impotence caused by his wound and the not always helpful impersonality of the system that tries to care for him.

In both cases, however, the protagonists' private problems are objectified and solved in a social context. The films prominently feature fatherly psychiatrist/therapist figures who help the wounded men relive and come to terms with the past. The ironic center of Miller's conception, of course, is that much of the real drama of Willy's consciousness cannot by its very nature be made apparent to those around him, who are nonetheless deeply affected. The salesman's inner life, his having come "unstuck in time" like Kurt Vonnegut's Billy Pilgrim, is objectified only for the spectator. With its juxtaposition of scenes representing the reality all characters share with those representing only Willy's sense of the real, the play offered structural and thematic complexities with which Kramer, by no means a "literary" producer, had had no experience and for which he likely had little appreciation.

Yet Kramer could hardly alter the most characteristic feature of one of the era's best-known plays. Faced with choosing between realist and modernist approaches, Kramer attempted a compromise. He opened Willy's drama out into a series of authentically detailed settings. Nothing remains in the film of the innovative expressionistic staging by Jo Mielziner – a house that was the objective correlative of Willy's inhabiting of the present and past, a playspace whose time reference could be instantly shifted. As many reviewers noted, the hardly happy result is that Willy's movement toward recognition seems more madness than hyperconsciousness.

Simply put, the problems posed by cinematic adaptation proved too difficult for the bargain basement creative team Kramer assembled. Stanley Roberts had written only a few films before beginning this project. In his brief Hollywood career, he enjoyed only one real success – adapting

Herman Wouk's *The Caine Mutiny* for Kramer and Edward Dmytryk. Similarly, director Laslo Benedek was largely unknown before his work on *Salesman*; his most significant project had been a low-budget noir/realist thriller, *Port of New York* (1948), to which he imparted an interesting semi-documentary look. If he had originally intended to make Willy a "social problem," then a plus for Kramer may have been the director's leftist sympathies and social realist proclivities. In his own words Benedek was eventually "greylisted" for his politics, only to return to Europe where his career did not flourish.

Except for music director Morris W. Stoloff, the only seasoned professional involved in the filming of *Death of a Salesman* was photographer Franz Planer, who had been successful with a deglamorized, chiaroscuro style in a number of noir and noir/realist films. His work on *Death of a Salesman* is generally effective; most scenes have a low-key flat look, with occasional expressive shadows and areas of light. A flaw is that the subjective moments are not lit more consistently in an expressionist manner, highlighting dramaturgical changes through stylistic contrast. However this was probably Benedek's idea; he attempted, somewhat misguidedly, to emphasize throughout the realistic nature of Willy's restagings of experience. Like Roberts and Benedek, much of Planer's experience had been in "B" productions; none of the group had ever been involved in the crafting of a prestige literary adaptation.

Political difficulties may also have impaired the project. In the middle of production, Carl Foreman, Kramer's collaborator, appeared before the House Un-American Activities Committee as an unfriendly witness. Attempting to salvage his career, Kramer bought out Foreman's interest, but the scrutiny of right-wing groups fell heavily upon him and his projects. Matters were not helped by Miller's well-known leftist associations. Filming was at times picketed by members of the American Legion, who suspected that *Death of a Salesman* was an anti-American work. Columbia planned to forestall further trouble upon release by prefacing the film with an explanatory short consisting of, in Miller's words, "interviews with professors who blithely explained that Willy Loman was entirely atypical, a throwback to the past when salesmen did indeed have some hard problems."[2] Threatened by Miller with legal action should they proceed with a plan he thought would certainly compromise the artistic integrity of the work, Columbia abandoned the idea of a filmic disclaimer. Yet it is likely, as Miller himself believes, that the play's social critique, its revelation of false promises at the heart of the American dream, was blunted because Columbia pressured Kramer to do so.

This aspect of the film was not helped by the casting of Fredric March as

Willy Loman. The complexity of Willy's self, for which memory has become strangely present and is dramatically reenacted, demands a multi-layered, subjective interpretation. Blessed (or perhaps cursed) with hyper-consciousness, Willy is compelled to produce in the theatre of his own mind a series of dramatic encounters that critically examine his life; the ripe circumstance that brings on this state of mind is the imminent loss of his job and, by extension, his role as family provider. In *All My Sons*, by way of contrast, the past lives again for Joe because others, like George and Chris, revivify it and because, even in the face of death, it cannot be erased, as Larry's letter objectifies. For Willy the present of familial relationships offers mostly misunderstanding, sometimes perhaps a deliberate failure of understanding. In its present tense, the play dramatizes a series of mis-connections, epitomized by the misbegotten restaurant celebration Hap and Biff plan for their father. Only the spectator, afforded access to an objectification of Willy's waking reveries, understands the character's complex progress toward self-annihilation. In short, Willy Loman is a main character vastly different from Joe Keller, who can be and was played effectively by an objective actor like Edward G. Robinson.

Although he garnered some good notices at the time, March is simply wrong for the part. His career had been built on objective not subjective performances: first, as a young man in starring, romantic parts, such as the eponymous hero of *Anthony Adverse* (Mervyn Le Roy, 1936); then in character roles, most famously as a tipsy ex-serviceman who returns to his dull job as a bank executive in *The Best Years of Our Lives* (William Wyler, 1946). Often on Broadway in such productions as *Long Day's Journey into Night* and *A Bell for Adano*, March provided able and sensitive support to an ensemble cast, but as one critic put it, he was "never a star who dominated audiences. The bulk of his work is nonassertive."[3]

March could play a stolid, yet sensitive upper-middle-class type, a man capable of intense emotion in a crisis; the proof is his success, among other similar roles in the fifties, as the respectable businessman besieged by Humphrey Bogart in *The Desperate Hours* (William Wyler, 1955). But Willy Loman is a more demanding role. Instead of being marvelously disoriented by his moment of ripeness, March's Willy appears simply confused by visions of the past. Either March proved unable to commu-nicate the character's Bergsonian complexity, his divided loyalty to what is now and what was, or Benedek encouraged him to play Willy as a pathetic misfit.

In any event, his performance is neither sympathetic nor engaging. Despite an able supporting cast – Kevin McCarthy as Biff is especially good – and Benedek's often successful attempts to manage Miller's complex dramaturgy, the film fails to offer a significant version of the play. The viewer feels only pity, not terror, as Willy in the film's final scene speeds madly toward his own demise. Ben sits beside him approvingly as the car disappears into an expressionistic sky of stars metamorphosizing into diamonds. Willy's last sale, the exchange of his life for the insurance money needed to support his family, is transformed from a bitter, practical choice into the deluded gesture of a madman still delirious with hopes of striking it rich.

The Misfits: a personal film

Tennessee Williams had the good fortune to have his best play – *A Streetcar Named Desire* – filmed by Elia Kazan. Kazan had directed the original Broadway production, cooperated with the playwright in writing the screenplay, and had a good deal of valuable Hollywood experience before beginning the project. Kazan also benefited from an outstanding cast, including Marlon Brando, Kim Hunter, Karl Malden, and Vivien Leigh, most with stage experience in either the New York or London productions of the play. Furthermore, with its steamy sexual undercurrents, the film version of *Streetcar* hit movie theatres at an advantageous cultural moment, just when the industry concept of wholesome family entertainment was making way for a sensationally profitable new area of production: the adult film, a genre based on the linked themes of sex and violence that were to become a Williams trademark during the era.

Miller's luck with the film version of *Salesman* could hardly have been worse. His property purchased by a realist-minded, "engaged" producer charged with making six cheap films a year for five years, Miller saw his masterpiece entrusted to a writer and director with little experience and less talent. Although those involved were initially sympathetic to the play's social critique, they were either forced to downplay its political themes or were simply incapable of mounting them effectively. *Salesman* by its very nature required careful casting in the lead role, which must carry the production. At the end of a distinguished career, Fredric March could not (or was not directed to) play Willy Loman as Miller had imagined him. In comparison with the raw sensationalism of Williams's themes, Miller's explorations of lower-middle-class discontents appeared positively wholesome. There was no trouble getting this material past the censors at the Production Code Administration. For all these reasons, the film version of *Salesman* made little impact on the American cinema; igniting neither scandal nor enthusiasm, it soon disappeared from critical and popular memory. While the films made during the period from Williams plays have enjoyed a new life and popularity in videocassette form, *Salesman* has not been rereleased. At the moment, apparently lacking any confidence in the film, Columbia plans no such release, even though the classic film market is steadily profitable. Nor, so I was told, do they rent 16mm prints. Were it not for archive holdings, the original film version of Miller's most noted play – arguably the greatest American play ever written – would be inaccessible, not only to the general public but to scholars as well.

Though he disliked the film, Miller was not unduly concerned about its failure. He continued to regard the cinema as a medium inferior to the theatre, one to which he intended devoting little energy and concern even though, he was not hesitant to admit, the fluid handling of time in *Salesman* was in large measure cinematic. After the kind of experience he had had with Stanley Kramer and Harry Cohn, the head of Columbia, it is difficult to fault his disdain for Hollywood. In contrast, Williams never severed his creative links to filmmaking. *The Glass Menagerie*, his first theatrical success, had actually been written as a screenplay while Williams was employed in Hollywood. The triumph of the film version of *Streetcar* was due in large measure to the playwright's direct involvement with the project. The Hollywood *Salesman*, deserving a better fate, offered an inferior version of Miller's masterpiece at least in part because of the author's indifference and uninvolvement. During the fifties, the period of his greatest theatrical and popular success, Arthur Miller did not follow Williams and other dramatists of the time into a creative cooperation with the Hollywood literary establishment. Thus Miller's early career offers no analogy to Williams's work with Kazan on the rewriting project that would eventually come to the screen as the notorious and celebrated *Baby Doll*. Nor would he have ever thought to suggest, as Williams once did, that a screen version of one of his plays (*Sweet Bird of Youth* is the case in point) was in fact superior to the original stage production.

And yet what he avoided for professional reasons, Miller was to do for personal ones. Devoting himself at decade's end to making a screenplay from his short story "The Misfits" and cooperating with renowned director John Huston, Miller in no way attempted to imitate the successful collaboration of Williams and Kazan on *Baby Doll*. On the contrary, Miller viewed the project as time away from his true artistic calling, as a loving gift of talent and labor his to then wife Marilyn Monroe, whose personal and professional life, he believed, could be redeemed from impending collapse through this penitential effort. At the peak of his popularity, with a name that could command creative collaborators and financial backers, Miller chose to expend his artistic energies and personal capital on writing a film he imagined less as a work than as occupational therapy. It is hardly surprising that the result is far from satisfactory. *The Misfits* was a critical and box office failure that occupies a significant place in Hollywood history only because it offers the last performances of three notable stars – Clark Gable, Marilyn Monroe, and Montgomery Clift – and because Miller was centrally involved. The film certainly did nothing to further or improve the playwright's relations with the commercial film industry, nor was Miller eager for this to happen. Noted film critic and scholar Leslie Halliwell pronounces the standard view of *The Misfits*: "A sad film . . . this kind of pseudo-highbrow non-money-maker would in the old days have been vetoed at script stage by the studio's front office; failures like this are the price of independence."[4]

The screen versions of *All My Sons* and *Death of a Salesman* were produced with little or no involvement from their author (the two movies barely rate a mention in either Miller's long autobiography *Timebends*[5] or in his extensive body of critical writings). And so the success of the one and the failure of the other must be accounted for by reasons proper to the cinema, not Miller. His material assigned to film producers for financial consideration, the author awaited in each instance an outcome that only minimally interested him. From the viewpoint of the playwright, these films are entirely impersonal. In contrast, *The Misfits* is perhaps too personal, its structures and content – not to mention the creative team that Miller was able to select – all dictated by the likes, dislikes, fears, and abilities (as her husband interpreted them) of the film's intended feature performer, Marilyn Monroe.

Because the film was truly Miller's project, *Timebends* offers the most reliable extended and detailed account of its production. Miller reveals that he was simply more interested in how *The Misfits* could repair his disintegrating marriage than in overseeing a successful film. The project was suggested by Miller's photographer friend Sam Shaw, who remarked that "it would make a great movie . . . and that's a woman's part she could kick into the stands" (*Timebends*, p. 458). Shaw's comment is difficult to understand because Roslyn isn't a realized character in the story; the only presence she is allowed is in the minds of Gay and Perce as they set about their hunt for wild horses. The evident unsuitability of the story as a vehicle for Marilyn did not deter Miller, who reports jumping at the suggestion. Having just suffered a miscarriage, Marilyn was despondent, "sad beyond sadness"; her husband "felt an urgency about making something for her" (p. 458). As he confesses, Miller's purpose was in some sense to restore her "original idealization" of him as an intellectual and writer; he would "never have dreamed of writing a movie otherwise" (p. 460). And yet though he "was constructing a gift for her," the message of love took them away from the private world of their relationship: ". . . it was she who would have to play the role, and this inevitably began to push the project into a different, coolly professional sphere" (p. 459). The result was that the filming, instead of drawing the Millers together, actually widened the breach.

First – and appropriately – published in the men's magazine *Esquire*, the original story was ill suited to Miller's desire to create a showcase for Marilyn's recently acquired skills as a serious actress (painstakingly nourished by Lee and Paula Strasberg from the Actors' Studio; Paula even accompanied Marilyn to the filming in Nevada as a coach). Like most of Miller's work, "The Misfits" evokes a man's world and men's problems; Guido, Perce, and Gay are three rootless inhabitants of the contemporary West who, to avoid having to work for "wages," hunt down wild mustangs to sell for processing into dog food. The story is, in part, a mood piece that carefully delineates the subtle and difficult connections the men share; in part, an action/adventure story that, with a Hemingwayesque love of detail, precisely describes the successful hunt, imbuing it with both failed romanticism and heroic resignation. Like the horses they hunt, the three men are a dying breed unsuited to life in a modern, developed society; their success in capturing the ragged animals merely postpones the accommodation they must make to a world that insists they become employees. The opening movement of the story develops the characterizations that are given meaning by the following action. The structure is spare and effective, more dependent on the story-teller's painting of the scene than the dramatist's imagination of interesting dialogue and meaningful encounter. "The Misfits" gives substantial evidence of Miller's ability as a writer of short fiction, a genre dependent upon simple but intense effects.

The story presented Miller with two difficulties that were perhaps impossible to surmount as he strove to transform it into a "cinema novel" with a featured role for Marilyn. First, the material had been conceived not in dramatic but narrative terms; the characters are largely inarticulate – or obedient to a shared masculine code of silence – and therefore require a narrator to make sense of their relationships and reveal their thoughts. Miller refused to reformulate the story in traditional screenplay form, which would have provided the director with a series of dramatic scenes subdivided into shots. A screenplay would have had to discover how to dramatize passages such as the story's memorable initial description of Gay:

When there was something to be done in a place he stayed there, and when there was nothing to be done he went from it. He had a wife and two children less than a hundred miles from here whom he had not seen in more than three years. She had betrayed him and did not want him, but the children were naturally better off with their mother. When he felt lonely for them all he thought of them longingly, and when the feeling passed he was left without any question as to what he might do to bring them all back together again. He had been born and raised on rangeland, and he did not know that anything could be undone that was done, any more than falling rain could be stopped in mid-air.[6]

Though it is somewhat more dramatic, the cinema novel form still depends heavily on a narrative voice, as Miller suggests in the preface to the published edition: "it is a story conceived as a film, and every word is there for the purpose of telling the camera what to see and the actors what they are to say." Too much the artist to be blind to the problem, Miller recognized that the "sense" of his story "depends as much on the nuances of character and place as on the plot."[7]

But how could any director stage and film a passage such as the introduction of Isabelle – so much more dependent on the wry narrator's sympathy for his subject than on dramatizable, photographic elements? "Her nose and cheeks are faintly purpled, her voice cracks and pipes, and she looks on the world with an amused untidiness that approaches an air of wreckage and misspent intelligence . . . For people in general she has little but despair, yet she has never met an individual she couldn't forgive" ("The Misfits," p. 5). A theatrical version of this material could make effective use of an onstage narrator such as the one Miller employs in A View From the Bridge to solve a similar problem. Voice-over narration would be the cinematic equivalent, but even though the device was much used in Holly-wood, Miller avoided it.

Instead, exposition is handled in dialogue, as the other characters converse, mostly with Roslyn, thereby solving the second problem with the source material: its lack of a realized female character for Marilyn Monroe to portray. Because the cinema novel introduces two female characters – the recently divorced Roslyn and her erstwhile older companion Isabelle – who do not know the three men, much of its initial section, and the corresponding part of the resulting film, consists of rather static scenes where dialogue has no plot to advance. In short, Miller here abandons the Ibsenesque principles of dramatic construction that had served him so well; the circumstances in which these characters find themselves are unripe. The evocation of the characters' pasts therefore does not set into motion a set of actions whose impulse toward resolution had been halted by design or chance before the point of attack. Instead the slowly developing first hour of The Misfits brings to life the characters and circumstances to be resolved by the exciting action of the second hour. Miller's emphasis on characterization is understandable; the revised form of the story often poignantly evokes the misdirection and randomness of the characters' lives, including chance encounters that can make a fateful difference. His five misfits are like Roslyn's convertible, which, though almost brand new, bears the numerous marks of collisions with men who, like the trio of male protagonists, are eager to make her acquaintance. Such a looser form of narrative structure, however, did not accord with Hollywood story-telling principles. To audiences and critics alike the film seemed formless, directionless.

John Huston had proven his abilities to work well with ensemble casts in films that emphasized atmosphere and character as much as plot. His version of *The Maltese Falcon* (1941, with Huston also as screenwriter) depends on dialogue-heavy scenes to advance a complex plot involving five principal characters; but Huston's feel for the kinetics of acting along with the film's quick-paced editing gives the story the forward motion necessary for an effective Hollywood film. Much the same can be said about *The Asphalt Jungle* (1950), a caper film (a film that details the planning and execution of a crime) with a social realist agenda; Huston spends much time detailing the individual lives of the gangsters preparing to pull off a complex robbery, who, like Miller's misfits, are mostly meeting for the first time. If these two films are successful, however, it is because detailed characterization and the evocation of both mood and social milieu are accomplished while a plot sweeps the characters up into a classically Aristotelian chain of circumstances. This is not the case with *The Misfits*, where the plot's main enigma – who will Roslyn go with if she goes with anyone? – emerges late and is only inadequately connected to the mustang hunt. Huston was not enough of a visual stylist to transform the subtleties of the cinema novel into images that could support audience interest and communicate a sense of complex feelings and moods. Witness the failure of his last project, a version of James Joyce's *The Dead* (1987), to catch any more than the surface inanity of the party and evening that mean so much to the protagonist.

Centerpiece of the story, the hunt becomes pointless because Roslyn convinces Perce and Gay to let the captured animals go. Roslyn disrupts the resigned masculine world of the misfit cowboys by suggesting the possibility of a softer, more sentimental attitude toward life. But what does she release the captives, men and horses alike, to find? Where are they to go and what will they do if they renounce the hunt?

The film's lack of an effective conclusion resulted from Miller's indecisiveness about how the revised story should resolve itself; he wrote and rewrote as filming went forward. Eventually, production was halted by Marilyn's hospitalization for drug addiction, and it appeared the project was doomed. But then Marilyn and Miller each found the energies to complete the film. Not surprisingly, the playwright had Roslyn couple at the end with Gay (Clark Gable), the oldest of the trio, who is enthralled by her vivacity and physical charm. Yet for both his personal life and *The Misfits*, the presence of Roslyn/Marilyn posed a problem Miller was never adequately to solve. Inspired by his love for her, the husband intended to write a drama that would showcase the wife's newly acquired talents. Strangely, the resulting film is strikingly undramatic. Though, as one of Huston's admirers suggests, "the myth of *The Misfits* transcended the work of Miller and Huston," "there is an emptiness about the actual film. The actors' charisma so towers over the story they are supposed to enact that the viewer is kept waiting for extraordinary moments that never come."[8]

A View from the Bridge, The Crucible: European versions?

Unlike *All My Sons* and *Death of a Salesman*, *A View from the Bridge* was not an initial Broadway success. The original version was in one act and presented a starkly conceived drama, with little deep examination of character or motive, the doomed attraction of longshoreman Eddie Carbone for his niece. Despite its central theme of sexual obsession, Miller was determined that *A View from the Bridge* would not partake of what he termed the "psycho–sexual romanticism" so much in evidence on the 1955 Broadway stage – the not so oblique reference is to Tennessee Williams.[9] Thus the central character is the mirror image of Willy Loman, a rather unintelligent working-class man who refuses, or is unable, to account for or objectify his inner turmoil. Miller wrote a two-act version of the play for London and Paris production, and in those two cities it was quite successful, enjoying long runs. The two-act version deepens the human dimensions of Eddie's misfortune, but still requires the guiding presence of an onstage commentator, the lawyer Alfieri who fails to dissuade Eddie from a self-destructive course of action and addresses the audience as the designated chronicler of the tortured man's eventual downfall.

The two-year successful run of the French production persuaded producer Paul Graetz and Continental Distributing that a film version would be a profitable undertaking. Deciding on an international cast of actors barely known in the United States, Graetz realized that the film would hardly attract a general release and would play best in the art house circuit, then an important part of American exhibition. Miller's name and the grim, unglamorous realism of the story might ensure success; many similar European releases had done well, though the current fashion was more for modernist art films that showcased the stylistic flourishes and thematic obsessions of their directors. The early sixties witnessed the height of popularity for Ingmar Bergman, Federico Fellini, and the daring young experimentalists of the French New Wave like François Truffaut and Jean-Luc Godard. A French language version of *A View from the Bridge* was shot simultaneously for distribution in Europe.

Graetz made what seemed a wise choice for director, picking the American Sidney Lumet, who would shoot the exterior scenes on the streets of his native New York; interiors were done in a Paris studio. Lumet had been a success as a director of live TV theatre and with a small black and white production of one of the era's most famous live TV plays: *Twelve Angry Men* (1957). *A View from the Bridge* was to be the first in a series of Lumet films chronicling the less glamorous aspects of New York life: *The Pawnbroker* (1965), *Serpico* (1973), and *Dog Day Afternoon* (1975) are the best known. Raf Vallone, who starred in the Paris production, repeated his role as Eddie, though he knew no English, while two European actors, Jean Sorrel and Raymond Péllegrin, played Rodolpho and Marco. A Broadway actress of some note, Maureen Stapleton, appeared as Beatrice, and Carol Lawrence, most famous for her role in the original Broadway production of *West Side Story*, played Catherine. It is to Lumet's credit that he was able to extract competent performances from an ensemble cast of widely different backgrounds and training.

More than Miller's previous plays, *A View from the Bridge* draws on the *Kammerspiel* or "chamber play" tradition of late German Expressionist drama. The pessimistic naturalism of the playwright, given voice on stage by the cynical and world-weary Alfieri, is best suited to a claustrophobic, theatrical set. Lumet and writer Norman Rosten, however, chose to open the play to a variety of realistic locations on the New York docks. The naturalism of their approach is signaled by the credit sequence, which features artfully edited shots of longshoremen gracefully operating unloading vehicles that resemble giant hands with wheels. Though it allows its inhabitants a certain power and strength, this environment oppresses them as well. Rushing to the aid of a fellow worker injured in an accident, Eddie stands up to the uncaring representative of the company; he is respected and feared, a man of cunning as well as muscle, rather similar to the unloaders he and his companions operate. Eddie is generous as well. Taken covertly into the ship's hold, he meets for the first time the "submarines" who will share his home. He welcomes Marco and Rodolpho warmly, seems genuinely pleased at their arrival.

However, the film's emphasis on environment and Eddie's control of it is misplaced. *A View from the Bridge*, despite a title that apparently promises a sociocultural approach to its subject, does not centrally concern itself with environment since Eddie's obsession with Catherine is not construed psycho-culturally but as tragically inexplicable and unalterable. Furthermore, though Miller contrasts the laws contained in books with those written only in the human heart, his intent is not to push a social agenda, a code of behavior in a world of conflicting loyalties. With its condemnation of informing, Miller's play may have been intended as a kind of riposte to Elia Kazan's *On the Waterfront* (1954), a film whose subject is a longshoreman persuaded by his priest, his girl, and his better instincts to inform to a government commission on waterfront racketeers. Former collaborators and friends, Miller and Kazan had parted ways over the issue of cooperating with congressional witch-hunters; Kazan named names, but Miller refused, risking his reputation and freedom. In any event, *A View from the Bridge*, though perhaps a political gesture, does not treat a political subject. Eddie informs on the two men living in his house because Rodolpho has successfully wooed Catherine and plans to take the young girl away from the uncle who has raised her. His betrayal of personal and community loyalties is occasioned by jealousy and fear, not an evolving conscience, as in the case of Kazan's Terry Malloy. Eddie responds to an internal agenda he never comprehends, not to the pressures of his environment. His tragedy is registered by the community, not caused by it.

On the Waterfront was a critical and popular success, earning much money at the box office and garnering eight Academy awards and four other nominations. Released seven years later, *A View from the Bridge* was largely a failure with audiences in the US and abroad; as *Variety* correctly predicted "this looms mainly an arty bet with not too much entertainment value." Yet in many ways Miller's material is far superior to that supplied Kazan by Budd Schulberg, who adapted his own novel. Schulberg's portrait of waterfront life and politics is oversimplified at best, distorted at worst; *On the Waterfront* is a social problem film in the mainstream Hollywood tradition, replete with easy to identify good and bad guys, as well as a complex issue resolved unconvincingly by the good faith and endurance of the protagonist. In the manner of Greek tragedy, Miller more persuasively limns the familial and societal results of a compulsion the main character can neither understand nor control.

However, the reasons for Kazan's success and Miller's failure are easy to identify. Working with a big budget and a producer, Sam Spiegel, with much faith in the project, Kazan was able to cast Marlon Brando, Karl

Malden, Rod Steiger, Lee J. Cobb, and Eva Marie Saint, a gallery of Actors' Studio graduates who were able to provide a clinic on ensemble Method acting, a style very much in vogue with audiences after the screen success, of *Streetcar*. Leonard Bernstein, one of America's finest living composers, produced an outstanding score. Marketed for general release in first run houses, the film was afforded the fullest opportunity to succeed with audiences, which it did largely because of its production values and not its somewhat flimsy story. As was the case with *Salesman*, Miller's play was not given the prestige literary adaptation treatment. Though the international ensemble cast gives a creditable performance for Lumet, a lack of stylistic consistency is apparent and was noted by several reviewers. Lumet was unable to deal effectively with some of the play's longer scenes, which have a slow and stagy look in the completed film. These worked well on the confined theatrical set, but Lumet's realistic opening out of the play develops an unfortunate contrast between slowly evolving interior scenes and the often energetic exteriors. He was perhaps misguidedly persuaded by the success of *On the Waterfront* that this was the way to proceed. Lacking stars and a popular "pre-sold" property – most Americans had not heard of Miller's play – the film was consigned to art house exhibition and hence viewers with whom its gritty realism was out of fashion. Because the production was probably doomed to failure from the outset by its limited budget and the director's misinterpretation, it seems appropriate that Norman Rosten has Eddie kill himself at film's end with his longshoreman's hook. The suicidal gesture was perhaps appropriate for the screenwriter as well; this was his first and last important project.

A *View from the Bridge*, like the Greek tragedy it is modeled upon, treats timeless themes that do not depend upon specific cultural resonances for their development; this is why Lumet's social realist approach to the film version was a miscalculation. In contrast, *The Crucible*, like *Salesman*, thematizes a myth central to the American character; if the latter displays discontents that derive from a Constitutionally guaranteed right to pursue happiness, the former chronicles the failure of American experience to live up to a similarly guaranteed freedom of thought, the presupposition that every citizen has the right to speak the truth as he sees it. In comparison with *Salesman*, however, *The Crucible* evokes characters, events, and a social milieu less capable of universalization; it recreates a history that can only be properly understood within the parochial boundaries of American culture. Because of its facticity and attendant complex dramatic structure, the play is not easily accessible to audiences on the level of its engagement with American political history; yet the universal aspects of this dramatization of individual conscience in opposition to oppressive and unjust authority have made it a favorite around the world. In any event, the initial New York production was not a success; Miller would have to await a second for this masterpiece to be properly appreciated.

Though *The Crucible* deals with the seventeenth-century Salem witch trials, the subject matter and treatment seemed to many an extended commentary on an important current within recent American history, the "Red scare" and attendant search for Communists under every important bush that had preoccupied Americans since 1947. Itself the target of Congressional investigation, the filmmaking industry by the early fifties had been frightened away from any properties that even faintly smelled of political controversy. Miller's play was certainly one of these. Despite his increasing reputation as one of the most important voices within American literary culture, no studio was interested in filming *The Crucible*. It was left to a French producer to try. The result was not happy.

Like the screen version of *A View from the Bridge*, *The Witches of Salem* was prompted by a successful theatrical run, starring Yves Montand and Simone Signoret, who in the film repeat their roles as the Proctors. Montand and Signoret, paired here for the first time on screen, were then France's most popular film stars. Yet Miller's play is hardly suitable as a star vehicle. Though John Proctor is the featured character, the action is complex and diffuse, requiring the work of an ensemble cast. The very commercially minded producer, Pathé Cinema-Films Borderie, was determined to make the most of Montand's sex appeal, persuading screenwriter Jean-Paul Sartre to reorient the play's structure accordingly. As a result, the film's opening concentrates not on the bewilderment of Reverend Parris at the spectacle of his apparently bewitched daughter, but on the illicit liaison between John and Abigail, portrayed as a hysterical minx by Mylène Demongeot. Their coupling, only alluded to in the play, is here enacted; leaving the bed of his frigid wife – whose religious convictions prevent her from being a real woman – John falls into Abigail's willing embrace, only to be caught by an outraged Elizabeth. This triangle becomes fateful when Abigail, seeking vengeance, persuades her companions to "cry out" against Elizabeth. Needless to say, the moral center of Miller's conception is correspondingly shifted. To make matters worse, Sartre's screenplay emphasizes the class conflict only briefly alluded to by Miller, turning Proctor into a champion of individual rights in the face of oligarchic tyranny; late seventeenth-century America looks more like late eighteenth-century France. Raymond Rouleau's turgid and unimaginative direction, as well as the unfortunate editing decision to let the completed film run 143 minutes, compound the disaster. Only briefly exhibited at art houses in the US, the film received some good notices from reviewers – especially Bosley

Crowther for *The New York Times* – who, however, proved unable to persuade viewers that it was worth their time and money. Miller intended *The Crucible* to resurrect a history made relevant by recent developments in American culture. Raymond Rouleau's film, in contrast, offers a costume melodrama that makes very Gallic points about the connection between sexual weakness and good faith in the class struggle. The version now being filmed, it is to be hoped, will do better by the brilliance and importance of Miller's conception.

Conclusion

The commercial films made from Arthur Miller works during the period of the author's greatest popularity in the fifties and early sixties certainly did nothing to advance his reputation. With the exception of *All My Sons*, they were all more or less critical and popular failures. None exerted any appreciable influence on the course of the cinema; none is much discussed by film scholars nor much viewed by *aficionados* of classic Hollywood films despite the increasingly popular presence of such films on videocassette and repertory television – the exception being *The Misfits*, which still arouses interest, though for its stars rather than its story. The fault, if fault there is, is partially Miller's. Unlike Tennessee Williams, he was at this time not very much interested in the cinema even when, because of his reputation and standing, he landed an opportunity never given Williams: writing an original screenplay and more or less co-producing the film itself. But the fault also lies with the commercial cinema, which failed to marshal the intellectual resources to make an appropriate version of one of America's greatest plays (*Salesman*) and lacked the courage to attempt a production of one of its most intellectually engaged and committed (*The Crucible*).

NOTES

I wish to extend my sincere thanks to Charles Silver and the extremely helpful staff at the Museum of Modern Art for providing me the opportunity to view three Miller films I could not otherwise have seen.

1 "Arthur Miller on *The Crucible*," *Audience* 2 (1972): 47.
2 As quoted in Brenda Murphy, *Miller: Death of a Salesman* (Cambridge: Cambridge University Press, 1995), p. 137.
3 David Thomson, *A Biographical Dictionary of Film*, 3rd edn. (New York: Alfred A. Knopf, 1994), p. 480.
4 *Halliwell's Filmgoer's Companion*, 7th edn. (New York: Charles Scribner's Sons, 1980), p. 558.
5 Arthur Miller, *Timebends* (New York: Grove Press, 1987).

6 Arthur Miller, "The Misfits," in Harold Clurman (ed.), *The Portable Arthur Miller* (New York: Viking Press, 1971), p. 448.
7 Arthur Miller, *The Misfits* (New York: Viking Press, 1961), p. ix.
8 Scott Hammen, *John Huston* (Boston: Twayne Publishers, 1985), p. 98.
9 I quote from the introduction to Arthur Miller, *A View from the Bridge* (New York: Viking Press, 1960), p. vi.

13

MALCOLM BRADBURY

Arthur Miller's fiction

There is, of course, no essential reason why our playwrights should also be our novelists, or vice versa. Certainly many of our finest writers – from Henry Fielding and Aphra Behn to Victor Hugo and Charles Dickens, from Oscar Wilde and Anton Chekhov to Samuel Beckett and Max Frisch – have made fine use of the double traffic, stepping from page to stage as the occasion demanded, the artistic stimulation prompted, the theatrical opportunity came. Some of our best novelists have been among our very best playwrights; some of our finest dramatists have excellently exploited the loose baggy monsterdom of the novel. Equally there have been a good number of major writers who failed with the alliance. A notable example was Henry James, whose unfortunate adventures in theatre at the start of the 1890s, when disillusionment with the novel led him to write various plays, including the costume-drama *Guy Domville* (promptly booed off the stage), cost us several important late fictional works from the Master – or so we like to believe.

James's example is a useful reminder that the arts of the novel, the short story, and the stage play are not necessarily close – except that all are produced by writers, and all share some basic skills and structures in common. Ever since the novel became a popular and central genre in the Europe of the early eighteenth century, it has often been thought useful to distinguish the activities and practices of the novel from those of theatrical discourse. In his preface to *The History of the Adventures of Joseph Andrews* (1742), a travesty of the work of the "new" novelist Samuel Richardson, Henry Fielding, by this date a well-established workaday playwright, with some thirty plays performed, emphasized the difference. Trained to think in terms of Aristotle's neo-classical poetics, he struggled to find a definition of the fledgling genre we have rightly come to call the novel. It resembled not the drama, with its two distinctive categories of tragedy and comedy, but the epic. If an Aristotelian generic description were needed of it, it would have to be defined as "a comic epic poem in prose." True, it depended on similar properties of scene, character, and dialogue as did drama, and dealt with the same kind of social spectacle, above all the universal presence of the ridiculous. But its freedoms were greater and its conventions looser. And as Fielding's own work in the novel led him onward to the vaster social reach and original comic benevolence of *Tom Jones* (1749), we can see the new genre making claims for itself that spare it any particular reliance on the rules and conventions of the stage.

Yet, throughout the modern history of the novel, the dramaturgical analogy – the sense that the shape of a novel is that of a drama, that its social landscape is that of a stage, that its characters are masks or performances, and so on – has stayed of crucial importance. Henry James drew constantly on the notion of fiction as theatre, one reason for his unfortunate engagement with the *Guy Domville* adventure. But theatre also represented the darker side of fictional writing: it signified the spectacular, the masked, the falsified, the unreal. The writer was constrained by the regulated nature of the stage's arched traffic, lured into its tricks of deception and inflation. So, when James wanted to compare the novel with a truly serious art, he preferred painting, which was formed from consciousness, impression, composition. In his engaging book *Aspects of the Novel* (1927), E. M. Forster came back again to what was now a long-established question, and spoke about the grand curtailments drama imposed, as against the simple, expansive humanity of fiction:

> [T]he novel is not capable of as much artistic development as the drama: its humanity or the grossness of its material (use whichever phrase you like) hinder it . . . The drama may look toward the pictorial arts, it may allow Aristotle to discipline it, for it is not so deeply committed to the claims of human beings. Human beings have their great chance in the novel.[1]

The potential of the different forms and genres, the contrasting freedoms they offer, the contrasting skills they require, have always been matters of high concern for writers. Critics assign them to this tradition, or that genre; in turn they frequently insist on stepping out of frame. When in 1967 Arthur Miller published a collection of stories, *I Don't Need You Any More*, he suitably added a preface containing his own reflections on the various forms and genres which are part of the repertory of writing, and the different ways and different kinds of occasion on which the writer might chose to employ them.[2] Miller writes with all the authority of a playwright, ever conscious of a public duty, clearly aware of the stage as a key cultural meeting place between the writer and his audience, but one who is tempted from time to time off the stage.

All these forms we have inherited – story, novel, play – are degrees of distance writers need to take between themselves and the dangerous audience which they must cajole, threaten, and, in one way or another, tame. The playwright is all but physically on stage, face to face with the monster; the writer of fiction, however meager his covering, is safe in this sense, but out of hearing of the applause, out of sight of the mass of strangers sitting spellbound in the theater, sucked out of themselves by his imaginings.

("Foreword," *I Don't Need You Any More*, p. xii)

But the chief task, Miller argues, is doing full justice to the kinds of dramatic arrangement that are appropriate to each different subject; the writer needs to find the form, the address, the tone due to each thing, each person, each event. Whatever form he chooses, every vision has to be rendered at its own due distance, with the appropriate method of attack on that elusive audience. By this reckoning, novel and short story occupy their own theatrical or dramatic spaces too. They too are means of distance, other, less direct ways of encountering what Miller calls "the terrible heat at the center of the stage" (p. xii).

Not all novelists and story-writers would agree that this theatrical heat, or a deliberate address between writer and audience, is important to the essence of fiction. Indeed many novelists who have been analytical about their art – and one of the great adventures of the novel has been, as Henry James said, its coming to a modern "self-consciousness" – have emphasized other aspects of their genre. Often it is just the absence of theatricality – of the need to dress up, paint, pretend, dramatize, or engage in any interactive process with an audience – and the unmasked, unstaged nature of the novel's confrontation with reality, humanity, or experience that explains the distinctive power of the form. So is the novel's capacity to meditate, digress, wander where it will, toward whatever knowledge is discovered; its unritualized dialogue, its refusal of confrontation and conflict, its essential freedom of scene and openness of structure; its sloppy humanity and random journalistic adventuring, which can informally lead the story in so many directions; its textual intensity and its verbal self-consciousness; its distinctive grammar, not necessarily of characters, scenes, and acts, but of selected consciousnesses, angles of vision, *points d'appui*; its construction of the author as maker, the prime and first participant in the action; its benign, meditative, and various audience, and hence its nature as an open drama that can be freely reconstructed and interpreted in the mind of the reader; and its pure fictiveness.

Any writer who has moved from the one medium to the other, or had reason to adapt a work of fiction (one's own or someone else's) from a narrative into a dramatic medium (novel to stage or screen), comes to understand that many of the practices that seem so central to the modern novel as we have it (authorial narration, consciousness presented without character, fundamental tonal devices like irony or distinctive linguistic stylization) possess no precise equivalents in stage drama or film narrative. In short, novels and short stories are more than other types of the same sort of drama we represent on stage, which for once happen to be written down rather than enacted. They are born not just from different conventions but different temperaments of writing. This, in his Foreword, Miller is concerned to acknowledge.

> Some of these stories could never be plays . . . The playwright, after all, is a performer *manqué*; thoroughly shy and self-effacing philosophers do not write plays – at least not playable ones. That is probably why playwrights at middle age so often turn to fiction and away from the unseemly masquerade. All the world's a stage, but the point comes when one would rather be real and at home . . . The mask, in short, is of another kind when one sits down to write a tale. (p. x)

What might be the difference between the kind of "mask" a writer puts on when he or she writes a play, and that assumed to write a novel or a story? Miller draws attention to several. He notes it is oddly hard to write dialogue in a story, since in prose not written to be performed one acquires a half-conscious objection to working through dialogue when it is not relevant or necessary. The spoken line in drama is a "speech," and it is generally presented dialectically: to summon a reply, lay bare a conflict, trigger an action. In writing a story, such dramatic transactions can distort all that lies around. So can exposition or situational development through direct speech. In the novel and the story, dialogue is cast toward the eye, not the ear; it becomes part of the work's overall textuality. The temptation for the playwright is to think that dialogue is always at the centre of fiction's drama; this is the high moment when the author ceases chattering and at last gets out of the way, the point at which the novel ceases to be an opinion or an impression and turns into a fact or an action.[3] Even when dialogue in fiction becomes a central mechanism of the narrative (as in James's *The Awkward Age*, or the work of Ivy Compton-Burnett), it is frequently not conceived in order to be "dramatic"; it becomes another aspect of the great textual repertory of fiction.

Miller's forewords are always instructive, and that to *I Don't Need You Any More* is especially so. It is a meditation on the frames and distances the different forms of writing offer an author: "No single form can do everything well; these stories are simply what I have seen, at another distance" (p. xiii). Yet the masks are different, the games not the same, the very sense of difference is a value. Over the course of a long writing career, Miller has made prodigious use of the different masks and distances. At various stages in that career, different points in his personal, his theatrical, his moral, and his political development, he has ventured on practically all of the fictional forms: the novel, the novella, the short and the long story. He has taken them on with notable success, but also in some significant relationship with the work he has been doing for the stage, or film (in Miller's view a far lesser medium, because of the simplicity of its distances and the passivity of its audience). The film screenplay of *The Misfits* (1960) began as one of his finest short stories. The most interesting published text of *The Crucible* (1953) has been in effect "novelized" by his own interpolations. A formidable dramatist who carries with him the great heritage of world-drama ("I've come out of that playwriting tradition which is Greek and Ibsen where the past is the burden of man and it's got to be placed on the stage so he can grapple with it"), Miller's contributions to fiction will always take their place in relation to a major dramatic career, where the great scenes, the most powerful artistic effects, and the largest moral moments are there to be delivered onstage. But he has taken fiction seriously enough and deployed it strongly enough for his contributions to be important ones: not just to the sum of his own literary career but to the development of modern American fiction.

It was at an early stage of his writing career that Miller brought out what is so far his only published novel, *Focus*.[4] The book was first published by Reynal and Hitchcock in 1945, and won a significant reputation; selling some 90,000 copies in hardback, it was widely exported and translated. Part of its significance is that it has some claim to being the first postwar Jewish–American novel, appearing at a time when that distinctive genre underwent a powerful, internationally influential revival. This was not least because the new work of the generation of Jewish–American novelists coincided with the tragic revelations of the Holocaust, now shocking the whole world. Miller's novel was not quite the first to capture the changing fictional atmosphere. A year earlier Saul Bellow – another writer who, like Miller, had begun to establish his career during the 1930s – also published a first novel, *Dangling Man* (1944), marking the beginning of an extraordinary career. *Dangling Man* is a wartime story, told in introverted journal form, exploring the existential uncertainty of a young intellectual in Chicago as he tries to fill the space between leaving behind his job (and with it the lost political world of the thirties) and his forthcoming military enlistment.[5] As Miller would also do, Bellow was drawing on a tradition of Jewish–American fiction that went back to the immigrant years of the 1890s, and developed in the work of Abraham Cahan, Mike Gold, Henry Roth, Isaac Bashevis Singer, and many others.

What made Bellow's book feel different was the nature of its subject matter and the breadth of its philosophical references. It was not concerned with migrant experience, the hard endurance of the urban ghetto, the loss of an ethnic past, or the transition to New World identity. Instead it was devoted to the realm of introverted solitude, the waning of the world of realism, politics, and significant forms of social action, and the problem, in such a vacant and purposeless world, of constructing the self as a sufficient agent of moral identity and action. Hence the book owes far more to works like Jean-Paul Sartre's then influential novel *La Nausée* (1938), and other earlier European existentialist fictions of self-awareness and superfluity, not least the stories of Gogol, Dostoevsky, and Kafka, than it does to earlier Jewish–American writing. Yet it is also powerfully concerned with the (wartime?) question of how to define personal, moral, and social responsibility. Set in a blanked-out city in a waiting time, and a mood of spiritual and moral dejection, the novel finally has the hero sacrifice his own lonely struggle: "I had not done well alone . . . Perhaps the war could teach me, by violence, what I had been unable to learn during those months in the room. Perhaps I could sound creation through other means. Perhaps" (*Dangling Man*, pp. 190–91). Bellow would later call the novel "timid," as it was in comparison with his own subsequent displays of fictional energy and invention. Still, it opened the door to a new surge of culturally central Jewish–American fiction which would make its mark over the immediate postwar years. The books included Isaac Rosenfeld's *Passage from Home* (1946), Lionel Trilling's *The Middle of the Journey* (1947), Bellow's second novel *The Victim* (1947), Isaac Bashevis Singer's *Gimpel the Fool* (1947), Delmore Schwartz's *The World is a Wedding* (1948), Norman Mailer's *The Barbary Shore* (1951), Bernard Malamud's *The Natural* (1952), and, not much later, the fiction of Philip Roth, Edgar Lewis Wallant, Stanley Elkin, Joseph Heller and others. For many readers inside and outside the USA, these works came to represent the exemplary new American novel of the postwar, Superpower age. The Jewish hero – introvert, underground man, urban wanderer, outsider, victim, survivor, schlemiel – was in process of turning into a key figure in American writing. His rhetoric of moral anxiety, social displacement, political alienation, and self-recovery became a central theme in a troubled era of existentialist doubt and conscious historical anguish.

This is the context in which Miller's own novel appeared. Like Bellow's book, *Focus* is set in the closing phase of the war, in an uneasy militarized America where the prospect of peace brings confusion of identity and doubt about the national future. A great success in its day, the novel undoubtedly played a part in constructing the climate in which the above-mentioned books were written. Yet, although the new Jewish–American fiction has been subject to vast critical commentary, Miller's book has come in for little attention. This surely has far less to do with any insufficiencies than the simple fact that Miller's subsequent theatrical success and international fame drew attention elsewhere; the center of his authority and his authorship moved from fiction to drama. However, at the time he wrote it, Miller was thirty, and neither an established novelist nor a fully established playwright. Born in Manhattan (indeed in Harlem), he had turned from laboring work to the theatre. In the later 1930s he worked with the Federal Theatre Project, with its drama of political issue and righteous anger, and imbibed some of the spirit of social drama represented by playwrights like Clifford Odets and Lillian Hellman. During wartime he wrote several successful and well-paid patriotic plays for radio, won various drama prizes, and completed five or six full-length plays. One of these, *The Man Who Had All the Luck* (of which he also wrote a novel version, still unpublished) was performed in 1944 on wartime Broadway, in an ineffective, botched production which ran for only four days. It was a disillusioning experience. "I would never write another play, that was sure," Miller notes of this episode in his autobiography, *Timebends*.[6]

These were the circumstances in which he left playwriting for three years, turned to the novel form, and wrote *Focus*. Not surprisingly, it carried forward a number of themes from the earlier plays, and shared their political urgency. It was written in a wartime Manhattan where Miller – who had been turned down for military service as a result of an injury, and worked in the New York Naval Yard repairing ships – felt displaced, uneasy, and politically indignant about the mood on the home front. At the yard, he was witness to a climate of anti-semitism and incipient Fascism, and was himself another Dangling Man. "I seemed to be part of nothing, no class, no influential group," he records of this period in *Timebends*.

> The city I knew was incoherent, yet its throttled speech seemed to implore some significance for the sacrifices that drenched the papers every day. And psychologically situated as I was – a young, fit man barred from a war others were dying in, equipped with a lifelong sense of self-blame that sometimes verged on a pathological sense of responsibility – it was probably inevitable that the selfishness, cheating, and economic rapacity on the home front should have cut into me with its contrast to the soldiers' sacrifices and the holiness of the Allied cause.
> (p. 223)

These comments are above all relevant to the writing of Miller's play *All My Sons* (1947), which directly deals with that contrast. But they are also clearly relevant to the mood in which he produced *Focus*.

Focus is a short, intense, and only gradually dramatic novel about the growing racial and anti-semitic tension its author observes on the home front as war abroad moves toward its close, national fears grow of a return to the conditions of the Depression, and America begins to face the social and ethnic changes that will emerge from the melting pot of war. It is a New York story, set in commercial downtown Manhattan and a very ordinary residential neighborhood of Queens, and, like Bellow's book, it is concerned with the question of how in a socially disordered time we define our responsibility for others. And, like most of Miller's early plays, it is placed in the world of the common man: those for whom the system must always be greater than the individual, the self has a small arena in which to act, a place in the sun is hard to win. The book starts with a dream-sequence, about a carnival somehow worked from below by a great subterranean machinery, which serves as an image of society itself. The novel is the story of one such small man, Mr. Newman. Appropriately he bears a very literary name (Christopher Newman in Henry James's *The American*), though it here has an ironic connotation. Newman himself is a gentile, of British stock, but the name he bears is one much taken up by immigrant Jews. A prim middle-aged bachelor who fought in the Great War, he now lives with his mother in a small house, and works as a minor personnel clerk for a huge Manhattan corporation. He is a repressed and private man, with exact and civil manners, a yearning for order, a great deal of social caution. He also cultivates a few self-conscious discrepancies by which he distinguishes himself from his no less ordinary neighbors. Thus their shutters are painted dark green, his are light green. These tiny separations from the larger tribe will eventually cost him dear.

Newman's uneasy dream, which starts the novel, is at once interrupted by reality; he hears a woman calling for help in the night as she is victimized on the street outside his home. He reacts with inaction, indifference. "Her accent satisfied Mr. Newman that she was abroad at night for no good purpose, and it somehow convinced him that she could take care of herself because she was used to this sort of treatment. Puerto Ricans were, he knew" (*Focus*, p. 9). This sets the theme of the book, which is concerned with the moral inertia felt by ordinary people about the secret racial tensions that are running through this massed and overcrowded metropolis, its neighborhoods and immigrant peoples ever on the move. When, in the morning, Newman goes to the subway station, to take his place among the crush of people going into Manhattan to work, anti-semitic graffiti on the subway pillars suggest to him an underground message – "a secret newspaper publishing what people really thought" (p. 12). Like Asa Leventhal in Bellow's next book *The Victim* (another tale of racial tension and responsibility in an over-massed, over-heated New York City), Newman is uneasy amid the moving crowd, and, waiting in the subway, is "academically" attentive to signs of class, position, and ethnicity. A survivor of the Depression who has kept his job in the offices of a great "corporation," his timid, anxious manner has much to do with the "mammoth" size of this company and his own powerless place within it ("He had seen other men defend themselves against it and he had seen them crushed" [p. 17]). Still, he has achieved an office of his own, where he can observe the working secretaries, and his task is hiring and firing. The company operates an anti-semitic policy, and his job is to weed out the female applicants, some of whom conceal their Jewish background by claiming Episcopelian or Unitarian faith.

It soon emerges that Newman has every reason for his anxieties. His sight is starting to fail, and he is losing his ability to read essential human signs and signatures. And he has delayed collecting his new spectacles, for the reason that they give a semitic appearance to his face: "The frames seemed to draw his flat, shiny-haired skull lower and set off his nose, so that where once it had appeared a trifle sharp it now beaked forth from the nosepiece" (p. 27). The spectacles change his life. In an increasingly surreal sequence of episodes, he now finds himself seen as Jewish – by his mother, female applicants at work, and the people in his neighborhood who are engaged in a social war to keep out the new "element" beginning to move out of the East Side and encroach on the street. The novel begins to turn analogically on the spectacles on Newman's nose. Not only do they give him a Jewish appearance, making him separate and increasingly shunned by others; they also let him see the world through new lenses, and hence from an increasingly Jewish point of view. The protected world he has made soon starts to collapse. Dismissed to a smaller office because of his newly ambiguous facial appearance, he resigns his job. Given his experience, he thinks it will be easy to find another, but finds himself rebuffed by the hidden web of anti-semitic suspicion: "A total stranger looking for a man with just his experience had taken him for a Jew, and therefore he had not gotten a job that was rightfully – and almost fatefully – waiting for him," he thinks as he walks down Wall Street. "But what shocked him into this dulled stupor was that he could not go back and explain to the man . . . What was there, exactly, that ought to be explained?" (pp. 61–62).

From here, rising unreality begins to move toward dangerous drama. "Hours come when the familiar seems about to change its shape, verging on the strange and unexplored," the book's measured prose advises (p. 107). His world begins to be upturned. He acquires a new job, with a Jewish corporation, helped by a girl he had once interviewed himself, and thought Jewish. Eventually he marries her, only to discover that, though she too appears semitic, she is fiercely defending a gentile identity. On honeymoon, they are refused accommodation at a select resort, and encounter increasing hostility in the neighborhood. As summer heat intensifies, there is a rising mood of menace, when the local campaign against the encroaching "element" increases. Newman's own position is deeply perplexing to him; he dislikes Jews, and attempts to distinguish himself from Finkelstein, the one Jew on the block, who keeps the corner store. But he refuses to join the rising hysteria, which puts him in further danger. When he goes to Finkelstein's store and suggests that, for his own safety, he should move out, Finkelstein poses his own problem to him: "Suppose I told you to move . . . suppose I said to you, there's too many people in this neighborhood who are looking like Jews?" (p. 160). At a meeting called by the Christian Front to Cleanse America, Newman is expelled for failing to applaud. Before long the underlying violence erupts, and he finds himself fighting off the street mob beside Finkelstein. Finally he accepts the challenge, refusing to return to the fold of the anti-semites, instead reporting the attack to the police. "How many of you people live there?" asks the police sergeant (p. 190). Newman, the small and naturally passive man under challenge, accepts the last change of focus: "Just them [the Finkelsteins] and myself," he says (p. 190).

Focus belongs to that kind of fiction Lionel Trilling, in his famous essay "Manners, Morals, and the Novel," describes as "moral realism," and identifies as the literature of "the liberal imagination." "The novel is a perpetual quest for reality, the field of its research being always the social world, the material of its analysis being always manners as the indication of the direction of man's soul," he argues, adding that the novel's liberal imagination and social curiosity best belong to a post-ideological age.[7] Such, suggests Trilling, is the post-1945 period, when the ideological and Marxist arguments of the thirties have dissolved into the ambiguity of new social and political conditions, putting the moral realities of social life under a new kind of pressure, giving a new challenge to the novel. *Focus* is indeed a work of fictional realism, with a liberal import; it is also concerned to express the surrealism – the rising unreality – of contemporary American life, which was to be remarked upon by so many novelists. Its prose is literary, considered, meditative:

> For nearly forty days the city had had no rain. It is an insidious pacifier, rain; the people stay at home and the pages of precinct blotters do not turn so often. But when the sky stays blue as it did this summer, say after a sweltering day, and the humid air chokes a man out of his sleep, it is the streets and

stoops of the city that become populated and the authority of the family
disintegrates for a time. The ice cream parlours crowd up, and the saloons;
the beaches are flattened down by more people than they were meant to hold
– the city empties out into its own swelling arteries.   (*Focus*, p. 134)

The structure is not intrinsically dramatic. There is considerable strong
dialogue, and a fine scenic sense, but most of the action is internal, kept
close to the consciousness or self-awareness of the passive, reflective
Lawrence Newman. The other characters in the novel are shadowy and
deceptive, and shift in meaning and emphasis according to Newman's
perception of them: his changing focus. This is especially true of Gertrude,
the woman he marries. In first focus, he sees her as Jewish and erotically
dangerous; later she is seen as gentile and desirable. She describes herself as
an "actress," and she is certainly a story-teller, who fictionalizes freely
about her own identity and her past. The only other major character whose
point of view we enter is Finkelstein, the secular Jewish storekeeper. His
family story is separately told, a counterpoint to Newman's, and he
becomes the formidable "other," the key object of attention and responsibility in the book. By the end, Newman has in effect acquired the condition
and self-awareness of Finkelstein, and has become not a natural inhabitant
of the city but one of its eternal strangers ("He *belonged* here. Or did he?"
[p. 157]).

In the early pages, the action is inward, slight, gestural. Graffiti in the
subway, the expression on someone's face, the overturning of a garbage
can: such small incidents are sufficient to upset Newman's feelings and stir
his anxieties. Only slowly does rising unreality turn into external threat.
Now the dramatic intensity, the direct impact of social conflict and dialogic
or action scene, increases. Newman faces an ever more complex set of
moral difficulties and ambiguities, and discovers the rising price of earlier
inaction:

> What seemed like one thing had turned into another. He had gone all his life
> bearing this revulsion toward the Jews and it had never been anything of
> importance to him . . . And then he had come to see how many others shared
> the feeling, and he had found stimulation around the subway pillars and all
> the time he had felt no great personal fear about what was looming up
> ahead."   (p. 118)

Finkelstein is summoned to moral action too; at his father's graveside he
recollects and contemplates the long story his father had told him of Itzik,
the Jewish pedlar in Poland who is unable to prevent a pogrom that kills his
family. Then, in a strong and vivid literary prose, Miller lays out the scene
of the Christian Front meeting, led by a racist Boston priest in a climate of

heat, sweating tension, social anxiety, rising extremism. Miller's gift for moral conflict is finally let loose in the most dramatic parts of the narrative: the dialogue scenes that take place between Newman and Finkelstein, where the deeper ambiguity of Newman's attitudes – his inert anti-semitism, his refusal to confront violence in others, his refusal to challenge himself – is explored. But the true drama lies in his change of focus: his shifting vision of the exterior world, in which he is ever more a stranger, and then his acceptance of this alien condition.

As contemporary reviewers did not fail to note, *Focus*, is also a "realist" work in the more obvious thirties, propagandistic sense. To suggest that the USA was an anti-semitic, fascistic society, when it was playing a major part in a World War against Fascism and totalitarianism, was plainly controversial. Miller was already setting off on a career that would prove rich in controversy and conscience, and the direct urgency of his book, the strength of its political critique, would distinguish it in emphasis from many subsequent Jewish–American novels, which explored the complex alienations and moral anxieties of a post-war America in an age of affluent conformity. In another place, I have explored the chastened mood of post-war realism, as novelists responded to the appalling revelations and realizations that followed the war – the news of the Holocaust, the onset of the nuclear age – and the rising sense of unreality that many writers felt as they experienced daily postwar American events. As the nation returned not to Depression but sudden affluence, as a new age of consumerism rose, modern mass-culture spread and society became increasingly suburbanized, the American writer too faced a change of focus, as the ideological and moral perspectives and responsibilities of the thirties yielded to an encounter with the postwar landscape of American and Un-American activities, of superpower status and a culture of individualized personal success.[8] Miller's novel hence has an explicitness and directness of implication later Jewish–American novels would revise, amend, and complicate, as the Jew in postwar America becomes a central witness to the conflict between moral selfhood and affluent emptiness. In Bellow's *The Victim*, published two years later, Asa Leventhal, another petty bourgeois office worker, ever alert to an anti-semitic slight, will discover there is a mutuality of suffering between Jew and gentile in an alienating history, where the world can no longer guarantee anyone's place, define the nature of society, take a respectful measure of man. In Malamud's *The Assistant* (1957), the small-time Italian hoodlum Frank Alpine, guilty after robbing a Jewish store, becomes an honorary Jew, advances down the path of Newman's revised sense of identity, and discovers the limits of honorable suffering. American fiction after 1945 would become a post-migrant writing that dissolved into a great many paradoxes of identity. As in Ralph Ellison's *Invisible Man* (1952), there were many invisible men and women, hidden from view not simply by ethnic origin but by skin color or gender, who would appear in the fictional landscape to seek their place in the American sun.

As for Miller himself, the direction of his writing would suddenly shift again. The wartime play he had written around the time of *Focus*, *All My Sons*, was presented on Broadway in 1947, at a time when a new and more radical spirit was emerging in mainstream American theatre. Here too Miller explored the tense relationship between the "heroic" war front and what was happening to the American soul at home, as the wartime economy revived not just commercial opportunities but the self-seeking culture of the twenties, and personal success came into conflict with the larger responsibility for others. Directed on commercial Broadway by Elia Kazan, the play ran for more than a year, and, despite or because of the controversy it stirred, won the Drama Critics' Circle Award. And, despite many tensions that were still to come, it established Miller as the major playwright of the postwar generation, and won him *his* place in the theatrical sun. Thus, when Miller slowly returned to the writing of fiction, his own and the cultural situation around him were already very different. He wrote nine short stories between 1951 and 1966, the period in which he wrote the plays *Death of a Salesman*, *A View from the Bridge*, *Incident at Vichy*, and *After the Fall*, and became America's leading playwright. First published in magazines, they were collected in *I Don't Need You Any More* in 1967, and, though they are placed in a different order in the collection, are probably best inspected in the sequence of their writing.

In 1947 Miller made a trip to a postwar but still wartorn Italy. "Monte Sant' Angelo" (1951) is a benign, reflective story, about the ambiguity of identity and ancestry, which doubtless arose from that journey. Two Americans, one of Italian stock, the other of Jewish origins, briefly visit a hilltop town in Italy, so that the Italian–American, Vinny Appello, can see the longtime home of his family. The town is ancient, remote, unused to strangers; the entire experience becomes strange and estranging. Apello finds his past, but is neither recognized nor welcomed by his surviving relative. In turn Bernstein finds he is affected and embarrassed by his own seeming lack of ancestors ("I have no relatives that I know of in Europe . . . And if I had they'd all have been wiped out by now" [*I Don't Need You Any More*, p. 55]). But when a local man comes into the restaurant as they eat lunch, he has a sudden odd sense of recognition – even imagining, though he knows no Italian, he can talk to him – and then perceives this man as Jewish. The man denies this in all innocence; but Bernstein believes he recognizes, in the way he packs up a parcel ("The whole history is packing bundles and getting away" [p.64]) and takes bread home on Friday night as if for *shabbas*, the trace of the Italian's now forgotten ancestry. "A past for me, Bernstein thought, astounded by its importance for him, when in fact he had never had a religion or even, he realized now, a history" (p. 68). The story ends on a note of brotherly intimacy and kinship between the half-alien, half-rooted American visitors.

In 1957, Miller took a different bearing with the story "The Misfits," written for *Esquire*. This was Miller's modern "Western" – "a kind of an Eastern Western," he later called it. In 1960 he would adapt it as a film, directed by John Huston, chiefly meant as a vehicle or a "gift" for Marilyn Monroe, whom he had married in 1956. The story itself was born out of that troubled year of change, when he traveled to Reno, Nevada, for his divorce, rented a cabin by a "prehistoric lake," with Saul Bellow as his one neighbor, and when, as he visited his divorce lawyer in Reno, he was served a subpoena to appear before the House Un-American Activities Committee (HUAC). During this episode he had gone out into the empty desert and mountains with two rodeo men who hunted wild mustangs; this experience had given him the story, which was partly finished off in England after his marriage to Monroe. In *Timebends* he describes the story as about "three men who cannot locate a home on earth for themselves and, for something to do, capture wild horses to be butchered for canned dog food; and a woman as homeless as they, but whose intact sense of life's sacredness suggests a meaning for existence" (*Timebends*, pp. 438–9). But this description imposes the film version on the original tale – largely contained within a single continuous episode, and firmly devoted to three male "misfits": two rodeo men, the older Gay Langland and his protégé, the youthful Perce Howland, and Guido Racanelli, the Italian–American pilot of the battered plane they also use for hunting. They are rootless, maverick figures from another America: in the world of conformity and commerce, they don't want anything, don't want to want anything. Nonetheless their freedom proves to be devoted to a cruel futility. Guido uses his plane to drive wild mustangs down from the mountains for the two cowboys to round up from their truck. These wild horses, too, are untameable, undomesticated misfits. Shackled with heavy tires, they are left overnight in the desert to be recaptured and sold for animal feed at virtually no profit to the men. Unlike the film, which necessarily becomes an extended and emotional narrative, with a shifted character focus (the girl friend Roslyn), the story condenses its point about waste, mechanized futility, and the corruption of the natural by telling of a single day's hunting and then returning, simply, to the horses, waiting in the desert cold to be slaughtered next day:

When the first pink glow of another morning lit the sky the colt stood up, and as it had always done at dawn it walked waywardly for water. The [shackled] mare shifted and her bone hoofs ticked the clay. The colt turned its head and returned to her and stood at her side with vacant eyes, its nostrils sniffing the warming air. *(I Don't Need You Any More*, p. 111)

In 1959, Miller published the delicate long story "I Don't Need You Any More," about a five-year-old Jewish boy whose consciousness has just come to the point of self-individualization. The day is a Jewish holiday, when his father and brother are fasting and praying with the men at the synagogue; it is the last year of his childish independence, which he longs to leave behind. He is departing the world of his mother for the world of the patriarchs; he doesn't need her any more. This is a tale of profound, gentle intimacy with childhood: with the certainties of innocence, a growing but confused apprehension of the contradictory adult world, the sacredness and ordinariness of things, the child's belief that he has his own visionary insights and can protect his family from danger and too much knowledge. His world constantly explodes into confusion, upset, and danger; he knows his own difference from others. His father protects him, but he is an illiterate; he can protect his father. In the ocean out there is God, his beard drifting in the shallows toward the beach, and he requires obedience. The story begins and ends on the beach, where the sea sends moral and religious messages he tries to understand. Among Miller's finest pieces, this is a story of powerful evocation, about the way we struggle through life to some sort of respectful, obedient, half-known moral consciousness: "He would let them laugh and not believe him, while secretly, unknown to anyone but the eyes that watched everything from the sea, he would by the power of his silence keep them from badness and harm" (*I Don't Need You Any More*, p. 50).

"Please Don't Kill Anything" (1960) is a vignette, also set on the beach, and evidently based on the author's life with Marilyn Monroe – who, like the story's central figure, would walk along the seashore rescuing live fish fisherman had rejected and throwing them back into the sea. In 1961, Miller published another long, substantial story, "The Prophecy." This is the work of an intensely mature writer, penetrating beneath the familiar self-knowledge of individuals and their conception of themselves, into the deepest elements of unease and disorder. A famous international architect, living in the country, leaves his wife, Cleota, for a few days, over the misty winter season when people are rendered touchy and uncomfortable. In his absence, Cleota holds a dinner party for an old female friend, and her friends. Cleota is strong and self-shaped, but almost unknowingly disappointed that her life has flattened and not found fulfillment. The friends bring with them a sense of sexual chaos, and of prophecy. The most formidable disturbance in the story is an ugly old woman, Madame Lhevine, who seems to carry some authentic power of prospecting the spirit and the future. Cleota is strongly affected both by her influence and the (carefully worked) emotional shape the long evening takes on. A writer who weekends locally, Joseph, visits the party late, after dinner, when the question of life's purpose has overtaken the table. Each character has a clear moral character: Cleota possesses an aristocrat's indifference ("her blind stare, her inattention to details, her total absence of discrimination. She seemed not to realize that people ordinarily judged others" [*I Don't Need You Any More*, p. 126–27]) but the evening upsets it. Meanwhile Joseph has an emotional understanding of others, but also knows somewhere in his mind "that real truths only came out of disaster, and he would do his best to avoid disaster in all the departments of his life" (*I Don't Need You Any More*, p. 143). The evening ends with Cleota and Joseph exposed to each other, and there is the possibility of sexual fulfillment. Joseph rejects it; when the story ends in the summer, the world of order and good sense has returned, the prophecy of anarchy is unfulfilled. The story's density of thought, the careful combination of characters and their significances and challenges to each other, the vivid presence of every moment, compose its energy. In one sense nothing happens: a sexual opportunity is not taken, a prophecy proves false. In another the sensation of life, its moments of senselessness, its challenge, and its metaphysical difficulty, all are unlocked as it unfolds.

"Glimpse at a Jockey" (1962) is a short character-revealing monologue; "Fame" (1966) a cunning story with a twist, is about a famous playwright, constantly recognized, who is hailed in a bar by someone who remembers him from school but has not linked him to his fame. "Fitter's Night," also 1966, goes in the other direction. It takes us back to the New York Naval Shipyard in wartime, where Miller was employed. Here thousands of men not accepted for military service work in confusion, getting damaged ships back into the war. The central character is Tony Calabrese, a fitter of Italian–American background who has a feckless and at times criminal history, and is skilled in working the system. Miller always writes well about work and working techniques, but layered into all this is another tale – about Tony's arranged marriage to a girl he dislikes, which has been imposed on him by a grandfather come over from the Old Country who has promised to reward him with a fortune. Only after Tony has dutifully fathered twins does it emerge that the Mussolini money is worth nothing at all in the Depression. Now a disappointed man, cynical, racist, and self-interested, Tony uses the system; but on the harsh, freezing night of the story he gets a difficult job to deal with on a damaged destroyer that is waiting to get back into convoy duty, and he comes through. "Fitter's Night" is a work of realism, a backward look at a world of Depression survival and hard labor. "A Search for a Future," also published in 1966, is a fable for a more modern, enfeebled America, and uses the contrast between the theatrical world and the real history beyond to explore Miller's dismay with the nation of the day. The story is the first-person narrative of an actor who has lost that earlier, urgent sense of reality. An unhappy unmarried man, he visits his father, who, stricken with a stroke and in a nursing home, is scarcely able to speak, can hardly make himself understood. His son, used to persuading with words, finds it hard to express any truth in them. But he sees in his failing father an attachment to life he can never have: "He has a future they will never be able to rip away from him. He does not have to teach himself or remind himself of it. As long as he can actually walk they are going to have trouble with him, keeping him from going where he wants to go and has to go" (*I Don't Need You Any More*, p. 236).

In 1992, amid the writing of the later plays, Miller returned once more to fiction, this time with *Homely Girl: A Life*, a short novella that was published in the USA with illustrations by Louise Bourgeois. In Britain it appeared in 1995, retitled as *Plain Girl* (divided from the US by a common language, Britain gives a different meaning to the word "homely").[9] This is the (condensed) life story of Janice Sessions, the child of a rich and aristocratic Jewish refugee who settles in New York in the 1930s and then dies as Hitler invades Poland. Janice is the "homely girl" of the title; her looks are no recommendation, but her style and her life-instinct are strong. After the funeral of her father, she loses his ashes in a bar: it stirs her to think she must start living. She is married to Sam Fink, a devoted Communist, but now their marriage is beginning to split, under the pressure of world events, above all the Nazi–Soviet Pact. His views are no longer convincing; she feels a new need for independence. During wartime, as Sam serves abroad, she begins to discover a life and an education of her own; when Sam returns home from war with a story of having raped a German woman, a Nazi, she at once leaves him. America has now reentered the age of commodity capitalism, and the ideological world she has matured in has emptied of meaning. Janice's life falters again. It recovers when she falls in love with Charles Buckman, a blind musician, for whom her character is not her looks. She then wins back fourteen years of mature happiness in the sixties and seventies, until Charlie dies.

Plain Girl is a modest, retrospective allegory that reaches back across the world of Miller's writing, touching on the big political events and cultural changes that have shaped it, and the sense of moral maturing, and of loss, it has left behind. It reminds us that a strong part of Miller's overall narrative has been told not only in drama but in fiction, and that the concerns that have driven his writing – a strong sense of moral hunger for life and meaning, an awareness that life is always lived against history, and its crises, persecutions, and evasions, a feeling that there is always a potential for decency and self-knowledge – have been as vigorously created there as they have been on the stage. More than fifty years old now, *Focus* remains an important novel, as well as a signpost on the way to a significant post-war fiction that would prove a lasting way of telling America's troubled, often alienating modern story. Four at least of the shorter pieces – "I Don't Need You Any More," "The Misfits," "The Prophecy," "Fitter's Night" – are by any standards remarkable pieces of original prose writing, taken from a repertory of literary skill and awareness that can reach alike into the world of immigrant poverty and labor and the moral and intellectual anxieties of those who bear cultural responsibility. In his fiction, Miller has indeed been "real and at home." He has brought to the novel and the short story, as he has to the modern theatre, a distinctive artistry that is also an original strength of vision.

NOTES

1 E. M. Forster, *Aspects of the Novel* (London: 1927: reissued New York: Harvest Books, 1954), pp. 164, 168–69.

2 Arthur Miller, "Foreword: About Distances," in *I Don't Need You Any More: Stories* (London: Secker and Warburg, 1967), pp. ix–xiii.

3 Miller's thoughts on the subject bear some resemblance to those of Henry James's famous meditation on dialogue in his "Preface" to *The Awkward Age* (1899), a novel in which James sought to apply many of the lessons and conventions of theatre to fiction ("The beauty of the conception was in this approximation of the respective division of my own form to the successive Acts of a Play"). James wished to make a primary distinction between his own mannered discourse and the strong demands made by contemporary editors and publishers for dialogue in fiction: "'Dialogue,' always 'dialogue'! I had seemed from far back to hear them mostly cry: 'We can't have enough of it, and no excess of it, in the form of no matter what savourless dilution, or what boneless dispersion, ever began to injure a book so much as even the very scantest claim put in for form and substance.' The wisdom had always been in one's ears; but it had at the same time been equally in one's eyes that really constructive dialogue, dialogue organic and dramatic, speaking for itself, representing and embodying substance and form, is among us an uncanny and abhorrent thing . . . " Henry James, *The Art of the Novel: Critical Prefaces* (New York: Scribner, 1934), pp. 106–07.

4 Arthur Miller, *Focus* (New York: Reynal and Hitchcock, 1945; London:

Gollancz, 1949; paperback, London: Panther, 1964 [all quotations are from this edition]).

5 Saul Bellow, *Dangling Man* (New York: Vanguard, 1944; London: John Lehmann, 1946).

6 Arthur Miller, *Timebends* (London: Methuen, 1987), p. 105.

7 Lionel Trilling, "Manners, Morals, and the Novel," in *The Liberal Imagination* (Garden City, NY: Doubleday Anchor, 1950), pp. 200–15.

8 Malcolm Bradbury, "Neo-Realist Fiction," in Emory Elliott (ed.), *Columbia Literary History of the United States* (New York: Columbia University Press, 1988), pp. 1126–41.

9 Arthur Miller, *Homely Girl: A Life* (New York: Peter Blum, 1992); *Plain Girl: A Life* (London: Methuen, 1995).

14

STEPHEN BARKER

Critic, criticism, critics

From the very beginning of his career, Arthur Miller has engaged with the critical enterprise, but perhaps even more interestingly he has himself been a relentless and passionate critic, in all of his plays, of the human social and psychological condition, and has consistently ascribed a high value to that critical engagement. In fact, Miller's is a remarkably diverse yet tautly consistent group of major works that have made him, without doubt, the major American dramatic writer of his time, perhaps of the twentieth century.[1] And yet, perhaps not surprisingly, given the nature of the expectations of American theatre audiences, Miller's critical reception, particularly in his native America, has been mixed, at times downright hostile; Miller has irked critics from the beginning of his career and continues to do so, and it is precisely this irksomeness, along with his relentless will to excavate his own and the general human psyche and to place his discoveries into hypotheses about the human experience that draw broad (and often very critical) conclusions, that make his plays so compelling and powerful. "Great drama," he declares, "is great questions or it is nothing but technique."[2] It is this notion of "great questions" that Miller has been most interested to explore, throughout his work. Though many of his plays show a flexibility of form, Miller has on the whole not been primarily interested in attempts at radical innovation in form, or indeed in content, but despite this relative conservatism in an experimental age, most evident in his rigorous and prevailing belief in structure, content, and meaningful communication, Miller has energetically explored a committed liberal humanist agenda, whose great questions are always critical ones, frequently working against the grain of prevailing taste, both critical and public.

I want here briefly to explore Miller's complex relationship with the critical enterprise – from his notion of cultural, ideological, and social criticism, as a philosophical activity, to that of acts of theatre and aesthetic criticism itself, to his perennially interesting and provocative relationship to critics *per se*, in order to examine how this complex set of themes has stimulated and interacted with his dramatic writing and production. Such an investigation reveals that Miller's thematic tenacity and subtle experimentation, taken in its social, political, and psychological contexts, has resulted in a body of work that significantly contributes to a definition of the American psyche but that stretches the critical enterprise far beyond American shores.

Drama and critique

A drama rises in stature and intensity in proportion to the weight of its application to all men.[3]

Miller's critique is committed to personal awareness and social change, obsessed with the process by which these can be achieved. But Miller's subtlety in excavating the individual and social psyche is predicated on the possibility of successful communication, of theatrical language as a tool for human contact and understanding. He has been accused of being mechanical in his structure (Ronald Hayman calls him a "carpenter"[4]), but this is always directed toward a sense of unity that can only be discovered in the passionate, structured, theatrical critique of lived life aimed at "the true condition of man," which is a life lived in "comradely embrace, people helping one another rather than looking for ways to trip each other up" (*Timebends*, p. 111). This benevolent unity is, of course, a function of desire in Miller, and the catalyst for conflict. Miller's dilemma centers on the reliability of the social fabric by which the individual is bound to the group and by which society is created out of the weave of individual wills. This fabric is always a function of language; in Miller's plays, language and its reliability are central. From *All My Sons* on, the ability to use and manipulate language determines the nature of the world. Indeed, Miller's plays have become increasingly oriented toward talk, acknowledging the centrality of language as a social index: "drama . . . must represent a well-defined expression of profound social needs, needs which transcend any particular form of society or any particular historic moment," Miller declares,[5] since it is "an organism" (*Collected Plays*, p. 16) that expands one's awareness to life's continuity and meaning. For Miller, this is a contentious issue. When he says that "the fortress which *All My Sons* lays siege to is the fortress of unrelatedness" (*Collected Plays*, p. 19), he could be writing about any of his works.

This fundamental link between rhetoric and social – even metaphysical – meaning, has significant ramifications. It produces in Miller a deep aversion to the arbitrary, which he considers "indulgence" (*Collected Plays*, p. 8), and thus to a long series of avant-garde experimental enterprises in drama and the other arts during the twentieth century, from surrealism ("naturalism disguised" [*Timebends*, p. 562]) to the postmodern. It also produces an increasing tendency toward self-justification or self-explanation, seen most clearly in, for example, *The Price*'s set-piece speeches, which move momentarily away from the heated exchange of the dialogic and toward the greater solipsism of the monologic, wherein Miller's characters attempt to define their identities (often, seemingly, for themselves). Echoing, with his customary ironic overtones, that originary conservative text, the Bible, Miller claims that since "in the beginning was the word," "they're trying to name themselves; they're trying to define themselves because the moral situation is so nebulous and few people can ever know what side they're on, or if there are sides. So they talk themselves into positions"[6] from which they then operate.

Miller's great mentor for the critical analysis of existence, of course, was Ibsen, who was always concerned with the "possibilities" of accomplishment and empowerment, linked to the ideal of the rugged individual who finds it "intolerable that anybody should tell him what to do" (Centola, *Arthur Miller in Conversation*, p. 52). Miller, in his work, is quite clear that this condition of autonomy, which he considers basic for human life and which he calls "precious naiveté" (Centola, *Arthur Miller in Conversation*, p. 53), is, despite its preciousness, extraordinarily valuable precisely because it is an antidote to the dangers of mindlessly following directives of the herd's need for organization and structure, set against individual expression. This world of communicative self-determination and social responsibility, acknowledged even in the face of our clear limitations and shortcomings, is always aimed at the high ideal of critique: "I take it as a truth," Miller says, "that the end of drama is the creation of a higher consciousness and not merely a subjective attack upon the audience's nerves and feelings. What is precious in the Ibsen method is its insistence upon valid causation" (*Collected Plays*, p. 21). Ibsen is echoing the Greeks' tragic sense of causality, further echoed by Miller in his insistence on the primacy of causality; indeed, this Ibsenesque causal linkage provides the two fundamental building blocks of Miller's critical method: meaning and history.

Causation as the core of meaning is the driving engine of Miller's critique, and this always entails what Miller, in his Harvard lecture on Expressionism, calls the manifestation of "hidden forces."[7] Life has meaning and that meaning can be articulated and communicated. In common with Ibsen's conservative-tragic sense, Miller's is always "unveiling a truth already known but unrecognized as such" (*Collected Plays*, p. 11), which leads us back, as it were, to the shared "mutuality" of our existence, enacted both metaphysically and pragmatically. C. W. E. Bigsby points out that it is precisely this penetration to the "metaphysical implications" of social and cultural issues that made and makes Miller so unique in and to postwar American theatre.[8] So pervaded by the notion of causative critique is Miller's work that a play devoid of an intentional presentation of ideas linking the metaphysical realm with lived experience would be an "aesthetic nullity" (*Collected Plays*, p. 9). It is important to notice here how radically this view distances Miller from any tinge of the postmodern and its categorical stance with regard to human disconnectedness. When Miller went to China to direct *Death of a Salesman* in 1983, the American critical community, thinking that the play could never be successfully staged in a Communist country, predicted a fiasco; Miller's view that only one humanity exists made him sure it would reach the Chinese, and of course he was spectacularly correct.

In his pragmatic sense of causality, Miller takes a very interesting attitude toward the eminently culpable parents portrayed in many of his longer plays. They are finally not to blame for their ruinous actions, he asserts: the parents are "after all, but the shadows of the gods."[9] Miller claims that the hidden forces behind the figures' actions must be discovered, labeled, and held accountable for the horrifying failures of the authority figures who are, ironically, their puppets. According to Miller, these hidden forces are pervasive throughout human culture; they are the root causes of the loss of innocence, of transgression, and of the blindness with which his characters (and we all) act. In this respect, the process of discovery through which one must go to articulate these "gods" defines the development of Miller's protagonists over the course of his major plays, from the inarticulately tragic figures of the early works to over-articulate later figures such as Quentin in *After the Fall*, who is too important to Miller not to speak portentously but who, in so doing, undermines his own value as a critical analyst.

This sense of the causal link, in action, between invisible forces and visible consequences leads Miller to a second causal link at the center of his pervasively social critique: that between history and experience. "A new poem on the stage," he asserts, "is a new concept of relationships between the one and the many and the many and history, and to create it requires greater attention, not less, to the inexorable, common, pervasive conditions of existence in this time and this hour. Otherwise, only a new self-indulgence is created" (*Collected Plays*, p. 53). Given that "social drama" is the main stream of cultural identification, as opposed to the self-indulgence of postmodernists and absurdists whose solipsistic exercises should never, according to Miller, be confused with art, the playwright's job is to show history being made, in the minutiae of past events insinuated into present experience. This is central to Miller for two reasons: because of his links to his own past and because America must constantly be reminded that it has one. Miller confesses that like Willy Loman he has always been "kind of temporary" about himself, feeling that the "here and now was always melting before the head of a dream coming toward me or its tail going away" (*Timebends*, p. 69). Miller's Jewish history, his sense of the role of victimization and of the victim's relationship to a larger societal unit, and his sense of the oneness of the individual and society all contribute to complicate this picture. His great fear for America – and this is one of Miller's explanations for his greater success in England than in the United States in recent years – is that, as he told Mark Lamos in an interview in 1986, "we don't have any past anymore."[10] To have no real awareness of a continuity with the past is to have no real culture, to be "invisible in [one's] own land" (*Timebends*, p. 589). Timebends are indeed for Miller those overlappings of time by which the so-called past and the present melt together into a composite time that informs a more total notion of experience. It is the past and the present collapsed together, inseparable and yet discrete sense–memory layerings, that give us the sense of "unity" over any sense of disparateness or separation. Theatrically, this means a constant critique of the commercial theatre devoted to the money, lies, shallowness, and elitism Miller hates so deeply, and its displacement by a committed theatre that investigates and critically analyses the genuine human experience of the common person whose sensitivities are shared – and validated in that sharing.

History is thus the perpetual validation of experience; it is particularly ironic that Miller, the most passionate critic of the rejection or ignoring of history, should face a threatened reputation because he himself "could not hear the tempo of the time anymore" (*Timebends*, p. 445). In the latter twentieth century, Miller's notion of our rootedness in a substantial and objectified past of which the present is a result has given way to a double notion of fracture with history: in the commercial theatre audience, the sense of history has been replaced by an easy forgetfulness compensated by the self-centeredness of the capitalist ethic; at a more theoretical level, thinkers and writers have dispensed with the past altogether as a gauge or measure of identity or reality. Miller passionately rejects both of these options, but, in so doing, he places himself "outside of history," alien to the evolution of historical context: his own sense of history threatens his historical relevancy. In offering a critique of, and rejecting, what he calls the "cold pessimism of the absurd" (Bigsby, *Confrontation*, p. 49), with its unaccommodatable abjectness, terrors, and anomie, he rejects the solipsistic (or self-less) darkness of non-history to couch his critique in the very historical groundedness of common perception, desiring "to write so that people of common sense *would mistake my play for life itself* and not be required to lend it some poetic license before it could be believed" (*Collected Plays*, p. 19, emphasis added). This mimesis is itself a central idea in Miller's work, since the more generalizable the conflict, the more tragic and relevant it will be. As for Aristotle, for Miller the building of character is far less important than the construction of challenges placed in the way of the individual caught in the collective swirl (e.g. Willy Loman, the exemplum and instrument of social critique, echoed by Phillip Gellburg in *Broken Glass*, who fulfills the same role). "Americans," Miller laments, "don't want to be separated from the mask," and therefore "adopt a mask in order to be like everybody else" (Bigsby, *Confrontation*, p. 24). The dilemma for the Modernist/humanist Miller here is that adoption of this mask-identity represents the establishment of a sense of universal and ordinary identity and simultaneously a radical loss of it.

The pulls and pulses of criticism

to locate the individual in a social context which goes some way to explain but never wholly to define his or her identity. . .[11]

While his language declares a strategic unity of theme and experience among all, Miller's writing is made much more dynamic by its relationship to the action of criticism itself, which relies not on similarity and unity but on difference and division. Miller was and is simultaneously the loner and the gregarious man, a part of the whole but somehow apart from it, acknowledging that self-knowledge and self-empowerment are not inherent nor immanent but functions of "skepticism, of self-removal, that presages the radical separation of man from society which the American drama expresses ultimately through themes of frustration."[12] This emphasis on critical difference is not in contradiction to his view of unity, but a development of it. After all, any concept of history or of time itself is predicated on difference and division. For Miller, any such division relates to the association between the individual and the larger group, which is always a critical relationship. Indeed, this critical distance is the corollary to the mask of conformity by which Miller suggests derisively that Americans identify themselves: for him, the real self is the private one, often lost in the welter of social pressures and forces, that will not permit, without a passionate struggle, the lobotomized collectivism he saw during the McCarthy era. To be properly self-conscious is to come to understand the dialectic of choice, commitment, responsibility, conscience, morality, ethics, and, finally, tragic failure. Indeed, it is just these pulls and pushes of the critical enterprise that ostensibly make us successful (or unsuccessful) beings, and the appropriate subjects of serious drama.

Passionate commitment is the first step toward critical understanding: "to imagine that a play can be written disinterestedly is to believe that one can make love disinterestedly" (*Collected Plays*, p. 13). We must be committed if we are to be anything. Passion is of course moderated by the "god of Reason," whose chief power is "the power to choose" (*Timebends*, p. 71), and in making choices we take stands which identify us. Thus the "collective vision" Miller posits is actually a double vision, consisting of the dangerous but compelling mask of convention and the conflicting (critical) individuality of seeing with one's own eyes; commitment to ideas is always, finally, commitment to difference. And commitment to ideas designed to alienate an audience oriented toward its mask has always been central in Miller's work. He refers to himself as "the bringer of bad news" (*Timebends*, p. 534), the only mode in which the responsible artist can work. Referring to the particularly bad news he brings in *After the Fall*, that innocence can be lethal, he says that "I was soon widely hated, but the play had spoken its truth as, after all, it was obliged to do, and if the truth was clothed in pain, perhaps it was important for the audience to confront it uncomfortably and even in the anger of denial. In time, and with much difficulty, I saw the justification for the hostility toward me, for I had indeed brought very bad news" (*Timebends*, p. 534).

The "responsible" criticism in which Miller engages reveals his disappointment with a country – indeed, a humanity in general – that has managed assiduously to avoid its responsibility to itself. Tragic enlightenment is possible only if one accepts one's accountability and culpability. Taking responsibility is a choice that one may make, as do Quentin in *After the Fall*, Von Berg in *Incident at Vichy*, Fenelon in *Playing for Time*, Kroll in *Clara*, John Proctor in *The Crucible*. If one is not able to make this choice, one undergoes the tragic transformation into the deluded, nightmare-beleaguered, suicidal *doppelgänger* of the responsible individual, so evident in Miller's earlier plays, characters such as Joe Keller, Willy Loman, Eddie Carbone, Maggie, and latterly Phillip Gellburg. For these characters, only a non-choice exists, in which they are unable to understand their accountability. They are ruined by their inability to separate themselves from the dominant social forces that control them.

Given his penchant for exploring the universal and metaphysical in the individual and concrete, Miller always discovers what is already there, beneath the various accommodations and mask-appropriations of which we consist. This disclosure leads not only to a dialectic with responsibility, but also with guilt – guilt at having lived, in a Camusesque sense, and not died; guilt at the evil we harbor within us; guilt at not being able to take responsibility. This may be a central reason why Miller's critical parables have been problematic for a Broadway audience.

Here one reaches the core of Miller's morality, which runs like a vein of cultural criticism through all his plays: the relationship of individual accountability to the forces against which we must struggle in order to maintain that individuality on the basis of which meaningful action is possible. Miller's is a pragmatic morality, bringing us "into the direct path of the consequences" we produce (*Collected Plays*, p. 18), since reality lies in consequence *as* action. *After the Fall*, for example, intimates that the original fall, from Eden, is recapitulated by each individual through the fall into consciousness, and thus into choice (i.e. the Cain or Abel choice). Miller draws moral distinction clearly, in order to show how vital the issues of choice and accountability are; he calls himself an "impatient moralist," and attempts to heighten viewer/reader awareness of the moral and ethical relationships within which people live (Bigsby, ed., *File on Miller*, p. 66).[13] Choice is an allegory for autonomy, the hegemonic marker sustaining the autonomous individual. The actions of choice are vitally moral.

But just as in the Greek drama, in Miller no successful path to right choice and actions exists; it is a matter of choosing the correct incorrect path to an idea, and that idea is always the failure and betrayal of the purity and perfection for which his characters strive. This failure is the tragic lesson Miller always teaches, and which grounds his critical dialectic. It is an ineluctable fact of life that we are alienated, that we desire not to be, that we search for a way not to be, that this search is itself ineluctable, and that it will always be unsuccessful. The desire to be "at home," no longer in a condition of unrestful, psychological nomadism, is a natural and unsatisfiable desire. While Richard Gilman does not consider Miller to be a tragic writer (*The Making of Modern Drama* [New York: Da Capo Press: 1974]) (but rather a melodramatist), Raymond Williams does, placing Miller in the "liberal tragedy" tradition exemplified by Ibsen, albeit a "late revival" of this tradition (*Modern Tragedy* [California: Stanford University Press], pp. 88ff.). The juxtaposing of tragedy and failure highlights Miller's dialectical rejoinder to his universal "we are all one": in our tragic nature is the individual struggle against the self that declares "we are all separate" from each other and from ourselves. Miller's tragic sense undergoes a clear evolution from his early to his most recent plays, his characters learning to accept their lives (which his early protagonists could never do) after undergoing some sort of revelation. This evolution has made Miller's tragic vision more traditional, in that the weight of the characters' conscious tragic sense gives them added insight, in the Greek sense. Indeed, tragic human will is the ability to accept things as they are, despite the resultant elation and/or despair. To attempt to change things is to fall victim to hubris, frustration, and madness. Thus, since one is inevitably always striving for the purity the world and human life deny, this resignation requires the dialectical acknowledgment of tragic failure.

Miller and the critics

> I have often rescued a sense of reality by recalling Chekhov's remark: "If I had listened to the critics I'd have died drunk in the gutter." (*Timebends*, p. 534)

Miller's vision, then, consists of a critique of the universal human situation and a critical dialectic with the human and social conditions of difference and alienation within which we live and work. Each of Miller's plays is a critique of his work and life, and of the life of people, American and otherwise. Since for Miller humans are not perfectible, despite the false idealism of the social theatre, we must accept our flawed, venal nature in any program for social improvement. These abstract and theoretical considerations place his work within the writer's larger cultural spectrum. Miller sees himself as an arbiter of the social fabric; all the more interesting, then, that those arbiters of the dramatic fabric, critics, have had such a complex relationship with Miller and his work. Miller has received a remarkably (and famously) wide variety of critical responses; the tragic social message he has sent has not been uniformly received. If the critics have sometimes been dismissive, so has Miller: "critics and commentators, like most of the rest of us, are lazy people, and once I had been labeled it seemed no longer necessary for them to look twice at the plays that followed";[14] it was not that critics knew "more than others but that they could write better about the little they did know" (*Timebends*, p. 137). The result has been, to use Miller's interestingly pugilistic metaphor for it, "I exist as a playwright without a major reviewer in my corner" (*Timebends*, p. 534). While it is true that since what several unfriendly reviewers refer to as "the Marilyn plays" (thus quite completely and dramatically misunderstanding them, from Miller's point of view), Miller's reviews in America have been remarkably consistently negative (except for some revivals in New York and elsewhere); in England, and elsewhere outside America, they have been just as consistently positive. Miller accounts for this by suggesting that no single British critic is sufficiently powerful to close a play, leading to much more balanced reviewing. This is good, according to Miller: since critics have no special insight, they should have no inordinate power. But Miller is respectful of the critical community's power as well, acknowledging that the theatre we have "is the theatre the critics have permitted us to have, since they filter out what they consider we ought not see, enforcing laws that have never been written, laws, among others, of taste and even ideological content" (*Timebends*, p. 136). This critical paradox relates closely to Miller's thematic focus, since though the critic is no more nor less than a member of the audience, the critic's individual view, received by "the crowd," can be life-giving or lethal. Finally, the playwright's special task requires obedience to "laws" of "the physiological limits of attention in a seated position" (*Collected Plays*, p. 4), which pertain to newspaper critic and lay critic alike.

If this sort of absolutely practical shift seems jarring, considering Miller's attention to critique, it shouldn't, given the centrality of *praxis* in his aesthetic world view. It is refreshing to note, as many critics have, that a play must be a play before it is a set of ideas. Indeed this is yet another aspect of the critical dialectic in which Miller engages: he is poised between important, critical writing and theatre. His training in commercial theatre, and his life-long fascination with commerce and the business ethic, enforce a certain delight in the notion of selling, *per se*; he wants to be well-enough liked to sell on that basis.[15] But at the same time, he desires to rise above the shallowness and escapism of the commercial theatre to something he could acknowledge as universally true and valid. While they must deal centrally with the great questions of human life and society, plays themselves cannot be philosophical in nature, but must always attach to the actions of people "pre-philosophically" (*Collected Plays*, p. 36). He himself, in fact, claims that he does not write philosophically nor even methodically but rather – and we have to do our best to understand him here – "out of instinct" (Centola, *Arthur Miller in Conversation*, p. 22). This claim to instinctuality and its attendant anti-intellectual framework, is a particularly fascinating part of Miller's relationship to criticism: on the one hand, he is a highly sophisticated critic of American politics, business, social life, mores, and psyche; on the other hand, in this claim to work directly from instinct he eschews any direct link to a theoretical or critical matrix from which to work. This can have its downside, as in Gilman's claim (*The Making of Modern Drama*) that he does not rise to the tragic level or in Hayman's assertion that Miller's instinctual writing results in loss of control over the relationship between plots and ideas, so that they are not successfully integrated. The epitome of this view was expressed by Eleanor Clark in her review of *Death of a Salesman* in which she claimed that the play, "a hodge-podge of dated materials and facile new ones," "an intellectual muddle" of "contemporary fellow-traveling," is "clumsy," "specious," "unpleasantly pompous," "flat," "a very dull business, which departs in no way that is to its credit from the general mediocrity of our commercial theatre."[16] So much, according to Ms. Clark, for instinct.

Part of the curious relationship Miller has had with the critics has been his own reaction to criticism in the form of altering his work. He says that this is a result, in America, of "the frightened theatre" (*Timebends*, p. 586) of the critical mainstream, for which he has had to "contaminate" the early version of his plays to satisfy a benighted audience of critics (chiefly, for Miller, those of *The New York Times*) and the readers of critics. British productions have tended to use these earlier, purer versions of the works, which have never or seldom received a Broadway showing. Though the more one knows about his theatrical ideas the less certain one is of why he would want a Broadway production of any of his work, this too is part of Miller's complex critical enterprise. Since there is frequently now no serious drama on Broadway, one can hardly disagree with Miller about the narrowness of this theatrical venue. This has partly to do with Miller's history as well as with the history of his plays and their revivals. European critics have been willing to judge Miller on his works one at a time, assessing each of the most recent of his works as a new entity; American critics have persistently, and very unfavorably, compared his recent work with his early work which, one must again remember, was always seen in altered versions. Furthermore, American critics have fairly consistently seen the recent work as vastly inferior to the best of the earlier work.

Treatment of several of Miller's plays shows the complexity of the American and British reaction. *The Price* has been interesting from this point of view:[17] it has improved with time for reviewers and critics alike, now being considered very pertinent to the tenor of its time and richly depictive of a constellation of themes. *After the Fall* has suffered a more complex fate. The American critics' reaction to it when it was first presented in 1964 is legendary: they saw it as a tasteless and obsessive revelation of the Miller/Monroe relationship, and the fact that it appeared hot on the heels of Monroe's death did it and Miller further harm, making it (from that point of view) seem even more crassly tasteless. When the play was revived off-Broadway in 1984, however, it failed to alter that original reaction: the American critics were still unable to see the play as capable of being separated from the biographical details purportedly surrounding its original production – details always denied by Miller. The English, not bound by "celebrity speculation" (Centola, *Arthur Miller in Conversation*, p. 12) to nearly the same extent, have come increasingly to respect the play. Michael Blakemore's 1990 London production, in which Maggie was played by a black woman, thus demonstrating complete freedom from the historical myth to which Americans attach the character, was a great critical success.

A moment of metacriticism

Inevitably, to one degree or another, we see what we see on the stage not only with our own eyes but with the eyes of others.   (*Collected Plays*, p. 10)

The "others" through whom we see what we see include, in a dramatically optimal position, the critical community, whose eyes introduce us to art. And, as it happens, critical ambivalence to his work remains one of Miller's most arresting traits. On the one hand vilified by a highly vocal portion of his critical audience (led over the years by Robert Brustein, who is perpetually irritated by Miller's work), Miller remains on the other hand the doyen of living American playwrights. Explanations for this ambiguous position are fascinating in what they reveal of Miller as a playwright and artist. Miller clashes and concurs with critical themes on three important fronts: innocence, individuality, and hope. All three are problems for Miller's characters and for the society the critical community sees itself as representing. According to C. W. E. Bigsby, America finally does not want to be told that innocence can ever be lost, that a condition of "after the fall" exists, and so cannot accept Miller's world-view; in America, Miller's vision is thus incompatible with the individualistic (yet mask-oriented) American dream. But in Miller's latter works, the expansive capacities of the individual are increasingly attended to. Another suggestion is that Miller's "tragic vision is more compatible with the perspective of Europeans who accept human imperfection and recognize the need to offset it with responsible social action" (Centola, *Arthur Miller in Conversation*, p. 12). Yet Miller has from the beginning suggested in his plays, at least implicitly and frequently explicitly, that audience action in response to the shortcomings of his characters is a needed corollary to the dramatic presentation.

The spur to action for Miller is hope which, though it may be denied by characters who are unable to choose to perceive it, is immanently present in Miller's ethos. Even where one can see the refusal of hope by characters destroyed by their blindness, one can also see the other side of the dialectic, looming behind or stated in the play. The courage to face oneself and to be ruthlessly honest in that confrontation marks the ability to perceive that hope. In a future comprising infinite possibilities for the empowered, insightful, and willful individual, a play presenting this structural or dialectical element of hope is accomplishing its critical social goal.

Critique and criticism are, for Miller, the structural functions of the playwright. Had Miller not attempted to bring his message to the market-place in an essentially mainstream way, he would not have suffered the sort of response he has occasionally received. His desire to be successful for the masses has meant that he has been forced to accept the slings and arrows of critics whose portfolio has been to arbitrate the "taste of record" of the day. Despite the generally subtle innovations in technique, style, and content with which he has worked in his major plays, Miller has never tried to present himself as anything but a patently public, "Broadway" playwright; indeed, during much of his writing career he had no alternative, since until the 1960s no real national alternative to Broadway existed. By that time, Miller's target audience had been established in his mind, so that he has never attempted to appeal to a more experimental audience, not the *cognoscenti* nor the so-called but always elusive mainstream. In point of fact, Miller has always emulated Ibsen, desiring to be successful at the level of theatrical presentation and dramatic/symbolic content; he has been less speedy, however, to take the final step to Ibsen's universal appeal. Miller is finally a playwright attempting to appeal beyond the barrier of professional criticism to the critical masses; certainly, starting with *Death of a Salesman*, and moving through a number of later works (very much including Miller's most popular play, *The Crucible*, and the recent *Broken Glass*), many plays from Miller's *oeuvre* do rise to the level of universality for which he has, ultimately, striven. Meanwhile, many of the rest of his plays, not as unsuccessful as is sometimes claimed nor as successful as some rejoinders might indicate, are at least consistently intimate experiments, in theme and treatment; Miller is a deeply thoughtful craftsman who in his own self-critique has always desired and striven to be more, in an attempt to "try to capture some of the smell and sense of this very vagrant thing we call existence" (Centola, *Arthur Miller in Conversation*, p. 54), the source and the end of all critique and all criticism.

NOTES

1 Despite Eugene O'Neill's Nobel Prize and numerous Pulitzers, his reputation has contracted over time, while Miller's has expanded. With the possible exception of Tennessee Williams, no other figure, at this point, rivals Miller and O'Neill in terms of impact and quality of work, as theatregoers, critics, and scholars increasingly agree.

2 Arthur Miller, *Timebends* (New York: Grove Press, 1987), p. 180.

3 ARthur Miller, cited in Henry Popkin, "Arthur Miller: The Strange Encounter," in Alan S. Downer (ed.), *American Drama and Its Critics* (Chicago: University of Chicago Press, 1965), p. 222. It is impossible to avoid the persistent reference Miller makes to "man," speaking of "human beings"; without doubt, his chief concern is with men, with notable exceptions (e.g. *Playing for Time*), since the vast bulk of his writing is based in exploration of his own life and feelings.

4 Ronald Hayman, *Arthur Miller* (New York: Frederick Ungar, 1972), p. 111.

5 Introduction, *Arthur Miller's Collected Plays* (New York: Viking Press, 1971), p. 3.

6 Miller in conversation, cited in Steven R. Centola, *Arthur Miller in Conversation* (Dallas: Contemporary Research Associates, 1993), p. 54. At the same time, Miller's critique is from the point of view of what he calls a "bridge" figure, the European Jew accommodating to the new world, embracing and rejecting the new society around him, simultaneously trusting and distrusting the institutions around him, hoping for the best but never surprised by the venality and self-centered paranoia he confronts.

7 Published in the *Atlantic Monthly*, April 1956.

8 *Confrontation and Commitment* (Columbia: University of Missouri Press, 1968), p. 26.

9 Cited by Henry Popkin, "Arthur Miller: The Strange Encounter," in Alan S. Downer (ed.), *American Drama and Its Critics* (Chicago: University of Chicago Press, 1965), p. 227.

10 Mark Lamos, "An Afternoon with Arthur Miller," *American Theatre* 3 (1986): 21.

11 C. W. E. Bigsby, "Drama from a Living Center," in Harold Bloom (ed.), *Modern Critical Views: Arthur Miller* (New York: Chelsea House, 1987), p. 122.

12 "On Social Plays," Introduction to *A View from the Bridge* (New York: Viking Press, 1955), p. 6.

13 C. W. E. Bigsby (ed.), *File on Miller* (London: Methuen, 1987).

14 June Schlueter and James K. Flanagan (eds.), *Arthur Miller* (New York: Frederick Ungar, 1987), p. 135.

15 By training from earliest youth – and in terms of his relationship to American culture, Miller is very concerned with the modern morality of the corporate society: he asks if it is possible that we might become so much "a function of production and distribution" that "personality becomes divorced from the actions it propels" (*Collected Plays*, Introduction, p. 19). And of course one cannot forget the wonderful story that as *All My Sons* became a success on Broadway, Miller became worried that "my identification with life's failures was being menaced by my fame" (*Timebends*, p. 138); he went out and got a minimum-wage job assembling beer-box dividers – for a very short period of time – in order not to become detached from what mattered. Later in his life, of course, Miller's idealism took other forms, but the main concern with business and its ethos remains (as witness *The Price*, *A View from the Bridge*, and latterly, *Broken Glass*, one of whose major themes is an echo of that business-orientation).

16 *Partisan Review* (June 1949): 632.

17 See Robert Brustein's vitriolic "The Unseriousness of Arthur Miller" in *The New Republic*, 24 February 1968, and contrast it with the exaltation of Miller in David Richards's "*The Price* is Right for These Days" in *The New York Times*, 28 June 1992.

15

SUSAN HAEDICKE

Arthur Miller: a bibliographic essay

After nearly five decades of writing for the theatre, Arthur Miller continues to have new plays produced on New York and London stages, and the number of revivals of his plays increases annually in professional and academic theatres where they reinvigorate American audiences and enthrall international ones. "No other American dramatist," writes C. W. E. Bigsby, "has so directly engaged the anxieties and fears, the myths and dreams, of a people desperate to believe in a freedom for which they see ever less evidence. No other American writer has so successfully touched a nerve of the national consciousness" (*A Critical Introduction to Twentieth-Century American Drama*, vol. II [Cambridge: Cambridge University Press, 1984], p. 248). Best known for his stage plays, Miller has also made important contributions to dramatic theory and criticism, and he has written radio and television plays, film scripts, novels, and travel journals. In addition, Miller continues to extend his political activities beyond the stage as he fights for the freedom of artists worldwide. His work still provokes scholarly debate.

Bibliographies

Several bibliographies on Arthur Miller are readily available. The most comprehensive is John H. Ferres, *Arthur Miller: A Reference Guide* (Boston: G. K. Hall, 1979) which lists primary and secondary sources, including books, essays, theatre reviews, book reviews, bibliographies, and dissertations from 1944 through May 1978 in chronological order. Each citation includes a brief abstract. Other helpful, although somewhat dated, bibliographies are Martha Turnquist Eissenstat, "Arthur Miller: A Bibliography," *Modern Drama* 5 (1962): 93–106; Tetsumaro Hayashi, *An Index to Arthur Miller Criticism*, second edition (Metuchen: Scarecrow, 1976); George H. Jensen, *Arthur Miller: A Bibliographic Checklist* (Columbia: Faust, 1976); and Harriet Ungar, "The Writings of and about Arthur Miller: A Checklist

1936–1967," *Bulletin of the New York Public Library* (1970): 107–34. Tetsumaro Hayashi also edited *Arthur Miller and Tennessee Williams: Research Opportunities and Dissertation Abstracts* (Jefferson: McFarland, 1983) which reprints dissertation abstracts from 1952–80 which mention Miller. This volume is exceedingly helpful to students. Charles A. Carpenter, "Studies of Arthur Miller's Drama: a Selective International Bibliography, 1966–79," in Robert A. Martin (ed.), *Arthur Miller: New Perspectives* (Englewood Cliffs: Prentice-Hall, 1982), offers many foreign entries. The *MLA Bibliography*, now available online through First Search, and the annual bibliography published in *Modern Drama* list current works on Miller. "A Bibliography of Works (1936–1977) by Arthur Miller," in Robert A. Martin (ed.), *The Theater Essays of Arthur Miller* (New York: Viking Press, 1978), lists Miller's work in chronological order by genre and locates unpublished manuscripts and manuscript/typescript collections, and C. W. E. Bigsby's *File on Miller* (London and New York: Methuen, 1987), part of Methuen's Writer-Files Series, lists all of Miller's writings and includes a brief summary of the work and excerpts of reactions at the time of production or publication.

Four important bibliographic essays provide more detailed information on Miller scholarship. James J. Martine's introduction to his volume entitled *Critical Essays on Arthur Miller* (Boston: G. K. Hall, 1979) comments on the major works by and about Miller through the late 1970s. The bibliographic essays by Alvin Goldfarb, in Philip C. Kolin (ed.), *American Playwrights Since 1945: A Guide to Scholarship, Criticism, and Performance* (Westport, CT: Greenwood, 1989), and by June Schlueter, in Matthew C. Roudané (ed.), *Contemporary Authors: Bibliographical Series*, vol. III (Detroit: Gale, 1989), add more recent entries to the sources cited by Martine. In addition, each essay offers an extensive coverage of one area of Miller scholarship. Goldfarb summarizes the production history of Miller's plays, and Schlueter offers a chronological guide through almost fifty of the interviews Miller granted up to 1989. Schlueter's very thorough essay is difficult to find, but well worth the work. The most recent bibliographic essay, published in 1995, is Matthew C. Roudané's examination of sources on Miller in his edition of *Approaches to Teaching Miller's "Death of a Salesman"* (New York: The Modern Language Association of America, 1995). This essay, while emphasizing works pertinent to the study of *Death of a Salesman*, also adds sections on "Text and Performance" and on "Further Selected Readings" which categorizes titles, including those not specifically on Miller, under the headings of "Language and Psychology," "American Myths and the Family," "Public Issues, Private Tensions," and "Dramatic Innovations."

Biographical dimensions

Many books on Arthur Miller include a biographical chronology. One of the most detailed appears in *Arthur Miller*, edited by June Schlueter and James K. Flanagan (New York: Frederick Ungar, 1987). Full-length critical studies of Miller's plays (see section on general books) often include chronologies or biographical chapters. Benjamin Nelson's *Arthur Miller: Portrait of a Playwright* (London: Owen; New York: David McKay, 1970) emphasizes biographical information in the critical study of the plays, and Schlueter and Flanagan's *Arthur Miller* (mentioned above) explores connections between his life and work.

Although no book-length biography exists on Miller to date, *Timebends* (New York: Grove, 1987), Miller's autobiography, begins to fill this gap with subjective, but insightful accounts of experiences Miller found significant in his own life and art. And in a recent interview with Susan Cheever, "The One Thing That Keeps Us From Chaos," *New Choices for Retirement Living* 34.8 (1994): 22–25, Miller discusses his family, his marriage, and his attitudes toward the United States. A different type of personal account appears in Kenneth T. Rowe's "Shadows Cast Before," in Martin, *Arthur Miller: New Perspectives*. His playwriting teacher at the University of Michigan, Rowe describes their professor/student relationship as he examines Miller's earliest plays. *Arthur Miller and Company: Arthur Miller Talks About His Work in the Company of Actors, Designers, Directors, Reviewers, and Writers*, edited by Christopher Bigsby (London: Methuen, 1990), offers insights into the man and his work in an interview and comments by eighty writers.

Miller has commented that all his plays are, in a sense, autobiographical, so scholars have used them, especially *After the Fall*, as a potential source of information. Harold Clurman wrote a series of essays, later published as "Arthur Miller's Later Plays," in Robert Corrigan (ed.), *Arthur Miller: A Collection of Critical Essays* (Englewood Cliffs: Prentice-Hall, 1969), which examines the plays through *After the Fall* for autobiographical material. Leonard Moss, on the other hand, asserts that Miller's "autoplagiarism" results in recurring characters and ideas rather than specific autobiographical anecdotes, in "Biographical and Literary Allusion in *After the Fall*," *Educational Theatre Journal* 18 (1966): 34–40.

Through the nearly half-century that Miller has written for the stage, he has granted frequent and informative interviews discussing personal details and offering insights into his dramaturgy, his intentions on specific plays, his sociopolitical concerns, and his reactions to the critical responses his plays aroused. The interviews provide another perspective on Miller the man, and, taken together, they form a coherent and perceptive commentary on American theatre in the second half of the twentieth century. As already mentioned, Schlueter's bibliographic essay organizes many important interviews from 1947 to 1989 in chronological order and highlights the original material explored in each. Matthew C. Roudané collected thirty-five of the most significant interviews in *Conversations with Arthur Miller* (Jackson: University Press of Mississippi, 1987), and Steven R. Centola edited his interviews with the playwright for *Arthur Miller in Conversation* (Dallas: Contemporary Research Associates, 1993). Other recent interviews include those conducted by Jide Guo, "My Interview with Arthur Miller," *Foreign Literatures* 5 (1987): 31–38 (in Chinese); Jan Balakian, "A Conversation with Arthur Miller," *Michigan Quarterly Review* 29.2 (1990): 158–71; Robert Feldman, "Arthur Miller on the Theme of Evil: An Interview," *Resources for American Literary Study* (1990): 87–93; Steven R. Centola, "Just Looking for a Home: A Conversation with Arthur Miller," *American Drama* (1991): 85–94; "The Talk of the Town: Miller's Tales," *New Yorker* 70.8 (11 April 1994): 35–36; and Heather Neill, "Leading Role," *Times Educational Supplement* (9 September 1994): A15. In the last two interviews, Miller discusses his most recent play, *Broken Glass*, as well as the respect bordering on veneration he receives in England.

Miller's dramatic theories and thoughts on the American theatre, discussed informally in the interviews, receive a more formal consideration in the many theatre essays written by Miller. Robert A. Martin collected some of these essays in *The Theater Essays of Arthur Miller*. A new collection of theatre essays, edited by Robert A. Martin and Steven R. Centola, also entitled *The Theater Essays of Arthur Miller* (New York: DaCapa Press), appeared in 1996. A bibliography of the essays written through 1987 appears in Schlueter's bibliographic essay and in Bigsby's *File on Miller*. In 1987, Miller participated in "A Round-Table Discussion: Talking About Writing for the Theatre" with Athol Fugard, David Mamet, and Wallace Shawn, *Foreign Literatures* 5 (1987): 44–47.

In many of the interviews and essays, Miller gives his thoughts on the importance of an artist's political responsibility. Continuing a life-long commitment to the freedom of artists, Miller published "Ibsen's Warning," *Index on Censorship* 18.6–7 (1988): 74–76 and "On Censorship," in Nicholas J. Karolides, Lee Burress, and John M. Kean (eds.), *Censored Books: Critical Viewpoints* (Metuchen: Scarecrow, 1993). This volume includes essays on the censorship of *The Crucible* and *Death of a Salesman*. Melvin Maddocks explores the responses of several dramatists, including Miller, to political injustice in "Words and Deeds," *World Monitor* 2.3 (1989): 18–19.

Critical studies

Miller scholarship is very extensive, and the bibliographic essays of Martine, Goldfarb, Schlueter, and Roudané, cited earlier, provide an excellent guide through the critical material by organizing the secondary sources primarily into categories of books, collections of essays, and works specific to individual plays. Roudané's addition of the section on "Further Selected Readings" and the observation at the end of Schlueter's essay that hopefully "the next generation of Miller scholarship will bring special critical perspectives to his work" (p. 270) inspired the organization of the secondary sources found here. After briefly citing the major general books on Miller and the collections of critical essays, the present bibliographic essay which comprises this chapter will work its way through Miller scholarship by focusing on "critical perspectives." These categories have flexible boundaries, and, in fact, many sources are mentioned in more than one. Given the enormous number of sources, selection for inclusion forced very difficult choices and necessitated leaving out many solid critical studies. In no way, however, does this omission intend to diminish the contributions to Miller scholarship that are not included.

General books and collections of essays

Dennis Welland's *Arthur Miller* (Edinburgh: Oliver and Boyd, 1961) marks the beginning of book-length studies of Miller's work and establishes the format that was to become the standard in Miller scholarship: an overview chapter on the playwright and then separate chapters devoted to analyses of each of the plays. Welland returned to an examination of Miller's plays in *Miller: A Study of his Plays* (London: Methuen, 1979) which he revised and updated in *Miller: The Playwright* (London: Methuen, 1983). The 1983 edition examines plays through *The Archbishop's Ceiling* and *Fame* and includes a listing of American and British premieres. Sheila Huftel, in *Arthur Miller: The Burning Glass* (New York: Citadel, 1965), following Welland's format, focuses on the characters' quest for self-knowledge in plays through *Incident at Vichy*, and offers an appendix with cast lists for the New York and London premieres. *Arthur Miller: Dramatist* (New York: Frederick Ungar, 1967), by Edward Murray, adds few new insights and no overview chapter. Leonard Moss in *Arthur Miller* (New York: Twayne, 1967), expanded in 1980 to include the later plays and a 1979 interview, focuses on the psychological dimensions of Miller's work. Ronald Hayman's *Arthur Miller* (New York: Frederick Ungar, 1972, reprinted 1983) concludes with a chapter on Miller within the context of modern European and American drama where he emphasizes Miller as a social dramatist. Neil Carson, in *Arthur Miller* (New York: St. Martin's Press, 1982), extends the play-by-play format through *The Creation of the World and Other Business* and *Playing for Time*. Biographical chapters precede the play analyses, which are followed by a concluding chapter on Miller's contributions and his vision as both a social and religious writer. The most recent study, *Arthur Miller* (1987) by Schlueter and Flanagan, already mentioned, offers insightful analyses of the plays through *Danger! Memory*, and examines his social commitment, dramatic innovations, and the interplay between his personal experiences and his dramatic works. Also of importance are the long sections on Miller in C. W. E. Bigsby's *A Critical Introduction to Twentieth-Century American Drama*, vol. II (1984), already mentioned, and *Modern American Drama, 1945–1990* (Cambridge: Cambridge University Press, 1992).

A number of collections of critical essays have been published over the last three decades. Those specific to *Death of a Salesman* include John D. Hurrell, *Two Modern American Tragedies: Reviews and Criticism of Death of a Salesman and Streetcar Named Desire* (New York: Scribner's, 1961); Gerald Weales, *Arthur Miller: Death of a Salesman: Text and Criticism* (New York: Viking Press, 1967, reprinted Harmondsworth: Penguin, 1977); Walter J. Meserve, *The Merrill Studies in Death of a Salesman* (Columbus, Ohio: Merrill, 1972) which includes some foreign reviews; Helen Wickham Koon, *Twentieth Century Interpretations of Death of a Salesman: A Collection of Critical Essays* (Englewoods Cliffs: Prentice-Hall, 1983); and Harold Bloom's *Arthur Miller's Death of a Salesman* (New York: Chelsea House, 1988) and *Willy Loman* (New York: Chelsea House, 1991). Two volumes focus on *The Crucible*: Gerald Weales, *The Crucible: Text and Criticism* (New York: Viking Press, 1971, reprinted 1982), and John H. Ferres, *Twentieth Century Interpretations of The Crucible* (Englewood Cliffs: Prentice-Hall, 1972). Other collections cover a wider range of Miller's work: Robert W. Corrigan, *Arthur Miller: A Collection of Critical Essays* (Englewood Cliffs: Prentice-Hall, 1969); James J. Martine, *Critical Essays on Arthur Miller* (Boston: G. K. Hall, 1979); Robert A. Martin, *Arthur Miller: New Perspectives* (Englewood Cliffs: Prentice-Hall, 1982); Harold Bloom, *Modern Critical Views: Arthur Miller* (New York: Chelsea House, 1987); Steven R. Centola, *The Achievement of Arthur Miller: New Essays* (Dallas: Contemporary Research Associates, 1995). Only the last name of the editor and short title will appear in future references to these collections.

Critical perspectives: comparative analyses

Miller's plays began to attract the attention of theatre critics with the production of *Death of a Salesman*. The first articles to appear compare his work to that of Tennessee Williams, a comparison that continues to interest scholars. Alan Downer in "Mr. Williams and Mr. Miller," *Furioso* 4 (1949): 66–70, praises both playwrights for making substantial contributions to American drama, but highlights the differences between the two, and Kenneth Tynan in "American Blues: The Plays of Arthur Miller and Tennessee Williams," *Encounter* 2 (1954): 13–19, recognizes the power of both dramatists. Allan Lewis includes a chapter, "The American Scene: Williams and Miller," in *The Contemporary Theatre: The Significant Playwrights of our Time* (New York: Crown, 1962). Ralph Willett compares "The Ideas of Miller and Williams," *Theatre Annual* 22 (1965): 31–40, as does Michael P. Steppat in "Self-Choice and Aesthetic Despair in Arthur Miller and Tennessee Williams," *Literary Criterion* 20.3 (1985): 49–59. Anthony S. Abbott included "Arthur Miller and Tennessee Williams" in *The Vital Lie: Reality and Illusion in Modern Drama* (Tuscaloosa: University of Alabama Press, 1989), pp. 129–47. And in 1992, David Savran published *Communists, Cowboys, and Queers: The Politics of Masculinity in the Work of Arthur Miller and Tennessee Williams* (Minneapolis: University of Minnesota Press, 1992).

While Miller is most often paired with Williams, themes that appear in his work have often been examined in relation to other writers as well. Not surprisingly, *The Crucible* is often studied with *The Scarlet Letter*, notably in David Bergeron's "Arthur Miller's *The Crucible* and Nathaniel Hawthorne: Some Parallels," *English Journal* 58 (1969): 47–55, which compares Proctor and Dimmesdale; and an interesting publication from Budapest entitled *The Origins and Originality of American Culture* (Budapest: Akadémiai Kradó, 1984), edited by Frank Tibor, includes Miklos Trocsanyi's "Two Views of American Puritanism: Hawthorne's *The Scarlet Letter* and Miller's *The Crucible*." Jeanne-Marie A. Miller, in "Odets, Miller, and Communism," *CLA Journal* 19 (1976): 484–93, examines *The Crucible* and Odets's *Till the Day I Die* as warnings to the American people. Christopher Innes contrasts the role of the salesman in *Death of a Salesman*, O'Neill's *The Iceman Cometh*, and Gelber's *The Connection* in "The Salesman on Stage: A Study of the Social Influence of Drama," *English Studies in Canada* 3 (1977): 336–50, collected in Bloom, *Arthur Miller's Death of a Salesman*, pp. 59–75. More recent comparative studies include: Steven R. Centola, "Compromise as Bad Faith: Arthur Miller's *A View from the Bridge* and William Inge's *Come Back, Little Sheba*,"

Midwest Quarterly: A Journal of Contemporary Thought 28 (1986): 100–13; Thomas P. Adler, "The Embrace of Silence: Pinter, Miller, and the Response to Power," *The Pinter Review* (1991): 4–9; Yun-choel Kim, "The Degradation of the American Success Ethic: *Death of a Salesman, That Championship Season*, and *Glengarry Glen Ross*," *The Journal of English Language and Literature* 37.1 (1991): 233–48 (in Korean); and Leslie Kane, "Dreamers and Drunks: Moral and Social Consciousness in Arthur Miller and Sam Shepard," *American Drama* (1991): 27–45.

Critical perspectives: genre considerations

Much of the scholarship on Miller has focused on questions of genre, particularly on the concept of tragedy which Miller himself initiated with his essays "Tragedy and the Common Man" and "Arthur Miller on 'The Nature of Tragedy,'" both originally published in 1949 and reprinted in Robert A. Martin (ed.), *The Theater Essays of Arthur Miller* (1978). Alvin Whitely responds to these ideas as he evaluates *All My Sons* and *Death of a Salesman* in "Arthur Miller: An Attempt at Modern Tragedy," *Transactions of the Wisconsin Academy of Sciences, Arts, and Letters* 42 (1953): 257–62. M. W. Steinberg, in "Arthur Miller and the Idea of Modern Tragedy," *Dalhousie Review* 40 (1960): 329–40, collected in Corrigan, *Arthur Miller*, pp. 81–94 and Ferres, *Twentieth Century Interpretations: The Crucible*, pp. 98–100, uses the playwright's definition of modern tragedy to examine his plays. Another important essay is Emile G. McAnany's "The Tragic Commitment: Some Notes on Arthur Miller," *Modern Drama* 5 (1962): 11–20, where the author offers a different interpretation of Willy Loman as a tragic hero. Other discussions of Miller's writing of tragedy are John Prudhoe's "Arthur Miller and the Tradition of Tragedy," *English Studies* 43 (1962): 430–39, which examines the stylistic possibilities of tragedy within the conventions of realism; and Clinton W. Trowbridge's "Arthur Miller: Between Pathos and Tragedy," *Modern Drama* 10 (1967): 221–32, collected in Martine, *Critical Essays*, pp. 125–35 and Bloom, *Modern Critical Views: Arthur Miller*, pp. 39–50, which argues that Miller's plays move from pathos to tragedy. Robert Hogan's monograph *Arthur Miller* (Minneapolis: University of Minnesota Press, 1964) claims that the significance of Miller's work is in the tragic spirit that the plays embody.

Other scholars have attempted to examine Miller's process of playwriting and to define his dramatic form. Orm Overland, in "The Action and its Significance: Arthur Miller's Struggle with Dramatic Form," *Modern Drama* 18 (1975): 1–14, collected in Bloom, *Modern Critical Views:*

Arthur Miller, pp. 51–64, and Martin, *New Perspectives*, pp. 33–47, summarizes Miller's development as a dramatist. Other articles include: Leah Hadomi, "Fantasy and Reality: Dramatic Rhythm in *Death of a Salesman*," *Modern Drama* 31.2 (1988): 157–74, collected in Bloom, *Willy Loman*, pp. 112–28; Peter Szondi, "Memory and Dramatic Form in *Death of a Salesman*," in his *Theory of the Modern Drama* (Minneapolis: University of Minnesota Press, 1987), collected in Bloom, *Arthur Miller's Death of a Salesman*, pp. 19–23; and Michael Kuckwara, "Miller Defines Drama," *English Journal* 83.7 (1994): 109.

Much of the criticism of *Death of a Salesman* focuses on a definition of tragedy and how this play achieves or fails to achieve the tragic form. Articles that explore the play from this perspective include Remy G. Saisselin, "Is Tragic Drama Possible in the Twentieth Century," *Theatre Annual* 17 (1960): 12–21, collected in Meserve, *Merrill Studies*, pp. 44–45; George de Schweinitz, "*Death of a Salesman*: A Note on Epic and Tragedy," *Western Humanities Review* 14 (1960): 91–96, collected in Meserve, *Merrill Studies*, pp. 52–57 and in Weales, *Death of a Salesman: Text and Criticism*, pp. 272–79; Richard J. Foster, "Confusion and Tragedy: The Failure of Miller's *Salesman*," collected in Hurrell, *Two Modern American Tragedies*; Ester Merle Jackson, "*Death of a Salesman*: Tragic Myth in the Modern Theater," *CLA Journal* 7 (1963): 63–76, collected in Bloom, *Modern Critical Views*, pp. 27–38; in Meserve, *Merrill Studies*, pp. 57–68; and in Bloom, *Arthur Miller's Death of a Salesman*, pp. 7–18; Charlotte F. Otten, "Who am I? . . . A Re-Investigation of Arthur Miller's *Death of a Salesman*," *Cresset* 26 (1963): 11–13, collected in Koon, *Twentieth Century Interpretations: Death of a Salesman*, pp. 85–91; Lois Gordon, "*Death of a Salesman*: An Appreciation," in Warren French (ed.), *The Forties: Fiction, Poetry, Drama* (DeLand, FL: Everett/Edwards, 1969), pp. 273–83, collected in Koon, *Twentieth Century Interpretations: Death of a Salesman*, pp. 98–108; B. S. Field, Jr., "Hamartia in *Death of a Salesman*," *Twentieth Century Literature* 18 (1972): 19–24, collected in Koon, *Twentieth Century Interpretations: Death of a Salesman*, pp. 79–84; William Aarnes, "Tragic Form and the Possibility of Meaning in *Death of a Salesman*," *Furman Studies* 29 (1983): 57–80, collected in Bloom, *Arthur Miller's Death of a Salesman*, pp. 95–111; Dan Vogel, "Willy Tyrannos," from his *The Three Masks of American Tragedy* (Baton Rouge: Louisiana State University Press, 1974), collected in Bloom, *Willy Loman*, pp. 58–65; and Rita Di Giuseppe, "The Shadow of the Gods: Tragedy and Commitment in *Death of a Salesman*," *Quaderni di Lingue e Letterature* 14 (1989): 109–28.

Other plays receive genre considerations as well. Philip Walker, in

"Arthur Miller's *The Crucible*: Tragedy or Allegory?," *Western Speech* 20 (1956): 222–24 posits that this play falls between the categories of tragedy and allegory and thus falls short of both, and Arthur D. Epstein's "A Look at *A View from the Bridge*," *Texas Studies in Literature and Language* 7 (1965): 109–22, collected in Martine, *Critical Essays*, pp. 107–118, also discusses tragedy. Steven R. Centola relies on Joseph Campbell's concept of the "monomyth" to show how *After the Fall* transforms the personal into the symbolic, in "The Monomyth and Arthur Miller's *After the Fall*," *Studies in American Drama 1945 – Present* (1986): 49–60. Many more studies exist which explore the concept of tragedy and other genre considerations which cannot be included here.

Theatrical perspective

Virtually all of Miller's plays, beginning with *The Man Who Had All the Luck*, have been produced in New York and reviewed in local publications. The best source for these reviews is *The New York Theatre Critics' Reviews*, published annually. Citations of the reviews are also available online in the *Expanded Academic Index*. Bigsby's *File on Miller* offers an overview of the critical reception of the plays by reprinting excerpts of reviews, including some outside New York. Many of the reviews discuss the acting, scenery, lighting, costumes, and music and thus provide an important source for understanding the performance.

Almost all of the many sources available that look at the plays from a theatrical perspective are specific to a particular production. Excerpts from the notebooks of Elia Kazan, director of the original production of *Death of a Salesman*, are published in *A Theatre in Your Head* (New York: Funk and Wagnalls, 1960), edited by Kenneth Thorpe Rowe; and Jo Mielziner, original set and lighting designer, included "Designing a Play: *Death of a Salesman*" in his *Designing for the Theatre* (New York: Atheneum, 1965). An extensive, and quite recent, work in this area is Brenda Murphy's *Miller: Death of a Salesman* (Cambridge: Cambridge University Press, 1995). This book divides the four chapters into "The Broadway Production," "Productions in English," "Productions in Other Languages," and "Media Productions" and includes a Production Chronology, Discography, Videography, and Bibliography with extensive sections on collections of archival material and on reviews and criticism of specific productions of *Death of a Salesman*. Herbert Blau, as co-director of the Repertory Theatre of Lincoln Center, investigates the production values of *The Crucible* in "The Whole Man and the Real Witch" (in Corrigan, *Arthur Miller*, pp. 122–30), and Joseph N. Calarco discusses the production process of the

Hilberry Repertory Theatre's *The Crucible*, performed in repertory from 1972–74, in "Production as Criticism: Miller's *The Crucible*," *Educational Theatre Journal* 29 (1977): 354–61. Three articles offer insights into the New York production of *After the Fall*: Richard Schechner and Theodore Hoffman's interview with Elia Kazan, "Look, There's the American Theatre," *Tulane Drama Review* 9 (1964): 61–83; and Nancy and Richard Meyer, "Setting the Stage for Lincoln Center," *Theatre Arts* 48 (1964): 12–16, and "*After the Fall*: A View from the Director's Notebook," *Theatre (Lincoln Center)* 2 (1965): 43–73. Similarly, Harold Clurman's "Director's Notes: *Incident at Vichy*," *The Drama Review* 9 (1965): 77–90, collected in Corrigan, *Arthur Miller*, pp. 143–68, describes the production process of the ANTA–Washington Square Theatre production of that play. J. L. Styan analyzes the success of Peter Brook's production of *A View from the Bridge* in "Why *A View from the Bridge* Went Down Well in London: The Story of a Revision," in Martin, *New Perspectives*, pp. 139–48.

Other sources attempt to understand the theatricality inherent in the plays. William Heyen explores the disparity between the strength of the text and its effect in the theatre in "Arthur Miller's *Death of a Salesman* and the American Dream," in *Amerikanisches Drama und Theater im 20 Jahrhundert* (1975), collected in Bloom, *Arthur Miller's Death of a Salesman*, pp. 47–58, and Enoch Brater in "Miller's Realism and *Death of a Salesman*" (Martin, *New Perspectives*, pp. 115–26), insists that "the set *is* Miller's play" (p. 119) and explores its significance. Bernard F. Dukore's *Death of a Salesman and The Crucible: Text and Performance* (Atlantic Highlands: Humanities, 1989) emphasizes the significance of moving from page to stage and, in the second half of the book, "Performance," he focuses on the theatrical elements of these two plays. John Ditsky, in "Stone, Fire, and Light: Approaches to *The Crucible*," *North Dakota Quarterly* 46.2 (1978): 65–72, hints that the play's theatricality contributes to its lasting popularity; and James J. Martine includes an insightful chapter on *mise-en-scène* in *The Crucible: Politics, Property, and Pretense* (New York: Twayne, 1993). One other avenue to understanding the performative aspects of *The Crucible* is to look into The Wooster Group's *LSD*, a pirated adaptation of the play. Several sources exist on this production, notably David Savran, *The Wooster Group, 1975–1985: Breaking the Rules* (Ann Arbor: University of Michigan Research Press, 1986, reprinted 1990) and his earlier article, "The Wooster Group, Arthur Miller, and *The Crucible*," *The Drama Review* 29 (1985): 99–110.

Two articles in Matthew C. Roudané's *Approaches to Teaching Miller's Death of a Salesman* explore the pedagogical value of a performative approach: Thomas P. Adler, "Miller's Mindscape: A Scenic Approach to *Death of a Salesman*" (pp. 45–51), and Susan C. Haedicke, "Celebrating Stylistic Contradictions: *Death of a Salesman* from a Theatrical Perspective" (pp. 37–44). Also helpful for teaching from a theatrical perspective are videos of the televised plays (see John Hiett, "Video Reviews: Arthur Miller," *Library Journal* 114.13 [1989]: 175) and the CD ROM of *The Crucible*, Penguin Electronic Publishing (1995); see also Dudley Barlow, "Education Resources," *Education Digest* 60.6 (1995): 78–79.

Many books not specifically on Miller can aid those interested in this approach. J. L. Styan, consistently pointing out the performative elements of a play, offers an example of analysis from a theatrical perspective in his three-volume study, *Modern Drama in Theory and Practice* (Cambridge: Cambridge University Press, 1981). His books, *Shakespeare's Stagecraft* (Cambridge: Cambridge University Press, 1967), *Chekhov in Performance* (Cambridge: Cambridge University Press, 1971), and *Restoration Comedy in Performance* (Cambridge: Cambridge University Press, 1986), offer even better models of this type of analysis, although none of these books mention Miller. Styan's *The Elements of Drama* (Cambridge: Cambridge University Press, 1969) and *Drama, Stage, and Audience* (Cambridge: Cambridge University Press, 1975), offer the tools necessary for this type of approach. Two other texts, David Ball, *Backwards and Forwards: A Technical Manual for Reading Plays* (Carbondale: Southern Illinois University Press, 1983) and David Scanlon, *Reading Drama* (Mountain View, CA: Mayfield Publishing Company, 1988) are extremely helpful to students in understanding the very different analytic process needed for play analysis. For the adventurous scholar, Bernard Beckerman's *Dynamics of Drama: Theory and Method of Analysis* (New York: Drama Book Specialists, 1970) offers a more complex but rewarding analytic approach which acknowledges the performative elements of drama.

Critical perspective: gender studies

A relatively recent critical approach offering new insights into Miller's work is that of gender studies. Two volumes exploring the plays from a feminist perspective are both edited by June Schlueter. *Feminist Rereadings of Modern American Drama* (Rutherford, NJ: Farleigh Dickinson University Press, 1989) includes Iska Alter, "Betrayal and Blessedness: Explorations of Feminine Power in *The Crucible, A View from the Bridge*, and *After the Fall*"; Gayle Austin, "The Exchange of Women and Male Homosocial Desire in Arthur Miller's *Death of a Salesman* and Lillian Hellman's *Another Part of the Forest*"; Jeffrey Mason, "Paper Dolls:

Melodrama and Sexual Politics in Miller's Early Plays"; and Kay Stanton, "Women and the American Dream of *Death of a Salesman*" (also collected in Bloom, *Willy Loman*, pp. 129–56). *Modern American Drama: The Female Canon* (Rutherford, NJ: Farleigh Dickinson University Press, 1990) includes Charlotte Goodman's "The Fox's Cubs: Lillian Hellman, Arthur Miller, and Tennessee Williams." Carol Billman in "Women and the Family in American Drama," *Arizona Quarterly* 36.1 (1980): 35–48, explores how women occupy a key role in family dramas, like *Death of a Salesman*, but their suffering is often overlooked. Beverly Hume explores "Linda Loman as 'The Woman' in Miller's *Death of a Salesman*," *NMAL: Notes on Modern American Literature* 9.3 (1985): Item 14; Charlotte Canning writes "Is This a Play About Women? A Feminist Reading of *Death of a Salesman*," in Centola, *The Achievement of Arthur Miller*, pp. 69–76; and Wendy Schissel has recently reexamined the roles of Abigail and Elizabeth Proctor as witches and unseated John Proctor as the hero in "Re(dis)covering the Witches in Arthur Miller's *The Crucible*: A Feminist Reading," *Modern Drama* 37.3 (1994): 461–73. Linda Ben-Zvi tackles the idea of the frontier in "Home Sweet Home: Deconstructing the Masculine Myth of the Frontier in Modern American Drama," in David Morgan, Mark Busby, and Paul Bryant (eds.), *The Frontier Experience and the American Dream: Essays in American Literature* (College Station: Texas A & M University Press, 1989), pp. 217–25. Nada Zeineddine writes a comparative study of women's identity in *Because It Is My Name: Problems of Identity Experienced by Women, Artists, and Breadwinners in the Plays of Henrik Ibsen, Tennessee Williams, and Arthur Miller* (Braunton, Devon: Merlin Books, 1991).

Critical attention has also focused on men's issues. Eugene R. August introduced the idea with "*Death of a Salesman*: A Men's Studies Approach," *Western Ohio Journal* 7 (1986): 53–71. More sophisticated is David Savran's *Communists, Cowboys, and Queers*, which offers a fresh interpretation of the plays through a consideration of the "authoritative Cold War masculinity for which Miller's protagonists yearn" (p. 41). And Stefan Tai published "Arthur Miller's 'Last Yankee': A Male Depressive," *Contemporary Review* (1994): 147–48.

Steven R. Centola has written an article with a provocative title for the 1990s: "Family Values in *Death of a Salesman*," *College Language Association Journal* 37.1 (1993): 29–41. Another tantalizing title is Granger Babcock's "What's the Secret?: Willy Loman as Desiring Machine," *American Drama* 2.1 (1992): 59–83.

Interdisciplinary approaches: sociology, psychology, business and law, history, and ethnic studies

Sociology

Miller insists that the value of art arises from its usefulness for a changing society, and a large majority of scholars working on Miller investigate or at least touch upon the social concerns raised in his plays, thus making the selection for this section very difficult. The few sources mentioned here offer analyses specifically from a sociological perspective. A general text that is helpful in understanding this perspective is Elizabeth and Tom Burns (eds.), *Sociology of Literature and Drama* (Harmondsworth: Penguin Books, 1973). More directly related to Miller is Lois Gordon's "*Death of a Salesman*: An Appreciation," in Warren French (ed.), *The Forties: Fiction, Poetry, Drama* (DeLand, FL: Everett/Edwards, 1969), collected in Koon, *Twentieth Century Interpretations: Death of a Salesman*, pp. 98–108, which defines two primary opposing critical perspectives, the tragic and the social. Arvin R. Wells, however, questions the sociological approach in "The Living and the Dead in *All My Sons*," *Insight* 1 (1962): 165–74, collected in Martine, *Critical Essays*, pp. 5–9, and Bloom, *Arthur Miller's All My Sons* (New York: Chelsea House, 1988), pp. 27–32.

At the time of the initial runs of *Death of a Salesman* in New York and London, Ivor Brown in "As London Sees Willy Loman," *New York Times Magazine*, 28 August 1949, pp. 11, 59, collected in Weales, *Death of a Salesman: Text and Criticism*, pp. 244–49, contrasted the audience responses to the play in the two cities, and the resulting analysis offers a sociological survey of the two cultures. Henry Popkin, in "Arthur Miller: The Strange Encounter," *Sewanee Review* 68 (1960): 34–60, excerpted in Bloom, *Willy Loman*, pp. 10–13, sees *Death of a Salesman*, *The Crucible*, and *A View from the Bridge* as parables of the social and political climate of their time. Working from a sociological perspective, Eric Mottram in "Arthur Miller: The Development of a Political Dramatist in America," in John Russell Brown and Bernard Harris (eds.), *American Theatre* (New York: St. Martin's Press, 1967), collected in Corrigan, *Arthur Miller*, pp. 23–58, claims that Miller oversimplifies social issues, whereas Paul Blumberg claims that Miller has a great deal to say to sociologists, in "Sociology and Social Literature: Work Alienation in the Plays of Arthur Miller," *American Quarterly* 21 (1969): 291–310, collected in Martin, *New Perspectives*, pp. 48–64. Leonard Moss struggles with a definition of social drama in "A Social Play" (collected in Ferres, *Twentieth Century Interpretations: The Crucible*, pp. 37–45); and S. K. Bhatia analyzes "*Death of a Salesman* as a Social Document," *Banasthali Patrika* 20 (1976): 45–49. More recently, Donald P. Costello, in "Arthur Miller's Circles of Responsibility: A View from the Bridge and Beyond," *Modern Drama* 36.3 (1993): 443–53, examines Miller's ideas of social responsibility in relation to the heroes in his plays. Normann Helge Nilsen examines the controlling influence of Marxism and the portrayal of characters as products of American capitalism in the early plays, in *"From Honors at Dawn to Death of a Salesman*: Marxism and the Early Plays of Arthur Miller," *English Studies* 75.2 (1994): 146–56.

Psychology

Death of a Salesman, in particular, aroused the curiosity of psychologists. Soon after the play appeared on Broadway, psychoanalyst Daniel E. Schneider analyzed Willy's "flashbacks" in "Play of Dreams," *Theatre Arts* 33 (1949): 18–21, collected as "A Modern Playwright" in his *The Psychoanalyst and the Artist* (New York: Ferrar, Strauss, 1950), pp. 246–55, and in Weales, *Death of a Salesman: Text and Criticism*, pp. 250–58. *Psychology and Arthur Miller* (New York: Dutton, 1969), a book-length dialogue between psychologist Richard I. Evans and Miller, first appeared in 1969 and was republished as *Dialogue with Arthur Miller* (New York: Praeger, 1981). Literary scholars soon began to borrow terminology and methodologies from psychologists to explore the play. As early as the mid-1950s, George G. Kernodle urged finding a balance between psychological and sociological approaches to the play, in "The Death of the Little Man," *Tulane Drama Review* 1 (1955–56): 47–60, but psychological analyses of the Lomans continued to fascinate scholars, as in W. David Sievers, *Freud on Broadway: A History of Psychoanalysis and American Drama* (New York: Hermitage, 1955). John V. Hagopian, in *"Death of a Salesman,"* *Insight* 1 (1962): 174–86, collected in Meserve, *Merrill Studies*, pp. 34–42, calls the play itself schizophrenic, and Joel Shatzky borrows terms from psychology in "'The Reactive Image' and Miller's *Death of a Salesman*," *Players* 48 (1973): 104–10, to analyze both the structure of the play and the author's intentions. Tony Manocchio and Patrick Roberts explore "The Loman Family" in their *Families Under Stress: A Psychological Interpretation* (London and Boston: Routledge and Kegan Paul, 1975). Frederick L. Rusch uses a psychological approach in his analysis of Miller's plays in "Approaching Literature through the Social Psychology of Erich Fromm," in Joseph Natoli (ed.), *Psychological Perspectives in Literature: Freudian Dissidents and Non-Freudians: A Casebook* (Hamden, CT: Archon, 1984), pp. 79–99.

Albert Rothenberg and Eugene D. Shapiro apply this perspective to another play in "The Defense of Psychoanalysis in Literature: *Long Day's Journey into Night* and *A View from the Bridge*," *Comparative Drama* 7 (1973): 51–67, collected in John H. Stroupe (ed.), *Critical Approaches to O'Neill* (New York: AMS, 1988), pp. 169–85.

Business and Law

Death of a Salesman also initiated discussion on American business ethics. A. Howard Fuller, president of the Fuller Brush Company, drew attention to business issues in *Death of a Salesman* as he defended the salesman as an appropriate representation of American society, in "A Salesman is Everybody," *Fortune* 39 (1949): 79–80, collected in Weales, *Death of a Salesman: Text and Criticism*, pp. 240–43. Several sources explore the success ethic, especially in relation to *Death of a Salesman*, notably Thomas E. Porter, "Acres of Diamonds: Death of a Salesman," in his *Myth and Modern Drama* (Detroit: Wayne State University Press, 1969), pp. 127–52; Gordon W. Couchman, "Arthur Miller's Tragedy of Babbitt," *Educational Theatre Journal* 7 (1955): 206–11, collected in Meserve, *Merrill Studies*, pp. 68–75; M. Gilbert Porter, "From Babbitt to Rabbit: The Materialist in Search of a Soul," in Gilbert Debusscher (ed.), *American Literature in Belgium* (Amsterdam: Rodopi, 1988), pp. 185–96; and Yunchoel Kim's "The Degradation of the American Success Ethic: *Death of a Salesman, That Championship Season*, and *Glengarry Glen Ross*." Frank W. Shelton examines "Sports and the Competitive Ethic: *Death of a Salesman* and *That Championship Season*," *Ball State University Forum* 20.2 (1979): 17–21. Michael Spindler explores consumerism in "Consumer Man in Crisis: Arthur Miller's *Death of a Salesman*," in his *American Literature and Social Change: William Dean Howells to Arthur Miller* (Bloomington: Indiana University Press, 1983). John S. Shockley compares Willy Loman and Ronald Reagan in "*Death of a Salesman* and American Leadership: Life Imitates Art," *Journal of American Culture* 17 (1994): 49–56.

Thomas E. Porter, in "The Mills of the Gods: Economics and Law in the Plays of Arthur Miller," collected in Martin, *New Perspectives*, pp. 75–96, separates the issues of business and law in part by categorizing *All My Sons, Death of a Salesman*, and *The Price* as "business plays" and *The Crucible, A View from the Bridge*, and *After the Fall* as "judicial plays." He addresses the topic of the law in "The Long Shadow of the Law: *The Crucible*," in his *Myth and Modern Drama*, pp. 177–99, collected in

Martine, *Critical Essays*, pp. 75–92 as he explores the notion of a "fair trial." John D. Engle treats "The Metaphor of Law in *After the Fall*," *Notes on Contemporary Literature* 9.3 (1979): 11–12.

History

Just as *Death of a Salesman* encouraged a psychological perspective, *The Crucible* sparked studies examining the historical precedents of the play, what James J. Martine in *The Crucible: Politics, Property, and Pretense* (New York: Twayne, 1993) calls the two "matrices: distant and near" of Colonial America and the United States of the 1950s. The primary focus in studies examining *The Crucible* and the Salem witch trials revolves around Miller's historical accuracy. David Levin's "Salem Witchcraft in Recent Fiction and Drama," *New England Quarterly* 28 (1955), 537–42, points out Miller's historical inaccuracies and oversimplification of the actual events. Robert A. Martin's "Arthur Miller's *The Crucible*: Background and Sources," *Modern Drama* 20 (1977): 279–92, collected in Martine, *Critical Essays*, pp. 93–104, explores Miller's use and alterations of historical facts. William J. McGill, Jr., in "The Crucible of History: Arthur Miller's John Proctor," *New England Quarterly* 54.2 (1981): 258–64, finds Miller's Proctor is not historically accurate. E. Miller Budick, in "History and Other Spectres in Arthur Miller's *The Crucible*," *Modern Drama* 28.4 (1985): 535–52, collected in Bloom, *Modern Critical Views: Arthur Miller*, pp. 127–44, reads the play as the story of American Puritanism in spite of historical fabrications, whereas Edmund S. Morgan finds seventeenth-century Puritanism quite different from that portrayed in the play, in "Arthur Miller's *The Crucible* and the Salem Witch Trials: A Historian's View," in John M. Wallace (ed.), *The Golden and Brazen World: Papers in Literature and History 1650–1800* (Berkeley: University of California Press, 1985), pp. 171–86.

Parallels between the events of the play and McCarthyism have received critical attention as well. Peter A. Foulkes, in "Arthur Miller's *The Crucible*: Contexts of Understanding and Misunderstanding," in Edgar Lohner and Rudolf Hass (eds.), *Theater und Drama in Amerika: Aspekte und Interpretationen* (Berlin: E. Schmidt, 1978), pp. 295–309, and again in "Demystifying the Witch Hunt (Arthur Miller)," in his *Literature and Propaganda* (London and New York: Methuen, 1983), pp. 83–104, focuses on the parallels between the play and the 1950s as he reviews McCarthyism and interprets the play as anti-propaganda. Tosao Kanamaru takes up the subject in "McCarthyism and Arthur Miller," *American Literature in the 1950s* (Tokyo: Tokyo Chapter, American Literature

Society of Japan, 1977), pp. 140–46. C. W. E. Bigsby's section on Miller in vol. II of *A Critical Introduction to Twentieth-Century American Drama* relates the play to Miller's HUAC experiences, as does Herbert Blau's essay "The Whole Man and the Real Witch" (in Corrigan, *Arthur Miller*, pp. 123–30). Blau values the exposure of the parallels between the witch trials and the Communists' hearings. Robert Warshow, on the other hand, attacks the parallels that the play makes between the events at Salem and those of the 1950s, in "The Liberal Conscience in *The Crucible*" (collected in Corrigan, *Arthur Miller*, pp. 111–21). Gary P. Hendrickson explores the topic again in "The Last Analogy: Arthur Miller's Witches and America's Domestic Communists," *Midwest Quarterly* 33.4 (1992): 447–56, as does P. G. Rama Rao in "Reflections of Twentieth Century America in a Seventeenth Century Witches Cauldron," in J. L. Plakkootam and Prashant K. Sinha (eds.), *Literature and Politics in Twentieth Century America, 11–12 Oct. 1991* (Hyderabad: American Studies Research Centre, 1993), pp. 71–78.

None of Miller's other plays has inspired such a detailed historical approach, although Leslie Epstein, in "The Unhappiness of Arthur Miller," *Tri-Quarterly* 1 (1965): 165–73, accuses Miller of a lack of understanding of the historical situation dramatized in *Incident at Vichy*.

Ethnic studies

Not surprisingly, several scholars have examined Miller's work in relation to his Jewish heritage. Inspired by an early Yiddish theatre production of *Death of a Salesman*, George Ross, in "*Death of a Salesman* in the Original," *Commentary* 11 (1951): 184–86, collected in Weales, *Death of a Salesman: Text and Criticism*, pp. 259–64, concludes that the play grows out of the Jewish–American experience. Mary McCarthy accuses Miller of concealing that the characters in *Death of a Salesman* are Jewish, in *Sights and Spectacles* (New York: Ferrar, Strauss, & Cudany, 1956), and Leslie Fiedler claims the characters are Jewish, but are "presented as something else," in *Waiting for the End* (New York: Stein and Day, 1964). Morris Freedman expands on these ideas in "The Jewishness of Arthur Miller: His Family Epic," in his *American Drama in Social Context* (Carbondale: Southern Illinois University Press, 1971), pp. 43–58, where he explores the treatment of guilt and Jewish–American values in *All My Sons*, *Death of a Salesman*, *After the Fall*, and *The Price*. Joel Shatzky returns the focus to *Death of a Salesman* in "Arthur Miller's 'Jewish' Salesman," *Studies in American Jewish Literature* 2.1 (1976): 1–9. *From Hester Street to Hollywood: The Jewish–American Stage and Screen* (Bloomington: Indiana

University Press, 1983), edited by Sarah Blacher Cohen, includes two articles: Enoch Brater's "Ethics and Ethnicity in the Plays of Arthur Miller" (pp. 123–36), and Lawrence Langer's "The Americanization of the Holocaust on Stage and Screen" (pp. 213–30) on *Incident at Vichy*. Two other articles exploring Miller and the Holocaust are Edward Isser, "Arthur Miller and the Holocaust," *Essays in Theatre* 10.2 (1992): 155–64; and Joyce Antler, who examines how Miller and others have relocated the horror of the Holocaust in the American psyche, in "The Americanization of the Holocaust," *American Theatre* 12.2 (1995): 16–20. Dan Vogel explores Jewish identity in "From Milkman to Salesman: Glimpses of the Galut," *Studies in American Jewish Literature* 10.2 (1991): 172–78.

Some reviews, notably Mel Gussow's review of the 1972 Center Stage production of *Death of a Salesman* with an African–American cast ("Stage: Black *Salesman*," *The New York Times*, 9 April 1972, p. 69), focus on issues of ethnicity and race as directors began to experiment with non-traditional casting. Brenda Murphy's *Miller: Death of a Salesman* documents those productions which employed African–American or interracial casts (pp. 83–92).

Cross-cultural perspective: potential new direction

Another recent critical approach examines Miller's work cross-culturally, either exploring the impact of productions in another culture or interpreting the plays from a cultural perspective different from the author and the initial audiences. One important text looking at productions abroad is Miller's *Salesman in Beijing* (New York: Viking Press, 1984), which documents the rehearsal process of the Chinese production of *Death of a Salesman* as it explores cultural difference. The Chinese production, notes Miller in a 1986 interview with Mark Lamos, who directed the Hartford Stage revival of the play, focused the attention on Linda ("An Afternoon with Arthur Miller," *American Theatre* 3 (1986): 18–23, 44, collected in Roudané, *Conversations*, pp. 376–88. Henian Yuan also comments on this production in "*Death of a Salesman* in Beijing," *Chinese Literature* 10 (1983): 103–09. As already mentioned, Brenda Murphy's *Miller: Death of a Salesman* has a complete chapter devoted to productions of this play in other languages. Two articles collected in Meserve, *Merrill Studies*, describe other performances of this play abroad: Paul Rajinder's "*Death of a Salesman* in India" (pp. 23–27) and Freidrich Luft's "Arthur Miller's *Death of a Salesman*: Hebbel-Theater (Berlin)" (pp. 19–22). C. W. E. Bigsby examines Miller's work from a British perspective in "A British View of an American Playwright," in Centola, *The Achievement of Arthur Miller*, pp. 17–30.

Other scholars have interpreted the dramatic texts drawing on world views outside the mainstream Anglo–American cultural perspective. N. Bhaskara Panikkar's *Individual Morality and Social Happiness in Arthur Miller* (New Delhi: Milind Publications Private Limited; Atlantic Highlands, NJ: Humanities Press, 1982) examines types of morality and tensions found in Miller's plays and exposes American values from a cross-cultural perspective. Kiyoe Ohtsuka also explores morality in *"The Price: Two Different Attitudes Toward Life," Chu-Shikoku Studies in American Literature* 24 (1988): 66–80. Maria Kurdi's "The Deceptive Nature of Reality in Arthur Miller's *Two-Way Mirror*" appears in Mirko Jurak (ed.), *Cross-Cultural Studies: American, Canadian, and European Literatures: 1945–1985* (Ljubljana: English Department, Filozofska Fakulteta, 1988). *Understanding the USA: A Cross-Cultural Perspective* (Tubingen: Narr, 1989), edited by Peter Funke, includes Lothar Bredella's "Literary Texts and Intercultural Understanding: Arthur Miller's Play *Death of a Salesman*."

Several articles have been written on Miller from this perspective in foreign languages. Some have already been mentioned, but also of interest is Antonio Rodriguez Celada, "Buero, Miller y el 'Common Man.'" *Estreno: Cuadernos del Teatro Espanol Contemporaneo* 10.1 (1984): 25–28 (in Spanish), which offers a cross-cultural treatment of the common man as tragic hero. Other foreign language articles and several dissertations looking at the plays cross-culturally are indexed in the *MLA Bibliography*.

A great deal of work still needs to be done in this area, but these works offer promising beginnings. *Interculturalism and Performance* (New York: PAJ Publications, 1991), edited by Bonnie Marranca and Gautam Dasgupta, while it has no selections on Miller, is a very helpful text for understanding this critical perspective.

Fiction and screenplays

The scholarly community has largely overlooked Miller's fiction and screenplays although much of this work has received numerous reviews. The best source for reviews of works written before 1979 is Ferres, *Arthur Miller: A Reference Guide*. The most efficient way to access reviews after 1979 is through the online database First Search, which cites references to thousands of scholarly journals, weekly and bi-weekly publications, and newspapers. The easiest way to access many of the reviews on the screenplays is by title and director.

Miller's first novel, *Focus*, received numerous reviews, notably Iris Barry, "Look Through this Glass," *New York Herald Tribune Weekly Book*

Review (18 Nov. 1945): 4, which compares *Focus* to other propaganda novels. A more scholarly treatment appeared in David R. Mesher, "Arthur Miller's *Focus*: The First American Novel of the Holocaust?," *Judaism: A Quarterly Journal of Jewish Life and Thought* 29.4 (1980): 469–78.

The short stories, collected as *I Don't Need You Any More*, have attracted more attention. In addition to the numerous reviews, notably Stanley Koven, "*I Don't Need You Any More*," *Commonweal* 85 (1967): 686–87, several scholars have explored Miller's themes and techniques as a short story writer. While most agree that the short stories add little to Miller's reputation, they differ in their evaluations of them. In "Arthur Miller's Constancy: A Note on Miller as a Short Story Writer," *Revue des Langues Vivantes* 36 (1970): 62–71, Edmond Schraepen notes that the themes of the stories closely resemble the early plays. Brooks Atkinson, in "A Theatre of Life," *Saturday Review* 50 (1971): 53, compares Miller's fiction to that of Tennessee Williams, and Allen Shepherd criticizes the short stories in "'What Comes Easier': The Short Stories of Arthur Miller," *Illinois Quarterly* 34 (1972): 37–49. Irving Jacobson analyzes one story from the collection in "The Vestigial Jews on Mont Sant' Angelo," *Studies in Short Fiction* 13 (1976): 507–12, and praises Miller's thematic treatment of the family in "The Child as Guilty Witness," *Literature and Psychology* 24 (1974): 12–23.

Although not really fiction, it is important to mention Miller's anecdotal autobiography, *Timebends*, which has been frequently reviewed. Some of the most helpful reviews include Enoch Brater, "*Timebends*," *Michigan Quarterly Review* 28 (1989): 298–303; and Bernard F. Dukore, "*Timebends*," *Theatre Research International* 14 (1989): 219–20. Also of importance is Robert Lee Feldman's essay on "Arthur Miller's Neglected Article on the Nazi War Criminals' Trials: A Vision of Evil," *Resources for American Literary Study* 15.2 (1985): 187–96.

Miller's screenplay, *The Misfits*, received a great deal of critical attention, with most writers criticizing the film's characters, dialogue, and Western movie format. Lawrence Grauman, Jr.'s "*The Misfits*," *Film Quarterly* 14 (1961): 51–53; Philip T. Hartung's "The Screen: Woe, Woe, Whoa," *Commonweal* 73 (1961): 532–33; Stanley Kauffman's "Across the Great Divide," *New Republic* 144 (1961): 26, 28; and Henry Popkin's "Arthur Miller Out West," *Commentary* 31 (1961): 433–36, all censure the film with varying degrees of intensity. William Hamilton's "Of God and Woman," *Christian Century* 78 (1961): 424–25, and Dennis Welland's section on *The Misfits* in *Arthur Miller* (New York: Grove Press, 1961) are much kinder. James Goode, *The Story of The Misfits* (Indianapolis: Bobbs-Merrill, 1963) gives detailed background information on the film, including

Miller's role in the project. Edward Murray examines *"Death of a Salesman, The Misfits,* and *After the Fall"* in his book *The Cinematic Imagination: Writers and the Motion Pictures* (New York: Frederick Ungar, 1972).

Other screenplays have received reviews only. Lewis Funke gives an account of the filming of *The Reason Why* on Miller's Connecticut estate in "Stars Help Miller Film TV Antiwar Allegory," *The New York Times* (17 Nov. 1969), p. 58. *Everybody Wins* received numerous reviews, including Kirk Johnson, "Arthur Miller's Version of Love Becomes a Movie," *The New York Times* (11 June 1989), 2, p. 19:1; Peter Travers, *"Everybody Wins," Rolling Stone* 572 (1990): 39; and Pauline Kael, "The Current Cinema: New Age Daydreams," *New Yorker* 66.44 (1990): 115–21. *Playing for Time* got a brief mention in L. Kessel's "Casting Call," *Television Quarterly* 17.3 (1980).

Finally, film versions of some of the plays are worthy of mention. Arthur Miller discusses the television adaptations of some of his plays with Susan King in "Arthur Miller's 'Enemy' Has Found a Friend," *Los Angeles Times* (11 June 1990), F, p. 1:5. Best known of the film versions is Dustin Hoffman's televised performance of *Death of a Salesman,* reviewed by Helen McNeil, *Times Literary Supplement* 4456 (1988): 932. Jean Paul Sartre's *Witches of Salem,* based on *The Crucible,* received numerous reviews, notably John McCarten, "The Current Cinema," *New Yorker* 34 (1958): 209–10; Philip T. Hartung, "The Screen: Many Things to Many People," *Commonweal* 69 (1959): 363–64; and Eugen Weber, *"The Crucible," Film Quarterly* 12 (1959): 44–45. The film version of *A View from the Bridge* also received several reviews: Norman Rosten, "Scenarist Eyes His *View from the Bridge," The New York Times* (21 Jan. 1962), Sec. II, p. 9; Stanley Kauffman, "The Unadaptable Adapted," *New Republic* 146 (1962): 26–27; and Pauline Kael, "Review of *A View from the Bridge," Film Quarterly* 15 (1962): 27–29. Most recently, Miller has rewritten *The Crucible* for the screen to be directed by Nicholas Hytner. David Gritten discusses this project in "A Timely Return for 'Crucible,'" *Los Angeles Times* (30 April 1995), CAL, p. 25:5. Other discussions of the film include Daniel Voll, "The Devil and Arthur Miller," *George* (1996): 118–21; Holly Sorensen, "Miller's Crossing," *Première* 9.7 (1996): 41; and Victor Navasky, "The Demons of Salem, With Us Still," *The New York Times* (8 September 1996), pp. 2, 37:1. These references represent just a sampling of writings on the television and film versions of the plays.

INDEX